Martin Meyerson

The Fiscal System of Venezuela: A Report

THE FISCAL SYSTEM OF
Venezuela

A REPORT

CARL S. SHOUP, *Director*
of the Commission to Study
the Fiscal System of Venezuela

JOHN F. DUE
LYLE C. FITCH
Sir DONALD MacDOUGALL
OLIVER S. OLDMAN
STANLEY S. SURREY

THE JOHNS HOPKINS PRESS: BALTIMORE, 1959

: Foreword

At the request of the Minister of Finance of the Republic of Venezuela, a Commission to Study the Fiscal System of Venezuela was
formed by the Director of this project, with the approval of the Minister, in May, 1958. Research and writing occupied the summer
months. The report was submitted on August 22, 1958, then mimeographed, translated into Spanish, and circulated within the Government.
Additional information thus obtained led to some revision and expansion of the report in June, 1959, in the course of a three-weeks visit to
Caracas by two members of the Commission (Professors Shoup and
Surrey). Changes that have occurred in the Venezuelan tax law since
August, 1958, are described in footnotes and, with respect to the income tax reform of December 19, 1958, in Appendix C. The text of
the tax chapters therefore remains a description and analysis of the
Venezuelan tax system as it was in August, 1958.[1] Some minor administrative changes that have been made since that date, mostly
along lines recommended in the report, are not specifically noted. A
Spanish-language edition of the report is being printed by the Government of Venezuela.

The study is focused on the tax system of Venezuela in the comprehensive sense of including national, state, and local taxes. Both tax
policy and tax administration are covered. In the first two chapters, the
Venezuelan economy is described and analyzed with respect to characteristics important for tax policy: distribution of income, rate of investment, and sources of its finance, and optimum uses of capital. Estimates of costs for certain goals are given for education and public
health. The Government accounting system is analyzed with a view to
changes that would provide data for national income accounts.

The thought that such a study should be made of the Venezuelan
fiscal system originated with Dr. Tomás Enrique Carrillo-Batalla, while

[1] This date also applies to Chapters I, II, XII, XIII, and XV. Most of Chapter XIV and all of Chapter XVI were written in June, 1959.

he was attending graduate courses in economics, particularly public finance, at Columbia University. In discussions with Professor Shoup, Dr. Carrillo contributed significantly to the planning of the proposed project; it was at his suggestion that the study was broadened to include a description of the Venezuelan economy (Chapters I and II).

Following the Revolution of January 23, 1958, Dr. Arturo Sosa became Minister of Finance. Upon his invitation, Professors Shoup and Surrey spent a week in Caracas early in May, 1958, conferring with him, with Dr. Carrillo, and with others, in and out of Government, on the practicability of the project. As a result, it was decided that the project should be undertaken. In late May, 1958, Dr. José Antonio Mayobre became Minister of Finance, upon the appointment of Dr. Sosa to the Presidential Junta. The Commission has enjoyed the active and understanding support of Dr. Mayobre throughout the course of the study.

As the work progressed, Dr. Carrillo gave unstintingly of his time and thought. Whatever beneficial results may flow from this project will be due largely to his help, starting with the original idea and continuing through more than two years of discussion, planning, arranging of conferences, reading of manuscript, and making of comments on factual statements and policy conclusions reached by the Commission. We of the Commission are greatly in Dr. Carrillo's debt.

We wish to note particularly the cooperation we have received from Dr. Leopoldo J. Bello and Dr. Amadeo Araujo, Directors of the Commission for Financial and Administrative Studies, of the Ministry of Finance, and to recall their thoughtful attention and aid with respect to staffing, travel within Venezuela, and similar matters. The printing of the Spanish-language edition of the report is being carried through under Dr. Araujo's supervision.

Much benefit was obtained from counsel given by the Fiscal Reform Commission appointed by the Minister of Finance, Dr. Mayobre, who acted as president of the Commission. The other members of the Commission were: Dr. Carlos D'Ascoli, Dr. Tomás Enrique Carrillo-Batalla (chairman), Dr. Alfredo Machado, and Dr. José Andrés Octavio. This advisory Commission met every week with our Commission, suggesting ways of obtaining information that otherwise would have remained inaccessible, planning trips for our Commission to various regions of Venezuela, and discussing technical and policy issues. After the report had been submitted in August, 1958, the Fiscal Reform Commission studied the manuscript, assisted in circulating it within the Government, and gathered and forwarded comments and suggestions from others, as well as their own. Dr. Octavio wrote a valuable analysis of our recommendations respecting the income tax, and Dr. Carrillo kindly supplied a summary of the Fiscal Reform Commission's comments on the entire report. In the summer of 1959, those members of the Commission who were available at that time, Dr. Carrillo and Dr. Octavio, and also Dr. Juan A. Gil of Puerto Rico, who had written a memorandum on certain aspects of our report, assisted in the conferences on revision of the 1958 draft. We acknowledge a special indebtedness to the members of this Fiscal Reform Commission, who spared so much time from their pressing business and professional affairs to aid us. The report, as published, is thus the result of close cooperation between the undersigned and the members of the Fiscal Reform Commission.

Dr. Iván Senior did much to help the study get under way in 1958, arranging contacts for us in Government and business circles.

We are also obligated to the Central Bank of Venezuela for a memorandum commenting on several of the points made in our description of the Venezuelan economy. The Central Bank, and particularly Dr. Enrique Landaeta, were most helpful in responding to our requests for information in the summer of 1958.

Particular thanks are due to the national tax officials of Venezuela, and to officials in other ministries, who have given much time and effort to the task of informing us precisely how the several taxes are administered. We have drawn most heavily on the time of Dr. Jesús Briceño Guedez, in charge of the income tax, and the members of his staff; they have cooperated generously and effectively.

The complex task of organizing the mimeographing of the entire report in 1958 within a very short period was accomplished through most skillful planning and unremitting effort by Dr. Juan Antoni and Mr. Jerónimo Sotillo, on leave from the Central Bank (to which organization we are correspondingly grateful). Dr. Antoni and Mr. Sotillo also assisted notably in earlier phases of the study.

We wish to acknowledge with appreciation the important contributions made by Mr. Guillermo Castro, Mr. Héctor Gouverneur, and Mr. Juan Vidago, as interpreters and translators who also rendered research assistance; and the secretarial and office direction and assistance provided throughout the study by Mrs. Margarita Carnevali, Mrs. Robert S. Digweed, Miss Isabel Francis, Mrs. Mercedes Senior, and Miss Louise Tutsnah.

In the course of our study we visited various sectors of Venezuela, including cities and rural areas in the states of Bolívar, Carabobo, Guárico, Mérida, Miranda, Táchira, and Zulia. We received useful information and suggestions in interviews with the governors and municipal officials in these states, and with officials of the Federal District.

We have also held a number of meetings with business executives, lawyers, accountants, representatives of labor, and scholars of public finance, in Venezuela, all of whom have been cooperative in supplying information and views.

Miss Consuelo Maldonado, Director of the Office of Accounting Systems of the Treasury Department of the Commonwealth of Puerto Rico, added substantially to the report in June, 1959, by revising and expanding Chapter XIV, on government accounting, in the course of a month's stay in Caracas. Miss Maldonado was given most helpful co-operation by the Controller, Dr. Luis A. Pietri, and the Treasurer, Dr. Pedro Enrique Aguerrevere, and members of their staffs.

Significant contributions to various factual and analytical sections of the report were made by Dr. Jean Due, Research Associate, and Mr. Anthony H. Pascal, Research Assistant.

For the translation of the report into Spanish we are indebted to Dr. Raúl Villasana of the Central Bank, who gave generously of his time and energy to this end.

Miss Ruth Harwood, Secretary to the Commission since October, 1958, has had charge of preparing the manuscript of both the English and the Spanish editions of this report for the printers.

> *John F. Due*
> Professor of Economics, University of Illinois
>
> *Lyle C. Fitch*
> First Deputy City Administrator,
> City of New York
>
> *Sir Donald MacDougall*
> Official Fellow, Nuffield College,
> Oxford University
>
> *Oliver S. Oldman*
> Assistant Professor of Law,
> Harvard Law School;
> Director of Training, Harvard Law School
> International Program in Taxation
>
> *Carl S. Shoup* (Director of the Study)
> Professor of Economics, Columbia University
>
> *Stanley S. Surrey*
> Professor of Law, Harvard Law School;
> Director, Harvard Law School
> International Program in Taxation

Caracas, June 20, 1959

Contents

List of Diagrams

List of Tables

NOTE : The term "billion," wherever used in this report, means one thousand million (1,000,000,000), not one million million.

Summary

A. Scope of the Report

A reform of the structure of the income tax, with certain changes in administrative procedure; a revision of the customs duties and customs administration; repeal of the "cinco por mil" tax; an increase in the tax on gasoline; and a strengthening of the municipal real estate tax in urban areas: these are the major tax recommendations in the report of the Commission for a Study of the Fiscal System of Venezuela, submitted August 22, 1958.

Suggestions are offered in the report for revision of the system of grants-in-aid from the national government to subordinate units of government (states, *distritos*).

The amount of tax, direct and indirect, that is borne by some typical Venezuelan families is estimated, though with a considerable margin of possible error.

The report also calculates how much it would cost to put every child of school age in elementary school by 1963-64, and 300,000 young men and women in secondary schools by the same date. The rates of income tax that would be necessary to initiate this program in its earliest phase, 1959-60, are given.

The economic background against which these recommendations have been formulated is described and analyzed in the two opening chapters of the report. One of them presents, for the first time, a comprehensive estimate of the way in which the national income of Venezuela is distributed among broad income classes. The other chapter discusses the problem of capital accumulation, and economic development in general, in Venezuela. To integrate the government's budgetary totals with analyses of the nation's income and capital, techniques are suggested with respect to certain features of governmental accounting, in a later chapter. The role—it turns out to be a minor one—that may be played by the tax system in helping assure economic stability within Venezuela

1

is appraised in another chapter of the report.

Attention is given to the importance of the petroleum companies in the economy of Venezuela and, accordingly, in the tax revenue of the national and local governments. The practical working of the so-called 50-50 principle of sharing the oil profits is described. The report makes no recommendation, one way or another, on change from the 50-50 formula to some other ratio; this matter of national policy involves so many important issues other than taxation that it lies outside the scope of the commission's technical recommendations. To facilitate discussion and decision by others, some of the relevant issues are discussed, especially as they bear directly on tax policy, and certain data are presented.

B.   The Revenue System of Venezuela

The revenue system of Venezuela possesses four striking features.

First, practically all of the tax revenue flows to the national government. The states have virtually no tax sources of their own. The Federal District (Caracas) imposes a few taxes at low rates. The municipalities other than Caracas collect little tax revenue in the aggregate.

Second, by far the major part of the national government's tax revenue comes from taxes on the petroleum companies [1] operating in Venezuela.

Third, the remaining national tax revenue, that is, the revenue from taxes levied on the non-oil sector of the Venezuelan economy, comes chiefly from indirect taxation, notably customs duties. Income tax revenue from the non-oil sector is a small part of the total revenue from that sector. And it is, as a corollary, a very minor source of revenue for the national budget as a whole.

Fourth, the tax system seems to be erratically progressive in a mild sort of way, but with many exceptions; this result reflects, of course, chiefly the distribution of the indirect taxes.

These points will now be amplified.

The tax revenues of the national government, as estimated in the budget for the fiscal year July 1, 1958–June 30, 1959, total Bs.3,809 million, according to the system of classification employed here; a good deal less than that, if we follow the budget classification. The classifi-

---

[1] For purposes of the present analysis, the iron-ore mining companies are to be grouped with the petroleum companies, and in the remaining part of Section B of this Summary, the term "oil" or "petroleum" is to be understood as including "ore," except where obviously inapplicable. Quantitatively, the oil companies in the aggregate dwarf the iron-ore mining companies. Thus, on 1956 incomes, the total income tax paid by oil companies amounted to Bs.927 million, against Bs.40 million paid by mining companies (see Table III-6 at end of Chapter III).

cation employed here includes in tax revenues the production tax (royalty tax) on petroleum companies (and a relatively small amount arising from initial exploitation taxes, sales of concessions, etc., which does not come to a large figure, it appears, for 1958-59). It also includes as a tax the profits realized by the government from selling bolivars to the oil companies at 3.09 per dollar (or 3.046 for some part), and reselling them to the commercial banks or the public at 3.32 or 3.35, respectively. Finally, it includes consular fees in the tax totals. The reasons for including these items in tax revenue are given below, in Chapter III (production tax), Appendix A (exchange profit), and Chapter IX (consular fees).

In contrast to the national government, the state governments of Venezuela will collect only a few millions of tax revenue; the Federal District, probably something between Bs.50 million and Bs.100 million; and the rest of the municipalities (strictly, *distritos*) less than Bs.100 million.[2]

As to the second point above, the petroleum companies pay about two-thirds of the national tax revenues. They will pay at least 70 per cent of the income tax estimated for 1958-59 (about Bs.900 million);[3] at least Bs.100 million of the customs duties; all, of course, of the oil production tax and related charges; perhaps some Bs.30 million of the consular fees; and probably some Bs.10 million of stamp taxes. On these counts, the oil companies will pay almost Bs.2,300 million. If in addition we assume that the bulk of the "tax" represented by the profit on foreign exchange is a burden on the oil companies (although any assumption whatsoever on this point is dubious),[4] we conclude that the oil companies account for some Bs.2,500 million, or 66 per cent of the total revenues that are here classified as coming from national taxes.

Table S-1. Estimated Revenues, 1958-59 Fiscal Year, National Government

Taxes	Millions of Bs.
Income tax (includes income taxes on oil and mining companies)	1,270[1]
Inheritance and gift taxes	13

[2] For details on state and local revenue sources, see Chapter XII below.

[3] And most of this will be paid by the three largest petroleum companies. On 1956 income, the largest petroleum company paid slightly over Bs.400 million in income tax (thus, somewhat more than the entire non-oil sector); the three largest together paid nearly Bs.700 million.

[4] See Appendix A below.

Table S-1 (cont.)

Taxes	Millions of Bs.
Import duties and related charges	530
Liquor tax	126
Cigarette tax	95
Match tax	2
Tax on gasoline and certain other petroleum products	24
Stamp taxes	62[1]
Vehicle license tax	15
Production tax (royalty tax) on oil and mining companies, and concession charges, etc.	1,280[2, 3]
Profit on foreign exchange transactions	238[3, 4]
Consular fees	154[3, 5]
Total revenue classified here as tax revenue	3,809
Income from the public domain	13[6]
Fees	167[7]
Miscellaneous revenue	33
Total, current revenue	4,022[9]
To be covered by drawing down reserves, and borrowing	1,793[8]
Total	5,814[9]

[1] The "cinco por mil" tax (see Chapter X below), which has been yielding nearly Bs.120 million a year, and is still in force at this writing (August, 1958), is, in the official budget estimates for 1958-59, from which the present table is drawn, assumed to be repealed; and the income tax estimate includes the effect of an assumed increase in rates to make up for the repeal of the "cinco por mil."

[2] The category includes a certain amount of charges on grants of oil concessions, but for 1958-59 the amount will apparently not be significant, relative to the total.

[3] Not officially classified as a "tax" in the budget estimates.

[4] For the reasons for classifying this item as a tax, see Appendix A to this report.

[5] For the reasons for classifying this item as a tax, see Chapter IX below.

[6] In the budget, items 10 and 11 are included under this heading.

[7] In the budget, item 12 is included under this heading.

[8] In the budget, this is termed "Otros recursos especiales" (plus Bs.2 million, "Acuñación de Monedas").

[9] Constituent items do not add to total, owing to rounding.

With respect to the third point, the non-oil sector contributes, in tax revenue, under the estimates and assumptions just noted (see Table S-1):

	Millions of Bs.	Percent of Total
Income tax, approximately	370	29
Inheritance tax	13	1

Import duties, consular fees	554	43
Liquor, cigarette, and match taxes . .	223	17
Gasoline tax and related taxes . . .	24	2
Stamp taxes	52	4
Vehicle license tax	15	1
Other	40	3
Total	1,291	100

Venezuela's national tax system, ex-oil, is thus seen to be essentially based on indirect taxes. They account for practically 70 per cent of total national tax revenues other than oil-company taxes.

This is so, because the income tax rates are quite modest, and the personal exemptions substantial. Thus a married couple with two children, with salary income of Bs.25,000 a year (= $7,508 at Bs.3.33 to the dollar), pays a total personal income tax of Bs.295, that is a tax of 1.2 per cent on income before subtracting exemptions. At Bs.100,000 (= $30,030), the married couple pays Bs.3,010 in tax, or 3.0 per cent of income. At Bs.500,000 (= $150,150), income tax is Bs.29,695, or 5.9 per cent of income. At Bs.1,000,000 the tax is still only 7.6 per cent of income. Slightly higher percentages apply to business income: 2.7 per cent, 4.5 per cent, 7.4 per cent, and 9.1 per cent, respectively.[5]

The corporation income tax utilizes the same rate scale. And dividends are exempt from the income tax.

Obviously, the income tax in Venezuela, apart from the oil sector, is little more than a token levy.

Accordingly, it is the indirect taxes, largely the customs duties, that determine the distribution of the total tax bill among the income groups. Some illustrative cases built up on a number of more or less dependable assumptions indicate that in the very lowest income groups somewhere between 5 per cent and 10 per cent of income is absorbed by taxation (all indirect), if we assume that indirect taxation is reflected in higher relative prices, that is, is shifted forward rather than backward to profits, wages, or rent. They also indicate that it is possible that some very wealthy persons pay between 15 per cent and 20 per cent of their incomes in tax—partly in income tax, but largely in indirect taxes. Other wealthy individuals, however, doubtless pay no more than from 10 per cent to 15 per cent. Indeed, the chief impression left by a study of these hypothetical cases (see Appendix B below) is the erratic manner

---

[5] See Table III-1 at end of Chapter III below.

in which the percentages vary. Thus, a certain hypothetical family with a disposable income of Bs.20,520 pays 11.33 per cent of total income in taxes, direct and indirect; another, with Bs.27,640 income, pays 17.67 per cent; another, with Bs.34,795, pays 11.38 per cent; another, with Bs.77,670, pays 18.41 per cent—and so on.

C.   Distribution of Income

A distribution of the tax bill among income classes must be viewed in the light of the distribution of income itself. But here we encounter a formidable obstacle in the lack of data. By piecing together bits of information from one source and another, it has been possible to construct a rough estimate, using broad income groups. However, this part of our study has demonstrated forcefully the need for expansion of data gathering in Venezuela, on a large scale. Basic information on incomes needs to be assembled before further progress can be made in understanding the social and economic aspects of the tax system.

Apparently, a little more than one-tenth of the families in Venezuela receive an annual income of more than Bs.12,000. The aggregate income they receive is about 50 per cent of the total private income of the country. At the lower end of the scale, nearly half the families in Venezuela get less than Bs.2,400 a year. They account, in the aggregate, for about one-tenth the total private income. These percentages are before subtracting taxes; but so mildly progressive is the tax system, that the percentages remain virtually unchanged when the computation is made in terms of incomes after taxes (direct and indirect).

The regional differences are no less striking: in Caracas the average income per income earner (not per head) seems to be about Bs.14,000 a year; 40 per cent of the private income in Venezuela goes to Caracas residents alone. In contrast, in other cities of more than 20,000 population, the average income per income earner is about Bs.9,000; and in the rural areas, excluding villages or towns of more than 500 population, it drops precipitously to something like Bs.1,500 a year. Most of the rural poor work their own small plots of land; with some paid work outside to supplement, a typical farm family of 6 persons may get a family real income of Bs.2,000 a year.

Poverty is not entirely a rural phenomenon, however. In some depressed areas (e.g. fish processing), daily wage rates can be found as low as those common in most of the rural area—Bs.6 or 7 a day. And in the larger cities, especially Caracas, there are thousands of unsuccessful job hunters, most perhaps recently from the rural areas, living in the "rancho" slums.

The explanation for these differences in income levels is to be found partly in differences in skill, chiefly skill acquired in schools. Since not much more than half the children of elementary school age go to school in Venezuela, and since only a very small number are able to enroll in the secondary schools, and a minute fraction, in universities in Venezuela or abroad, skilled persons of all descriptions are scarce, and consequently command a high premium in the manpower market.

In part, the explanation lies in the concentration of capital. Agricultural land, for example, is highly concentrated; it is estimated that 2½ per cent of the units of production are those which are over 500 hectares and account for 82 per cent of the total in area. But agriculture itself, on the whole, uses little capital equipment, relative to other sectors of the economy. Employing 43 per cent of the labor force of 2,100,000 persons, agriculture produces only 10 per cent of the national income (excluding oil profits, except the government's share). The petroleum industry, employing only 2 per cent of the labor force, produces 24 per cent of the national income (again, ex-oil profits, except the government's share).

The moral of all this for tax policy seems to be that there is room for a tax system that is more progressive, less erratic in its distribution of the tax bill, and less burdensome at the very lowest levels of income, than the one now in force. But before reaching a conclusion on this matter, we must look at the problem of capital accumulation, to ascertain whether such accumulation might be seriously affected by a change in the tax system.

D. Capital Accumulation

Venezuela has been investing a very large proportion of its annual gross national product—apparently as much as 30 per cent, taking one year with another. Of course, a great deal of investment is needed merely to continue to keep a rapidly growing population at the same standard of living, and Venezuela's population has been growing rapidly indeed: 4 per cent a year. The total annual investment has been more than enough for this, however. Even after allowing for some part of the investment that has proved ineffective or even wasted, there has been enough of it to allow some rise in the average level of consumption. Large segments of the populace, however, have probably shared little or not at all in that rise. If the problem of poverty is to be solved in Venezuela, anything that seriously impedes a continued rapid growth in capital formation must be avoided; but the problem of distributing the gains among all classes remains a problem.

This extraordinarily high rate of investment has been made possible largely by the fact that the government has received a substantial annual revenue from the oil sector of the economy and has devoted an amount not very far short of that revenue to investment in public works, broadly defined. This accounts for some 15 per cent of the national product. Also, Venezuela has been importing capital from abroad; this accounts for another 5 per cent. This leaves something more than 10 per cent of the national product to be contributed to investment by saving on the part of private individuals and corporations within Venezuela, if the 30 per cent rate of investment is to be accounted for. And this, apparently, is what has happened. But since virtually all of this 10 per cent must come from those with enough income to save, that is, roughly speaking, those with incomes above Bs.12,000, and since half the income goes to that group, their rate of gross saving must be about 20 per cent of their incomes.

The question thus arises, whether a more progressive tax system would endanger the contribution to the total of saving, and thus, directly or indirectly, to investment, made by the income group above Bs.12,000 a year.

No doubt, any increase in taxation on the group that are saving would be met in part out of saving, and thus make it necessary for the economy to find some replacement saving elsewhere (as through a larger excess of government current revenue over current expenditure, as distinct from capital expenditure), if the volume of investment were to be maintained without borrowing abroad. But there are countervailing considerations. The amount of decline in saving that would be caused by a moderate increase in progressivity of the tax system would be small, relative to total saving. The decrease in the tax bill of the lower income groups would free some income that they might "invest" in themselves, by increasing their vigor and skill through improved diet and more education (the former, in many instances, depends on the latter). Moreover, education is itself a form of investment, even though it is not counted as such by the technical rules of national income accounting. In Venezuela, education is one of the highest-yielding investments, even when we restrict our view to the sheer money-making aspects: some computations in Chapter XV indicate an annual return ranging from 17 per cent to as high as 130 per cent a year on investment in education.

Hence, additional government expenditure on education would be a form of investment (and saving); the rate of total true investment in Venezuela might not decline, and might even increase. On the whole, the data in Chapters I and II taken together do not suggest that the economy of Venezuela would be harmed by some increase in the progressiveness of the tax system. But it remains true that capital is scarce in Venezuela, with a consequent need for careful allocation of it among the many competing ends.

E. Economic Stability

A tax system can lessen somewhat the impact of depressive or inflationary forces on the economy if it reacts quickly to those forces, demanding much more money from business men and consumers in a period of boom, and slackening its demands on them when business is poor. The national government will accumulate cash reserves in periods of prosperity, and draw on them when revenues fall off. The taxes in question here are, of course, only those that affect the residents of the country. In Venezuela this limitation of the general rule is important. A large part, indeed a major part, of the tax revenues do not affect the disposable income of Venezuelan residents; they impinge on the owners of the petroleum companies (and iron-ore companies). Changes in the income-after-taxes of these persons do not affect business within Venezuela, at least not directly and immediately. Therefore, with respect to such taxes, sensitivity of tax yield to changes in the market for oil does not aid the Venezuelan economy to maintain its stability.

Whether a tax is sensitive to economic fluctuations depends on whether it is linked with magnitudes that change rapidly with business conditions, net profits for example, or, instead, with quantities that do not change rapidly—for example, assessed values of real estate.

We conclude (see Chapter XIII below) that the taxes that the Venezuelan Government takes from the residents of Venezuela are only moderately sensitive; moreover, they are not large in relation to the national income. Accordingly, they are not likely to be very effective in mitigating booms and depressions through automatic changes in yield. The measures we recommend for reforming the tax structure, when examined from this point of view, do enhance, on balance, the sensitivity of the tax system to business fluctuations, but the amounts involved are not large enough to be very significant. As to the taxes on the oil and iron-ore companies, there is a considerable element of sensitivity, owing to the fact that a large part of that taxation is based on profits. Stability of the Venezuelan economy is, to that extent, not promoted. But neither is it endangered, at least for fluctuations that are not too intense or long-lasting. The government may insulate the economy to a considerable degree from depressive or inflationary influences accompanying fluctuations in oil and ore revenues (it is the oil revenues, of course, that are of far the greater importance, quantitatively) by keeping its own expenditure level from fluctuating with its tax receipts from petroleum and iron ore. To do so, it must be prepared to draw on cash reserves, or to borrow from the banks at home, or to borrow abroad, when oil-tax revenues fall off; and when they rise, the government must proceed warily with plans to spend the excess.

Stability of the Venezuelan economy would also be enhanced by a substantial system of social security. Recommendations on the construction of such a system lie outside the scope of the present report. The existing taxes on payrolls for social security as that term is used here (as distinct from fringe benefits, including severance pay) are so light, and restricted to so moderate an area of the Venezuelan economy, that they have no appreciable effect on the economy as a whole (illustrations of amounts paid are given in the course of the computations of the tax bills of representative families in Appendix B), and we do not study them in detail in the chapters below. But at some stage, perhaps not far distant, it might be advisable to set up a special study of social security in Venezuela, especially to regularize payments to the unemployed, and to provide some assistance in old age.

Management of the public debt can be an important factor in the internal stability of the economy. Since arrangements for meeting the current year's deficit partly by borrowing from banks, both at home and abroad, are now nearing completion, we make no short-term recommendations on this score; but as Chapter II indicates, there may be a strong case for a moderate amount of long-term borrowing from abroad, in view of the great need for capital in this period of extremely rapid growth of the Venezuelan economy—capital for investment in the widest sense, including investment in the human resources of the country through education. The financial size of the task of assuring that every child is getting at least part of an elementary school education by, say, 1963 is not so great that it cannot be met by internal taxation; but the change in tax rates needed would mark an abrupt break with the past, and the possibility of borrowing to cover part of the cost need not be precluded from discussion.

These thoughts suggest the question of taxable capacity. In Venezuela at the present time, taxable capacity is limited perhaps more by social and political factors than by economic considerations. The chief question, again, is whether Venezuela should try to finance all her capital needs through her own tax system, and this point has been covered in the remarks above. Taxes, national and local on Venezuelan businesses and residents (that is, excluding foreign-owned companies, which means practically all the oil and all the iron ore sector), take approximately Bs.1.3 billion per year out of a national income of some Bs.17 billion (income received by Venezuelan residents, plus the government income from oil and ore and property), thus approximately 8 per cent. If the comparison is made instead with the Bs.13 billion of private national income (i.e. excluding the government income from oil, ore, and properties), the ratio is approximately 11 per cent. But if all national and local taxes, including those from oil and ore, a total of Bs.4 billion, are compared with net national income produced in Venezuela (including, that is, profits of oil and ore companies originating in Venezuela), about Bs.20 billion, the ratio is instead near 20 per cent. These ratios do not give much guidance for tax policy, but, by comparison with other countries, they indicate that Venezuela is not close to any economic limits, whatever they may be, on taxation. In more industrially advanced countries, the ratio comparable to the 8 to 11 per cent ratios above will be found in the range 25 to 35 per cent; but this in turn is not a safe guide for Venezuela, where the need for large amounts of capital formation is relatively more urgent (including, again, improvement in human skills and vigor as capital accumulation), and where a large part of the population lives at a very low economic level. The better procedure, in place of relying much on comparative ratios of this kind, is to return to the intensive analysis of the particular needs of the country, and the ways of meeting them that seem feasible in the particular environment of time and place.

F. *A Program of Immediate Tax Reform*

Increased progressivity in the tax system of Venezuela does not depend wholly on a change in the rates of income tax. Let us pass in review the major recommendations that the present report makes with respect to taxes other than the income tax, and observe the result. The reasoning that has led to these recommendations will not be reproduced here; it can be found in the respective chapters below.

Improvements in administration of the inheritance and gift tax should result in a substantial percentage increase in revenue, but the increase would be small, relative to the total budget. Rates might well be increased somewhat, but again, the revenue total would not be very significantly affected. The issue here is more one of social policy than of revenue.

The tax on distilled liquors might well be increased; if rates were raised by some 50 per cent or more, an additional Bs.40 million of revenue might be gained.

The tax on gasoline is extremely low in Venezuela. Although we are aware of the significant arguments made against any increase in the tax, we believe that an increase is necessary, perhaps inevitable. If the tax on regular grade gasoline were raised from (approximately) 1 céntimo a litre to 5 céntimos, and the tax on super-grade, from (approximately) 2 céntimos to 9 céntimos, an additional Bs.100 million might be obtained. Perhaps mass transportation for the lower income groups could be exempted from this increase.

Repeal of customs duties on a wide range of articles not domestically produced, now subject to low or moderate duties, should, directly and indirectly, lift some of the tax burden from the lower income groups. The revenue loss here might run to Bs.150 million a year. Some customs duties might well be increased, and changed to an ad valorem basis: the articles in question are consumers goods purchased almost entirely by those in the middle or upper income groups. There might be about Bs.100 million of added revenue from this source.

The gross receipts tax ("cinco por mil") should be repealed. Although the tax has been yielding nearly Bs.120 million, its repeal would reduce total tax revenues by only some Bs.80 million, if that; repeal of the tax would automatically increase the yield of the income tax, for reasons explained in Chapter X below.

The revenue gains from these recommended changes amount to Bs.240 million; the losses, to Bs.260 million. The near equality of the two is coincidence; but it demonstrates that, even before taking the income tax into consideration, the tax system can be made somewhat more progressive by measures that can be supported not only for this reason but also on other grounds, explained in the chapters below.

Is there, then, any need for income tax reform? The answer is clearly yes, for two reasons. First, even if the income tax were not to be required to produce more revenue, it is in need of structural reform; and second, the information given in Chapter XV below suggests that Venezuela may soon decide to spend substantial additional sums on education, and, to a lesser degree, perhaps, on public health. All this is without taking into account the fact that the national budget indicates a deficit of nearly Bs.1,000 million for the current fiscal year apart from paying off past obligations. Such a deficit may be appropriate at the present moment, given the current slackening in business activity, but the possibility must be envisaged that for 1959-60 measures may need to be adopted to reduce it or eliminate it, either by reducing outlays or by gaining more tax revenue. Accordingly, Chapter XV below makes a suggestion, only one of many feasible and appropriate patterns of income tax increase, for starting on an enhanced education program; and Chapter III below discusses some of the general principles to be observed if rates of the income tax are raised or exemptions lowered. There is little point in attempting to be still more specific on the subject of income tax increases until the demands to be made on the tax system become clearer, as they no doubt will be by the turn of the year, if not before. In general, we believe that the personal income tax system can yield about Bs.200 million more without raising rates or lowering exemptions to levels that could be reasonably objected to, assuming, of course, that the structural reforms recommended below are also carried through. The corporation income tax might yield some Bs.40 million more under a rate scale of say 10 per cent on the first Bs.100,000, and 20 per cent on the bracket Bs.100,000 to Bs.10,000,000, without increasing the top rate; since the top rate affects almost none but the oil companies, a change there brings up the question of a change in the 50-50 minimum formula, a problem of great complexity that involves so many non-tax considerations that it has been understood to be outside the scope of the present report. Tables to Chapter III supply data for computing possible results of increases in tax in this area, if any are decided on.

One thing is troublesome, however, at the moment: the statistics on which to base adequate estimates of income tax yield under increased rates and lower exemptions simply do not exist. The yield estimates given here and in Chapter XV are of a highly uncertain quality. So, about all we can say is that if rate schedules of the type we mention here, in Chapter III, and in Chapter XV were adopted, experience would show us what they would yield, and it is almost sure that the increment in yield would be on the order of from Bs.100 million to Bs.300 million. And of course much more could be obtained with somewhat larger increases.

Although it is not feasible to summarize here the many recommendations made for every tax in the Venezuelan system (for information the reader is referred to the chapters below), income tax reform is of such significance that an exception is made in its case, in the following paragraphs. The customs duties, and the fiscal position of state and municipal governments also deserve an attempt at summary.

G. Income Tax Reform

STRUCTURE OF THE TAX

Three major reforms are recommended in the income tax structure: replacement of the nine schedular taxes and the complementary tax by a single, unified income tax; a freeing of the rate schedule of the corporation income tax from absolute conformity to the rate scale of the personal income tax; and taxation to Venezuelan shareholders of the dividends they receive from Venezuelan corporations, with some allowance, either at the corporate level or the individual level, to avert substantial overtaxation of corporate income. These measures will represent a maturing of the Venezuelan income tax structure, following the fifteen years of introduction and assimilation since the tax was enacted.

The chief purpose of the schedular taxes, namely, to treat different kinds of income differently, can be maintained, to the degree justified, in a much simpler way under a unified income tax. Thus, an earned income credit can be allowed for wages and salaries, and, if it is desired (though the case seems a weak one), a similar credit can be granted to profits of agriculturists.

The need to allocate income precisely among the nine different schedules is a source of dispute between taxpayer and tax administrator, and increases noticeably the mechanical task of handling the returns as they flow through the various stages in the Income Tax Administration. The differing rules as to what may or may not be deducted in computing net income taxable under the schedules make for unequal treatment among taxpayers. The failure to take account of the number of the taxpayer's children, or his marital status, is only partly offset by the provisions of the complementary tax. Schedular tax is withheld at the source on wages and salaries, but by a crude method that often forces the wage earner to accept a lower personal exemption than the Bs.12,000 a year granted under all the other schedules. Finally, the public can scarcely understand what the income tax rate schedule as a whole comes to, so complicated is the mental task of adding the schedular rates and the complementary tax rates, with due allowance for the differences in family exemptions, definition of taxable income, and so on.

It is probably not just a coincidence that those countries that make heavy and successful use of the personal income tax do not use a system of schedular rates (the British tax is in essence a unified tax, even though the taxpayer's income is reported in terms of schedules), while some of the other countries where the income tax has encountered grave difficulties are adherents of the schedular system (France comes especially to mind).

The single scale of progressive tax rates that applies to corporate income and to personal income in Venezuela has become inappropriate for the fast growing, more complex Venezuelan economy of today. If the personal income tax scale is to be adjusted in the years ahead, the adjustment should not be hampered by the requirement that the new rate scale also be suitable for corporations. Similarly, an increase in the corporate income tax should not automatically require a simultaneous increase of just the same amount in the individual income tax. Separate rate scales should be established for individuals and corporations. Both rate scales should be progressive, but the corporation tax should start at a higher rate, and carry only two or three steps in its progression; otherwise, the splitting of a large corporation into several small ones—already a feature of the Venezuelan fiscal scene—would further weaken the tax.

The present exclusion of dividends from an individual's taxable income is a relic of the earlier days of the income tax in Venezuela when virtually all domestic corporations were family affairs, and the common rate scale (corporate and individual) taxed corporate profits much as if they were already in the hands of the stockholders. But today, a wealthy or even just well-to-do family often owns shares in many corporations, and it holds income-yielding property in other forms too. Moreover, under different rate scales for corporations and individuals, as proposed here, no argument remains for exempting dividends from tax. Accordingly, we recommend that dividends from Venezuelan corporations be included in the taxable net income of individuals resident in Venezuela.

To mitigate the problem of overtaxation of corporate income, a problem that has never been completely solved in any tax system that we are aware of, corporations should be allowed to deduct a fractional part of dividends paid to shareholders, in computing the corporate net income subject to tax, or, alternatively, shareholders should be given some credit for income tax paid by the corporation.

Other technical issues in income taxation that are covered in this report will be noted only briefly here; they are discussed in detail in

Chapters III and IV below.

Venezuela should move gradually toward taxing income received by its residents and its domestic corporations from sources abroad. At present, income from foreign investments or from work abroad is not subject to tax in Venezuela.

Capital gains should continue to be taxable, though with elimination of certain deductions now allowed; on the other hand, the individual taxpayer should have the right to average the gain back over the preceding three or four years, to avoid being thrown unfairly into high bracket rates erratically in one year or another; and capital losses should be deductible, and, if not fully absorbed in the year of realization, carried forward to be offset against future years' income. Gain accrued during the taxpayer's lifetime should not escape income tax entirely, as it now does, when he passes the property on to others.

The existing mechanical limitation on deduction of salaries in computing corporate income, and the accompanying exemption granted to the employee with respect to the salary so disallowed as a corporate deduction, are too arbitrary, and will not be needed anyway under the tax structure recommended in this report.

A business loss for a given year should be carried back and offset against the profit, if any, of the two preceding years, thus giving rise to a tax refund. If not fully absorbed this way, the remainder of the loss should be carried forward to subsequent years of profit.

Accounting rules for income tax should be liberalized to allow installment-method accounting; and deduction for certain reserves should be permitted. Transactions between taxpayer corporations controlled by the same interests need close examination. The statute of limitations that sets a time limit for action against the taxpayer by the government, when he has submitted an erroneous return, needs revision.

ADMINISTRATION OF THE TAX

Administration of the income tax has made a good record in Venezuela, and the suggestions offered in our report for changes are chiefly designed to simplify administration under the proposed unification of the income tax, and to prepare the administrative body to handle the larger task that lies ahead as the Venezuelan economy becomes still more complex, and as the income tax is called upon to play a larger relative role. An expanded staff of income tax personnel is needed, especially in the intermediate supervisory positions; and an increase in technical training will more than pay for itself.

Many of the changes are too technical to be summarized readily here, especially those dealing with methods of processing the tax declarations within the Administrative Division and the Technical Division of the Income Tax Administration. This remark is applicable also to suggestions for change in methods of checking on whether everyone who should file a declaration has in fact done so (for this purpose, an extension of the system of certificates of solvency is recommended) and of collecting information from payors, vendors, and others, to match against the taxpayers' declarations.

Of more interest to the general public are the recommendations in Chapter VI that taxpayers be required to keep themselves more nearly current in their payment of income tax. This necessitates measures that will make it easier, on the one hand, for the taxpayer to pay his taxes (a greatly increased use of checks in the Venezuelan economy would be one of the most important means of inducing taxpayers under all Venezuelan taxes to pay promptly what they owe), and, on the other hand, collecting delinquent accounts more promptly and thoroughly. Moreover, taxpayers who do not have their income tax withheld at the source should be required to pay on account, on an estimated basis, during the same year they are receiving the income—that is, on a pay-as-you-go basis. (Care must be taken not to lose a whole year's taxes, in the year of transition; the extra payment in the year of change can be spread over a few years.) A final reckoning should be made for each taxpayer, whether withheld on or not, soon after the close of the year. Where tax has been overpaid, either because of over-estimate or over-withholding, refund of the overpaid tax should be automatic and prompt. A rapid and completely fair system of refunds of taxes that have been overpaid for whatever reason (including errors made by the taxpayer against himself on his declaration) is one of the most powerful means of building up a willingness of taxpayers to comply with income tax law and creating an atmosphere of mutual confidence without which no modern income tax can function properly.

Appeals by taxpayers against additional assessment, following examination of their declarations, or books, by the tax agents, need to be facilitated by discussion between the taxpayer and the officials of the Tax Administration before resort is had to the courts.

A Tax Research Group is needed in the Ministry of Finance to advise the Minister on economic policy and legal aspects of taxation, especially to anticipate problems that will be coming over the tax horizon. (It is important not to dissipate such a Group's time and energy on a large number of day-to-day problems.) Efficient functioning of such a Group will require, among other things, the gathering of still more statistical data from the tax declarations.

H. Reform of the Customs Duties and Administration

Whether or not Venezuela should pursue a policy of protection for manufacturing industries, and if so, how intensively, is a problem that is analyzed in Chapter II below, where it is urged that the immediate costs of such a program be kept well in mind, and weighed against the assumed, and by no means certain, benefits that are expected over the long run. In Chapter IX, on the other hand, the revenue aspects of the duties are considered, from the point of view of the distribution of the tax burden on various classes of consumers. Some of the duties on consumer goods seem to serve no aim of protection, and could well be repealed as part of a plan to lower the total tax bill of the lowest-income groups. The same remark applies to duties on imports of many capital goods, including certain chemicals, and machinery and equipment. Exonerations do allow a considerable import, duty-free, of capital goods and basic materials not produced in Venezuela, but a less cumbersome approach would be simple repeal of the duties. In any event, exonerations might well be granted for longer periods of time than they are at present.

Some customs duties could be increased, to yield appreciable additional revenue, without imposing a burden at low-income levels. Included in this group in the recommendations in Chapter IX are automobiles, parts and accessories (with compensating domestic excise taxes, if further protection is not an issue); television sets; radios and phonographs; watches and clocks; cameras and film; and electrical appliances and lamps. The rates suggested range from 10 per cent to 30 per cent ad valorem.

These suggestions for rates on such articles bring to mind another important, and general, improvement that could be made in the customs duties: replacing the present duties based simply on weight (so many Bs. per kilogram) by duties based on value of the article. The valuation problem would not be difficult in many instances, and, in fact, there is already an ad valorem duty on all imports, a duty that ranges from 2 per cent to 3½ per cent, labelled (misleadingly) a "consular fee." Such necessities as flour should be exempt from this "fee," and, indeed, perhaps the entire consular fee could be consolidated with the tariff proper.

Administratively, the greatest need in customs, as in indirect tax administration generally, is to prohibit in the future the granting of positions in the tax administration on a political basis. By no means all personnel have obtained their positions in this manner, and there are many able and devoted individuals performing difficult tasks in these areas; but the problem just noted is well recognized.

One feature of compensation of customs officials is probably, on balance, unfortunate; the practice, sanctioned by the law, of awarding customs officials a portion of the fines assessed, up to a certain maximum per month, depending on the base pay. But of course elimination of this feature requires an improvement in base pay, and in supervision.

A good many recommendations on other administrative features of customs administration are given in Chapter IX, which cannot be easily summarized here, including problems arising from classification, the imposition of fines, expansion of physical facilities for customs inspection and storage at the ports, use of trust funds to hold bond-money, possible adjustment of duties to a net weight basis if specific duties are retained, and codification of customs regulations. One further change is of great importance to the formulation of tax policy: information on how much of the customs revenue comes from each of the categories of imports. At the present time no records are compiled of duty revenue by class of import.

I. State and Local Finance

The financial role to be assigned to the states and municipalities of Venezuela in the years ahead is still by no means clear. It depends on some weighty decisions that must be made soon on centralization versus decentralization of the governmental structure. At the present time, the state and municipal governments are struggling to emerge from the state of impotence into which they were thrown by neglect and, perhaps just as often, arbitrary personal intervention of the central government under the late regime. And many of the tasks that local governments undertake so extensively in other countries, notably provision of education and public health, are so great in Venezuela because of the accumulation of unmet needs, that it is difficult to see how these subordinate units of government can play much of a role without extensive grants from the central government. These remarks probably do not apply to the few large, relatively wealthy municipalities, including the Federal District (Caracas), the city of Maracaibo, and perhaps two or three others. They seem to have the economic resources to enable them to achieve a notable degree of self-sufficiency and local initiative, by means of improvement in their administration of the real estate tax (such improvement is already well under way in Maracaibo), and a substantial increase in rates. This tax, which in virtually all other countries with active local governments is an important source of revenue, is in Venezuela imposed at rates so low as in many cases to be almost negligible. And rural land is, in general, not taxed at all; but here, real estate taxation is probably best suited to be taken in hand by the state governments, just as soon as surveys of areas owned are made.

In the larger cities, increased use could well be made of special assessments (betterment taxes, to help defray the cost of paving, sewers, and other improvements that enhance the value of land in particular areas); and, as the real estate tax proper is increased, land might well be required to carry more of the increased tax bill than buildings or improvements of the land (grading, etc.).

The *patente,* the local business tax common to Venezuelan municipalities, is a crude form of taxation, and should be repealed as soon as local ability to strengthen the real estate tax has been demonstrated.

Motor vehicle quarterly taxes need to be made uniform to prevent widespread evasion through registration of automobiles in low-taxing states where they are scarcely if ever, in fact, used.

But none of these tax measures will be enough (outside the few larger cities), if local units are to become effective organs of government. A system of grants-in-aid is already in force, from the national government to the states; and the states pass on a little money to the municipalities; but the formula for grants to the states needs revision, and the municipalities will have to get more, perhaps directly from the national government, if they are to be revitalized. A permanent Local Government Commission, set up so as to be outside of political influences, needs to be created at the national-government level, to help develop the system of grants-in-aid and to supply the municipalities with a great deal of technical information on administration (tax and other). But the process of rebuilding municipal vigor, though it can be made a sure one, is not likely to be accomplished within a year or two or three; and if a frontal attack is to be made within a short time on the great problem of educating the growing numbers of children (not to speak of the not far from half of the adult population who are said to be illiterate), it cannot very well be left to the states and municipalities. They should, of course, be able to continue much of the program, once it is well under way.

CHAPTER I : **The Distribution of Income**

Introduction

In studying the tax structure of any country it is essential to form some idea, in quantitative terms, of the distribution of income. So far as we are aware no comprehensive study of this problem has been made in Venezuela. We have therefore had to make for ourselves the best estimates we could in the time available and with the limited material at our disposal.

We have relied mainly on material collected by the Banco Central in connection with its estimates of national income and expenditure; on the results of various sample surveys carried out by "Datos," a market research organization, in the course of which certain information on incomes was obtained; on statistics of the Ministerio de Hacienda arising out of the collection of income tax; on the results of the National Agricultural Inquiry (Encuesta Agropecuaria Nacional) of 1956, carried out by the Ministerio de Agricultura y Cría with the assistance of a technical staff provided by the Food and Agriculture Organization; on details of payrolls in a number of establishments shown to us by the Ministerio del Trabajo; on the results of an inquiry into the conditions of "The Venezuelan Peasant Farmer" recently carried out by Dr. George W. Hill and some of his students in the Central University, Caracas; [1] and on conversations with numerous people in various parts of the country.

While our estimates are inevitably subject to a margin of error it is reassuring that, when the problem is approached from various angles, and independent sources are used, the same general picture emerges.

The income of Venezuela is unevenly distributed—between town and countryside, between regions of the country, between sectors of the economy, and between the individual members of the population—to

[1] Some preliminary findings were presented to the 8th Annual Convention of the Venezuelan Association for the Advancement of Science at Caracas, 28 May 1958.

21

an extent that inevitably impresses a visitor from the United States or the United Kingdom.

A. Town and Country

Income is heavily concentrated in Caracas and, to a lesser extent, in the other larger towns. In general, the larger the town the larger the average income tends to be; and it is lowest of all in the rural areas. According to our estimates, presented in Table I-1, the average income in Caracas per income earner (not *per capita*) is Bs.14,000-15,000 a year. In other towns of more than 20,000 it probably approaches Bs.9,000. And so on down the scale until we come to people living outside towns of over 500 inhabitants; they have an estimated average income of only Bs.1,500 a year, one-tenth of that in Caracas.

Table I-1. Estimated Distribution of Private Incomes: Rural and Urban, by Size of Towns, 1957

Population of town or area	Number of incomes (thousands)	Average income (Bs. per annum)	Total income (Bs. million)	Per cent of number of incomes	Per cent of total income
Over 1,000,000 (Caracas)........	350	14,500	5,100	17	40
20,000-1,000,000....	470	8,750	4,100	22	32
5,000-20,000......	210	6,250	1,300	10	10
500-5,000.......	280	4,000	1,100	13	9
Under 500 (rural areas)..........	800	1,500	1,200	38	9
Total.........	2,110	6,000	12,800	100	100

SOURCES: Information obtained in the course of constructing Tables I-5 and I-6. The item "Profits, etc., not reported in survey" in Table I-6 was mainly, but not wholly, attributed to the larger towns.

Looking at the matter in another way we find that Caracas, with only one-sixth of the country's population, has about two-fifths of the income (and this does not, of course, include the Government's income from oil; we are considering only private incomes). Adding in the other larger towns we find that about two-fifths of the population live in the twenty to twenty-five towns of over 20,000 people; yet they have nearly three-quarters of the income. At the other extreme we find nearly two-fifths of the population living in rural areas; yet they have only about one-tenth of the income.

It is true that prices are higher in Caracas, and to a lesser extent in the other larger towns, than they are in the small towns and in the countryside, so that the differences in *real* incomes tend to be less marked than our figures suggest. But, apart from rents, the differences in prices are perhaps not so great as is sometimes thought; many branded goods, for example, have a uniform price throughout the country. Moreover, Government expenditure on such things as roads and schools has probably brought greater benefits to the larger towns than to the rural areas. These greater benefits, which are not reflected in money incomes, may quite possibly offset the higher prices. If so, the figures in our table may, after all, give a fair indication of relative real incomes in towns of various sizes and in the countryside.

B. *Regional Differences*

The size of a town is not, of course, the sole determinant of the average income of its inhabitants. Much depends on the region of the country in which it is situated. Thus, for example, in the group of towns with a population of between 20,000 and 1,000,000, those connected with the petroleum industry—such as Maracaibo, Cabimas-Lagunillas, Punto Fijo—have an average income between two-thirds and four-fifths of that in Caracas,[2] while in those situated in relatively depressed agricultural areas—such as Valera, Mérida, and San Cristóbal in the Andes—the average income is well under half that in Caracas; in Cumaná, in the Sucre fishing region, it is only one-quarter. (This is a depressed region in which, in a large fish-processing factory, the commonest wage is Bs.6 a day for women and Bs.6-7 for men.)

Similarly, among the smaller towns and in the rural areas there are patches of prosperity: for example, around the oil fields (in small towns such as Valle de la Pascua) or at Calabozo, the site of a large irrigation and flood control scheme where farmers, many with considerable experience, are being settled on specially prepared farms of about 200 hectares.

---

[2] The figures quoted in this paragraph are based on data provided by "Datos."

C. Industrial Distribution of Income

The level of income generated per head varies greatly from one sector of the economy to another. In particular, there is a marked contrast between the two extremes: agriculture (which is taken to include animal husbandry throughout this chapter) and petroleum. Agriculture, as is shown in Table I-2, may employ over two-fifths of the economically active population but generates only one-tenth of the national income. The petroleum industry employs only 2% of the country's labor force but generates one-quarter of the national income, if we include the taxes and royalties paid to the Government (other than payments for new concessions, which we have excluded as they are of a non-recurrent nature).

Table I-2. Industrial Origin of National Income, 1957

	Income generated		Active population	
	Bs. thousand million	%	Thousands	%
Agriculture..............................	1.5	10	900	43
Petroleum:				
Remuneration of labor.......... 0.9				
Government taxes and royalties (ex. new concessions)......... 2.9[1]	3.8	24	46	2
Other private activities[2]....................	10.4	66	1164	55
Total..............................	15.7[2]	100	2110	100

[1] 4.1 Government income from oil *accruing* during year (this is more than the income received) less 1.2 new concessions. Banco Central.

[2] Excludes Government income from property other than petroleum.

SOURCES: Table I-3 and notes above.

These comparisons are less striking if we exclude the oil industry's payments to the Government, as we should do in an analysis of private income. But even then we find incomes in agriculture to be only 12% of the national total and the earnings of oil workers alone to be 7% although they comprise only 2% of the labor force. (In addition, of course, the oil industry has important effects on private incomes in other sectors of the economy. It provides a market for contracting work and supplies generally; the oil workers provide a market for consumer goods; and the large sums turned over to the Government enable it to employ many Venezuelan firms and workers on public works and the like.)

D.   *A More Detailed Analysis*

We shall now look in more detail at the way in which private income is distributed between various classes of the population, using figures calculated by the Banco Central for the purpose of estimating the national income. (*Private* income falls short of the total national income by the amount of Government income from the oil companies and from various forms of Government property.)

The last column of Table I-3 gives estimates of the income of various classes of the community. These correspond to figures given in the 1957 *Memoria* of the Banco Central (Tables 14-6 and 14-7), except that they have been further subdivided and brought up to 1957 through the courtesy of the Banco Central, who have provided us with provisional estimates. In the first column there are estimates of the number of incomes in the various classes. Most of these figures too are derived from information provided by the Banco Central with the exception of those for Government service and agriculture, where the method of estimation is explained in the notes below the table.

We have assumed that the active population was about 2,100,000 in

Table I-3.   Analysis of Private Income, 1957

(Round figures are used throughout)

	Number of incomes (thousands)	Average income (Bs.)	Total income (Bs. thousand million)
1. Independent professionals[1,2]....	4.5	80,000	0.35
2. Petroleum workers[2]............	46	20,000	0.9
3. Industry, commerce, mining, services, construction[2,3]:			
a. Salary earners: Federal Dist.	60 ⎫	16,000	1.0 ⎫
b. Salary earners: Interior.....	150 ⎬ 850	8,000	1.2 ⎬ 5.1
c. Wage earners: Federal Dist...	180 ⎪	7,000	1.3 ⎪
d. Wage earners: Interior......	460 ⎭	3,500	1.6 ⎭

Table I-3 (cont.)

	Number of incomes (thousands)	Average income (Bs.)	Total Income (Bs. thousand million)
4. Domestic servants[2]:			
a. Federal District............	40 } 165	3,000 }	0.3
b. Interior..................	125 }	1,250 }	
5. Government service...........	145[4]	10,000	1.5[2]
6. Agriculture:			
a. Remuneration of labor......	750 }	1,100	0.8 }
b. Remuneration of capital and enterprise.................	150 } 900[5]	5,000	0.7 } 1.5[2]
7. Profits in industry, commerce, mining, services & construction..	—[6]		2.15[2]
8. Rent & interest not elsewhere included.......................	—	—	1.0[2]
Total..................	2,110	6,000	12.8[7]

[1] Doctors, dentists, veterinarians and lawyers only.   Excludes those employed in Government service, by business concerns, etc.

[2] Source: Banco Central de Venezuela.

[3] Includes employers and workers on their own account, the average remuneration of whose labor (as distinct from their capital and enterprise) is assumed to be equal to that of wage and salary earners. See note 6 to this table.

[4] According to the estimates of the Banco Central, the total remuneration of labor in Government service rose by 43% between 1950 and 1957. During the same period the average rate of wages and salaries in industry, etc., rose by about 60%; but salaries rose less than wages, and the proportion of salary earners is substantially higher in Government service than it is in industry. It thus seems reasonable to assume that employment in Government service is of the same order as it was in 1950 when, according to the Census, it appears to have been about 145,000.

[5] It is difficult to estimate the numbers engaged in agriculture. We give below two methods that may give high and low limits.

One method is to estimate the total active population and then subtract those accounted for in the non-agricultural sectors. In 1950, according to the Census, the total active population was rather more than 34% of the total population of the country. If the proportion was the same in 1957 and the population at mid-1957 as high as 6.6 million (see footnote 3 which follows in text below), the total active population would be about 2.25 million. Subtracting 1.2 million already accounted for in lines 1-5 of the table (and ignoring unemployment) we are left with about 1,050,000 engaged in agriculture. This may seem high, as it is 50% above the number enumerated in agriculture in the 1950 Census, while agricultural production rose by only about 50% between 1950 and 1957 (Banco Central *Memoria* 1957, page 102), so that no increase in productivity per worker is allowed for. (The 1950 Census may, however, have understated the numbers in agriculture.)

Another method of calculation is as follows. It is estimated in *Encuesta Agropecuaria Nacional 1956* that there were in 1956 nearly 400,000 units of exploitation in agriculture, of which about 320,000 were of less than ten hectares and nearly 80,000 of more than ten hectares. Assuming six persons to a family this gives a total population of 1,920,000 associated with the smaller units. Assuming that rather more than one-third of these were active (the proportion for the nation as a whole in 1950), we have 650,000 workers whom we may, as a first approximation, assume to be engaged on the family holdings and as workers on the larger farms. Adding 80,000 larger farmers and, say, 70,000 members of their families, and others not from the smaller holdings, working on their farms, we get a total of 800,000 engaged in agriculture. (Alternatively, we might assume rather fewer members of the average family on a small unit at work but rather more laborers on the larger farms and get the same total number.)

We have taken a figure between these two estimates, namely 900,000. In the light of the figures in the previous paragraph, and bearing in mind that they refer to 1956, we assume that the Bs.800 million estimated by the Banco Central as "remuneration of labor" in agriculture (which is intended to include production of small holdings as well as wages of hired labor) is shared between 750,000 workers, and the Bs.700 million estimated as "remuneration of capital and enterprise" between the remaining 150,000.

6 In 1950, according to the Census, there were roughly 30,000 employers and 160,000 workers on their own account in industry, services, etc. Such people have, however, already been included in the first column under item 3. (See Note 3 to this table.)

7 This is equal to the sum of the remuneration of labor and of capital and enterprise (as given in the Banco Central *Memoria* for 1957, tables 14-6 and 14-7 but brought up to 1957), excluding Government income from petroleum and other Government property, which should not be included in an estimate of private income. The small item "employers' contributions to Social Security" has been ignored.

1957 or about one-third of a total population of perhaps 6-1/3 million (approximately the proportion in the Census of 1950). The remaining 4 million or so were dependents: wives, children, old people, etc. There is some uncertainty about the size of the total population of Venezuela but this does not affect the general picture.[3]

The middle column shows the average annual income of the various classes, the average for the active population as a whole being Bs.6,000. Some groups are well above this figure but some are well below.

3 The official estimate of total population at mid-1957 is 6,130,000, based on the assumption that the annual percentage rate of growth of the population since 1950 has been the same as that between 1941 and 1950 as shown by the Censuses of those years. On the other hand we have been given figures by the Dirección General de Estadística of the Ministerio de Fomento which imply a population in the middle of 1957 of about 6.6 million. This is estimated by starting with the 1950 Census figure and allowing for subsequently recorded births, deaths and net immigration. Estimates made by "Datos" for the end of 1957 imply a figure for mid-1957 between these two extremes of about 6.35 million. See also Chapter II, below.

INCOMES WELL ABOVE THE AVERAGE

Let us start with those that are well above. First, there are 4,000-5,000 *independent professionals*—doctors, dentists, lawyers and veterinarians only—working on their own account (line 1 of the table) with an estimated average income of about Bs.80,000. The 46,000 *petroleum workers* (line 2) have an average income of Bs.20,000 a year. Some are well above this figure and, with a minimum wage of Bs.20 a day, every worker in regular employment must have an income far in excess of the national average when account is taken of various supplements and benefits.

In line 3a we find 60,000 *salary earners in industry, commerce, etc., in the Federal District* with an average income of Bs.16,000 a year. Since many of these are junior office staff, shop assistants and the like earning much less than this figure, there must be a substantial number earning far more. In the payrolls shown to us by the Ministry of Labor we did find a fair number of senior executives earning Bs.50,000 or more and a good many more earning less than this but still considerably more than Bs.16,000. There must also be a number of salary earners getting high figures in the Interior, but here the general level of salaries tends to be much lower. (For high salaries in all occupations reference may be made to Table III-16 which gives details of salaries declared for Income Tax in *1956*. This shows 22,000 salaries of between Bs.30,000 and Bs.50,000; 7,000 between Bs.50,000 and Bs.100,000; and nearly 1,000 over Bs.100,000, including 2 of over Bs.1,000,000.)

While the average income of *wage earners in industry, etc.* (lines 3c and 3d) is relatively low, especially outside Caracas, there is a minority earning substantially more. In the Ministry of Labor's payroll figures we found some workers classified as wage earners who appeared to be earning between Bs.15,000 and Bs.20,000 a year, including supplements, mainly in large, well-managed firms. But Bs.20,000 seemed to be a virtual ceiling; we found only one wage earner with a higher figure. There are also some very high wage earnings in iron mining comparable with those in petroleum.

In *Government service* (line 5) we find 145,000 with an average income of Bs.10,000. A good many of these have an income little if at all above the national average, and some get less; but a fair number have salaries far in excess of Bs.10,000. According to the Budget for 1958/9 a Minister gets Bs.96,000 plus Bs.60,000 for expenses of representation; a senior official gets a basic salary of over Bs.57,000; and so on down the scale.

In line 6b, there are included some prosperous *farmers* earning good incomes and, as we shall see shortly, a small number of people owning huge estates from which they must derive very large incomes.

Finally, there is a very considerable number of people earning large incomes, some very large, from *profits, interest and rent* (lines 7 & 8).

INCOMES WELL BELOW THE AVERAGE

Let us now go to the opposite extreme and consider those who are earning well below the national average.

The first group that springs to attention is that of the 460,000 *wage earners in industry, etc. outside the Federal District* (line 3d) with an estimated *average* income of only Bs.3,500 a year. This means that a good half of the group is probably getting less. The fish-processing workers in Sucre, already mentioned, provide examples. There must also be a good many *salary earners in the Interior* (line 3b) earning very low incomes. For example, the Ministry of Labor showed us payroll figures for a store in Barquisimeto where the commonest rate for a female assistant was only Bs.100 per month, or Bs.1,200 a year apart from supplements. In Caracas, on the other hand, there seem to be rather few wage or salary earners with less than Bs.3,500 a year. This is the impression formed from a perusal of the Ministry of Labor figures, and it is confirmed by the results of the "Datos" sample survey; of those interviewed only 5% reported incomes of under Bs.300 a month. It is true that only men were interrogated, but the Ministry of Labor figures suggest that, although there was a fair number of women in this group, the bulk of the women earned more; and it is estimated that even a domestic servant in Caracas (line 4a) gets, on average, about Bs.3,000 a year, including the value of board and lodging where provided; a chamber-maid in a first-class hotel may make substantially more. The bulk of the really low incomes, outside agriculture which we shall consider in a moment, are thus to be found among the wage and lower salary earners in the Interior, and with these we may include the 125,000 *domestic servants in the Interior* with an estimated average income of Bs.1,250 a year (line 4b). In Table I-5 below we estimate, from quite independent sources, that there were about 400,000 people living in towns of over 500 inhabitants who had incomes of under Bs.3,600 a year, a result that is broadly consistent with the analysis in this paragraph.

We now come to *agriculture*. It is here that the great bulk of the really low incomes are to be found. We estimate (line 6a) that there are around three-quarters of a million *campesinos* and agricultural workers (supporting a population, including themselves, of over 2,000,000) with an average income of little more than Bs.1,000 a year. This is earned partly by working for wages on the larger farms and partly by cultivating their own small plots. Let us consider these two sources of income in turn.

AGRICULTURAL WAGES

We are told that, in many parts of the country, not too near the cities or the oil camps where the competition for labor is greater, the usual wage for unskilled farm labor is around Bs.5 a day. But in many instances work is available during only part of the year, say 120-150 days during the period of the sugar crop. Annual earnings would then be only Bs.600-750 a year.

In the more modern, better-managed estates, however, especially if they are near cities or oil camps, the wage may be Bs.7-8 or even up to Bs.10 a day or more. (We have visited, or been told of, farms where a wage of Bs.10 or more was being paid, or at least demanded. These were all fairly close to cities or, for example, near Calabozo, where the irrigation works and influx of medium-sized farmers needing labor have helped to drive wages up.) A skilled worker, such as a tractor driver, may get Bs.12, Bs.15, or even up to Bs.20 a day, but often for only part of the year, and it is safe to say that exceedingly few agricultural workers will get as much as the national average of Bs.6,000 a year.

PRODUCTION ON SMALL FAMILY PLOTS

The bulk of the poor agricultural workers are, however, employed most of the time on the small family plots. (The Census of 1950, which is, however, not easy to interpret on this matter, showed only 245,000 employed workers [*obreros*] in agriculture.)

The National Agricultural Inquiry for 1956 estimated that there were about 320,000 units of exploitation of under 10 hectares. The sample survey of Dr. George Hill, to which we referred above, was concerned mainly with the *campesino* living on these small holdings. The survey, which was made in five different regions of the country, showed that the *campesino* "tills the soil with his hands, aided sometimes with the traditional pico, planting stick and machete; 66% of them have no other tools." Nearly half had gross sales of under Bs.800 a year. Since nearly one-quarter of the holdings in the survey were of more than 10 hectares, we may perhaps take Bs.800 as an average gross income from sales on holdings of less than 10 hectares. Dr. Hill has suggested to us that, on average, Bs.300-400 might be deducted for cash expenses of production and Bs.300-400 added for production consumed by the family, leaving a net income (including income in kind) of about Bs.800 a year for the small family holding.

WAGES AND PRODUCTION TOGETHER

If we think of a typical family as consisting of six, with two working, of whom one works full-time on the holding and the other works for half the year as a laborer at, say, Bs.7 a day, we get a total family income of rather more than Bs.2,000 a year, or just above Bs.1,000 per person working. This also happens to be the average figure obtained if we take the Banco Central's estimate of "remuneration of labor" in agriculture (which is intended to include production on the small holdings as well as wage-earnings) and divide it by the estimated number of workers involved (see line 6a and note 5, Table I-3).

E. Reasons for the Inequality of Incomes

We have already seen that the inequality of personal incomes in Venezuela results in part from geographical differences: some regions are highly prosperous, others depressed; and incomes are generally higher in the larger towns than they are in the smaller ones or in the countryside. Secondly, there are industrial differences: income per head is much higher in some sectors of the economy than it is in others; and this helps to a considerable extent to explain the geographical differences. Thirdly, there are marked differences in personal incomes within a given economic sector in a given part of the country. These result, first, from differences in the earnings of labor (in the widest sense) and, secondly, from the uneven distribution of ownership of capital and land.

DIFFERENCES IN THE EARNINGS OF LABOR

These can be explained in part by differences in age, sex, length of service in a given employment, and luck. But most important are the differences in ability and skill. And the premium on skill is high in a country like Venezuela where many do not go to school, or stay only for a few grades, and where high school education is confined to a tiny fraction of the population. (A more detailed description of the educational situation will be found in Chapter XV below.)

Our study of the Ministry of Labor's payroll figures suggested that, leaving out young people and women, skilled workers in the most responsible positions typically earn some three to four times as much as the lowest paid general laborer in the same business enterprise, and that the top executives typically get three to four times as much again. We have seen that, in Government service, a Minister gets Bs.96,000 a year and a top official Bs.57,000; in the same Ministry a junior official may get only Bs.7,000 and a laborer or servant only half as much. In agriculture we have seen that a tractor driver may get twice as much as a general laborer.

THE UNEQUAL OWNERSHIP OF CAPITAL AND LAND

This is perhaps even more important in explaining the unequal distribution of incomes than differences in the earnings of "labor." It also helps to explain the latter since better-off families can afford better education for their children.

The great bulk of the population has little or no *capital.* Among those who have significant amounts, there is a vast difference between the considerable number of small shopkeepers and owners of workshops on the one hand and, on the other, the few families who control large businesses with profits running into many millions of bolivars a year. Moreover, given the very low income and inheritance taxes in Venezuela, these inequalities in ownership can be perpetuated, and even perhaps intensified, in a way that is hardly possible in countries with much more severe taxation. (Low taxation also, of course, helps enterprising, gifted and lucky people to move fairly rapidly from a lower income group to a much higher one, and a substantial middle class has grown up over quite a short period.)

AGRICULTURAL LAND

This is also most unevenly distributed. Table I-4 and the accompanying Diagram I-1 (which are based on the National Agricultural Inquiry of 1956) show that a mere 2½% of the "units of exploitation" (those of over 500 hectares) account for 82% of the total area. At the other extreme we have 81% of the units of exploitation (those of

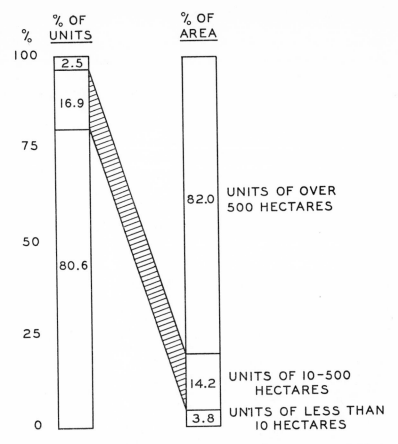

Diagram I-1. Agriculture: Size of Units of Exploitation, 1956
(Source: Table I-4)

under 10 hectares) accounting for only 4% of the total land. This is the share of the poor *campesinos* of whom we wrote above. It is possible that their share of the total value of agriculture output may be greater, and that of the larger estates smaller, than these figures would suggest. For the small holdings of under 10 hectares have as much as 23% of the area sown to crops and hardly any of the pasture land, the great bulk of which is in the large farms; and the value of output per hectare, other things being equal, is substantially higher in crop production than it is in animal husbandry. But against this must be set the inefficient methods and primitive equipment employed by the peasant farmer. In any case, it is clear that the very uneven distribution of agricultural land is bound to lead to great inequalities in income from it.

Table I-4. Agriculture: Size of Units of Exploitation, 1956 (Hectares)

	All sizes	Under 1	1-5	5-10	10-20	20-50	50-100	100-200	200-500	500-1,000	1,000-2,500	2,500-10,000	Over 10,000
No. of units (000's)	397.8	54.2	212.1	54.5	29.3	18.8	8.3	5.5	5.3	3.1	2.8	3.4	0.5
Per cent of total	100.0	13.6	53.3	13.7	7.4	4.7	2.1	1.4	1.3	0.8	0.7	0.9	0.1
Area:													
Sown	2,925	31	444	188	176	165	260	301	291	244	279	542	5
Fallow	864	—	12	24	30	68	41	45	78	71	118	194	181
Natural pasture	15,165	1	5	5	38	75	185	243	549	1,339	2,720	4,992	4,996
Artificial pasture	2,604	1	7	14	39	36	69	106	270	275	425	954	408
Other uses[1]	7,972	14	147	210	218	325	113	212	226	330	978	4,114	1,085
Total	29,530	47	615	458	501	669	668	907	1,414	2,259	4,520	10,796	6,675
Per cent of area by size of units:													
Sown	100.0	1.06	15.2	6.4	6.0	5.7	8.9	10.3	9.9	8.4	9.5	18.5	0.2
Fallow	100.0	0.03	1.4	2.8	3.5	7.9	4.7	5.2	9.1	8.2	13.7	22.5	21.0
Natural pasture	100.0	0.01	0.0	0.1	0.3	0.5	1.2	1.6	3.6	8.8	17.9	32.9	33.0
Artificial pasture	100.0	0.05	0.3	0.5	1.5	1.4	2.7	4.1	10.4	10.6	16.3	36.6	15.6
Other uses[1]	100.0	0.18	0.8	2.6	2.7	4.1	1.4	2.7	2.8	4.1	12.3	51.6	13.6
Total	100.0	0.2	2.1	1.5	1.7	2.3	2.3	3.1	4.8	7.7	15.3	36.5	22.5
Per cent of area by type of land use:													
Sown	9.9	66	72	41	35	25	39	33	21	11	6	5	—
Fallow	2.9	—	2	5	6	10	6	5	5	3	3	2	3
Natural pasture	51.4	2	1	3	8	11	28	27	39	59	60	46	75
Artificial pasture	8.8	2	5	8	8	5	10	12	19	12	9	9	6
Other uses[1]	27.0	30	24	46	43	49	17	23	16	15	22	38	16
Total	100.0	100	100	100	100	100	100	100	100	100	100	100	100

[1] Land productive but not cultivated; non-agricultural uses (houses, stables, corrals, buildings, granaries, mills, roads, etc.); woods; unproductive land.
SOURCE: Encuesta Agropecuaria Nacional, 1956 (Caracas, Sept. 1957). Ministerio de Agricultura y Cria.

F. A Quantitative Estimate
of the Personal Distribution of Income

We shall now attempt to make a quantitative estimate of the personal distribution of income. This is not easy, as the data are rather scanty. This is perhaps inevitable in a country like Venezuela where (1) the income tax covers only a small fraction of the population and, moreover, is levied on corporation profits but not on dividends, so that the personal distribution of the latter is not known, (2) the coverage of the Social Security System is as yet rather limited; in other countries this can yield valuable information about employment. The problem will be easier to handle as more basic data are collected but, in the meantime, there does seem to be scope for more analysis of the information that already exists than has been possible in the time available to us, and for more use of sample surveys of income.

We start with the results of the sample survey, already mentioned, that was carried out by "Datos" in 1957. This will be supplemented later by further information and, finally, we shall attempt briefly to see whether our results are consistent with the information given earlier in this chapter.

The "Datos" survey covered males only in all cities with more than 20,000 inhabitants and in a considerable number of towns of between 500 and 20,000 people. Those interviewed were shown a list of monthly income groups and asked to say in which group their own income fell. The groups were: under Bs.200 per month, Bs. 201-300, Bs.301-400, and so on up to Bs.2,001-4,000 and, finally, Bs. 4,001 or more.

Apart from the usual shortcomings of such inquiries (which did not, however, affect the original purposes for which "Datos" collected the information), this one was not constructed to include females and so tended to overstate the general level of incomes of males and females taken together. On the other hand, many of those interviewed probably did not allow for profit-sharing bonuses [4] at the end of the year (or for funds being put aside by their employers for their future benefit in the form of separation and termination pay).[5] After some reflection on the orders of magnitude involved it seemed not unreasonable to assume that this would broadly offset the omission of women from the

---

[4] *Utilidades.*
[5] *Antigüedades* and *Cesantía.*

Table I-5. Estimated Distribution of Private Income in 1957 in Towns of Over 500 People[1]

Range of income (Bs. per annum)	Assumed average income in range[2] (Bs. per annum)	Numbers of incomes[3] (thousands)	Total income[3] (Million Bs.)
			((2) x (3))
(1)	(2)	(3)	(4)
Under 2,400.....................	1,800	210	380
2,401-3600.......................	2,900	185	540
3,601-4800.......................	4,100	165	680
4,801-6,000......................	5,300	125	660
6,001-7,200......................	6,500	115	750
7,201-9,000......................	7,800	115	900
9,001-12,000.....................	10,000	155	1,550
12,001-15,000....................	13,000	75	980
1,5001-24,000....................	18,000	100	1,800
24,001-48,000....................	30,000	50	1,500
Over 48,000......................	80,000	15	1,200
Total........................		1,310	10,940

[1] This table does *not* cover those living outside towns of over 500 inhabitants. Moreover, the figures probably allow incompletely for income other than from wages and salaries. These omissions are discussed in the text and an attempt is made to repair them. The results are given in Tables I-6 and I-7.

[2] In estimating the average incomes in the various groups, account was taken of the fact that the original questions referred to groups such as Bs. 201-300, Bs.301-400, etc., and that a good many monthly salaries are in terms of a round number of bolívars. The assumed average for the last group is partly a guess but seems reasonable in the light of various figures given earlier in this chapter and in a table in Chapter III giving the distribution of salaries declared for income tax purposes.

[3] In round numbers.

inquiry.[6] We therefore multiplied the monthly income ranges by twelve and assumed that the resulting figures would give a fair indication (apart

[6] Outside agriculture there are about three men at work for every woman. If women's earnings were on average, say, 60 per cent of men's, the average for men and women together would be 90 per cent of that for men alone. An overstatement of average basic earnings of this order would be broadly offset by the failure of a good many men to include supplements when saying what their earnings were.

Table I-6. Allocation of Certain Incomes among Broad Income Groups

	Number of incomes (thousands)			Total income (Bs.million)			
Bs. per annum	In towns (from Table I-5)	In rural areas	Total	In towns (from Table I-5)	In rural areas	Profits, etc., not reported in survey	Total
(1)	(2)	(3)	(4)	(5)	(6)	(7)	(8)
Under 2,400..	210	750	960	380	800	—	1,180
2,400-12,000..	860	40	900	5,080	200	60	5,340
Over 12,000..	240	10	250	5,480	200	600	6,280
Total....	1,310	800	2,110	10,940	1200	660	12,800

NOTE:

The task is to allocate to three income groups 800,000 members of the active population living in rural areas and Bs.1,860 million of income not included in the figures from Table I-5 shown in columns 2 and 5.

As a first step it seems that one would not go very far wrong in allocating to the lowest group the whole of the 750,000 people and Bs.800 million of income shown in line 6a of Table I-3 for the "remuneration of labor" in agriculture. This leaves 50,000 living in rural areas to be allocated, in column 3, between the two higher income groups. Since a fairly high proportion of the larger farmers and landlords presumably live in towns, and in the light of the distribution of landholdings shown in Table I-4, it is likely that most of these 50,000 would be in the middle income group. Keeping to round figures we put 40,000 in the middle group and 10,000 in the upper one. The corresponding figures for total income in column 6 assume an average income of Bs.5,000 in the middle group and Bs.20,000 in the upper one.

We have now allocated Bs.1,200 million of the income, leaving Bs.660 million for profits, etc. not reported in the survey. It seems reasonable to put the great bulk of this, say Bs.600 million, in the upper group and the remaining Bs.60 million in the middle one.

Columns 4 and 8 show the final results when these additions are combined with the figures from Table I-5. They represent our estimates of the distribution of all private income among the whole active population.

from a further qualification to be mentioned later) of the distribution of annual incomes among males and females taken together.

We then estimated the economically active population in each of the towns of over 20,000 (taking one-third of the total estimated population at mid-1957 [7]) and, applying the proportions in the appropriate samples

[7] We used figures derived from "Datos" estimates which implied a total population in the whole country of about 6.35 million. See footnote 3, above. The

falling within each income group,[8] estimated the actual number of incomes within each group in each town and then, by addition, in all towns of over 20,000. A similar procedure was followed with the smaller towns, which were divided into two groups of 5,000-20,000 and 500-5,000. But, here, since the sample did not cover all towns, we divided the country into a number of economic regions and then applied proportions based on the towns where the survey was made. When the results for towns of all sizes over 500 were added up we obtained the figures shown in columns 1 and 3 of Table I-5. Finally, we assumed average incomes for each income group (column 2) and thus obtained estimates of the total income in each group (column 4).

Looking at the totals at the bottom of the table, it will be seen, first, that we have accounted for about 1,300,000 out of the total active population of about 2,100,000 shown in Table I-3. The remaining 800,000 comprise the active population in rural areas outside towns of 500 and over, areas which contain a total population of nearly 2½ million. Secondly, the total of incomes is Bs.10,940 million, compared with the total of private incomes of Bs.12,800 million derived from the Banco Central's estimates and shown in Table I-3, a difference of Bs.1,860 million. This does not look unreasonable since we still have two sums to add to the total shown in Table I-5. First, there is the income of dwellers in the rural areas. Secondly, some part of the income from profits, interest and rent was probably not included in the replies to the questions of the survey and not fully allowed for when we estimated the average income of those reporting incomes in the highest group. Almost certainly the *undistributed* profits of corporations have not yet been included in our figures although they must be included in an estimate of total private, as distinct from personal, income, and attributed to the shareholders on whose behalf they are being accumulated.

It is impossible to allocate our 800,000 people and Bs.1,860 million between the rather fine income groups in Table I-5, but we have made an attempt to do so between three broad groups—under Bs.2,400 a year, Bs.2,400-12,000 and over Bs.12,000. (The figure of Bs.12,000 has been chosen as a dividing line partly because it is the present income tax exemption limit for certain purposes.) The calculation is shown in Table I-6 and explained in detail in the notes to that table. Broadly

---

assumption that the ratio of active to total population does not vary with the size of towns may involve some error, but it is hoped that this is not quantitatively very important.

[8] The data were kindly supplied by "Datos."

speaking, we have assumed that most of the 800,000 in rural areas are poor *campesinos* and agricultural laborers in the lowest income group and that the bulk of the profits, etc. not reported in the survey (which are derived as a residual) is received by those in the highest group.

For clarity of exposition we have brought together the main results in Table I-7 where we also calculate percentages and round the figures off to avoid an impression of spurious accuracy.

Table I-7. Estimated Distribution of Private Income in Venezuela, 1957
(In round figures)

Income (Bs. per annum)	Number of incomes (thousands)	Total income (Bs.thousand million)	Per cent of total	
			Number of incomes	Total income
Under 2,400..............	950	1.2	45	9
2,400-12,000..............	900	5.3	43	42
Over 12,000..............	250	6.3	12	49
Total................	2,100	12.8	100	100

This table shows that, according to our estimates, about one-eighth of the income receivers get one-half of total income. At the other extreme, 45% get about one-tenth of the income.

Looking at Table I-7 in conjunction with Table I-5, the broad picture portrayed does not seem inconsistent with the evidence given in the earlier part of the chapter and in other parts of the report. First, we have seen that there are good reasons for expecting a high degree of inequality of income in Venezuela. Secondly, to turn to more quantitative aspects, we have seen (page 38) that our estimates of the number of low incomes (under Bs.3,600) in urban areas is not inconsistent with the analysis by social classes given in Table I-3. Thirdly, our figures for the higher income groups (over Bs.12,000 a year) do not seem inconsistent with the analysis in Table I-3. The reader who wishes will make his own comparison but we have shown in the footnote below, purely for purposes of illustration, one of various possible ways in which our estimated 250,000 incomes of over Bs.12,000 a year, yielding a total of Bs.6,300 million, might be distributed among the

Table I-8. Taxes Paid Directly and Indirectly by Typical Families in Venezuela

	Assumed income of head of family[1] (Bs.)	Taxes as percentage of total family income[4]		
		Direct taxes	Indirect taxes	Total taxes (round numbers)
Conuquero and peon.......	1,500[2]	—	7.1	7
Domestic servant[3]	2,500	—	7.8	8
Unskilled laborer (*Caracas*).	3,820	—	10.1	10
Machine tender, textile mill..	8,220	—	9.25	9
Petroleum field worker.....	15,000	0.2	13.0	13
Bookkeeper, food factory...	15,750	0.2	12.0	12
Iron-mine worker..........	19,000	0.35	11.0	11
Wholesale grocery executive.	28,000	1.3	16.4	18
Independent farmer........	35,000	0.6	10.8	11
Attorney.................	80,000	2.9	15.5	18
Large landowner..........	100,000	2.8	10.6	13
Real estate speculator and owner.................	350,000	6.6	13.2	20

[1] Including fringe and extraordinary benefits.

[2] Assumed to have son earning Bs.500 a year as laborer, making family income of Bs.2,000, or Bs.1,000 per person working.

[3] This domestic servant, though assumed to be in the Interior, is earning much more than the average for that category shown in Table I-3, line 4b.

[4] Includes, in a few cases, income of other members of the family.

NOTE: See Appendix B for full details and method of calculation.

groups in Table I-3, in the light of the analysis earlier in the chapter.[9]

Finally, while our estimated number of incomes of over Bs.12,000 may seem high in relation to the numbers declared for tax purposes shown later in the report (e.g. in Table III-8), the differences may be readily explicable. First, there is the possibility of tax evasion. Secondly,

[9] We give only the results since it would be tedious to justify them in detail and because there are several plausible ways in which the totals might be made up. The 250,000 incomes of over Bs.12,000 a year might be distributed as follows:

(1) *4,500* independent professionals at Bs.80,000, total *Bs.350 million.*

(2) Two-thirds of the petroleum workers, one-third of the salary earners in the Federal District and one-tenth of those in the Interior in industry, etc., and one-fifth of those in Government service give a total of *95,000.* Assuming an average of Bs.25,000 a year yields a total income of about *Bs.2,400 million.*

a good many salary earners getting between, say, Bs.12,000 and Bs.24,000 (who have already had schedular tax withheld by their employers) may fail to file a return for complementary tax since they know that they would not have to pay any on account of allowances for dependents. Thirdly, a corporation's profit counts as one income for tax purposes while it may distribute dividends to a number of shareholders.

G. *The Effects of Taxation and Public Expenditure*

Finally, it should be noted that all the incomes in this chapter are reckoned before tax and also exclude the non-monetary benefits of government expenditure. We have attempted to estimate the total burden of taxation, direct and indirect, on various classes of the community by considering the position of typical families. Full details and a description of the method of calculation will be found in Appendix B. The main results are given in Table I-8.

This table, which should of course be used only as an indication of broad trends, shows that the tax structure in Venezuela tends to be progressive, but only moderately so; and if the range of incomes in the table were extended further it would be seen that it is still possible to get an annual income, after all taxes, of several million bolivars. (See Table III-18 for some details of such high incomes. It is true that the figures there include capital gains, which may occur only infrequently, but they exclude dividends, which may be very large.) If taxes are subtracted from the figures of income given in Tables I-5, I-6, and I-7, it makes little difference to the general picture. We have attempted to estimate roughly the total tax burden falling on each of the three income groups distinguished in Table I-7, taking account of the data in Table I-8, and of the total collection of taxes from Venezuelan citizens. The results are given in Table I-9, which also shows, in the last column,

---

(3) Six per cent of the wage earners in industry, etc. in the Federal District and two per cent of those in the Interior give *20,000*. Assuming an average of Bs.15,000 a year yields a total income of *Bs.300 million*.

(4) *30,000* farmers and landlords with an average of Bs.15,000 yields *Bs.450 million*.

(5) *100,000* business men [not already included in (2)], shareholders and receivers of interest and rent, with an average of Bs.28,000 yields *Bs.2,800 million*.

The total is 250,000 incomes yielding Bs.6,300 million as in Table I-7.

the percentages of total private income, after all taxes, going to each group. It will be seen that these percentages are very little different from those relating to income before tax. The percentage going to the top group drops a couple of points and that going to each of the two lower groups rises a point; but that is all.

Table I-9. Income Before and After Taxes, 1957

(Bs. thousand million)

Income (Bs. per year)	Total income before taxes[1]	Total taxes	Total income after taxes (2) minus (3)	Percentage of total income after taxes
(1)	(2)	(3)	(4)	(5)
Under 2,400............	1.2	0.1	1.1	10
2,400-12,000............	5.3	0.4	4.9	43
Over 12,000............	6.3	0.9	5.4	47
Totals.............	12.8	1.4	11.4	100

[1] From Table I-7.

Moreover, as mentioned earlier, government expenditure probably tends to benefit disproportionately the larger—more prosperous—towns rather than the smaller ones and the countryside; and expenditure on trunk roads, hotels and the like probably tends to benefit particularly the richer classes. It is thus quite possible that taxation and government expenditure taken together have no redistributive effects.

CHAPTER II : **General Economic Considerations**
: **Relevant to Public Finance**

In this chapter we discuss a number of general questions and general principles, confining ourselves so far as possible to those that have a bearing, directly or indirectly, on public finance, under which term we include government revenue, expenditure, and borrowing. We begin by describing some of the features of the Venezuelan economy—in addition to the distribution of income discussed in Chapter I above—that seem most relevant to our study.

A. Capital Requirements

Foremost is the great need for capital investment. This arises, first, from the high rate of growth of the population. Secondly, there is need for a rapid growth in output per head of the population; for a very substantial part of the citizens of Venezuela still lives in comparative poverty. The more rapid the growth in average income per head, the easier will it be to achieve a rapid improvement in the condition of the less fortunate groups, for the less likely will it be that this would involve an absolute worsening in the condition of the more fortunate and a consequent resistance on their part.

Moreover, Venezuela has become so used to a very high rate of growth, and the structure of its economy has become so adjusted to it, that a substantial slowing down, even if some progress continued, might well cause considerable dislocation, disappointment, and even disillusionment. For many reasons, both economic and non-economic, a continuation of something like the rapid growth achieved in the last decade or so is thus an important goal of policy. Let us look at a few orders of magnitude, and make some very rough calculations, in order to illustrate the size of the capital requirements involved.

According to estimates of the Banco Central, the real national income

43

of Venezuela, even excluding the government's income from oil, rose by an average of no less than 9% per annum between 1950 and 1957.[1] Since 1950 may be regarded as a year of rather less than normal prosperity and 1957 as an abnormally prosperous one, let us say, to avoid overstating the argument, that the trend of growth was 8% per annum, an extremely high rate by world standards.

Now in many countries it is reckoned that every additional unit of output requires, on average, about three times as much additional capital, reckoned in money terms (and sometimes even more). In the jargon of economists, the marginal capital/output ratio is 3:1. If this was so in Venezuela, a growth of 8% per annum in the national income (excluding oil) would require a *net* investment each year equal to 24% of this national income.[2] This is an exceedingly high rate. In many countries 10% is considered normal.

It is true that the marginal capital/output ratio in Venezuela during the last decade or so has been reckoned by some at only about 2:1; this would require a net investment equal to 16% of the national income, still a high rate. The ratio may possibly be as low as 2:1 in a country beginning to develop. Such a country may be able to achieve a large increase in output with a comparatively small capital investment because, among other things, it can at the same time take over, in quite a short period, technical knowledge from the advanced nations that they have taken many years to acquire. Secondly, by improving communications and in other ways, it can open up resources hitherto inaccessible and create a single national market, thereby achieving great economic returns. Venezuela has done both of these things in a striking manner since the war. But, though there is much more to be done, the most marked gains may now have been achieved; for both the processes mentioned are essentially of a once-for-all nature. A further striking gain may come from an improvement in the educational system, which at present leaves a large part of Venezuela's *human* resources undeveloped, but this may be rather a long-term investment. For all these reasons, even if the marginal ratio of capital to output has been as low as, say, 2:1, it may well in future rise to, say, 3:1 or even more.

We have seen that ratios of 2:1 and 3:1 would require *net* investment equal to 16% or 24% of the national income to achieve a growth rate

[1] Calculated from figures given on pages 334, 335, 339, and 345 of the Banco Central's *Memoria* for 1957, and from figures for government oil income accruing in 1957, supplied by the Banco Central.

[2] If the national income is 100 and has to grow to 108, net investment must be 24.

of 8% per annum. Allowing for replacement expenditure to offset the depreciation of existing capital, this would mean that *gross* investment (excluding investment in the petroleum industry) would have to be of the order of 25-30% of the gross national product (excluding the government's income from oil),[3] and, for reasons just given, the true proportion may well be nearer 30%.

Now let us approach the problem by another route and see what capital investment is required to look after the rapidly rising population and to allow for an increase in the average standard of living. According to the official records of births, deaths and net immigration, the population of Venezuela has been growing by well over 4% per annum in recent years (see Table II-1). The birth rate has been very high, births having added 4½% to the population each year. Deaths have taken away only 1% and net immigration has added well over ½% a year. Net immigration continued at a high rate in 1957 but complete figures for the year were not available at the time of writing. In 1958 it fell off sharply and may even have been negative as many people left the country and restrictions on immigration were imposed; but this may be merely a temporary phase. The birth rate may fall, as it has done in many countries as they have become urbanized and industrialized and improved their educational system; but, if this happens in Venezuela, it seems unlikely to be a very rapid process. It is thus quite possible that the population will continue to grow by about 4% per annum for some time. Taking the population in 1957 at about 6½ million, this would mean an annual increase of 260,000 (and the increase would, of course, itself grow at 4% a year).

What are the annual capital requirements for such an increase in population? [4] First, they have to be housed. Reckoning 6 persons on

---

[3] The net national income at factor cost, excluding the government's income from oil, is estimated at Bs.13,660 million in 1957. Adding Bs.1,350 million for depreciation we get gross national product, at factor cost, of about Bs.15,000 million. (The estimate for depreciation outside the oil industry is a rough one derived by subtracting amortization during the year by the oil companies—Banco Central *Memoria* 1957, page 27—from the figure for total consumption of fixed capital shown on page 345 of that publication; another estimate we have seen suggests that depreciation outside the oil industry may be less than Bs.1,000 million). Adding Bs.1,350 million to 16% and 24% of the net national income, excluding the government's oil income, we get sums equal to 24% and 31% respectively of the gross national product, excluding oil. We have rounded these figures to 25% and 30%.

[4] We assume that any increase in employment in the petroleum industry will not be significant in relation to the total increase in population and labor force.

Table II-1. The Population of Venezuela, 1951-57

	Thousands						Per cent of population at beginning of year				
	Population, beginning of year	Recorded births	Recorded deaths	Natural increase (2) minus (3)	Net immigration	Total increase in population (4) plus (5)	Births	Deaths	Natural increase	Net immigration	Total increase in population
	(1)	(2)	(3)	(4)	(5)	(6)	(7)	(8)	(9)	(10)	(11)
1951.....	5056	225	57	168	23	191	4.4	1.1	3.3	0.4	3.8
1952.....	5247	231	57	174	27	201	4.4	1.1	3.3	0.5	3.8
1953.....	5447	251	54	197	41	238	4.6	1.0	3.6	0.7	4.4
1954.....	5685	262	57	205	44	249	4.6	1.0	3.6	0.8	4.4
1955.....	5933	272	59	213	54	267	4.6	1.0	3.6	0.9	4.5
1956.....	6200	278	59	219	41	260	4.5	1.0	3.5	0.7	4.2
1957.....	6460										

SOURCE: Dirección General de Estadística, Ministerio de Fomento.

average to a family, about 43,000 homes will be required.[5] If the new houses built are to be of a reasonable standard which, though better than the present average for the country as a whole, will still be quite modest, the cost per house can hardly be much less than, say, Bs.15,000, including services. This would be much less than the cost of *obreros'* houses built by the petroleum and iron-mining companies, according to some figures given to us. We have, it is true, been told of an interesting scheme near Maracay in which people are building their own houses with materials that cost much less than Bs.15,000, but allowance must also be made for the cost of their labor, for administration, and for the remuneration of capital and enterprise; and most houses will probably not be built in this way. Moreover, since Bs.15,000 is an average figure, and includes the cost of houses built for better-off families, the cost of most of the new houses will have to be less. Forty-three thousand houses at Bs.15,000 would cost about Bs.650 million.

Secondly, the increased population has to be employed. Assuming that, as shown in the census of 1950, about one-third of the population is economically active (the rest being housewives, children, students, old people, etc.) work places will have to be found for 87,000 people. We have made a good many inquiries about the investment required to establish one worker in reasonably well-paid employment, and we have looked at estimates on this matter prepared by others. The figures naturally vary a great deal, from one sector of the economy to another and between undertakings in the same sector, from a few thousand bolivars to well over one hundred thousand. With any likely pattern of economic development we suggest that the average figure could hardly be much less than, say, Bs.25,000. This is substantially higher than the average cost of an *existing* work place in Venezuela today—as is necessary to achieve a growth in average output per head. But it is substantially lower than the capital requirement in some more economically advanced countries, at least when allowance is made for the higher costs in Venezuela. With 87,000 people to be employed, the cost would then be Bs.2,175 million. Adding in housing costs, this gives a total of approximately Bs.2,500 million.

We still have to allow for (a) the gradual replacement, at higher standards, of the existing houses and places of work, (b) public investment in new roads, hospitals, schools, water systems, sewerage and all the rest; these have been quite inadequately allowed for in our estimate

[5] Strictly speaking, one should have an estimate of the number of houses required based on the number of new families being formed, but we do not have this information.

of the cost of work places. These additions (to say nothing of the increase in stocks and work in progress and in international reserves that is required over a period of years and will be discussed below) could easily bring the total gross investment requirements up to well over Bs.4,500 million a year. (Annual depreciation outside the oil industry, which may give some rough idea of replacement requirements, is probably of the order of Bs.1,000 million or more;[6] and a further Bs.700 million would be quite a modest sum for net public investment in the light of recent experience.) But even Bs.4,500 million a year would be 30% of the gross national product, excluding government income from oil.[7]

It is possible, of course, that the population will not grow by as much as 4% per annum.

First, the recent rate of growth may have been less than the figures in Table II-1 would suggest, because deaths have been under-recorded. A recent United Nations report suggested that the true death rate in Venezuela may have been 2% rather than the 1% recorded.[8] If this is so, the annual increase in population may have been rather more than 3%[9] instead of over 4%. (It may be, of course, that if deaths have been under-recorded, especially in the country districts, births have been under-recorded in these areas too; but the United Nations experts do not appear to take this view.)[10] Secondly, the birth rate may in fact fall significantly for reasons given above, and immigration may not be resumed at the high rate prevailing until 1957.

If, in fact, the population rose by only 3% per annum the gross investment requirements, as just calculated, might be, not 30% of the gross national product (excluding government income from oil) but something nearer 25%.[11]

This rough calculation thus tends to confirm the previous one. Both

---

[6] See footnote 3, Chap. II. Since quality of capital equipment tends to improve over the years as a result of technical progress, the mere reinvestment of accumulated depreciation funds when the equipment reaches the end of its life should normally make possible the installation of better equipment, except in so far as there has been a fall in the value of money since the original investment took place.

[7] See footnote 3, Chap. II.

[8] *Report on the World Social Situation 1957*, page 16.

[9] This is, in fact, the average rate of growth recorded between the Censuses of 1941 and 1950 which is still used to calculate the official estimates of population after 1950.

[10] *Op. cit.*, page 6.

[11] If we reduce the Bs.2,800 million required for the additional population by one-quarter to Bs.2,100 million, and keep the remaining Bs.1,700 million un-

suggest a range of 25-30%, and, in the light of all that has been said, the true figure in future may well be near the upper end of that range.

B.   The Actual Rate of Investment in Venezuela

In fact, according to some calculations shown in Table II-2 (which are derived largely from estimates of the Banco Central), gross investment, other than in oil, has averaged about 30% of the gross national product, excluding government income from oil, over the six years 1952-57. The actual figure shown is 29% (line 4) but no significance should be attached to a difference of a point or two since estimates on this matter are inevitably rough and ready (though it is to be hoped that they will be improved). The average conceals the fact that the proportion was lower in the earlier years of the period and higher in the later ones.

Investment in fixed capital alone (line 1) is shown as about 23% of the gross national product (we shall from now on stop repeating every time that we are excluding the government income from oil and investment in the oil industry). It was around one-fifth in 1952-54 but rose to one-quarter in 1955 and 1956 and to one-third in 1957. (Since the rate of growth of output has shown no corresponding increase, this may conceivably reflect a falling marginal ratio of output to capital, a possibility mentioned above; but it would be rash to base conclusions on such a short period and until the productivity of the high investment in the later years is more clearly reflected in the years ahead.)

There was also an increase in inventories (stocks and work in progress) which averaged 2% of the national product (line 2). This was heavily concentrated in 1957, but changes in inventories usually take place unevenly and an average increase of this order must be reckoned with as part of the nation's capital requirements. A country normally needs stocks and work in progress equivalent to at least three or four months' national output and, if the latter is growing by 8% per annum,

changed, the total gross investment requirements are Bs.3,800 million or 25% of the gross national product, excluding government income from oil. Rather more would in fact be required to maintain the same growth in average output per head because, in our calculation, this depends to a considerable extent on the fact that the investment deemed to be utilized for the increase in population is substantially higher than the existing capital per head.

Table II-2. Gross Investment (excluding petroleum) and Gross Savings as Percentages of Gross National Product[1], excluding Government Income from Oil

	1952	1953	1954	1955	1956	1957	Rough averages
Forms of Investment							
1. Fixed........................	19	20	20½	24	25½	32	23
2. Inventories................	–1	—	1	—	1	9	2
3. International reserves....	2	1	—	1	9½	10	4
4. TOTAL......................	20½	21	21	25	36	51	29
Sources of Finances							
5. Government oil income—regular..	14	13	13	14	15	17½	14½
6. Government oil income—occasional[2]..	—	—	—	—	7½	8	2½
7. Government savings excluding oil income[3]..	–4½	–4	–3	–4	–3	–4½	–4
8. Private internal savings (gross)..	9½	8	9	11	12	20	11½
9. Capital from abroad, excluding oil (gross)......	3	4	2	3	4½	10	4½
10. TOTAL......................	22	21	21	24	36	51	29

[1] At factor cost.
[2] New concessions.
[3] Government capital expenditures plus budget surplus (which together make up total government savings), less government income from oil. This is the same as the government's revenue other than from oil less its expenditures on current consumption.
NOTE: These are rough estimates based on data given in the various *Memoria* of the Banco Central. The figures in lines four and ten do not always agree exactly, as they should do in principle, because of the inevitable inadequacy of the data. Details do not always add to totals because of rounding.

2–3% of the national output will have to be set aside, on average, for increases in inventories.[12]

Finally, there was an increase in international reserves equivalent to 4% of national output (line 3). This was heavily concentrated in 1956 and 1957, the years in which new oil concessions were granted. But there are inevitably fluctuations in such reserves and they will have to be increased, over an average of years, by an amount equal to perhaps 2–3% of the national product in order to keep pace with the rise in the value of international transactions,[13] for the bigger this value is, the bigger the fluctuations, in absolute terms, that the reserves have to cope with.

C. Sources of Finance

All these various methods of approach suggest that investment in Venezuela must be at a very high rate if the momentum achieved since 1950—and indeed since the end of the War[14]—is to be maintained. Gross investment outside the oil industry will probably have to approach 30% of the national product excluding the government's income from oil. How can Venezuela achieve such a high rate of investment, a rate that would be regarded as impossible in most other countries, because they could not generate sufficient savings?

The main answer is, of course, that the government receives a large

[12] If the national output grows from 100 in one year to 108 in the next and stocks are 25 (three months) or 33 1/3 (four months) in the first year they will, if they are to represent the same number of months' output, have to be raised to 27 (three months) or 36 (four months), increases of 2 and 2.7% respectively.

[13] The international reserves at the end of 1957 were about Bs.4,500 million (*Memoria* 1957 of the Banco Central, page 268), including Bs.200 million of gold belonging to the National Government. Let us take, say, Bs.4,000 million as an adequate figure for reserves, given the recent value of international transactions, although they could of course be run down well below this level to meet a temporary deficit; this gives a better ratio of reserves to imports than in many other countries but their reserves are often too low and Venezuela must aim to keep high reserves since she is so vulnerable to international fluctuations. If international transactions grew as fast as the real national product (8%), the reserves would then have to be increased by Bs.320 million a year on average to keep in line. This is over 2% of the gross national product in 1957, and the value of international transactions may well grow faster than the real national product, especially if there is an upward trend in world prices.

[14] What estimates we have seen suggest that the average annual rate of growth was at least as high between 1945 and 1950 as it was between 1950 and 1957.

income from the oil companies equivalent, over the years 1950-57, to nearly 15% of the national product excluding such income (line 5 of Table II-2); and this does not include receipts from the sale of new concessions in 1956 and 1957 (line 6). The fact that the government, rather than private individuals, receives this income is of great importance; for it can, if it chooses, decide not to spend it on current consumption and so contribute to the national savings available for financing the nation's investment as a whole. (To do this the government would not necessarily have to spend all its income from oil on investment in public works and the like; it could lend some of it to private enterprise or simply, by running a budget surplus and piling up a reserve in the banks, allow private investment—provided it were forthcoming—to exceed private savings without causing inflation or a deficit in the balance of payments. In fact, the government has had a large budget surplus only in 1956 and 1957 when it was roughly equal to the receipts from the sale of new oil concessions; and, moreover, allowing for obligations' being piled up, the surpluses in these years may have been more apparent than real.)

If, as is conceivable, the oil had been owned by private individuals who themselves had made, say, 50-50 profit-sharing arrangements with foreign oil companies, it would have been much more difficult to use the income from oil for national investment. For the private individuals would no doubt have wished to spend a large part of it on consumption. If the government had tried to take it from them by taxation in order to finance investment, the rates might have had to be very high indeed; and this would have discouraged enterprise, on which the development of Venezuela so greatly depends.

Secondly, Venezuela has in recent years been receiving capital from abroad, other than from the oil companies, equivalent (gross) to nearly 5% of the gross national product, excluding the government's income from oil (see line 9, Table II-2). This investment, which has been growing relatively much faster than investment in the oil industry, is attracted partly by the existence of other minerals (chiefly iron to date), but also by the possibilities of making profits in such a rapidly growing economy in manufacturing, construction, banking, services, insurance, etc. (Foreign investment in manufacturing depends to a large extent on protection, which we shall discuss later in this chapter.)

If, then, the government gets income from the oil companies equivalent to 15% of the rest of the national output, and if foreign investors other than in oil provide savings from outside the country equal to another 5%, we have a total of 20%, leaving only 10% to be found from other sources to bring the total up to 30%; and this is a much more manageable proposition. In fact, the government does not save all its income from oil (line 7, Table II-2) but spends some of it on current consumption, so that private savers within Venezuela (including corporations) must save rather more than 10% (gross) of their income, as they appear to have done, on average, in recent years (line 8, Table II-2).[15]

It is particularly difficult to be confident about this 10% figure; it does not wholly accord with impressions we have formed as a result of conversations with some people. But if it is near the mark, and if it is assumed that the great bulk of the savings comes from the richest 12% of the population who are estimated to have incomes of over Bs.12,000 a year and to receive about one-half of the national total (Table I-7 in Chapter I), then these people must on average be saving (gross) 20% or more of their incomes, including undistributed profits being accumulated by companies on their behalf, *and* before deducting at least part of the depreciation on the capital they own. The figures of the Banco Central are very hard to interpret on this point (and it is hoped that the matter will be further explored). A correct allowance for depreciation might put the *net* savings ratio of the higher income groups very substantially lower. But even so it may still be relatively high. If so, this seems likely to be dependent on the unequal distribution of incomes and on the relatively low tax rates on the higher ones. (These savings are, of course, helping to finance not only more "essential" investment but also a good deal of "luxury" investment in expensive houses and the like.)

D. A Diagrammatic Presentation

It may be useful at this stage to portray in diagrammatic form some of the salient features of the Venezuelan economy to which we wish to draw attention. The analysis in Diagram II-1 is simplified, it ignores certain complications and the figures are intended only to be illustrative, but it is hoped that they give a correct general impression of relative orders of magnitude and that they may help to clarify some of the

---

[15] According to Table II-2, total internal savings, government and private, averaged about 7½% of the national product excluding the government's income from oil (lines 7 and 8), but the government's receipts from new concessions averaged 2½% over the six years (line 6) and we have taken no account of these receipts in this paragraph.

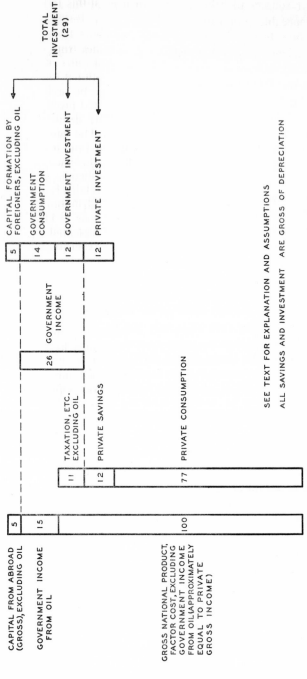

Diagram II-1.   Income, Saving, Investment, etc. in a Typical Year

discussion in this chapter. We consider what might be a typical year in Venezuela, assuming that the future is not too unlike the past. We have taken into account, but not reproduced exactly, the figures in Table II-2, and added figures for some items not shown there.

The gross national product, at factor cost, excluding the government's income from oil, is put at 100. This may be taken as roughly equivalent to the total of private gross incomes,[16] including, of course, the incomes of Venezuelans working directly or indirectly for the oil companies.

The first column shows the resources available to the country. At the bottom we have the 100 units just referred to, above it the government's income from oil of 15 (we assume that no new concessions are sold in the year), and at the top 5 units of capital (gross) from abroad, other than in oil, making a total of 120.

The second column shows how the private income of 100 is disposed of. Eleven goes in direct and indirect taxes, etc. (This may be taken to include fees, a substantial part of which should in any case be regarded as taxes—see Chapter IX—and the relatively small amount of revenue raised by the States and Municipalities.)[17] A further 12 represents private savings (gross of depreciation and including undistributed profits of companies). This leaves 77 for private expenditure on consumption.

The third column shows a total government income of 26, made up of 15 from the oil companies and 11 from taxes, etc., on private incomes.

The fourth column shows, in the two middle sections, how the government's income is used. It is assumed that the budget is balanced. Fourteen is spent on current consumption and 12 on investment. This 12 also represents government saving as the budget is in balance. Excluding the government's income from oil, it is dissaving 3 (i.e. spending 3 more on current consumption than it is raising from taxes, etc. other than on oil).

The fourth column also shows other forms of investment. At the

---

[16] Strictly it includes the government's income from property other than oil, but we ignore this complication. The Banco Central, in computing the national income, includes a figure for this item which has been running at around Bs. 1,000 million per annum in recent years (see Banco Central *Memoria* for 1957, page 339). We have, however, been told that this figure represents *gross* receipts and that the *net* income is very much smaller; otherwise, it would be an important source of saving.

[17] We have ignored, for simplicity, the problem of taxation of foreign companies other than those engaged in the petroleum industry.

top we have 5 units of gross capital formation by foreigners other than in oil (which is assumed to be equal to the inflow of foreign capital in the first column). At the bottom we have 12 units of private gross investment by Venezuelan residents. (This is equal to their private gross savings, but only because we have assumed that the budget is in balance and that, leaving out oil, the inflow of capital from abroad is equal to capital formation by foreigners.) It will be seen that total investment adds up to 29 (5 plus 12 plus 12).

E.   A Recapitulation of the Main Facts

Let us now recapitulate some of the main facts that have emerged from our analysis. Foremost is the need for a very high rate of capital formation to take care of the rapid population growth and allow for a continuation of the rapid improvement in income per head that has been achieved since the War. The benefits of this improvement may have been rather unevenly spread, between the various regions of the country, the various sectors of the economy, and the various classes of the community, but the nation can, if it so desires, change the pattern of investment in the years ahead (and reckon education, for example, as an investment, although it is not counted as such in the figures given here). The rapid growth in the past has been made possible mainly by the government's income from the oil companies but also, to a lesser extent, by an inflow of capital from abroad for investment in other activities; and private savings also appear to have been relatively high, partly as a result of the unequal distribution of income and of the low tax rates on high incomes.

The fact that the income from the oil companies goes to the government is also important. This makes possible at the same time a low level of taxation (other than on oil and other minerals) and a high level of government revenue. It almost certainly means, for reasons mentioned above, that total national investment and the rate of economic development have been greater than they would have been had the oil income gone to private Venezuelan citizens; and it is one reason why the government has been responsible for such a high fraction of the nation's investment.

Finally, an important fact is the nature of the distribution of income, described in Chapter I. This is more unequal than it is in many other countries, even before taxes have been paid there. In addition, whereas in other countries taxes and government expenditure often redistribute

incomes very substantially, in Venezuela they make rather little difference. Income taxes on Venezuelans are low and the rates go up very
slowly with income. Indirect taxes, which are much more important
revenue-raisers (in the non-oil sector), are only moderately progressive;
the rich are hit by high taxes on luxuries but the poor have to spend a
substantial part of their incomes on taxes on necessities. And government expenditure does not appear to have any very significant redistributive effects.

We shall now consider some of the morals that appear to emerge
from these facts and, in the light of them, analyse some general problems that relate directly or indirectly to public finance.

F. The Importance of the Oil Industry for Growth

The pace of economic development in Venezuela will clearly depend
to a large extent on the future course of the government's income from
oil. It will not be easy, at least for some time to come, for the national
product to grow at a rate faster than the rate of growth of this oil income.
The growth of the petroleum industry is also important for growth in
the economy as a whole because of the oil companies' investments in
housing, education, and the like, and because they pay out large sums
to Venezuelan workers, suppliers, and contractors. A failure of the
petroleum industry to expand rapidly may be reflected in budgetary and
balance of payments difficulties.

Quite apart from considerations other than those of revenue, this
raises two major problems of fiscal policy. First, would an increase in
the rates of taxation on the oil companies bring a greater or smaller
income to the government over a period of years? This question lies
outside our terms of reference and we can only list without comment,
for the convenience of the general reader, some of the main arguments
we have heard on either side.

On the one hand, it is claimed that an increase in taxation—at least
if it were substantial and especially if it were not part of a general
increase in taxation of Venezuelan citizens—would have psychological
and political repercussions in the United States and might adversely
affect United States commercial policy on Venezuelan oil which has recently been restricted far less severely than oil in Texas; and that higher
taxation would induce foreign oil companies to direct a higher proportion
of their new investment in the years ahead to the Middle East (where
costs are lower), the United States, and elsewhere.

On the other hand, it is argued that the Western World cannot do without a rapid increase in Venezuelan oil; that political uncertainties in the Middle East will continue to make it vital to have large alternative sources of supply; that other producing countries might follow Venezuela's example if she raised the level of her oil taxation so that her competitive position would not be affected; that if sales to the United States fell, new expanding markets could be found elsewhere; and that, even if increased taxation retarded the growth of Venezuelan oil output, the revenue from it might still be greater than it would otherwise have been because of the higher rates.

A second fiscal problem raised by the importance of oil to Venezuela concerns her Reciprocal Trade Agreement with the United States. The question is whether, if she attempted to revise this Agreement in order to give greater protection to certain industries where this is now precluded by the Agreement, this might lead to less favorable United States treatment of Venezuelan oil. We are not in a position to pass judgment on this political question but shall discuss the problem of protection generally later in this chapter.

G.   The Importance of Other Foreign Capital and Know-how

We have seen that foreign capital, other than in the petroleum industry, provides an important and growing supplement to domestic savings and so helps very substantially to finance the large investments required. The know-how that often comes with capital from abroad can also play an important role in the country's economic development. Three fiscal problems may be considered in this context.

First, there is the taxation of the profits of foreign enterprises. Apart from minerals, the rates are at present low, being the same as those levied on resident Venezuelan corporations. If income taxes on residents were raised, and with them the taxes on foreign enterprises, and if this discouraged the latter, it would be a serious matter for the development of the country. Fortunately, however, even quite a sharp *relative* increase would still leave taxes low by world standards and would be unlikely to deter foreign capitalists who saw a chance of good profits in Venezuela, especially as in many cases there would be an offsetting reduction in the taxes payable to their own governments.

The second fiscal problem is of quite a different nature. It has been suggested to us that foreign enterprises are often deterred from coming to Venezuela because of the high costs, and that one reason is the need to build houses, roads, hospitals, schools, etc., sometimes when the site is not very near existing centers of population. Such expenditures, which are not normally borne by the private industrialist, can greatly increase the investment required, perhaps adding up to 50% to the cost of the plant. The petroleum and iron-mining industries may be able to afford such investments but other firms often cannot. If, in order to encourage foreign enterprises, the government (either directly or through some agency) undertook these tasks in the areas involved, or even in some cases built factories to rent to foreign concerns, this would obviously place an additional burden on government finance.

Thirdly, we may consider in this section the possibility of borrowing abroad by the government or by one of its agencies. The borrowing might be done in foreign capital markets, from foreign government agencies or from an international organization such as the International Bank for Reconstruction and Development. Venezuelans have understandable prejudices against borrowing abroad, and they are justifiably proud of their record in this respect. But the capital needs are so great that such borrowing might have to be considered; and a start has been made in recent months, though in a rather special context.

There are, of course, objections to foreign borrowing. It creates an obligation to make interest and amortization payments and in this respect places a burden on the future balance of payments. But the borrowing may make possible—and it is important that it normally should make possible—developments in the fields of export, or import-saving, that will bring at least as great offsetting gains to the balance of payments. Even when it does not, the problem is no more serious than it is with private capital from abroad, which is not discouraged by the government even if it leads to no direct earning or saving of foreign exchange; indeed, the rate of profit on private investments is normally much higher than the rate of interest payable on government loans. This rate is also usually much lower than the likely return to the nation, including indirect benefits, on social investments of various kinds; see, for example, the calculations in Chapter XV on the possible return on investment in education in Venezuela.

Foreign borrowing (like borrowing at home) also, of course, places a burden on future budgets, but this need not be very great if, as is hoped, the national income rises rapidly and with it taxable capacity and government revenues. Other countries have certainly borrowed abroad on a large scale without ill effects when, as in Venezuela in the past decade or so, they have been going through a period of rapid development, with a high rate of population growth and heavy immigration. But few, of course, have had advantages comparable to Venezuela's large income from oil, and this, so long as it continues to grow sufficiently rapidly, will make foreign borrowing much less essential.

The government will not, of course, wish to borrow money abroad, and pay interest to foreigners, if it considers that the resources necessary for an adequate rate of development can be found without it, if necessary by cutting down luxury consumption by the richer classes through higher taxation (another example will be given in a later section). A judgment between these two methods of financing depends on one's political philosophy and on how far it is thought that a chance to earn very high incomes, after taxes have been paid, is necessary for rapid development. We shall now consider this general problem.

H. Taxation of the Higher Income Groups

The government might wish to increase taxation of the higher income groups in order to secure a more equitable distribution of income, or simply because its growing fiscal needs made necessary additional revenue and it was thought that this could be most easily provided by the richest classes. What effects would this have on enterprise? The present low rates of income tax very probably do encourage enterprise among Venezuelan residents (and also attract a good deal of foreign skill and enterprise to the country). The low rates may also, however, leave some people so rich that they have little incentive to try to make more by risking their capital in the hope of profit; the fact that quite a high proportion of Venezuelan private savings appears to go into mortgages [18] is not inconsistent with this hypothesis. The large opportunities for gain on real estate speculation also, no doubt, divert enterprise away from fields where it would be more useful to the nation; and this results partly from the low rate of tax on such gains. Then again the absence of a tax on agricultural land may lead to parts of large estates being held idle, while if they were taxed they might be developed by their owners or sold to others who would develop them. (The possibility that a tax on rural land might be imposed by the states of Venezuela is discussed in Chapter XII below.)

If, despite all this, higher taxation of the richer classes substantially discouraged enterprise on balance, this would be a serious matter, for rapid growth will depend to a large extent on the enterprise and initia-

[18] See the *Memoria* for 1957 of the Banco Central, page 351.

tive of private citizens. The present rates of direct tax are, however, still so low that they could probably be increased *relatively* a good deal without serious ill-effects and certainly without raising them to anywhere near the rates imposed on the higher income groups in many other countries. There could also be substantial increases in indirect taxes on less essential goods and services. These do not necessarily have any adverse effects on the enterprise and effort of those who have to pay them as consumers. They may indeed stimulate effort since more money must be earned to buy luxuries.

While, however, taxation of the higher income groups might be increased substantially in Venezuela without adversely affecting *private enterprise* to any significant extent, it is much more likely that *private saving* would be reduced. We have seen that the richer classes appear to save quite a high proportion of their incomes. If they were taxed more heavily they would thus be unlikely to reduce their consumption of luxuries to the same extent; they would probably find part of the extra taxes by cutting into their annual saving or by living on their capital, i.e. *dis*saving. This means that if the government wanted to set free, say, Bs.70 million of national resources (labor, materials, foreign exchange, etc.) at present being used for the production or importation of luxuries and to use these resources instead for, say, agricultural development or education, it might have to collect substantially more than Bs.70 million of additional taxation from the rich. The government might have to take, shall we say, Bs.100 million in additional taxes from them in order to set free Bs.70 million of resources, for they might cut their consumption by only Bs.70 million and find the remaining Bs.30 million by reducing their annual savings. (The 70:30 ratio is used purely to illustrate a principle; we have no evidence about what might actually happen.)

It is possible, of course, that if they saved less they might also decide to invest less because, for example, their profits for reinvestment had been reduced. Suppose, for example, that they had to pay an additional Bs.90 million of taxes and that they cut their consumption by Bs.63 million and thus their saving by Bs.27 million (the relative reductions in consumption and saving being the same as in the first case), but that they at the same time cut their investment in factories or houses by Bs.7 million. The government would then have to raise only Bs.90 million in additional taxes to set free Bs.70 million of resources for other purposes (63 from less luxury consumption and 7 from fewer houses or factories). If the reduction in investment were in expensive houses (or in other things designed to produce goods and services only for the high-income groups), this would presumably be considered as on a par with a cut in luxury consumption. But if it meant that fewer new essential factories would be built, the government would have to decide whether Bs.7 million of such factories (and Bs.63 million of luxury consumption) was more or less important than Bs.70 million in agriculture or education. It might, for this purpose, regard education as an investment for which it was worth sacrificing some investment in other fields.

If the government wished to have the factories as well, it could increase taxes further by the amount required to set free the necessary resources (to Bs.100 million in all, as before [19]) and build them itself. If it preferred to have them built by private enterprise it might attempt to bring this about in other ways, for example, by granting subsidies (see also Section I A below).

In general, while increased taxation of the higher income groups would probably reduce *private* saving in Venezuela, this could, in principle at least, be offset by increased *government* saving, i.e. by an increase in the excess of government revenue over government expenditure on current consumption. This means that the government would have either to devote part of its increased revenue to investment purposes, however defined, or run a budget surplus which could be used, directly or indirectly, to finance private investment.

It might also be possible to offset any tendency for private saving to fall by measures designed to stimulate the desire to save. Savings campaigns have been carried out in various countries. One possible fiscal device that could have the desired effect would be a progressive tax on personal expenditure rather than on personal income; but the administrative problems of such a change are very formidable indeed. It is chiefly because of the administrative task that would be involved in such a step, relative to the administrative resources available for the time being, that such a tax is not discussed in the succeeding chapters of the present report. But in one way or another, there is still a good deal of additional revenue to be derived from higher taxation of the richer classes. In this respect, Venezuela may possibly be compared with the United Kingdom before 1914. By contrast, the very high rates on large incomes that have been in force in that country since early in World

---

[19] Private individuals would then cut their consumption by Bs.70 million and their investment in factories by Bs.7.8 million (assuming, as before, that seven-ninetieths of the additional taxation is found by cutting investment). Resources valued at Bs.77.8 million would then be set free which the government would use by spending Bs.70 million on education and agriculture and Bs.7.8 million on factories.

War II have been mainly weapons of social policy designed to prevent what are regarded as excessively high incomes; a substantial reduction in these rates would not reduce government revenue very markedly.

The real resources that could be obtained for other purposes, even in Venezuela, by cutting the "luxury" consumption and investment of the richer classes must not, of course, be exaggerated. Our estimate in Chapter I that the richest 12 per cent of income earners may be getting about one-half of all private income may give a misleading impression of what might be done, unless interpreted carefully.

Let us go back to Table I-7, which suggested that there may be 250,000 income earners with more than Bs.12,000 a year getting a total of Bs.6,300 million. Now, first, these people are already paying perhaps Bs.900 million in taxes (see Table I-9), the bulk being indirect. This leaves Bs.5,400 million which represents the real control over the nation's resources [20] which their income gives them.

Secondly, they may be saving, gross of depreciation, around 20 per cent of their gross income. Even allowing for the saving required for depreciation and for "luxury" investment in expensive houses and the like, they may still have been financing, directly or indirectly, say Bs.500 million of "essential" net investment and thus contributing in an important manner to the nation's development. This leaves Bs.4,900 million as their expenditure on consumption and on "luxury" investment (reckoned at prices that exclude indirect taxation).

Finally, they must be left with a certain minimum standard of life. Even if we make the drastic, and quite unrealistic, assumption that they can all be cut down to an annual expenditure of Bs.12,000, excluding indirect taxes, this would use up Bs.3,000 million. Their "excess" expenditure over this level is thus under Bs.2,000 million.

In fact it would be impossible to take more than a fraction of this through taxation without severely affecting initiative and enterprise. Purely for purposes of illustration, a figure of Bs.500 million may be nearer the mark than one of Bs.1,000 million.

These are quite large figures in relation to the budget, especially as they refer to *real resources* set free by cutting "luxury" consumption and investment; the figures for additional tax revenue would be greater because the money to pay the taxes would be found partly by reducing annual saving that was going into "essential" investment, or by living on capital. The figures are large, too, relative to the amount of money that might be raised, from the illustrative scale of income tax rates in

[20] At factor cost.

Chapter XV below, to finance the first year of an expanded education program. For that year, at least, the effect of such a program on private saving would not be a matter of much consequence.

On the other hand the figures are rather small in relation to a total of private income of around Bs.13,000 million, which represents the source from which the government may draw taxation, direct and indirect, other than from the oil companies and other non-residents.

I.   The Scarcity of Capital
and the Need to Invest It Carefully

We have seen that the investment requirements of Venezuela are very high. This means that capital is scarce (which is no doubt one reason for the high return that can be obtained on it). Supplies of capital are also somewhat precarious since two of the main sources— government's income from oil and foreign investment in other sectors— are to a large extent outside Venezuela's control.

For these reasons it is vital that capital should be used carefully. This means, among other things, that any given investment should be executed in the most economical manner that is consistent with the achievement of the desired result—the question of public versus private enterprise is clearly relevant here; that unduly capital-intensive methods should be avoided; and that those projects should be selected, and those fields of investment emphasized, that give the highest return from a national point of view. Let us consider these three problems in turn, and especially their relevance for public finance.

A. PUBLIC VERSUS PRIVATE ENTERPRISES

The Venezuelan government is in business in a good many lines, including hotels, aviation, shipping, electricity, telephones, petrochemicals, steel, housing, railroads. Whether any of these could be more efficiently run by private enterprise, and whether or not future development should be left to private enterprise so far as possible, are in part economic questions but also in part political questions on which it would be inappropriate for us to pass judgment. But if waste and excessive costs are to be avoided in the future in government investments there may well have to be more careful accounting of expenditure, and more continuity in the execution of programs, than, we are told, there has sometimes been in the past. There may, quite frequently, be enterprises that are desirable from a national point of view but which private concerns will not undertake of their own accord, because the cost is too large, because the risk is too great or because, while the yield to the nation in the widest sense is substantial, the private profit to be earned is low or non-existent. It will not always, however, be essential that the enterprise should be run by the government. The latter might in appropriate cases subsidize private enterprise, at least for a period; it might grant loans on favorable terms; it might negotiate management contracts with private concerns, perhaps giving them an option to buy the enterprise at a later date if it became profitable; and so on. All these would raise problems of government finance, but the amounts required would be limited in so far as options to purchase were exercised and loans repaid; the sums returned could then be used to help start further enterprises. There would in fact be a revolving fund.

The more purely public enterprise there is, the more taxes will have to be raised or the more money will have to be borrowed, either directly by the government or by a government agency, except where the latter can finance its investments out of its own profits (in some cases, it may actually produce revenue for the government). If public and private enterprise are equally efficient, the matter has importance *only* in relation to problems of the budget, of the capital market and of the laws relating to government borrowing, important as all these are. People sometimes talk as though to turn an undertaking over from government to private enterprise will save national resources merely because it reduces the need for the government to raise finance. This is not so unless private enterprise is more efficient than public enterprise or unless foreign capital is attracted.

B. THE NEED TO AVOID UNDULY CAPITAL-INTENSIVE METHODS

This is a complicated question and we put it forward with some diffidence. Labor in Venezuela is expensive, especially when account is taken of the large supplements to wages payable by employers and of the inexperience of much of the labor. Capital equipment, on the other hand, is relatively cheap; much of it pays very low import duties while most other goods are taxed much more heavily. These two facts often encourage enterprises to buy the latest possible, most labor-saving, equipment. Given the scarcity of capital in Venezuela it may be asked whether this is always justifiable especially as, taking a longer view, the cost of labor may give an exaggerated impression of its scarcity. For, if vigorous steps are taken to increase agricultural productivity, the growing food needs of the country may be met without much if any increase in employment in agriculture, so that most, or the whole, of the increase in the labor force may be available for, and have to be employed in, the non-agricultural sectors; and if equally vigorous steps are taken to improve education, both general and vocational, this growing labor force will be better trained.

For these reasons it is conceivable that any changes in the direction of raising the relative price of capital equipment, for example through higher import duties (which would also raise government revenue [21]) and of reducing the cost of labor to the employer, for example through the assumption by the government of more responsibility for any future "fringe benefits" (which would increase government expenditure) would lead to a more rational use of the country's scarce capital resources. On the other hand, of course, there is the danger that making capital goods more expensive would retard economic development. And it may be that, for intangible reasons, such development is best fostered on balance by creating an atmosphere in which only the very latest equipment is considered good enough for Venezuela, even if this does involve a rather lavish use of capital.

C. THE NEED TO SELECT THE MOST PROFITABLE PROJECTS AND FIELDS OF INVESTMENT

With capital scarce, it is essential that the costs and profits, including the non-monetary profits, of various government-sponsored projects should be carefully assessed before they are put into operation and the most profitable, in the widest sense, selected. This is true both of the selection of projects within a given sector of the economy and in determining the emphasis to be given to investment in the various sectors.

It seems likely that, in the past, there has been a relative under-investment of resources in certain sectors, because they involved no spectacular projects or yielded no direct monetary return or only a small one. An example is *education*. Some calculations in Chapter XV suggest that the return on investment (using the term in a wide sense) in education is very high both from a private and from a national point of view; but the government gets no direct monetary return itself. (For investment in education to yield these high returns there must also, of

---

[21] Aside from this possible reason for import duties on capital equipment, such duties are inadvisable. From a distributive point of view they act something like a general sales tax on necessities and luxuries alike. See Chapter IX below.

course, be complementary investment in capital of all sorts with which the newly trained people may work.) A large increase in expenditure on education must almost inevitably come mainly out of government funds and will thus raise budgetary problems, some of which have already been mentioned.

Many people feel that another area of under-investment has been *agriculture*. Investment in this sector certainly seems to have been low—as has government expenditure on it, including expenditure by government agencies—considering the large fraction of the population engaged in it. From a national point of view, moreover, it is essential that agricultural production be expanded to meet the food needs of a rapidly growing population and to cater, in addition, for a rapidly growing demand for food per head as incomes rise; otherwise, a serious balance of payments problem will be created. On the other hand, it must be recognized that agricultural production is estimated to have increased by as much as one-half between 1950 and 1957; but a still faster increase may be necessary in future if there is a relative rise in the incomes of the poorer sections of the community; for they will spend a higher-than-average proportion of their additional income on food. It is important, in addition, to reduce costs of production which are now high and in many cases not competitive with prices in world markets.

We have been given a number of striking examples of the very high return that may be obtained on quite limited investment in agricultural research and extension services, provided these are backed up by adequate supplies of credit. Several people have also expressed the opinion that, within agriculture, more emphasis should be placed on the small poor *campesinos* who constitute by far the greater part of the agricultural population; the great bulk of the government's expenditure in the past appears to have been directed to the larger farmers, who admittedly, however, produce most of the nation's food. This is partly a social question and if it involves higher taxation of the more prosperous citizens, or rather less aid to the larger farmers (although such aid may have to be increased as well), it may be regarded as a form of redistribution. But it may also be a profitable proposition, in part at least, from a purely economic point of view, apart from any question of social justice. The methods used by the small *campesino* are so primitive that one would *a priori* expect a high return from investment in teaching him better methods, provided he is also given a better general education, finance to buy better equipment, fertilizers, seeds, weed-killers, insecticides, livestock and all the rest, and sufficient land to cultivate; at present he is often incapable of cultivating more than the small plot that he has. (The small *campesino* may perhaps be compared with an underdeveloped country that can get an unusually high return on capital investment if at the same time it takes over the accumulated knowledge of the more advanced nations.)

By contrast, some of the more spectacular agricultural schemes seem sometimes, judging by what figures we have been given, to have yielded a very moderate return on the capital invested. This is not, of course, to say that large schemes are unnecessary but only that their profitability in the widest sense should be carefully assessed and compared with that on other investments before they are started.

More investment in the widest sense in agriculture will almost certainly involve additional public funds (although in some cases a monetary return may be collected from farmers who profit). There are some things that only the government can do. These include the great bulk of agricultural research, of extension services and schools to train agricultural teachers, of feeder roads, flood control, and irrigation schemes. The government will also have to provide credit. Financial institutions will not in general lend to the small *campesino* and some inducement is often required to get the necessary investment even in larger farms when quicker profits are to be obtained in other, perhaps more exciting, sectors of the economy. The financial burden on the government can, however, be limited by the creation of revolving funds which are lent out again and again. Even the small *campesino* can repay if the credit advanced to him is properly supervised; we have been told of a private non-profit-making organization which recovered 95% of its advances in one experimental scheme.

J. Budget Surpluses and Deficits

Before going on to consider factors affecting the future level of taxation in Venezuela it will be useful to discuss the circumstances in which budget surpluses or deficits may be desirable. In this context we shall also discuss briefly the problem of government borrowing. To begin with we shall abstract from the legal and political aspects.

There is nothing magic about a balanced budget. Indeed, what it means is largely dependent on somewhat arbitrary definitions. Let us give two examples.

First, it might mean a balance between total government revenue and expenditure or simply that *current* expenditure should be covered by revenue, leaving capital expenditure to be financed by borrowing. Quite a plausible case might be made out for the latter but in economic terms it might make nonsense. For example, the Venezuelan government has for many years had a large surplus on current account in the sense that its total revenue has greatly exceeded its expenditures for current purposes (see Table II-2 and Diagram II-1). But if it were to limit its revenue to the amounts necessary to cover these expenditures, this would be equivalent, broadly speaking, to abolishing all taxation other than on the oil companies. It will be generally agreed that this would almost certainly lead to inflation and balance of payments difficulties.

On the other hand, it is not obvious that the government should necessarily raise enough revenue to pay for all its expenditures. Equally, it might have to raise more than enough and run a budget surplus. For example, when the Venezuelan government raises large sums through the sale of oil concessions, as it does at infrequent intervals, it will normally be appropriate to put a part at least to reserve. More generally it may happen that, with the overall budget only just in balance, the country would suffer from inflation or balance of payments difficulties, or both, because total demand would exceed the supplies available. It may then be necessary for the government to restrain demand by reducing expenditure, or by raising taxes on Venezuelan citizens and so reducing their purchasing power, and this will create a budget surplus.

To give another example, a balanced budget might mean the equality of the revenue and expenditure of the government narrowly defined or of the government and all government agencies taken together. If it were the rule that the budget should be in balance, and need only be in balance, in the narrower sense, this might lead to strange results. Suppose, for example, that in one year a balanced budget so defined was accompanied by a satisfactory level of employment, a stable price level and equilibrium in the balance of payments. Then suppose that, in the next year, everything remained the same except that funds for some regular annual investment that had previously been provided out of government revenue were now raised through a loan issued by a government agency. If, following the rule postulated above, the government now felt it could spend the money set free on some new project, there would be an increase in total demand which would quite possibly lead to inflation or to a deficit in the balance of payments, *unless* the borrowing by the agency reduced private investment, or consumption, by an equivalent amount. But it might well not do so. At least part of the funds raised might come out of idle balances.

Conversely, if in the second year the government took over responsibility for meeting, out of its revenue, expenditure that had previously been found through borrowing by a government agency, and cut down its expenditure on other things correspondingly, this could create unemployment and unnecessarily slow down the rate of economic development. (A rule that the budget of the government and its agencies taken together should be in balance could lead to equally strange results.)

Examples of this kind could be multiplied, but this is unnecessary for our present purpose which is simply to illustrate the need, from an economic point of view, to look at the revenue and expenditure of the government and of its agencies in relation to the economy as a whole and not merely in relation to rather arbitrary accounting conventions.

It is probably unlikely that a budget deficit (as at present defined) will often be appropriate in a country like Venezuela where the rapidly rising population, and the experience of rapid growth in the past, may normally be expected to stimulate a large amount of private investment that is fully as much as private saving can absorb. Indeed, it is possible that private investment will tend to run ahead of private saving so that a budget surplus, over an average of years, may be necessary to restrain demand and prevent inflation.

But, even so, there could be years when a budget deficit was desirable. For example, the pressure of private investment might slacken temporarily and not be offset by an increase in private consumption, so that the productive resources of the country were not being fully used. There would then be a case for increased government expenditure (or perhaps for a temporary cut in tax rates on Venezuelans)[22] in order to increase demand and take up the slack.

Or again, there might be a temporary setback in the petroleum industry, as there has been on a number of occasions in the past, for example, in the 1930's, in the early part of the war, in 1949, in 1953, and again in 1958. The possibility of quite a sharp setback at some time must always be reckoned with; and, with both quantity and prices falling, profits could be quite severely squeezed and with them the government's revenue from oil.[23] Other revenue, from both direct and indirect taxes, would also be likely to fall as the result, first, of a reduction in the income (and purchasing power) of the oil workers. There would, in

[22] It will be less necessary to cut such tax *rates* the more sensitive is tax revenue from Venezuelans to business fluctuations at a given level of rates. The sensitivity of the tax structure in this respect is discussed in Chapter XIII below.

[23] See again Chapter XIII below for a discussion of the sensitivity of taxes, etc., on the petroleum industry to business fluctuations. Sensitivity in this field is de-stabilizing.

the second place, be a reduction in the incomes of businesses selling supplies to the oil companies or doing contracting work for them, and of those employed by these businesses. (All such incomes together add up to around Bs.1,500 million a year.[24]) This would tend to set in motion a downward spiral in activity and incomes throughout the country which, besides causing unemployment and retarding development, would bring about a further fall in government revenue.

If, previously, the budget had been in balance, or not greatly in surplus, it would now run into substantial deficit for all these reasons. In order to maintain activity the government would actually have to *increase* its deficit still further by raising expenditure or reducing tax rates on Venezuelans, or both. It is clear that if, on the other hand, it tried to balance the budget, by raising such tax rates or cutting expenditures, the recession in activity would be still further intensified.

If, however, the government tried to maintain activity by increasing expenditure or cutting tax rates, imports would tend to be maintained at the old level while receipts of foreign exchange from the oil companies fell away. This would not necessarily cause a balance of payments crisis if (a) the country had previously been running a surplus in its international accounts so that a substantial worsening was possible before it actually ran into international deficit, or (b) adequate reserves of gold and foreign exchange had been built up against such a contingency. It is vital that Venezuela should in fact make every effort to run an international surplus, and build up international reserves, in more prosperous years, so that this two-fold cushion may be provided against temporary emergencies. (This, it may be noted, is not necessarily the same thing at all as the government running a *budget surplus* and building up a Treasury reserve of bolivars. It is quite possible that the government might be running a budget deficit, and going into growing debt, year after year, while the international reserve of gold and foreign currencies was steadily piling up. Alternatively, the Banco Central's reserve of gold and foreign currency might be falling while the Treasury's reserve of bolivars was rising; such a reserve would be of use in meeting subsequent budget deficits but of no use as an international reserve to cope with a balance of payments deficit.)

---

[24] The "remuneration of labor" in the oil industry in 1957 was about Bs.900 million (see Table I-3) and in 1955 it is estimated that the *U.S.* oil companies spent roughly as much in Venezuela on materials, supplies and equipment as they paid in wages and salaries. (U.S. Dept. of Commerce, *U.S. Investments in the Latin American Economy,* page 186.) Part of these payments, however, no doubt represented imports of materials, etc., from abroad.

If the country had not been running an international surplus in the more prosperous years, or if the international reserves had not been built up to an adequate level, an attempt by the government to maintain activity in the face of a sharp setback in the petroleum industry, which would very probably involve a budget deficit, would lead to a serious balance of payments crisis. In the absence of alternative measures, to be mentioned in a moment, such a crisis could be avoided only by allowing unemployment and stagnation to cut down imports. The dilemma could be resolved only:

(1) by the imposition of import restrictions on less essential goods; these should not be ruled out in the circumstances since they would be a lesser evil than unemployment and stagnation, although it is unlikely that they would be sufficient to solve the problem by themselves;

(2) by devaluation of the bolivar in terms of foreign currencies; this might take a considerable time to right the balance of payments; it would strike a severe blow at one of Venezuela's major economic assets —world-wide faith in the stability of her currency; and it would be quite unnecessary if the deficit were temporary;

(3) by borrowing of foreign exchange from abroad.

This would be one set of circumstances in which government borrowing from abroad would have a good deal to recommend it. If, on the other hand, the international reserves were high, or if the country had been running a substantial international surplus before the trouble started, such borrowing would be unnecessary, and undesirable insofar as it created an obligation to pay interest to foreigners in the future. It would be unfortunate if, when borrowing abroad was recognized to be economically unnecessary and undesirable, the government was forced into it, in order to finance a budget deficit, by purely technical considerations relating to the Venezuelan laws or other standing arrangements or conventions.

It is possible that a substantial budget deficit might in some circumstances be difficult to finance either at home or abroad because of the law relating to government borrowing, and difficult to finance at home because of the law prohibiting direct loans from the Banco Central to the government (although indirect financing might be possible [25]), and because of other arrangements that may make it hard to maintain the public's liquidity at a level that makes possible the taking up of government securities without unduly limiting the funds needed for a high level of private activity.

[25] For example, if the government withdrew support from government agencies which in turn borrowed from the Banco Central.

A detailed discussion of such laws and arrangements is outside our terms of reference. We recognize that there are good reasons for them, including the need to prevent irresponsible government spending and to provide safeguards against inflation and disorders in the balance of payments. But it is not inconceivable that they might contribute to other evils—unemployment and stagnation—if, for example, they made it hard for the government to borrow at home at a time when this was desirable to maintain activity and borrowing abroad was, for some reason, economically or politically difficult; and they might force the government to borrow abroad when this was economically unnecessary and undesirable.

K. *Considerations Affecting the Future Level of Taxation*

It is not our task, nor are we competent, to assess what changes if any in the general level of taxation are likely to be necessary. We can only set out some general considerations in the hope that they may be of some use to those who will have the responsibility of analyzing the problem in practical terms and of making decisions.

We do not propose to discuss the current budgetary situation in any detail. There is certainly a large prospective deficit in the current fiscal year, 1958-59, but this arises partly from heavy commitments incurred in the past; it is hoped that this rather poor year for the government's income from oil will prove to be abnormal; there are prospects of borrowing at home and abroad; and there is always a possibility—as with all budgets—that the estimates on which this one is based will prove conservative. It would thus be rash to make any assessment of the prospects for future years merely on the basis of the present one.

There is, however, one general proposition that can be made with some confidence. The need for taxation, other than on oil, will depend greatly on the future of the government's income from the petroleum industry which makes up such a large part of its total revenue. Here again we do not propose to make any forecast on what is a highly technical matter and on which there are so many experts in Venezuela. There are, of course, considerable differences of view among those to whom we have talked, but it seems to be fairly generally agreed that oil production, and oil profits, will continue to grow fairly rapidly after the recent setback. Whether, however, the growth will be as rapid as it has been over the past decade or so is a matter of opinion; it could be less rapid.

The outcome will depend partly on Venezuela itself; on the government's oil taxation policy; on any commercial agreements it may make with the United States or with other countries; on the degree of success achieved in keeping Venezuelan oil competitive, which depends, among other things, on the future course of wages and of the prices of supplies bought in Venezuela by the oil companies. But to a very considerable extent the future of oil income will depend on world forces outside Venezuela's control.

If the government's oil income goes up less quickly than in the past it will not be easy to maintain the past rate of growth in the national product; for we have seen that this oil income provides a large part of the resources required for the high rate of capital investment that is necessary. The past rate of growth in the national product could probably be maintained only if (1) the nation's investment could be made more productive so that a given capital expenditure yielded a greater increase in output (we have suggested some lines along which this problem might be tackled); or (2) more resources were obtained from elsewhere. These might come from borrowing abroad or from more foreign investment in Venezuela other than in oil. Otherwise, there would have to be a reduction in the proportion of the national product used for consumption, either by the government or by private citizens. Government economies in current expenditure on administration, defense and the like should be continually sought for, though they are seldom easy to make. There would probably have to be, in addition, a reduction in the proportion of private incomes spent on consumption.

Measures to encourage the desire to save might be of some help but "forced saving" might well have to be imposed by the government through higher taxation, the proceeds of which would either be spent on capital projects or allowed to create a budget surplus.

It should be noted that, even if private and public savings could be increased substantially to offset the relative fall in the oil income, so that there appeared to be sufficient resources available to continue investment at the old rate, there might still be a balance of payments problem. For the loss of oil income would be wholly in foreign exchange while the reduction of private and government consumption would fall only partly on imports of goods and services abroad. A balance of payments deficit might be prevented by other offsetting factors, but if such a deficit emerged it might well inhibit growth.

Let us now suppose that oil income in fact goes up as fast as in the past so that no problem arises on this score. Let us also suppose (merely to illustrate some general principles—the reverse might in fact occur) that there is a change in the pattern of investment, more being done by private enterprise and less by the government. This might possibly happen for two reasons. First, it might be in the national interest that less emphasis should be placed on investment of a type normally done by governments (such as road building) and more on investment of a type usually entrusted to private enterprise. (Some have indeed suggested that this should be the future trend in Venezuela—that "overhead" investment, which has been so heavy in the past decade or so, is now yielding diminishing returns and that it should give way somewhat to investments in direct production for which it has provided the necessary conditions.) Secondly, it might be desired, for political or other reasons, to have more investment done by private enterprise within a given sector of the economy and less by the government. What effect would such a change have on the need for taxation?

It might be thought that it would inevitably allow taxes to be reduced by the full amount of the contraction in the government's investment expenditure. But this is by no means necessarily so. For, as we have seen above (e.g. Table II-2 and Diagram II-1), the government has been performing a large part of the national saving and if it made an equal cut in taxes and in its capital expenditures, but no reduction in its expenditure on current consumption, it would be reducing its savings by a corresponding amount.

It is true that the reduction in taxes would allow private citizens to save more, but they would be most unlikely to do so to the full extent of the tax remission; a very substantial part would probably be spent on additional consumption. There would thus be a reduction in national savings as a whole so that, if the additional private investment were to be as great as the reduction in the government's investment (and this would seem necessary to keep up the rate of development except insofar as private enterprise may be more efficient), total investment would tend to outrun total savings, thus causing inflation or a deficit in the balance of payments. The government would thus be unable to reduce its taxation by nearly as much as it cut its capital expenditures. It would probably have to run a budget surplus and in this way help to keep up the level of the nation's savings to the extent required.

As a final illustration, let us suppose that oil income goes up as fast as in the past, that there is no change in the relative importance of public and private investment, but that it is desired to spend substantially more on education, agriculture, public health, and the like (which we shall not designate as investment in this context). It is then not improbable that more taxation will have to be raised. But if so, it will be necessary, as we saw earlier, to raise tax revenue by more than the increase in expenditure, since some of the extra taxes will be found by reducing savings by more than any reduction in private investment.

The illustrations in this section, together with those in other parts of the chapter, will, it is hoped, have made it clear that budget arithmetic is a complicated matter. It must be done in terms of the national accounts as a whole. It is not enough to look merely at the accounts of the government.

L. The Need for Better Statistics and for More Economic Research

It is not enough, of course, to appreciate the fact that budget arithmetic is complicated. It is essential to have adequate statistical data on which to base decisions. Much remains to be done in this field in Venezuela. The Banco Central deserves credit for its pioneering work in preparing estimates of national income and expenditure, of saving and investment. But there are still many important aspects of the national accounts for which no estimates are made, and the experts in the Banco Central would be the first to admit that the estimates they do make are sometimes, perforce, very rough and ready and that they often have to be based on quite arbitrary assumptions because of the inadequacy of basic data.

It would be helpful for the outsider, and no doubt useful for those producing the document, if a complete set of estimates of all the various magnitudes over a period of years could be prepared and published with a full explanation of the methods of calculation and a discussion of the inconsistencies that inevitably arise from the need to use inadequate data when making independent estimates of quantities that should be identical. This would also help the student to see what important gaps there were in the basic data and, it is hoped, encourage him to try to fill some of them by independent research.

The basic data are insufficient, not only for framing estimates of national income and the like, but for many other purposes. Let us give just a few examples. We have seen that estimates of the present population vary by as much as 7%. It may be growing by 3% per annum or, alternatively, by over 4%, an important difference when reckoning capital requirements of various kinds. Deaths may possibly be twice as high as those recorded. The number in various age groups is hard to estimate; this makes it difficult, for example, to calculate the cost of an educational program (see Chapter XV below) or the numbers that are likely to come on to the labor market in the years ahead. There are no reliable up-to-date figures of the occupational or industrial distribution of the labor force as a whole; this must make it difficult, for example, to analyze the implications of an extension of Social Security or to gauge the extent to which the various sectors of the economy have provided, and might in future provide, employment for the rapidly rising population.

For the latest comprehensive survey of many of these matters one has to go back to the Census of 1950 and it is hard to know what reliance to place on that. According to information based on data of the Oficina Nacional de Censo there were, in 1950, a total of 249,000 units of exploitation in agriculture. According to estimates in the National Agricultural Inquiry of 1956 (conducted by the Ministerio de Agricultura y Cría with the help of the Food and Agriculture Organization) there were 398,000; and the number can hardly have risen by over one-half in six years.

Information on wages and salaries is scanty (though there may be scope for more analysis of the data that exist). It is, as we have seen, not at all easy to estimate the number of people in the various income groups and how much income they receive in total. This clearly makes it difficult to calculate the yield of various possible income tax structures. Estimates of the yield of possible new indirect taxes of various kinds are likewise hard to make (see, for example, Chapter XI).

Many other examples could be given but these must suffice. Some of the gaps can be filled only by government inquiries: through well-organized censuses of population, production, and the like, and the collection of regular returns, many of them necessary for a proper up-to-date appraisal of the economic situation. Private individuals and research organizations can also help, for example by carrying out sample surveys. They also have an important role to play—it is to be hoped with the full cooperation of government servants and others with information useful to them—in the very difficult task of estimating important economic relationships, for example between investment and output and between income and savings, and in analyzing the innumerable aspects of the country's economic structure and problems.

Adequate and trusted factual information, both on the basic economic and social structure of the country and on the current situation, and informed public discussion of economic problems that is based so far as possible on agreed facts and is free to concentrate on differences in intellectual approach and in scales of value, are vital for a country that wishes to make the best use of its economic resources.

M. Protection

We conclude this chapter with a brief discussion of protection. This seems necessary in a fiscal study of Venezuela if only because customs duties form an important part of the tax structure. But the question of protection is also relevant to the problems of growth and of capital formation, to which we have devoted so much of this chapter. Chapter IX contains a detailed analysis of the customs duties and consular fees of Venezuela, of their administration, of their incidence on consumers, of the system of import licenses and exonerations, and of other related matters. In this chapter we shall concentrate on the question of protection.

In Chapter IX there will be found estimates of the proportion that customs duties bear to retail prices. For the purpose of the present chapter we have also calculated the approximate incidence of customs duties, in each tariff category, as a percentage of the wholesale price. This proportion is, of course, higher because the wholesale price falls short of the retail price by the amount of the duty and the cost of distribution. For each item we worked out from the foreign trade statistics the average import value, nearly always per kilogram, and divided this into the duty per kilogram. (We used the rates under the Trade Agreement with the United States for the relevant items and made appropriate adjustments when there was an *ad valorem* element in the duty.) There are various, fairly obvious, reasons why the results may be misleading for particular commodities but they should be sufficient for the purpose of the broad generalizations that we make below.

It is sometimes claimed that Venezuela is not a high tariff country. This is certainly the first impression obtained if one divides the revenue from customs duties by the total value of imports. This gives an "average" rate of under 10% in 1957, and of not much over 10% if consular fees are included (it is shown in Chapter IX that these should really be considered as taxes).[26]

Apart from the fact that similar calculations for earlier years yield higher percentages, and apart from the need to take account of direct import restrictions as well as customs duties, this method of calculation,

---

[26] The value of imports in 1957 was about Bs.5,600 million (Banco Central *Memoria* 1957, page 201), customs duties collected about Bs.500 million (*op. cit.*, page 275) and consular fees about Bs.150 million (see page 264 below where, however, the figures relate to the 1957-58 fiscal year).

as is well known, always understates the restrictive nature of a tariff. Take a simple hypothetical case of a country that imports only one commodity, and that free of duty, but would import large quantities of many others were it not for a prohibitive tariff of, say, 10,000% which it imposed on each of them. A division of the duties collected (zero) by the value of imports would give the answer 0% and suggest to the unwary user of the statistics that this was a free trade country.

The same sort of thing is true of Venezuela though, of course, in a very much less extreme form. The great bulk of Venezuela's imports, perhaps as much as three-quarters or four-fifths of the total value, either comes in free of duty or pays moderate duties of under 20%; the average duty for the group is well under 10% of their value. But at the other extreme there is quite a large number of goods on which the rates are very high, being usually equivalent to at least 50% and not at all infrequently to 100% or, sometimes, much more. Not surprisingly, however, these goods are not generally imported in large quantities and some are virtually not imported at all. The high rates thus tend to have little influence on an "average" of the type just described.

It would perhaps be a more meaningful measure of the restrictive nature of a tariff if one could give weights to the various items in accordance with what the relative value of their imports would be with completely free trade. Such a calculation is, of course, impossible, but it would certainly give a much higher figure for the average tariff level of Venezuela.

As a broad generalization we may say that most capital goods, which make up a large part of Venezuela's imports, are at present allowed to enter at moderate rates of duty or without paying any duty at all, although there are exceptions such as paint, which is important in building, where there is high protection. On the other hand, a large proportion of the basic consumer goods, such as most foods, textiles, clothing (including shoes), wooden furniture and soap, are protected quite heavily and form rather a small part of imports. For example, a straight unweighted average of the duties on the various food items works out at around 100% (although there is a great variation about this figure) and the same is true of clothing. The average is higher in some of the groups mentioned and lower in the rest but always about 50% or more. There is, however, at present little protection, if any, on a fair number of the more complicated consumer goods, such as electrical appliances, photographic goods and watches.

There is strong pressure for additional protection in Venezuela today. One obstacle is the Trade Agreement with the United States which, as we have already seen, precludes this for a number of articles. Table II-3 below shows that imports, *from all sources,* of items specified in this Agreement make up less than one-half of Venezuela's total imports. But a large part of the imports not subject to the Agreement consists of durable production goods. It may be that the bulk of these could at present be produced in Venezuela only with very great difficulty, or perhaps not at all, and that the same applies to a high proportion of the goods in the other categories.

Table II-3.   Imports from All Sources, 1957

(Bs. million)

	Included in Reciprocal Trade Agreement with U.S.	Not included	Total
Food................................	314	49	363
Other non-durable consumer goods........	89	194	283
Durable consumer goods................	327	92	419
Durable production goods..............	1597	1687	3284
Primary materials and intermediary products...........................	263	507	770
Luxury goods........................	54	417	471
Total............................	2644	2946	5590

SOURCE: Calculated from figures in Banco Central *Memoria* 1957, Chapter 7.

We have been unable, in the time available, to analyze this matter in detail but it is clearly important to know whether (a) the Agreement rules out a substantial number of important and promising candidates for protection, or (b) there are few of such candidates in any case since the most promising industries have already been protected and there are rather few more where the cost would not be virtually prohibitive at present, or (c) there are many good candidates of which the Agreement rules out only a few that are not economically indispensable. If (b) or (c) is the case—and we repeat that we do not know—it will be particularly important to weigh carefully the possible repercussions of an attempt to revise the Agreement on United States policy towards

Venezuelan oil, to which reference has already been made. Venezuela must also, of course, consider carefully the possible effects of any new protective measures on countries other than the United States that are customers for her petroleum and other exports.

Leaving aside foreign repercussions let us now look at some of the main arguments that are advanced for increased protection in Venezuela, and at some of the counter-arguments. We shall not attempt to reach any definite conclusions but only to set forth some of the considerations that should be taken into account, and to distinguish and classify some of the arguments.

The main arguments against protection are, of course, the classical ones that it reduces the international division of labor and imposes a direct burden on the country and on its people by causing goods to be produced at home which could be obtained with the use of less labor, capital and land by producing exports that could then be exchanged for these goods abroad. There is still a great deal of truth in these fundamental arguments but economists now recognize that many qualifications must be admitted.

One important argument for protection in Venezuela is that she must be more self-sufficient in case some future war or other emergency cuts off supplies from abroad. It is true that Venezuela depends greatly on imports; but she is much less vitally dependent than many other countries insofar as she is not so very far from self-sufficiency in food (partly, of course, because of the high agricultural protection that already exists). Even without any imports she could probably avoid starvation, at least if she kept reasonable stocks of, say, wheat and perhaps fertilizers. A large part of her imports consists of capital goods and this would help her, at least for a time, to keep up consumption and merely slow down investment. A shortage of capital goods and foreign raw materials could, however, create acute unemployment; this is perhaps the most serious danger. If the danger of war or other emergencies were the only argument for protection, the latter would obviously involve an economic cost because of the classical arguments mentioned above. It would then have to be decided how much cost the country was prepared to pay as an insurance, and alternative forms of insurance would have to be considered; it might, for example, be cheaper to build up a stockpile of the more vital imported articles. Protection would certainly not be granted to industries the absence of which in Venezuela would not cause serious trouble in an emergency.

Another argument, this one of an economic nature, is that protection is needed to give employment and prevent unemployment. It is not clear how much open (as distinct from concealed) unemployment there is, or has been, in Venezuela. Some people have expressed the opinion that what unemployment there is in 1958 is a temporary phenomenon connected, among other things, with the need to slow down public construction for a time. Others, particularly outside Caracas, seem to take the view that there has always been a good deal of unemployment but that it did not always reveal itself in the past. Whatever the truth it seems likely that open unemployment is not, and has not been, such a serious problem as in many other countries. Insofar as there is an emergency problem at the time of writing, it seems clear that no important contribution to its solution could be made in a short time by protecting new industries.

A more fundamental argument for protection to give employment takes account of "concealed" unemployment in agriculture and looks ahead to see how the growing labor force might be absorbed if vigorous steps were taken to improve education and productivity in the rural areas. In one sense, "concealed" unemployment in Venezuelan agriculture does not seem to be so severe as it is in certain other countries where acute shortage of land, in relation to the population on it, means that a good deal of labor could be withdrawn from agriculture without materially reducing output, even if there were no simultaneous changes in methods of production. In Venezuela, on the other hand, it seems that the small *campesino* often cannot till even the little land that he has because of the primitive methods used. But there is a great deal of concealed unemployment in the sense that, if better methods were used, the same amount could be produced with far fewer people or, alternatively, much more could be produced with the same number.

If then agricultural productivity could be rapidly improved, all the growing food needs of the country might be met without an appreciable increase in the agricultural labor force; there might even be a reduction. Nearly the whole, and perhaps more than the whole, of the growing labor force of the country would then have to be absorbed in non-agricultural pursuits. Moreover, it can be argued, since Venezuela cannot build up many new export industries because of her high costs, the extra population must be employed in industries that replace imports and this can only be done if more protection is granted.

There may turn out to be validity in this argument but it is difficult to be certain. In the first place, it is probable that there will be quite a substantial growth in import-competing industries, including those already established, even if no more protection is granted, and provided Venezuelan costs do not rise unduly. Moreover, an anti-protectionist might argue that, if the growing labor force cannot be absorbed because of the high cost level in Venezuela, the currency should be devalued so that her industries become more competitive. Protectionists, on the other hand, would argue that, quite apart from the other problems that would be created by devaluation, more protection is justified because the cost of labor to individual employers appears much higher than its social cost to the nation; if labor is becoming available as a result of educational and agricultural schemes that would be carried out in any case, and if it cannot be employed elsewhere, then its cost from a national point of view is zero.

In less theoretical terms it may be said that a great deal of extra employment will be provided, as in the past, in construction, in commerce and in services of various kinds (none of which need protection), both in the more prosperous, larger towns and in the smaller ones and the countryside as they become more prosperous; that trades serving a more efficient agriculture will grow up; that public construction could be increased if desired; that manufacturing, which is the main sector that desires more protection, may in any case employ relatively few extra people, at least if it continues to use such highly capital-intensive methods; and that it might be better, purely from an employment point of view and considering that capital is so scarce, to encourage sectors of the economy that use less capital per worker employed. Measures might also be taken to induce more labor-using and less capital-intensive methods of production in industry on the lines indicated earlier.

A further argument for protection is the need to diversify the economy of Venezuela so that she can become less dependent on oil. Two parts of this argument may be distinguished: that which draws attention to the danger of short-term fluctuations in oil income and that which looks at possible trends over a considerable period of years.

Any country that depends almost wholly for its foreign exchange on one commodity is clearly very vulnerable to fluctuations in world demand for it. If it had a number of equally important exports, fluctuations in demand for these might tend to cancel out, except, of course, when there was a general world depression. But Venezuela cannot hope to develop new exports that would be in the least comparable in magnitude to petroleum for many years to come. Therefore, so it is argued, she must reduce her dependence on imports. This will mean (1) that when oil income falls off, any necessary reduction in imports will cause less widespread dislocation, for more goods will be available at home, and possibly (2) that, in some way, it will be possible to let oil income become a less important part of the national income and of the government's budget, so that a temporary reduction in it need not cause so much unemployment.

It might, however, be less costly to invest in large international reserves, which could be used to maintain imports when oil income fell off temporarily, rather than in expensive domestic production.[27] And we have seen that, if this were done, the government could do a good deal to maintain employment by running a temporary budget deficit.

The long-term argument for diversification seems to be more powerful. It assumes that, even if there is oil in the ground to last for many years, the demand for it may not continue for nearly so long, or at least not go on rising nearly so rapidly as in the past. When this happens, Venezuela will be forced to produce for herself many things that she is now buying abroad with the foreign exchange obtained from oil. Basic economic forces will in some way bring about a reduction in her cost level in relation to costs abroad (by forcing a devaluation of the bolivar or in other ways) so that more import-competing production (and possibly more exports) will become economical even without any added protection. But it takes a long time to build up new industries so that a start must be made now if serious dislocation is to be avoided later.

The force of this argument depends greatly on the view taken of the future for Venezuelan oil, on the time that it is thought will be required to build up a given amount of new industry and on the burden that the country is prepared to bear now to provide a safeguard against future dangers.

The argument becomes a good deal stronger if it is combined with what economists call the "infant industry" argument for protection. This argument is that, although a new industry may be unable to compete with imports at the start without protection, it may be able to reduce its costs as its output grows and as it gains experience (often with the aid of foreign concerns that are induced to bring their know-how—and often capital—to the country) so that eventually it can compete without protection. One trouble in practice is, of course, that infants have a habit of not growing up, so that protection can never be reduced.

A similar argument can also be applied to the economy as a whole. Unindustrialized countries will never become industrialized unless they give an initial stimulus through protection (as a good many highly

---

[27] Policy on international reserves must of course take account of the fact that they are not directly productive and that they may depreciate in real value if import prices rise.

industrialized countries of today have done in the past). But as their industrial base grows, each individual industry will help the others, by developing specialized skills, by contributing to the general pool of industrially trained and disciplined labor, by providing nearby sources of supply for components, and so on, so that eventually most industries can compete with imports; some may even be able to begin exporting.

These arguments, together with that for diversification as a long-run policy, may constitute the most valid ones for the protection of Venezuelan industry. But they do not lead to the conclusion that the country should embark on a rapid program of protecting every industry that is physically capable of producing in Venezuela. The cost of such a policy would be very high, and it would absorb a great deal of the limited capital and energies that have to be shared between so many pressing needs. Candidates for protection will have to be selected with great care, the most important criterion being the level of protection required and the speed with which it may be reduced, although benefits to other parts of the economy will have to be taken into account. There is also a good deal to be said for avoiding protection that is so high as to exclude all imports; for competition from foreign producers is a useful spur to efficiency.

Venezuela will probably continue to import a large part of her manufactures, especially capital equipment, for many years. The cost of a high degree of self-sufficiency would be great if only because of the limited size of the internal market—and the possibility of enlarging the market by export is still a good way off for most Venezuelan manufacturing industries. It is true that, if her economy continues to grow at something like the rate achieved since the war, it will roughly double in a decade. But the market will still be small by world standards. For example, it is doubtful whether it will exceed one-half of the Canadian market today; and even Canada imports something like one-third of her manufactures.

There are undoubtedly gains or safeguards to be achieved from a policy of protection, but they are hard to evaluate, since they involve so much gazing into the future. There are also undoubtedly costs to be borne and dangers to be run, including, let us repeat, the danger that the commercial policy of foreign governments toward Venezuelan exports may be adversely affected. Since the extent to which Venezuela should pursue a protectionist policy in the years ahead must depend so much on an estimate of the future, and since it will involve a weighing of future possible gains against present sacrifices, it must clearly be a matter for political decision. But it is important that the costs as well as the benefits should be recognized, that they should be evaluated as carefully as possible, that partial arguments for protection which do not take account of all its implications should be rejected, and that possible alternative ways of achieving the same end at less cost should be fully explored before protection is embarked upon.

CHAPTER III : **Income Tax:**
: **General Considerations**

The present income tax was adopted in Venezuela in 1942, going into effect January 1, 1943. The law was amended in 1948 and revised in 1953. The 1956 law, published on August 8, 1955, and effective January 1, 1956, repealed prior legislation and is the present statutory law. The regulations for this 1956 law were published February 3, 1956, and replaced prior regulations. The income tax is imposed by the National Government and is national in scope. Under existing constitutional provisions, neither the states nor the local governments may adopt an income tax.

A. Description of the Income Tax

The income tax is composed of a series of schedular taxes at various flat rates and a complementary tax at progressive rates. There is a special additional tax applicable to oil production and mining, including oil royalties received by individuals and corporations. The same income tax is applied to corporations as to individuals. The income tax is essentially territorial in its jurisdictional application, applying only to income arising from sources within Venezuela as respects residents, citizens, and non-residents.

SCHEDULAR TAXES

All income subject to tax is classified into nine schedules. Each schedule (*cédula*) contains the description of the income items falling under that schedule, the deductions allowable, and the applicable rate. Individuals and corporations are equally subject to these schedules, with respect to rates, definition of income, and basic exemptions. As respects exemptions, a basic Bs.12,000 is allowed in total for schedules 1, 2, 3, 4, 6, and 8, as long as total income under those schedules does not

87

exceed Bs.19,200. If the total income exceeds that figure, no exemption is allowed for those schedules. The basic Bs.12,000 exemption is applied first to income in the schedules bearing the lowest tax rates. Special exemptions exist for schedule 5 (agriculture) and schedule 7 (wages and salaries). The exemptions are cumulative in the sense that a taxpayer having salary income may receive a schedule 7 exemption for the salary and also the Bs.12,000 exemption as respects any income he may have which falls under schedules 1, 2, 3, 4, 6, and 8. A similar cumulation exists as to schedule 5. Dividends are not subject to any schedule and therefore are not taxable. An excess of deductions over income in any one schedule may not, for schedular tax purposes, be applied against income in another schedule.

The schedular rates follow:

Schedule	Type of Income	Rate (%)
1	Rents from real property	2½
2	Interest, royalties	3
3	Business profits	2½
4	Oil and mining profits	2½
5	Agricultural profits	2
6	Profits from non-commercial professions	2
7	Salaries and wages	1
8	Gains from sales of real property	3
9	Lottery prizes and other chance winnings	10

Schedule 1: Rents. The schedular tax on rental income, schedule 1, is levied at a rate of 2½ %; it applies to rents from real property. In computing net income for this schedule, the following deductions are allowed: interest on mortgages on the property, taxes on the property, normal and necessary expenses of administration, and, up to 15% of gross income, maintenance expenses paid. Depreciation is not deductible. As indicated later, certain rents are excluded.

Schedule 2: Interest, Royalties, Annuities. This schedule, levied at a 3% rate, applies to income from personal property, and includes interest, royalties (including those from oil and mining), and annuities. Amortization of royalty and annuity costs is the only deduction permitted. Certain interest payments are excluded, as indicated later. Dividends are expressly excluded from tax.

Schedule 3: Industrial and Commercial Profits. This schedule, levied at a 2½ % rate, applies to industrial and commercial profits. In addition to business income, including that from forestry, it also covers gain from the sale of stocks and securities whether or not the seller is engaged in a business in the usual sense or in the business of selling securities, since, under the Commercial Law, the act of selling is a business; the sale of royalties; and any other gain not expressly taxed elsewhere nor expressly exempted. Taxable net income is determined by finding gross receipts, subtracting the cost of goods sold to provide gross income, and then subtracting the deductions allowed to provide net income. The deductions permitted are those normally found in the computation of business net income, including depreciation, interest, taxes (except income taxes), wages and salaries, losses, bad debts, and all other normal and necessary expenses.

The allowance of costs and deductions, however, is subject to the rule of territoriality under which, in general, the cost or expense must have been incurred in the country. There are various rules in this regard specifying that certain items are to be considered as incurred in Venezuela, such as the cost of goods purchased and of materials used, together with their transportation to Venezuela; the cost, in some situations, of transferring new employees from port of embarkation to Venezuela and return; and the transportation cost of goods exported if the goods are included in income at their price in the foreign destination. There are also special rules determining the amount of income attributable to Venezuela in certain cases, such as international transportation companies, foreign motion picture rentals, and imports on consignment. There is a two-year carry-forward of net losses under this schedule.

Schedule 4: Oil and Mining Activities. This schedule, levied at a 2½% rate, applies to income from hydrocarbon and mining activities, including production, refining, and transportation. In addition to the rules applicable to business income generally, there are provisions in the law and regulations relating to the special problems connected with these activities, such as the determination of depletion allowances (cost depletion but not percentage depletion is permitted), and the capitalization and amortization of concession and exploration costs and drilling expenditures. An especially difficult problem in the determination of the net income from oil production is the fixing of a price for the oil sold, since most sales are sales to other branches of the same company, or to related companies. An Interministerial Committee of representatives from the Ministry of Mines and Hydrocarbons and the Ministry of Finance exists to handle this problem.

Schedule 5: Agricultural Activities. This schedule, with a rate of 2%, applies to net income from agricultural activities. This includes, in addition to farming pursuits, livestock raising, fishing, and the initial processing in the farm area of agricultural or cattle products, including products obtained from others, but not fish processing. The computation of net income is in accordance with the business income schedule. However, if the Tax Administration does not find the taxpayer's records acceptable, it may compute net income by an estimate of his profit, and, if this is not feasible, it may fix net income at 10% of gross sales. The taxpayer, however, may not himself use this 10% computation. The special exemption for this schedule is Bs.30,000 as long as the net income under this schedule does not exceed Bs.50,000; beyond this point no exemption is allowed. A person receiving the Bs.30,000 exemption under this schedule may still receive the Bs.12,000 exemption for, say, interest income under schedule 2. There is a three-year carry-forward of net losses under this agricultural schedule.

Schedule 6: Non-commercial Professions. This schedule, levied at a 2% rate, applies to net income from non-commercial professions. In addition to the customary professions, such as law, medicine, architecture, engineering, accounting, etc. (provided the taxpayer conducts the activity on a professional basis and not as an employee), this schedule also covers copyright and patent sales or royalties, and income received by the self-employed if acting on an independent contractor basis, such as some taxi-drivers, etc., as long as the occupation does not involve an employer-employee relationship on the one hand (schedule 7) or an act of commerce (schedule 3) on the other. The deductions allowed are those permitted under the business income schedule, though certain accounting rules differ, in that under schedule 6 only the cash basis and calendar years are permitted.

As respects non-residents (in general—since there seems to be some uncertainty on this question—a resident is one who intends to reside in Venezuela and who is present within the country for 180 days, not necessarily continuously, over at least a two-year period and perhaps within one calendar year) subject to this schedule, the rate is 7%, no exemption is allowed, and only those expenses relating to fees, salaries, and taxes paid are deductible. Their income under this schedule is not, however, subject to complementary tax.

Schedule 7: Salaries and Wages. This schedule, levied at a 1% rate, applies to salaries, wages, and other employment income. Pensions, retirement pay, bonuses, profit-sharing, vacation pay, and the like are taxable. Indemnity payments upon dismissal, or payments in lieu thereof, are not taxable. Compensation in kind, such as housing, is taxable. The exemption for this schedule is Bs.1,000 monthly if the income under the schedule is not in excess of Bs.1,600 monthly; if it exceeds

Bs.1,600 monthly, no exemption is permitted. A person receiving these monthly exemptions may also receive the Bs.12,000 exemption for, say, interest received under schedule 2. No deductions are allowable under the salary and wage schedule. Non-residents (see the definition under schedule 6 above) are subject to a 4% rate and are not entitled to an exemption, but they are not subject to complementary tax on their compensation.

The employer is required to withhold tax under this schedule on all cash payments subject to tax. Since the exemption is on a monthly basis, the unused exemption of one month may not be applied against the income of another month. Thus, if a taxpayer earns Bs.700 in January, Bs.1,300 in February, and Bs.1,800 in March, the withheld tax would be zero, Bs.3, and Bs.18 respectively. (If a taxpayer works for more than one employer and receives amounts in excess of Bs.1,000, he must advise one of the payors of the total received so that the latter can withhold accordingly; the Tax Administration may authorize withholding by more than one employer in this situation.) Under this arrangement, there is no overwithholding or underwithholding as respects income subject to withholding. There are thus no credits against tax or under-payments of tax because of withheld income. As respects this schedule, therefore, most taxpayers will not have any schedular tax to pay when their annual declaration is filed. However, since some compensation is not subject to withholding—for example, compensation in kind in some situations—some schedular tax remains to be paid under the declaration at the end of the year for certain taxpayers.

Schedule 8: Gains from Sales of Real Property. This schedule, with a 3% rate, applies to gains from the sale of real property. In effect, this schedule covers capital gains on real property. The schedule is applicable to all such gains, including residential and agricultural property, except the gain on the sale of assets used in a business (schedule 3), sales made by one in the real estate business or one who purchases for resale at a profit (schedule 3), or sales of oil or mining concessions or assets (schedule 4). Capital gains on personal property are also taxable, presumably under schedule 3 either as constituting a gain from business or under the catchall paragraph of that schedule reaching all gains not expressly taxed elsewhere. However, it may be that some casual gains of personal property other than securities by one not in business may fall under schedule 2. In effect, all capital gains are thus subject to tax under some schedule.

The deductions permitted under this schedule are the initial cost of the asset, the initial cost of improvements, assumed interest at 6% a year on the above costs, and commissions paid on the sale if the payor withholds schedule 3 tax at 2½% on the commission. If the real property was acquired by the taxpayer prior to 1943, the portion of the gain allocable to the period prior to January 1, 1943, is excluded; this allocation is made on a pro-rated basis by days, without regard to actual 1943 values. There is no similar exclusion for personal property, or for real property sales falling under the other schedules. This tax, as well as that on personal property gains, does not apply where the transfer is by gift or inheritance. The donee or heir receives a tax cost or basis equal to the value of the property at the time of the transfer.

Schedule 9: Fortuitous Gains. This schedule, with a 10% rate, applies to fortuitous gains or chance winnings, such as lottery prizes and winnings on horse-racing bets. There is no exemption under this schedule and no deduction is permitted. The income, however, is not subject to complementary tax. The tax is withheld by those managing the lottery or betting before the winnings are paid to the taxpayers.

EXEMPT INCOME

The following are the principal income items specifically exempt from tax: all dividend payments; interest on Bs.10,000 of saving deposits per individual depositor; income of charitable institutions; indemnizations of employees such as dismissal pay; insurance proceeds (except amounts compensating for losses deducted in the computation of cost of goods sold); gifts and inheritances; rentals for five years from all new construction after July 15, 1958 (previously this exclusion was solely on a discretionary basis applicable to regions in which the exclusion was considered desirable).

In addition to these specific exclusions from income, there are certain items which may be excluded at the discretion of the National Executive. Under this discretion, exclusions exist for interest at a moderate rate on loans for agricultural development; interest not in excess of 6% on mortgage bonds relating to agricultural activities or industries producing articles of prime necessity or processing local raw materials; interest on mortgage bonds issued by banks owned at least 50% by the Government; rents for five years from new construction in areas where such a measure is advisable; income of savings institutions, credit and social welfare institutions, and cooperatives; income of religious, artistic, scientific, educational, cultural, sporting, and professional institutions or associations organized and operated on a non-profit basis (income from sources other than those related to the usual activities of these organizations is taxable). From time to time Government bonds or notes may be issued under special laws providing for a specific exemption of their interest from tax.

COMPLEMENTARY TAX

The complementary tax, applied at rates rising from 1.50% to 26%, is in general levied on all income subject to the schedular taxes. In effect, the net income for the complementary tax is determined by totalling the net amounts under each of the schedules. In this computation, net losses under one schedule may be applied against taxable amounts under other schedules, but no carry forward of net losses is here permitted, even though allowable in the computation of schedular incomes. Moreover, the various basic exemptions under the schedules are not allowed in computing the complementary tax, which has its own basic exemption. The amounts in schedule 9 (chance winnings), and as respects non-residents, the amounts in schedule 6 (non-commercial professions) and schedule 7 (salaries and wages), are not included in complementary tax income. Two additional deductions are allowed in computing complementary tax income—charitable contributions (not already deducted for the schedular tax as a normal and necessary expense) if the total is in excess of Bs.5,000, and medical and dental expenses of the taxpayer and his dependents if receipts are supplied.

As respects exemptions, individuals receive a Bs.12,000 exemption; corporations do not have any exemption. An individual also receives an allowance of Bs.4,000 for a spouse; Bs.3,000 for each parent, grandparent, child or grandchild supported by the taxpayer, except male descendants of legal age unless incapacitated; Bs.900 for any other person supported by the taxpayer.[1] If several persons contribute to the support of an individual, the allowance is pro-rated among them.

In brief, taxable income for the complementary tax is computed as follows:

(1) Total the schedular income before schedular basic exemptions, subtracting net losses (but disregarding net loss carry-overs), chance

[1] A man with wife and three children thus has an exemption of Bs.25,000. This is 9.5 times the national income per capita; see pp. 11 and 45 above. The corresponding ratio is higher in Burma, 1953 (20); India, 1950 (11); Ceylon (14); Philippines (14); it is lower in Japan (2.6), United States (1.4), United Kingdom (1.6), Australia (1.0), and Canada (1.9), in 1953. United Nations, *Economic Survey of Asia and the Far East, 1954,* p. 44, cited by A. H. Hanson, *Public Enterprise and Economic Development,* London, 1959, p. 76.

winnings, and the salary and professional income of non-residents.

(2) Subtract charitable contributions, if their total exceeds Bs.5,000, and medical expenses.

(3) Subtract Bs.12,000 personal exemption and the family allowances.

The rate scale for the complementary tax follows:

Brackets (Bs.)	Rate (%)	Brackets (Bs.)	Rate (%)
0–10,000	1.50	640,000–800,000	8.25
10,000–14,000	1.75	800,000–1,000,000	9.00
14,000–20,000	2.00	1,000,000–1,400,000	9.75
20,000–28,000	2.25	1,400,000–2,000,000	10.50
28,000–38,000	2.50	2,000,000–2,800,000	11.50
38,000–50,000	2.75	2,800,000–3,800,000	12.50
50,000–64,000	3.00	3,800,000–5,000,000	13.50
64,000–80,000	3.50	5,000,000–6,400,000	14.50
80,000–100,000	4.00	6,400,000–8,000,000	16.00
100,000–140,000	4.50	8,000,000–10,000,000	17.50
140,000–200,000	5.00	10,000,000–14,000,000	19.00
200,000–280,000	5.50	14,000,000–20,000,000	21.00
280,000–380,000	6.00	20,000,000–28,000,000	23.00
380,000–500,000	6.75	Over 28,000,000	26.00
500,000–640,000	7.50		

In the case of the last three brackets special rate reductions apply to reinvested income. Thus in the case of taxpayers in the bracket Bs.14,000,000–20,000,000 the rate is 19% on an income in that bracket equal to the amount of investment made during the year in Venezuela, up to Bs.3,000,000 of income; in the case of taxpayers in the bracket Bs.20,000,000–28,000,000 the rate is 20% on reinvested income up to Bs.4,000,000; in the case of taxpayers with income over Bs.28,000,000, the rate is 22% on reinvested income up to one-half the difference between the total taxable income and Bs.28,000,000. These lower rates are not cumulative; hence, for example, a taxpayer with an income of Bs.28,000,000.01 will lose the benefit for reinvested income applicable to the preceding bracket. Here, the last centimo of income results in an increase in tax of Bs.120,000.

SCHEDULAR AND COMPLEMENTARY TAXES
ON PARTICULAR CLASSES OF TAXPAYERS

Individuals. Individuals are subject to schedular and complementary taxes. As respects married couples, Venezuela has a community property system (called a "community of income") under which all income —the earnings of husband and wife and income from their property— is owned equally by the spouses. Property derived from such community income is also owned equally by the spouses. Property obtained by either spouse before marriage or acquired by either spouse as a gift or inheritance after marriage remains separate property, though the income from such property is community income. The husband administers the community income except the actual earnings of the wife, and administers the community property but not the separate property of the wife. However, this division of income and property does not carry over to the income tax. The husband in general must report all community income and pay tax thereon. For schedular purposes, however, though one return is filed, the tax is computed separately as to the wife's actual earnings and income from property she administers. As respects such earnings and income she has the right to obtain her own schedular exemptions. Under the complementary tax, the husband and wife are considered as a single taxpayer and together report all their income. They have a total basic exemption of Bs.12,000 plus the allowance of Bs.4,000 for a spouse. This joining of income applies to all community income, including the wife's actual earnings and income from separate property. In this latter respect the schedular tax rules and the complementary tax rules are inconsistent. However, for the complementary tax a wife may separately declare income actually earned by her as salary and professional earnings (schedules 7 and 6). In this event, while both husband and wife could obtain a Bs.12,000 exemption, neither may obtain the Bs.4,000 allowance, and only one may claim allowances for dependents. If the married couple have legally separated all of their property by court decree, then the parties are considered as two separate taxpayers. Also, if by pre-marital agreement the wife has kept her pre-marital property as separate property, she may report the income therefrom separately for both schedular and complementary taxes. Such agreements, however, are rare in Venezuela. The earnings of minor children and the income from the minor's property are included in the father's declaration, except in those situations in which by law he does not have the legal use of the earnings or income.

Partnerships. Partnerships are subject only to the schedular taxes. The partners include in their complementary tax income their respective shares of partnership income, whether or not actually distributed. These rules apply to joint interests *(comunidades)* but not to joint ventures *(cuentas en participación)*, in which each participant is treated separately for all income taxes. Foreign partnerships subject to tax are treated as taxpayers for both schedular and complementary taxes, and do not receive any exemption for the complementary tax.

Corporations. Corporations *(compañías anónimas)* are subject to schedular and complementary taxes, and do not receive any exemption for the complementary tax.

Limited Liability Companies. A limited liability company *(compañía de responsabilidad limitada)* is taxed as is a partnership. It is subject to the schedular taxes, and each member includes his proportional share of the income, whether distributed or not, for the complementary tax. A limited liability company must have a capital of at least Bs.20,000 but not in excess of Bs.2,000,000.

Non-Residents. Non-residents are taxed in the same manner as residents with the exceptions earlier noted respecting professional income (schedule 6) and salaries (schedule 7).

As respects the requirements for filing declarations, every person or entity having net income above Bs.12,000 or gross income above Bs.36,000 must file a tax declaration. A corporation must file a declaration of its net income even though it is less than Bs.12,000. The declaration form covers both schedular and complementary taxes. A married person with two children who receives, say, Bs.1,500 a month salary would be required to file a declaration, though his schedular tax would have been fully paid through withholding and he would have no complementary tax liability because of a total of exemption and allowances under that tax of Bs.22,000. Most exempt declarations are of this character; i.e., they relate to salary and wages income on which the schedular tax has been withheld and no complementary tax is due. If a person received Bs.12,000 rent from real property and a salary of Bs.1,000 a month, no schedular tax would be due because of the availability in this situation of schedular exemptions under both schedule 1 and schedule 7, and no complementary tax would be due if he were married with three children. A declaration would have to be filed, however. If a person received Bs.1,500 a month for 7 months and were unemployed for the other 5 months, he would be subject to schedular tax but this would be collected through withholding. He would not have to file a declaration at the end of the year.

Additional Income Tax on Oil and Mining. An additional income tax is applied to net income from the extractive hydrocarbon and mining industries, and from oil and mining royalties. Generally speaking, the tax is 50% of the excess of the net profits (i.e., after deducting taxes, including the schedular and complementary income taxes) over all taxes, including royalties, paid to the Government (other than the additional tax itself). The tax is sometimes referred to as the 50-50 tax. The tax was adopted in 1948, following special taxes in 1945-1947. The additional tax thus obtains for the Government a total return of at least 50% of the net income, computed before deducting any tax, realized from the natural resources of the country.

The principal taxpayers subject to this tax are those engaged in oil production and in mining. All of their income is potentially subject to the additional income tax, regardless of how much of their income is from production, as long as they are subject to the tax at all. In addition, where two or more taxpayers are controlled by the same interests and one is subject to the additional tax, the several taxpayers are combined for additional tax purposes even though the other taxpayers would not by themselves be subject to this tax, unless the National Executive excludes any of these taxpayers from such consolidation. The definition of net income used in computing the base for the additional tax is essentially that determined under the schedular taxes, with the following modifications: all income and expenses excluded by reason of territoriality rules from schedular income are here included if related with and applicable to operations in Venezuela, so that income items not having a Venezuelan source, and expenses incurred outside Venezuela, are covered (except that income taxes paid to other countries are not deductible); reserves for future expenses, such as termination pay, are deductible; dividends received from companies not subject to additional tax are excluded. In addition to taxpayers engaged in productive activities, those receiving oil or mining royalties are also subject to the additional tax but only on their net income from the royalties if they are not otherwise involved in oil or mining production. Those companies engaged in drilling or other service activities to the oil and mining industries, and not engaged in production, are not subject to the tax.

The Hydrocarbons Law imposes an annual surface tax on exploration concessions (Bs.2 per hectare) and an initial production tax (Bs.8 per hectare) for the first three years. However, in the recent bidding for concessions, additional amounts as first annual exploration tax or initial production tax have been required. Bonuses as high as $2,832 per acre have been paid (2.47 acres equal 1 hectare). A surface tax is also levied on production concessions; this is Bs.5 per hectare per year for the first ten years, increasing Bs.5 for each five years until it reaches Bs.30. If a production tax is paid, this surface tax is reduced by the former to a minimum of Bs.1.25 per hectare per quarter. There is a current monthly production *(explotación)* tax of 16-2/3% on crude oil or natural asphalt produced and on natural gas sold or used as fuel. This tax is sometimes referred to as a royalty. Some recent bidders have agreed to pay a higher rate of production tax. The tax may be collected in cash or in kind, and is usually collected in cash. Values are at present determined under an agreement between the Government and the companies, an agreement which establishes a figure higher than the now current posted prices of the companies. These latter posted prices are used by the companies in reporting gross income for income tax purposes.

The computation of the additional income tax, and the effect of the other income and oil taxes, is as follows:

(1) Net income is computed on the basis of the schedular incomes, with the modifications above noted. Included in this computation will be deductions for amortization of capitalized costs, including costs of concessions, initial exploration tax, the initial production tax, and customs duties and consular fees on capital items. There will also be included deductions for all current taxes not capitalized, such as the 16-2/3% production tax (royalty), other current hydrocarbon taxes, state and municipal taxes, and customs duties and consular fees which are properly expensed. Schedular and complementary income taxes are not deductible.

(2) From net income so computed the schedular and complementary income taxes are deducted to give net profits.

(3) There are then totalled all taxes currently being paid to the National Government, and to states and municipalities. These include schedular and complementary income taxes, 16-2/3% production tax (royalty), surface production tax, customs duties and consular fees (even though required to be capitalized for the purpose of net income computation), stamp taxes, gross receipts tax, and municipal *patentes,* and license and real property taxes (but not fees). They do not include any concession payments or initial production taxes paid during the year or amortized from prior years, or any exploration taxes, or the additional income tax itself. Nor do they include the various consumption taxes on products such as gasoline and oil, since these taxes are intended to be passed on.

(4) The total of these taxes is then subtracted from net profits.

(5) If any excess results, the excess is subject to a tax of 50%. This is the additional income tax.

When a taypayer's net income after deduction of schedular and complementary taxes does not exceed 10% of capital invested in production, the taxpayer is not subject to additional tax. If the net income after taxes is more than 10% of invested capital but not in excess of 15%, then the additional tax applies only to half of the taxable excess computed for the additional tax, so that the rate is, in effect, 25%. However, if the net income after taxes exceeds 15% of invested capital, then the full 50% additional tax rate applies to the entire taxable excess. Similarly, the 25% rate applies in full to a taxpayer whose net income after taxes just exceeds 10% of invested capital. As a consequence, a small increase in net income can result in a much larger additional income tax payment.

The purpose of the additional income tax is to obtain for the Government a total return of at least 50% of the net income, as computed before deducting any tax whatever (here referred to as operating income), realized from the oil and mineral natural resources of the country. It should be emphasized that the additional tax is a minimum tax and not a maximum limitation on the Government's share. In the case of some oil companies, the total taxes paid to the Government, essentially the 16-2/3% production tax (royalty), and the schedular and complementary taxes, will exceed 50% of the taxpayer's operating income as defined above. In these cases, no additional tax is payable, since there is no taxable excess for the purposes of that tax. At the same time, no reduction is made in the taxes paid to reduce the Government's share to 50%. These taxpayers are not subject to the additional tax, but the reason they are not so subject is that their other taxes paid already exceed 50% of operating income. Hence, an oil production company not subject in a given year to the additional tax is thus known to be paying taxes at a higher effective rate than 50% of operating income. Figures computed by Price, Waterhouse & Company for the principal companies engaged in the production of crude oil in Venezuela show that the Government's share of operating income, taken in royalty tax and other taxes, averaged 53% for the years 1947-1956. In 1956, the figure was 51%, in 1955, 52%, and in 1953, 53%. In 1956, when large amounts were paid for concessions, the percentage inclusive of these payments would have been 61% instead of 51%.

These figures do not vary appreciably from those published by the

Ministry of Mines and Hydrocarbons, if from the latter there is sub-tracted as an item of Government receipts the amount stated as repre-senting "exchange transactions." Whether the profit on exchange trans-actions can be regarded as a sort of tax is a question that is analyzed in Appendix A to the present report, below.

The figures reproduced here are based on unaudited tax declarations.

As Tables III–20 and III–21 at the end of the chapter indicate, there is considerable variation among the companies. Most of the oil com-panies paying additional tax, a group which included in 1957 the three largest companies in Venezuela, are close to the 50-50 dividing line, the largest company being the one farthest away (that is, before com-puting the additional tax). For these companies, a modest increase in the complementary income tax would be absorbed by a corresponding reduction in the additional income tax that they are now paying. But the 50-50 point would soon be passed with a further increase in the comple-mentary tax rates; thus any substantial increase in the complementary tax would give rise to an increase in total income tax payments by these companies.

The range of absorption of an increase in the complementary tax by a corresponding decrease in the additional income tax is apparently somewhere between an additional 1 to 3 percentage points in the com-plementary tax, the latter percentage applying for the largest oil com-pany. The absorption figure for this company drops to 1 percentage point for some prior years. For these companies, of course, any increase in the additional income tax itself, for example an increase from 50-50 to 55-45, would immediately cause their total tax bill to rise.

There are, on the other hand, a number of oil production companies that are not paying additional income tax, because their effective rates on operating income are over 50%. That is, the amount of taxes paid, in terms of those taxes taken into account in computing the offsets against net profits in calculating the taxable excess for the additional income tax, is, in the case of these companies, in excess of net income after all taxes except the additional tax. The reasons for this condition can vary considerably. It generally is the result of a low ratio of net income to gross income, so that the production tax of 16-2/3% based on gross weighs heavily in the offset. This low ratio may be the result of recent heavy investments in plant and equipment at high prices, yielding large annual amortization deductions, or of annual amortization of high concession costs. As another factor, the amount of taxes proper to be applied as an offset may be currently increased by large customs duties paid on extensive importations of equipment. For these taxpayers, an increase in complementary tax rates would at once be reflected in over-all increased tax payments. But an increase in the additional income tax to 55-45 or even, in some cases, to 60-40, would not result, point for point, in an overall increase in tax payments. The actual increase would vary from company to company.

Then there is a group of companies whose additional income tax is in each case quite large, so that any foreseeable increase in complementary tax rates is not likely to be reflected at all in an increase in overall tax payments. This group includes at least the largest mining company (whose production tax or royalty is 1%), and also those companies (and individuals) receiving only oil royalty payments, and hence having only income taxes to offset against net profits in computing the additional income tax. For these companies and individuals an increase in additional income tax would be immediately reflected in overall increased tax payments.

Hence, if it were decided to increase taxes on the oil companies, the method selected would obviously have a material effect on the distribution of the increase among the various companies. On the whole, the more appropriate method would appear to be an increase in the regular rates of tax (complementary tax) rather than in the additional income tax. However, special consideration might have to be given to the mining area, since an increase in regular rates is not likely to affect the total of the taxes paid by anyone in that area.

B. Basic Structural Suggestions

The above description of the Venezuelan income tax structure discloses two main aspects which require consideration. One aspect is that of the division of the income tax between the various schedular taxes and the complementary tax. The other is the application of almost identical rate structures to both corporations and individuals, together with the exclusion of dividends from taxable income. It is believed that both these structural features are undesirable and should be changed. This is so, even if the share of the fiscal burden to be borne by the income tax is not appreciably increased. And the changes are imperative if the income tax is to be required to produce considerably more revenue.

ELIMINATION OF SCHEDULAR TAXES

The present system of schedular taxation is a source of considerable complexity in the income tax. Initially, all income must be classified among the nine schedules. Since the rules for determination of net income in the various schedules are different, and also since the rates vary, even though the variations are minor, problems of definition and classification arise. Thus, the gain on the sale of real property bears a 3% rate if classified in schedule 8 but a 2½% rate if classified in schedule 3, a variation which presents a difficult definitional problem. Further, it is not clear whether rental income from personal property falls in schedule 2 with a 3% rate or schedule 3 with a 2½% rate; moreover, under schedule 2 none of the expenses incurred in the rental of the property would be allowed, although all such expenses may be deducted under schedule 3. It seems obvious that such problems of classification and definition should be eliminated as far as possible in an income tax. These legal problems could perhaps be tolerated if important consequences were to follow from the classification. In fact, however, the rate differences among the schedules are so minor that they cannot justify the resulting legal difficulties.

The division of a taxpayer's income among schedules tends to produce differences in technical rules that are not justified. Thus, only the cash method of accounting may be used in schedules 1, 2, 6, 7, and 9 but only the accrual method may be used in schedules 3, 4, 5, and 8. Taxpayers engaged in activities under schedules 3, 4, or 5 may use fiscal years, but other taxpayers must use only calendar years. Expenses allowed under one schedule are not allowed under another, though in both situations the expense is incurred in the production of income. Thus, depreciation is not allowed in computing rental income from real property under schedule 1 or from personal property under schedule 2, but depreciation is allowed in computing business income in schedule 3. Expenses such as interest and taxes that may be incurred in producing interest income under schedule 2 are not deductible, though such expenses are deductible in computing rental income under schedule 1. The inequities resulting from these disparities, apart from the problems of classification mentioned earlier, could be tolerated if they involved only the ½% to 1% variations among the schedules involved. But these rules for computing schedular income also govern the computation of income for the complementary tax, where the rates do go higher. The resulting inequities can thus be considerably more serious. But the very existence of the schedules and their low rates tends to conceal the importance of these technical rules and their significance for the complementary tax.

In addition to these aspects of classification, definition, and equity, the existence of nine schedules makes for a complicated declaration form and for a complicated tax computation. Separate taxes must be computed for each schedule in which the taxpayer has income. While most declarations involve income in only one schedule, principally schedule 7 relating to salaries and wages, a large number of declarations show income in several schedules. Thus, the total number of schedules showing taxable income in the declarations for 1957, for the Caracas Office, was 108,125, while the declarations involved were only about 75,000. For declarations having incomes under Bs.200,000, the tax computation is made by the Tax Administration on a machine. The schedular system requires that a separate card be punched and tax computed for each schedule, so that the computation of tax for a single taxpayer can involve a number of cards for the schedules and then another card for the complementary tax, and then the addition of the amounts on each card. Similar steps are involved in the hand computations for the returns over Bs.200,000. A later administrative recommendation suggests that the computation of tax be performed as far as possible by the taxpayers themselves. It will be simple to achieve this result if only the computation of a single tax is involved; and in fact the feasibility of the suggestion may depend on the change to a single tax.

Most important of all, perhaps, is the fact that the existence of a number of schedular taxes and a complementary tax makes it difficult to think clearly about the structure of the income tax, its impact upon taxpayers, and the burdens it involves. It is necessary to keep in mind several sets of exemptions for the various schedular taxes and a different set for the complementary tax. Moreover, the schedular exemptions do not take account of family status, while the complementary tax exemptions do vary with family status. Further, one must remember the different rates under the schedular taxes and the complementary tax. It becomes very difficult to grasp the cumulative effect of these taxes on any particular taxpayer or class of taxpayers, in order to perceive readily and clearly just what their tax burdens may be. Thus, one tends to think of the complementary tax as involving the heavier burden because its rates are progressive and rise to 26%. But for many taxpayers the schedular taxes are more important, since the schedular exemptions are lower and the rates higher. Thus, for a single person engaged in business, the tax under schedule 3 is higher than the complementary tax until the income rises somewhat above Bs.100,000; for a married person with two children the schedular tax continues to be higher even at Bs.200,000. But this is not so under schedule 7 relating to salaries. Here, for a single person the complementary tax is heavier until Bs.19,200; at Bs.19,201 the schedular tax is heavier; above Bs.30,000 the complementary tax again becomes the heavier. For a married person with two children the schedular tax is heavier until about Bs.50,000. As respects corporations in business, the complementary tax is heavier until Bs.19,200; at Bs.19,201 the schedular tax becomes the heavier; at about Bs.70,000 the complementary tax again becomes the heavier. (See Tables III-1 and III-2 at the end of this chapter.)

These differing impacts of the various taxes make it impossible clearly to visualize the Venezuelan tax system. The existence of these various taxes also makes it difficult to present statistical tax data in ways in which they can readily be grasped, for much the same reasons.

The only argument that appears to be advanced in favor of the present system is that it permits variations in the burden among the different types of incomes. This view, of course, assumes at the outset that meaningful qualitative distinctions exist between the various income sources, distinctions which can be quantitatively reflected in different tax rates. But it is not at all clear just why rents should be taxed less heavily than interest, or why patent royalties received by an inventor should be taxed less heavily than either. Moreover, excluding salaries and wages, the range in the schedular tax rates does not exceed 1%. As respects rents, interest, business income, and capital gains, the range is only ½%. Similarly, as respects professional income and business income, the variation is only ½%. Certainly, if significant qualitative differences exist, they are not adequately reflected in these quantitative figures. Put another way, the qualitative differences surely cannot be analyzed so finely as to justify or warrant ½% differentials. Put still another way, if the qualitative differences only warrant ½% differentials, or are to be accorded only ½% differentials, those qualitative differences are not worth worrying about. On the other hand, the adoption of large rate variations among the schedules would involve serious distortions in the economy. The result would be a hodgepodge of incentives and burdens that could materially affect the economic life of the country. For this reason the schedular variations must be confined to almost meaningless differences. So confined, they become hindrances to an effective tax system for the reasons earlier advanced.

The most significant variations in the present schedules involve the income of employees and agricultural income. As respects salaries and wages, the schedular rate is 1%. If variations are to exist among income sources, then the classification of income between earned and unearned income probably is the most defensible classification. It is this differential that is most strongly stressed in explanation of the present system. While a differential in favor of earned income necessarily involves technical complexity, there are many who think the equity factor outweighs that complexity, at least in the lower brackets and in the absence of a separate tax on wealth. It is not necessary at this point, however, to decide this policy issue. For if differentiation in favor of earned income is desired, it can readily be supplied without resort to a schedular system. Given a unitary tax rate structure applicable to all income, the differentiation can be supplied either by the exclusion of a percentage of earned income, or an absolute amount of earned income, or a percentage of earned income up to a ceiling amount. Thus (to illustrate the method and not as an indication of the actual figures), if one supposes a first bracket of Bs.5,000 taxed at an 8% rate, and if it were desired to tax earned income in this bracket at three-quarters of the rate on unearned income, then 25% of earned income could be exempted from gross income up to a total exemption of Bs.1,250. (This could also be expressed as a special deduction from gross income.) Or an earned income credit *against tax* could be used, under which there could be credited against the tax 2% of earned income up to a total credit of Bs.100. The figures, of course, depend on the actual rates of tax and on the differentiation desired. Necessarily, the amounts stated in the formula under the method that uses an earned income credit against tax are less than under the earned income exclusion or deduction method, for a given general level of earned income relief. The significant difference in the methods is that the deduction or exclusion method applies the benefit of the earned income differentiation at the taxpayer's top bracket rate of tax, while the credit-against-tax method applies the benefit at the initial bracket rates.

If an earned income differential is to be adopted, it should be restricted to salaries, wages and other compensation. The extension of the differential to professional income would in turn probably necessitate its further extension to all self-employed activity, including individually owned and operated business. But all income from self-employment arises, in varying degree, from both the taxpayer's capital and his labor, so that a division of the income between earned and unearned income is then required. This can only be done on some arbitrary rule-of-thumb basis which would hardly be supportable case by case, or by an attempted analysis of each case separately, which would be impossible from an administrative point of view. Moreover, under the present system, all business income is grouped together at a 2½% rate under schedule 3, and this is only ½% more than the schedule 6 professional rate. Thus, despite some claims by professional people and other self-employed for an earned income differential, it would be best to limit the differential to employment income.

As respects agricultural income, the differential exists partly in the rate, which under schedule 5 is 2% as compared with 2½% for business generally, and in the Bs.30,000 schedular exemption vanishing at Bs.50,000 as compared with the Bs.12,000 exemption vanishing at Bs.19,200 under the other schedules. Presumably this differential exists as an intended tax subsidy to those engaged in agricultural enterprises; it does not extend to agricultural labor. It is difficult to defend this differentiation in favor of agricultural activities and against other business. The tax system is basically not a suitable vehicle to provide a subsidy; grants and direct subsidies are preferable. Incidentally, the operation under the present system of this agricultural differential alongside the earned income differential is somewhat bizarre. A salary or wage earner pays more tax than a farmer up to Bs.50,001. Up to this figure, then, the agricultural subsidy argument outweighs the earned income argument; above this point, the earned income argument outweighs the agricultural subsidy argument.

Again, this matter of tax policy need not force a schedular tax system. If a tax subsidy is desired for agriculture, it likewise can be granted in the form of a special agricultural exclusion or deduction or credit against tax, as in the case of earned income. A possible, and simple, solution would be to treat agricultural income as earned income, and thus grant it any differential that may be accorded to earned income.

If the schedular taxes are to be eliminated, two steps are necessary. First, the schedular rates must be combined with the complementary rates to provide one unitary progressive rate structure. The shape of this structure, and the exemptions, tax rates and brackets used, depend of course on the revenue yield desired. A few considerations are noted here.

EXEMPTIONS

The exemption method now used under the schedular taxes is not as appropriate as that under the complementary tax. The schedular exemptions do not take account of family status; they are the same for a single person, a married couple, and a married couple with dependents. Further, at Bs.19,200, an exemption of Bs.12,000 exists, but at Bs.19,200.01 the exemption is lost. Hence an increase in income of Bs.0.01 can produce an increase in tax of Bs.120 under schedule 7, a tax increase of Bs.300 under schedule 3, of Bs.360 under schedules 2 and 8, and so on. While it may be appropriate to have basic exemptions vanish as income increases, so that only the lower brackets and not the higher brackets of income enjoy those exemptions, the mechanics should not involve such abrupt increases in tax. On the whole, it is simpler to allow the exemptions to remain constant, as under the complementary tax, especially if they are not too high, and if the top rates of tax are moderate, so that the equity aspect is not serious.

It is also desirable to recognize differences in family status in the exemptions used, as is done in the complementary tax. The relationships there followed are Bs.12,000 exemption for a single person, Bs.4,000 for a wife, and Bs.3,000 for close dependents (Bs.900 for other dependents). Thus the relationship rate is 1-1/3-1/4. It is not necessary that this precise relationship be used. It is arguable that the exemption for a single person is here too high in relation to that for a married couple, though this is counteracted by the relatively large exemption for dependents as the number of children in a family increases. Another question is whether a wife should receive an exemption greater or less than that of a dependent, and indeed greater or less than a single person. Also, if administrative convenience were the sole criterion, it would be simplest to have the same exemption for every person, so that the total exemptions in the family group would be ascertained by multiplying the basic exemption figure by the number in the group. The next simplest arrangement administratively is to have the wife's exemption the same as that of each dependent. Since most of the administrative problems created by varying exemption figures can normally be met in one way or another, equity aspects should generally weigh more. However, under present conditions, the figure used for the single person's exemption may be controlling. Thus, if it is decided to lower exemptions, the administrative problems involved as income tax coverage is increased will depend on how low the single person's exemption is made. If this must be kept at some minimum level, say Bs.5,000, Bs.6,000 or Bs.7,000, for administrative reasons, then the size of the exemptions for wife and dependents will largely be controlled by the revenue yield desired. Under such circumstances it is probable that the dependent's exemption must be kept relatively low. There may be greater flexibility in fixing the wife's exemption. In this light, the ratios used could be 1, 2/3, 1/3; 1, 1/2, 1/3; or possibly 1, 1/3, 1/3. It would also seem appropriate to maintain a differential, as at present, between close family dependents (parents, grandparents, children, grandchildren) and other dependents. The present ratio here is Bs.3,000 to Bs.900, or 1, 3/10. This ratio could be preserved, with a possible decrease to 1, 1/4.

The declaration filing requirements should be related to the single person's exemption, so that any person with net income over that exemption would have to file. Perhaps the filing requirement as respects married persons could be placed at the level of the combined exemptions for husband and wife. All persons with gross income above a certain level would also be required to file a declaration. All corporations should be required to file declarations.

RATES AND BRACKETS

As respects rates and brackets, these also depend on revenue yields desired. However, it may be pointed out that the present structure of the complementary tax utilizes more brackets than is necessary or desirable. There are 29 brackets in all, of which 9 are below Bs.100,000, and 20 above. In the lower parts of the scale, the rates vary only ¼% from bracket to bracket; thereafter, the variation rises slowly from ½% to 1%, until a few top brackets are reached. It never exceeds 3%. Frequent bracket changes create some complexity in tax computation, though this can generally be met by tax tables. From an equity standpoint, frequent changes are more justifiable at the lower end of the scale. An offsetting factor here is the administrative problems created for withholding of tax at the source on salaries and wages, especially if a significant part of the tax paid by the general run of employees is to be collected in this fashion. If there are too many rate graduations, the withholding tables become complex, and there is an increase in tax refunds at the end of the year because of overwithholding and also in bills sent to taxpayers for taxes still owed because of underwithholding.

The present first bracket is Bs.10,000 wide. It would appear desirable to reduce this bracket in size, especially if exemptions were to be lowered and rates increased. The latter steps would also involve larger variations in rates in the first few brackets. Thereafter, going higher in the rate scale, it would appear appropriate to reduce the number of brackets, since little is achieved at these levels by numerous brackets with only slight rate changes. Also, if tax rates were increased, the top rates would be reached more rapidly than is the case today, thus requiring fewer brackets in the middle and upper levels.

FAMILY TAXATION

It is appropriate to continue the main rules that now govern the treatment of family income. Thus, husband and wife would continue to be treated as a single taxpayer, with the additional allowance accorded to a spouse. This grouping should apply to all community income, including income from any separate property acquired before or after marriage and also any property kept separate by pre-marital agreement. On the latter point, the treatment would depart from that now existing in the relatively few cases in which agreements exist. As under present law, the wife could be permitted separately to declare her actual salary or professional earnings, if continuation of this feature were thought desirable. The husband would also include, as at present, any earnings of minor children and any income from any property owned by the minor children, except where he does not have the legal use of the earnings or income.

DEFINITION OF NET INCOME

The second step in constructing a unitary tax is the formulation, for the determination of net income, of a set of rules which are suitable to that end and which involve as few distinctions as possible respecting the various types of income. The following suggestions are made:

Gross Income

Gross income would include gains and profits from any source, subject to any territorial rule desired and subject to any special exclusions desired. The exclusions would be enumerated. Thus, gross income would be defined as any gain, profit or enrichment, whatever be its origin, nature or denomination (as expressed now in Art. 10, Ord. 5), including, as examples, salaries and wages, fees, commissions, rents, interest, business income, royalties and gains from sales of property. These examples would not limit the coverage of the general definition but would only be informative. Consequently, all income taxed at present would continue to be covered. The treatment of dividends is discussed later, as well as certain other exclusions from income.

Deductions

In computing net income, there would be allowed in general all the ordinary and necessary expenses incurred in the production of the gross income. This general rule would be subject to any limitations desired under the territoriality concept and to any items to be expressly disallowed. As respects business activities, the deductions currently enumerated for schedules 3, 4, and 5 would be permitted. As respects rental income, the general rule stated above would allow the deduction of interest and taxes related to the property involved, depreciation, and operating expenses. If desired, the deduction for maintenance expenses paid could be limited to a certain percentage of income, with the excess required to be capitalized unless clearly shown to be a maintenance item and not a capital item. The present 15% absolute ceiling is too rigid. As respects interest and royalties, the general rule would similarly allow deduction of administrative expenses and taxes relating to the income, interest paid on loans secured by the asset producing the income, and the amortization of any capital costs involved. Professional income would be subject to the same rules as business income. As respects employment income, no deductions would be allowed. Most employees do not incur expenses in the production of their income anyway, so the rule accords with the general situation. Moreover, it permits simplification of tax administration, including withholding, for this type of income and consequently for the larger part of all taxpayers. This rule would be especially appropriate if an earned income differential were used. It also permits simpler special declaration forms for this class of income, as suggested later under administrative aspects. Traveling and similar expenses would be an exception where the employee received a flat amount and did not account to his employer; such amounts would be includible in income, and actual expenses would be deducted. If the employee were merely reimbursed for expenses and the employer maintained records on these items, then the amounts involved would be excluded from the employee's computation.

The matter of capital losses is discussed later, as well as several special deductions. The accounting rules are also discussed later. As far as possible, uniform accounting rules should be applicable to the various classes of income. It may be appropriate, however, to permit only calendar years and the cash method for those having only wage and salary incomes, to simplify administrative and reporting aspects for these taxpayers.

FORTUITOUS GAINS

One recommended exception to the elimination of the schedular taxes is that of the 10% withheld tax on fortuitous gains or chance winnings. This tax was placed at this level, and the gains eliminated from complementary tax, in view of the difficulties in collecting directly from the recipient. Also, presumably, it was felt that this form of income could bear a higher rate of tax, since a 10% effective rate is now reached for individuals having other income only at about Bs.2,000,000. For these reasons, a flat rate tax should continue to be imposed at 10% (or higher rates, depending on the scale of individual tax rates). Such a tax could be regarded as simply a special tax on all lottery and betting pools and all prizes. At the same time, these gains and chance winnings could be treated as taxable income, to the extent they exceed a certain amount, such as Bs.2,000 or Bs.5,000. The payor of the winnings would be required to report the amounts won, and to withhold a tax at 10% if the 10% special tax had not previously been applied to the pool from which the winnings were paid. Thus, the 10% direct withholding would apply to television prizes. The recipient of any winnings would be required to include in his income only the amount actually received and would not have any credit for the 10% tax. The 10% tax would thus not be regarded as a withholding of tax from him in the usual sense in which a withholding tax operates.

It is thus possible to devise appropriate and relatively uniform rules for the determination of net income, eliminating thereby all the present variations from schedule to schedule. Any differences desired and any resulting special rules could simply be set forth in the statute and regulations, and would govern the effect to be given to the item involved in the computation of the taxpayer's total net income.

TAXATION OF CORPORATIONS

Under the present tax structure, individuals and corporations are subject to the same rates of tax as respects both the schedular taxes and the complementary tax. The only variation arises under the complementary tax, since here an individual obtains a basic Bs.12,000 exemption plus family allowances. Dividends are not included in the taxable income of the shareholder.

Need for Separate Corporate Rate Structure

The present system would be understandable perhaps in an economic society in which corporations were family-owned and family-managed. Consequently, under such circumstances an individual would, speaking generally, be taxed the same whether his wealth was in the corporate form or in individual ownership. But even this support for the present system would fall when individuals started to diversify their activities and to receive income from different sources. At this point the failure to tax dividends leads to the splitting of an individual's activities between himself and his corporation, and then in turn between himself and a number of corporations. This consequence of the present structure is already an aspect of Venezuelan economic organization, for knowledgeable taxpayers today engage in such splitting of income when the tax savings outweigh the factors making for unitary organization (such as stamp taxes and local *patente* taxes on gross receipts when intercompany transactions are involved, the corporate registration fee of Bs.1 per mil capital, and additional bookkeeping and administrative costs). This splitting of activities among various corporate enterprises and the individual himself through salaries and activities in his name is quite feasible when the various corporations are closely held.

The support for the present stucture earlier indicated also falls as corporations change from closely held, family-owned and family-managed affairs to large organizations in which management and ownership are separated and ownership is no longer closely held. This change has already occurred in Venezuela, as respects most of the larger and medium-sized corporations. The trend in the corporate area is steadily in the direction of the non-family corporation. As a consequence, on the whole, there is now probably little relationship between the tax brackets of the various shareholders and those of the corporate enterprise.

Thus, whatever the support that could originally have been advanced for the existing tax treatment of corporations, it is no longer available in the light of changed economic and business conditions. In addition, the present structure presents serious obstacles to any change in the revenue yield of the income tax. An increase in personal income tax revenues might require a lowering of exemptions or a rise in lower bracket rates. These changes, in turn, would, for equity reasons, require the top rates to rise. But as far as corporations are concerned, the factor governing their level would appear to be the treatment of the major oil companies. Any substantial increase in those rates, as long as the present annual 16-2/3% royalty (hydrocarbon production tax) is retained, would raise the Government's share of oil profits almost point for point above the 50-50 line. This being so, it is possible that the top corporate rates might not (for this reason alone) be increased substantially. It might also be thought inadvisable to increase these rates at this stage of economic development in Venezuela, wholly apart from the effect on the oil companies. Accordingly, the top corporate rates would have to be separated from the top individual rates, if the latter rose. At the other end of the scale, in the lower brackets, it is not appropriate to have the corporate rates determined automatically by the individual rates. Necessarily the individual rates, even under demands of increased revenues, will start at figures probably not higher than 5% to 8%. Such rates are inappropriate for corporations representing the collective ownership of shareholders in many different brackets. Further, if corporations are regarded as independent sources of tax revenue, wholly apart from their shareholders, rates as low as 5% or 10% are inappropriate. Also, while considerable progression is desirable within the individual rate scale, with a fairly large number of brackets, considerable progression and many brackets are not appropriate for corporate taxation, even when the corporations are regarded as taxable entities, for the fact that they are aggregates of shareholders cannot be disregarded too far.

In any case, much more flexibility in formulating tax policy is possible, if the corporate rate structure is not bound tightly to the individual rate structure.

For these reasons, it is desirable at this stage of Venezuelan economic growth to separate the tax-rate structure applicable to corporations from that applicable to individuals. Indeed, such separation will be a necessity if increased revenues are required from the income tax. This being so, it is imperative that dividends be included in the taxable income of the shareholders. This latter step is called for, wholly apart from any change in the corporate rates, because of the widespread splitting of income among family-owned enterprises.

As respects the corporate rate structure, it would be desirable to have at least two rate brackets, and probably three. Thus, the tax on corporations with incomes up to Bs.50,000 or Bs.100,000 could be 10%; the tax on the amount of income above this level and up to, say, Bs.10,000,000 could be 20%; the amount of income above Bs.10,000,000 would be taxed at the top rate, whatever it might be. Presumably this rate would be fixed so that it would at least maintain the present taxes obtained from the oil companies. The combined schedular and complementary top tax rate today is 28-1/2%. The first-bracket corporate rate should be fixed in relation to the individual initial bracket rates, but at a somewhat higher level. Such a three-bracket corporate rate structure might invite a minor amount of corporate splitting at the first-bracket level, but this would not be serious. It is unlikely that there would be much splitting at the Bs.10,000,000 level. If it did prove serious, it could be counteracted by requiring consolidation of the income of subsidiary corporations with that of the parent corporation, if the splitting took this form, or even with that of corporations owned by the same individual shareholder group, if the splitting took this latter form. Under this rate structure, as at present, there would be no exemption for corporations.

The present reductions in rates at the top three brackets for invested earnings should not be continued. As respects corporations at these levels, presumably the annual retained earnings are always sufficient to permit full utilization of the lower rates applicable to income that is reinvested. Consequently, the result is simply a somewhat lower rate structure expressed in this indirect fashion and always operative. This being so, the tax rates desired should be set forth directly as the actual rates, and the investment rate reductions should be discontinued.

Taxation of Dividends

As stated above, under the present treatment of corporations, and certainly under any separate rate structure for corporations, it is necessary to include dividends in the taxable income of shareholders. Without this step, it becomes impossible to maintain equitable taxation under the income tax. Dividends when received represent income to the shareholder and should be taxable to him. The matter of "double taxation" of corporate income will be discussed later.

The taxation of dividends as income will involve some technical and administrative rules, a few of which are here mentioned:

a. Definition. A dividend could be defined in terms of the corporate law, and presumably would cover distributions to shareholders out of corporate earnings and profits. Distributions from corporate earnings accumulated prior to these new rules would be considered as taxable dividends. Stock dividends would not be subject to tax, but their distribution would not capitalize the earnings for tax purposes, nor provide the shareholder with a tax cost for the stock dividend shares. Instead, the cost of his old shares would be pro-rated among those shares and the stock dividend shares.

b. Taxation of Shareholder. The Tax Administration would have to meet the problem of insuring full shareholder reporting of dividends. It may be desirable to require corporations to withhold some tax on dividends distributed, so that collection on the small shareholders would be assured, and also so that information would be available on the dividends received by the larger shareholders. (This aspect is considered in detail, below, in the discussion of "double taxation.") Splitting of stock among the family in order to escape tax should not be a serious problem in view of the rules of family taxation discussed earlier. If the stock were given to a wife or minor child, the husband would still be taxable. Outright gifts to adult children or other members of the family could reduce the tax if the donees were in lower brackets, but this is proper if the gifts are in good faith. Moreover, an effective gift tax would insure that some tax price was paid for any reduction in income tax so achieved. Treatment of foreign shareholders is discussed later.

c. Bearer Shares. Bearer shares would be a problem, but several solutions are possible. As respects publicly held corporations, the Stock Exchange rules could prohibit the listing of bearer shares. Perhaps the issuance of such shares could even be prohibited under corporate law. Another alternative would be the adoption of some device making the creation of bearer shares quite onerous, as through a very high stamp tax. The present inheritance tax has somewhat this effect, since it requires the corporation to pay an inheritance tax on the issuance of bearer shares if the shares constitute 50% or more of the shareholder's assets. Also, corporations could be required to withhold tax on dividends on bearer shares at a fairly high rate. At present bearer shares are not a prominent aspect of the corporate scene, though they do exist to a minor extent. Hence any effective steps taken to eliminate their use, in order to protect the taxation of dividends, would not injure corporate activity.

d. Retention of Corporate Earnings to Avoid Tax. If dividends are included in shareholder income, the shareholders of a closely held corporation may decide to retain the earnings in the corporation in order to reduce their taxes. This is not necessarily undesirable if the earnings are reinvested in actual operations. It is not desirable if they are simply invested in liquid assets. If capital gains on the sale of the shares are taxed in full, as is largely the case at present, the tax savings obtained are only those of postponement of tax. For these reasons, this aspect is not likely to be a serious problem. However, the corporate tax rates should be sufficiently high, in relation to individual rates, so that there is not a great inducement to retention of corporate earnings simply to reduce the tax on the shareholders. This preventive step is necessary to avoid too much temptation to the stockholder to fail to report his sales of corporate shares, and the capital gains, if any.

The Issue of "Double Taxation" of Corporate Income

Under the present structure, the so-called "double taxation" problem involved in having both a tax on corporations and the inclusion of dividends in shareholder income is not raised, since dividends are not taxed. Under the above proposal for a separate corporate tax and the taxation of dividends, the problem is created. There are several facets to this problem.

The first is that of the desirability or undesirability of taxing both corporations and dividends. Tax systems are divided on this point. There is, however, an increasing trend toward regarding the corporation as a separate entity from whom income tax may be obtained in addition to the tax on shareholders' dividends. The relative ease of collection of corporate taxes, the dominant role of corporations in business life, the separation of management from shareholders, are all factors in this trend. Thus, some may conclude that double taxation is either permissible or desirable. They would therefore be content to let the tax structure stand as above proposed. Others, however, who prefer to regard the corporation as an aggregate of shareholders and not as an ultimate tax entity would take the opposite point of view. They would therefore seek mechanisms to eliminate or reduce the double taxation. In this latter view, the question becomes that of the desirable mechanism, and also of the extent to which the double taxation should be reduced.

It is not necessary to elaborate on the various alternative mechanisms, since they are well known. One is not to tax the corporation at all, but instead to treat it like a partnership and to tax each shareholder on his share of corporate earnings whether or not distributed. While this method gives full recognition to the aggregate concept of a corporation, it presents probably insuperable difficulties in administration. This is certainly so for large corporations. As respects small corporations, present law treats the limited liability company as a partnership, and this treatment could be continued so that those desiring this result could use this form of organization. Another method, offering only a partial offset, is to credit a portion of the dividends received against the shareholder's tax. Thus, the shareholder would include the dividend received in his income and then credit against his total tax 5%, 10%, or more of the dividend. This method has the virtue of simplicity, but not much else. It is inequitable as between small and large taxpayers, since it does not "gross up" the dividend, though a credit for part of the corporate tax is granted, and also since the corporate tax may be larger in relation to the small shareholder's own rate than the credit allowed, but smaller in relation to the larger shareholder's rate.

The two most defensible methods are that of a deduction from income to the corporation for dividends which it distributes, or that of a credit against tax, allowed to a shareholder, of the amount of corporate tax on his dividend, with inclusion in his income of the dividend received, "grossed up," however, by that corporate tax. The latter method simply regards the corporate tax as a withheld tax, the same as the tax withheld by an employer on an employee. Thus, if a shareholder receives a Bs.100 dividend and the corporate rate of tax is 30%, then the dividend is increased, i.e. "grossed up" to an amount obtained by dividing the Bs.100 by 7/10, or Bs.142.86. The shareholder would include Bs.142.86 in his income, and receive a credit of 30% of that figure or Bs.42.86. Both mechanisms reach the same result (assuming that the corporate tax is borne by the shareholders as a matter of tax incidence, and is not passed on to consumers or back to employees). Hereafter in the discussion, the first method, that of a deduction to the distributing corporation, is referred to as the dividend deduction or deduction-to-corporation method. The second method, that of the credit against tax allowed to a shareholder, is referred to as the credit-to-shareholder method. The latter should be distinguished from the credit method earlier discussed which does not "gross up" the dividend but merely grants a credit against tax.

Both the credit-to-shareholder method and the dividend deduction method reach the same net tax result to the shareholders and corporation considered together. Both plans assume that the corporate tax is borne, or largely borne, by the shareholders as a matter of tax incidence, and is not passed on to consumers or back to employees. Under each plan, the tax benefit involved—deduction to the corporation or credit for the shareholder—becomes available only on the distribution of corporate profits to shareholders. These plans may therefore encourage management to distribute more corporate earnings than if there were full "double taxation" of corporate earnings. Whether or not this encouragement is so strong as to be undesirable is a difficult question. The possibility of encouragement becomes more likely as the degree of relief from "double taxation" increases. It also is probably more likely under the dividend deduction approach, especially if corporate managers look on the mechanism simply as one that imposes a tax higher on retained than on distributed corporate earnings. The credit plan may have a somewhat greater tendency to encourage investment in corporations, since superficially the shareholders may regard the tax on dividend income as being lighter than that on other income because of the credit. However, any possible differences between the two plans in these respects are not readily susceptible of evaluation, since they rest essentially on the attitudes and impressions of corporate managers and shareholders.

The deduction-to-corporation method involves a greater dependence, in comparison with the credit-to-shareholder method, on collecting to the full the amount due from the shareholders under the personal income tax, since the deduction method lessens the revenue importance of the corporate tax. The credit-to-shareholder method, on the other hand, safeguards the revenue if the shareholder does not report the dividend, as long as the shareholder's rate of tax is not greater than the credit allowed. Consequently, if the dividend deduction method is used, it would be very desirable to accompany it with a withholding tax on dividends similar to that described in Chapter V for wages and salaries.

This withholding tax would insure collection at least from shareholders in the low tax brackets. An actual withholding tax is not needed under the credit-to-shareholder method, since the corporate tax itself, to the extent credit is allowed to the shareholder, is in effect being regarded as a tax withheld from the shareholder. Moreover, if either method is used, it may be desirable to use it only to a partial extent, and not to permit complete elimination of the corporate tax in either case, until more experience is obtained respecting the taxation of dividends to shareholders. Thus, under the credit-to-shareholder method, many taxpayers with rates higher than the credit may not report their dividends, while those with rates below the credit would do so and thereby obtain a refund. This would equally be so under the dividend deduction method, since shareholders with rates above the withholding tax rate may not report their dividends while the shareholders with rates below the withholding rate would do so in order to get a refund.

As respects administration, the allowance of a dividend deduction to the corporation is simpler of administration, considered alone, since the mechanics—the allowance of the deduction—take place at the corporate level. Under the credit-to-shareholder method, the mechanics—the "grossing up" of the dividend and the taking of the credit—occur at the shareholder level. Moreover, corporations would probably have to provide shareholders with information as to dividends to be included and credits taken. The credit method also involves refunds to those shareholders whose tax rate is less than the portion of corporate tax rate to be credited, whereas refunds are not involved under the deduction-to-corporation method. But these administrative advantages of the deduction method disappear if there is coupled with it, as is suggested above is almost necessary, an actual withholding tax on dividends. In this event the mechanics under the two methods are virtually the same at the shareholder level, with the individual shareholder required to "gross up" the dividend received, include it in income, and then take his credit. The difference is simply in the amount of credit. Under the withholding tax the credit is the rate of that tax; under the credit-to-shareholder method the credit is the portion of the corporate tax to be allowed as the credit. It may be that the two rates would turn out to be the same though their function is different. (The withholding tax is a compliance measure attached to the deduction-to-corporation method, the latter being the method to reduce "double taxation"; the credit-to-shareholder for the portion of the corporate tax is a method to reduce "double taxation.")

The above discussion of administration relates to the effect on individual shareholders. Where corporate shareholders are involved, the problems are different. Here presumably the desire is not to subject the dividend to any greater tax as a consequence of its passing through intermediate corporations before it reaches the individual shareholders. Under the credit-to-shareholder approach this can be done simply. Intercorporate dividends, i.e., dividends received by corporations, would not be included in income and the receiving corporation would not be allowed any credit because of the dividend received. When the receiving corporation distributed a dividend in turn to its individual shareholders, then they would include the dividend ("grossed up") in income and receive the credit. This arrangement leaves the operating company fully subject to tax, leaves the corporation receiving dividends free of tax on the dividends, and gives the credit to the individual shareholders.

It is somewhat more complicated, however, to properly treat intercorporate dividends under the deduction-to-corporation method. Essentially, it is necessary to allow the deduction to the corporation first paying the dividend, then to tax the corporation receiving the dividend in an amount equal to the tax saved by the first corporation, and then to grant a deduction to the second corporation when it distributes a dividend, thereby relieving the latter corporation from that tax. This method thus leaves the operating corporation with the proper tax respecting operating profits, places a tax on the receiving corporation as long as it retains the dividend (so that parent-subsidiary corporations do not receive an advantage merely because a subsidiary pays a dividend to the parent), but then removes the latter tax if the receiving corporation later distributes the dividend (thus not subjecting parent-subsidiary corporations to any greater burden than single operating corporations as respects dividends paid to individual shareholders).[2] As a consequence of the differing treatments of intercorporate dividends, the credit-to-shareholder method may be somewhat simpler of administration.

As an overall administrative matter, the credit-to-shareholder method probably involves less compliance and avoidance risk for the government than the dividend deduction method, even when the latter is accompanied by a withholding tax. Under the credit-to-shareholder method the full corporate tax has been obtained and the relief from double taxation depends on shareholder initiative. Under the dividend deduction method, a lower corporate tax has been obtained and the relief from double taxation has been granted, so that the initiative of achieving the proper end result rests in this sense on the Tax Administration. In this light, the opportunities for avoidance and technical manipulation would seem somewhat greater under the dividend deduction method. Further, if the corporate rate schedule involves several brackets, the technical problems under the dividend deduction method

---

[2] The details of the treatment suggested in the text are:

(a) The distributing corporation would receive the dividend paid deduction.

(b) The receiving corporation would include in its income an amount equal to the actual dividend it received times the percentage dividend paid deduction allowed. This amount is thus the same as the deduction which the distributing corporation received. I.e., if the tax rate is 40% and the dividend paid deduction allowed is 33-1/3% of the dividend, then if a dividend of Bs.60 is paid, the distributing corporation will obtain a deduction of Bs.20 (33-1/3% of Bs.60) and the receiving corporation will include Bs.20 in its income (again, 33-1/3% of Bs.60). This step thus includes in the receiving corporation's income the deduction obtained by the distributing corporation. If the tax rate applicable to both corporations is the same, it thus requires the receiving corporation to pay the tax saved by the distributing corporation. But if the tax rates differ, it is the amount of the dividend paid deduction that is in effect being taxed to the receiving corporation.

(c) If the receiving corporation later distributed a dividend to its shareholders, it would receive the regular dividend paid deduction. The resulting tax saving thus offsets the tax which it earlier paid. I.e., using the figures above, if the receiving corporation then distributed Bs.60, it would receive a deduction of Bs.20 (33-1/3% of Bs.60), an amount equal to that previously included in its income. Where the receiving corporation distributes a dividend to its shareholders in a year later than the year in which it included in income the dividend it received, technical problems can arise which may affect the matching above described. Thus, the receiving corporation by reason of having paid a tax on the dividend it received may not be able in a later year to distribute in full the amount of that dividend. A similar problem can arise in the case of the distributing corporation, since if it pays a tax on operating profits in one year and does not then distribute a dividend it may not in a later year be able to distribute as large a dividend as it would if it had distributed a dividend in the earlier year and through the dividend deduction reduced the tax to be paid. Both situations can probably be met by appropriate technical rules regarding carrybacks of deductions and refunds, if thought desirable. These problems are not likely to arise unless a very large proportion of income is paid out in dividends. As respects a case in which profits earned are distributed in the same year, the maximum dividend distribution possible can be obtained from this formula:

$$\text{Dividend} = \frac{\text{Income } (1 - \text{tax rate})}{1 - (\text{tax rate}) \ (\% \text{ allowed for dividend paid deduction})}.$$

If a withholding tax is coupled for compliance purposes with the deduction-to-corporation method, it should apply to intercorporate dividends, so as to avoid the necessity for the distributing corporation to determine whether the recipient of the dividend is an individual or a corporation. In turn, this will require the receiving corporation to "gross up" the dividend to reflect the withheld tax and then to credit the tax against its tax. These steps will be in addition to the steps above outlined as necessary to take account of the dividend paid deduction.

It may be observed that an approach which would deny the deduction to the first corporation, exempt the intercorporate dividend from tax, and then allow the deduction to the receiving corporation if it distributed a dividend would not be satisfactory. In addition to requiring the first corporation to distinguish between dividends paid to individual shareholders (for which it could receive a deduction) and to corporate shareholders (for which it would not receive a deduction), the approach would place too large a tax on the operating company as a result of the denial of the deduction. Also, by granting the deduction to the receiving corporation the approach would be giving a benefit which would either be unusable by the receiving corporation, as where it was only a holding company and hence had no income, or which would be too favorable a benefit, as where the receiving corporation was itself an operating company having some stock investments. In this latter case the allocation of the corporate tax would be unfair to the first operating company, since it would not have received any deduction respecting these amounts.

are probably more troublesome than under the credit-to-shareholder method, assuming the credit is no higher than the lowest corporate rate.

The double taxation aspect of the corporate tax is thus a difficult problem, and does not yield readily to a satisfactory solution in Venezuela or elsewhere. It must, however, be remembered that the taxation of dividends to shareholders will be a distinct innovation in Venezuela. This being so, it may be appropriate to cushion the change through some offset against double taxation. At the same time, however, the concept that a corporation has a separate taxable capacity is not completely foreign to Venezuelan tax practice. This is shown by the fact that Venezuela does at present tax corporations at rates that in many situations are obviously higher than those that apply in fact to the corporation's shareholders, as in the case of publicly held corporations.

On balance, it is suggested that a mechanism to reduce double taxation be adopted, but that it not attempt fully to eliminate the effect of the corporate tax. If the mechanism utilized is that of affording the corporation a deduction from income for dividends distributed, the amount of the deduction should be in the range of 33-1/3% to 50% of the dividends distributed.[3] This method should be accompanied by a withholding tax on dividends for compliance purposes. If the mechanism utilized is that of affording the shareholder a credit against tax, after "grossing up" the dividend, the amount of the credit should be in the range of 33-1/3% to 50% of the corporate tax rate (the dividend would be "grossed up" by dividing the dividend by 1 minus the credit percentage). This would provide the same tax effect as the deduction method.[4] However, the credit-against-tax method which does *not* in-

---

[3] This does not mean, for example, that the result is relief of 1/3 or 1/2 of the "double taxation." Thus, if the corporate rate is 40%, and the deduction allowed is 50% of the dividend paid, then if a corporation earned a Bs.100 profit and distributed a Bs.75 dividend, it would receive a deduction of Bs.37.50 so that its tax would be Bs.25 instead of Bs.40. This is a corporate tax saving of 37½%. Thus the "double taxation" impact has been relieved to the extent of 37½% of the corporate tax otherwise applicable.

[4] Thus, if the corporate rate is 40%, and a credit of 20% is allowed (i.e., 50% of 40%), the result as far as relief from "double taxation" is concerned is the same as in the case of the allowance of a deduction of 50% of the dividend paid. If the corporation earned a Bs.100 profit, it would pay a tax of Bs.40 and could distribute a dividend of Bs.60. The shareholder would gross up the dividend to Bs.75 (i.e., $\frac{Bs.60}{1-.20}$) and receive a credit against his tax of Bs.15 (i.e., 20% of Bs.75). The relief from "double taxation" is thus Bs.15, which is the amount of the reduction in corporate tax obtained under the dividend deduction method (see footnote 3, *supra*).

volve "grossing up" the dividend would not be an appropriate method, and must be carefully distinguished from the credit-to-shareholder method here regarded as proper.

On balance, the credit-to-shareholder method may be somewhat simpler of administration than the dividend deduction, as indicated above, and could be preferred for this reason. But if it is thought desirable to use the dividend deduction method, it would be an appropriate method and could be administered.[5]

As respects foreign shareholders, if the credit-to-shareholder method is chosen, the foreign individual shareholder would receive the credit. As indicated in Chapter IV, such a non-resident shareholder should incur tax liability at the regular progressive rates. In Chapter IV a withholding tax is recommended generally for income going to non-residents and this withholding tax could equally apply to dividends. The result as to the non-resident individual shareholder would be that in effect there would be two withholdings, one the actual withholding tax on non-residents and the other the withholding implicit in the credit-to-shareholders method. Since non-resident individual shareholders of Venezuelan corporations are likely to be in the relatively higher brackets this combined withholding may be appropriate. At any event, by adjusting the rate of the actual withholding tax in the light of the amount of the credit, since the actual withholding rate need not necessarily be the same as the rate applied to salaries, wages, etc., going to non-residents, the desired combined rate can be obtained. If the foreign shareholder is itself a corporation, it would be proper to apply to it only the withholding tax and not to allow any credit against tax. Since intercorporate dividends are not taxed, it would not be proper to tax the foreign corporation as such. But since its income will ultimately go to individual shareholders who should be taxed (i.e., the non-taxation of intercorporate dividends assumes that the taxable recipients are the shareholders of the intermediate corporation, and hence the individual shareholders are regarded as receiving dividends from a Venezuelan source) it is proper to reach them by taxing the

---

[5] The above discussion assumes that the entire income of the corporations involved comes from a Venezuelan source and is thus taxable; it also assumes that there is no exempt corporate income involved. For situations in which these assumptions are not met, so that the corporation has non-taxable foreign source income or has exempt income, appropriate technical rules would have to be devised so that the credit to shareholders or the dividend deduction is granted only with respect to dividends regarded as derived (on a pro rata basis) from taxable corporate earnings.

foreign corporation at some composite or average rate. The withholding tax, coupled with a denial of the credit, achieves this result. If the foreign corporation does business in Venezuela as a branch, then, as discussed in Chapter IV, the branch would pay the regular corporate tax. The question remains whether an additional tax, corresponding to the withholding tax applied to the dividend paid by the Venezuelan subsidiary to its foreign parent, should be applicable to the profits of the branch. Unless this tax is applied there would be a lesser Venezuelan tax burden on the operation in branch form of a business owned by a foreign corporate investor than where the business is operated through a Venezuelan subsidiary. It might be said that this difference is a reflection of the existence of both a corporation tax and a shareholder tax. A somewhat similar difference would exist in this sense between businesses operated by Venezuelans in proprietorship form and in corporate form. But the Venezuelan proprietor does pay tax at the individual progressive rates, whereas the foreign corporation owning a Venezuelan branch would pay a tax only at the corporate tax rate. If the individual progressive rates are higher than the corporate tax rate, it can be said that some additional tax should be imposed on the shareholders of the foreign corporation as the ultimate owners of the profits of the branch. To the extent that the dividends they receive from their corporation are from those branch profits, the shareholders can be regarded as receiving income from a Venezuelan source. Hence it would be appropriate to apply the withholding tax (at the rate applicable to dividends paid to non-resident shareholders) to the branch profits when distributed to the home office (or when used for a purpose other than investment in the branch operation), and thus in effect regard those profits as equivalent to the dividends paid by a Venezuelan subsidiary to its parent. It must be recognized, however, that the application of such a tax to branch profits is more difficult in administration than in the case of dividends. Unless the lack of such a withholding tax on branch profits would contribute to avoidance situations in closely held corporations, it therefore may not be necessary to apply that tax to branch profits.

If the method chosen is that of a deduction to the corporation distributing a dividend, this deduction would be applicable whether the dividend is distributed to a foreign individual shareholder or to a foreign corporate shareholder. The dividend would be taxed to the foreign corporation as would an intercorporate dividend distributed to a Venezuelan corporation. While a Venezuelan corporation would in turn receive a deduction for dividend distributions to its shareholders, this latter deduction would not be allowed to the foreign corporation since the shareholders of the foreign corporation would not be taxed by Venezuela. If a withholding tax is applied to dividends in general in connection with this method, it would apply equally to dividends to foreign shareholders. In this event, it would not be necessary to apply to those dividends any withholding tax applicable to payments to non-residents generally except to the extent, if any, that the latter rate exceeded the withholding tax rate on dividends. As respects such withholding taxes, a foreign corporation receiving a dividend would not get any credit against its tax. The discussion above respecting branches is also pertinent here; if an additional tax is to be applied to branch profits, it would be at the rate of any withholding tax on dividends plus any additional withholding rate on non-residents.

Tables to Chapter III

Table III-1. Income Tax at Various Income Levels: Individuals

Net income in Bs. (Before exemptions)	Salary & Wages (in Bs.)		Total tax	Per cent of tax to net income
	Schedular tax	Complementary tax		
Single person:				
12,000............................	0	0	0	0
15,000............................	30.00	45.00	75.00	0.5
19,200............................	72.00	108.00	180.00	0.9
19,201 (1,600.08 monthly)............	192.01	108.01	300.02	1.6
25,000............................	250.00	202.05	452.05	1.7
30,000............................	300.00	300.00	600.00	2.0
50,000............................	500.00	770.00	1,270.00	2.5
50,001............................	500.01	770.03	1,270.04	2.5
75,000............................	750.00	1,490.00	2,240.00	3.0
100,000............................	1,000.00	2,400.00	3,400.00	3.4
200,000............................	2,000.00	7,080.00	9,080.00	4.5
500,000............................	5,000.00	25,370.00	30,370.00	6.1
1,000,000............................	10,000.00	66,800.00	76,800.00	7.7
Married person, two children:				
12,000............................	0	0	0	0
15,000............................	30.00	0	30.00	0.2
19,200............................	72.00	0	72.00	0.4
19,201 (1,600.08 monthly)............	192.01	0	192.01	1.0
25,000............................	250.00	45.00	295.00	1.2
30,000............................	300.00	120.00	420.00	1.4
50,000............................	500.00	520.00	1,020.00	2.0
50,001............................	500.01	520.02	1,020.03	2.0
75,000............................	750.00	1,190.00	1,940.00	2.6
100,000............................	1,000.00	2,010.00	3,010.00	3.0
200,000............................	2,000.00	6,580.00	8,580.00	4.3
500,000............................	5,000.00	24,695.00	29,695.00	5.9
1,000,000............................	10,000.00	65,900.00	75,900.00	7.6

Business income (in Bs.)			Per cent of tax to net income	Farm income (in Bs.)			Per cent of tax to net income
Schedular tax	Complementary tax	Total tax		Schedular tax	Complementary tax	Total tax	
0	0	0	0	0	0	0	0
75.00	45.00	120.00	0.8	0	45.00	45.00	0.3
180.00	108.00	288.00	1.5	0	108.00	108.00	0.6
480.02	108.01	588.03	3.1	0	108.01	108.01	0.6
625.00	202.50	827.50	3.3	0	202.50	202.50	0.8
750.00	300.00	1,050.00	3.5	0	300.00	300.00	1.0
,250.00	770.00	2,020.00	4.0	400.00	770.00	1,170.00	2.3
,250.02	770.03	2,020.05	4.0	1,000.02	770.03	1,770.05	3.5
,875.00	1,490.00	3,385.00	4.5	1,500.00	1,490.00	2,990.00	4.0
,500.00	2,400.00	4,900.00	4.9	2,000.00	2,400.00	4,400.00	4.4
,000.00	7,080.00	12,000.00	6.0	4,000.00	7,080.00	11,080.00	5.4
,500.00	25,370.00	37,870.00	7.6	10,000.00	25,370.00	35,370.00	7.1
,000.00	66,800.00	91,800.00	9.2	20,000.00	66,800.00	86,800.00	8.7
0	0	0	0	0	0	0	0
75.00	0	75.00	0.5	0	0	0	0
180.00	0	180.00	0.8	0	0	0	0
480.02	0	480.02	2.5	0	0	0	0
625.00	45.00	670.00	2.7	0	45.00	45.00	0.2
750.00	120.00	870.00	2.9	0	120.00	120.00	0.4
,250.00	520.00	1,770.00	3.5	400.00	520.00	920.00	1.8
,250.02	520.02	1,770.04	3.5	1,000.02	520.02	1,520.04	3.0
,875.00	1,190.00	3,065.00	4.1	1,500.00	1,190.00	2,690.00	3.6
,500.00	2,010.00	4,510.00	4.5	2,000.00	2,010.00	4,010.00	4.0
,000.00	6,580.00	11,580.00	5.8	4,000.00	6,580.00	10,580.00	5.3
,500.00	24,695.00	37,195.00	7.4	10,000.00	24,695.00	34,695.00	6.9
,000.00	65,900.00	90,900.00	9.1	20,000.00	65,900.00	85,900.00	8.6

Table III-2. Income Tax at Various Income Levels: Corporations (Compañia y Sociedades Anonimas)

Net income (Bs.)	Business income (Bs.)		Total tax (Bs.)
	Schedular tax	Complementary tax	
12,000.00........	0.00	185.00	185.00
15,000.00........	75.00	240.00	315.00
19,200.00........	180.00	324.00	504.00
19,201.00........	480.02	324.02	804.04
25,000.00........	625.00	452.50	1,077.50
30,000.00........	750.00	570.00	1,320.00
50,000.00........	1,250.00	1,100.00	2,350.00
50,001.00........	1,250.02	1,100.03	2,350.05
75,000.00........	1,875.00	1,905.00	3,780.00
100,000.00........	2,500.00	2,180.00	5,380.00
200,000.00........	5,000.00	7,680.00	12,680.00
500,000.00........	12,500.00	26,880.00	38,680.00
1,000,000.00........	25,000.00	67,880.00	92,880.00
5,000,000.00........	125,000.00	548,880.00	673,000.00
10,000,000.00........	250,000.00	1,357,880.00	1,607,880.00
20,000,000.00........	500,000.00	3,377,880.00	3,877,880.00
30,000,000.00........	750,000.00	5,737,880.00	6,487,880.00

Per cent tax to income	Farm income (Bs.)		Total tax (Bs.)	Per cent of tax to income
	Schedular tax	Complementary tax		
1.5	0	185.00	185.00	1.5
2.1	0	240.00	240.00	1.6
2.6	0	324.00	324.00	1.7
4.2	0	324.02	324.02	1.7
4.3	0	452.50	452.50	1.8
4.4	0	570.00	570.00	1.9
4.7	400.00	1,100.00	1,500.00	3.0
4.7	1,000.02	1,100.03	2,100.05	4.2
5.0	1,500.00	1,905.00	3,405.00	4.5
5.4	2,000.00	2,880.00	4,880.00	4.9
6.3	4,000.00	7,680.00	11,680.00	5.8
7.7	10,000.00	26,180.00	36,180.00	7.2
9.3	20,000.00	67,880.00	87,880.00	8.8
13.5	100,000.00	548,880.00	648,880.00	13.0
16.1	200,000.00	1,357,880.00	1,557,880.00	15.6
19.4	400,000.00	3,377,880.00	3,777,880.00	18.9
21.6	600,000.00	5,737,880.00	6,337,880.00	21.1

Table III-3. Total Income Taxes Received in Liquidation, Calendar Years 1949-57, Type of Tax
(Thousands of Bs.)

Type of Tax	1949	1950	1951	1952	1953	1954	1955	1956	1957
Schedular tax:									
1. Schedule 1 (real estate rentals)....	2,005	2,202	2,695	3,267	3,851	4,526	5,263	5,843	7,666
2. Schedule 2 (interest, etc.).......	1,856	1,509	2,022	2,270	2,421	2,664	3,275	3,802	4,861
3. Schedule 3 (business income)....	74,933	47,362	60,152	70,490	74,782	70,144	84,096	100,353	43,332
4. Schedule 4 (hydrocarbons & mining)[5]............	—	—	—	—	—	—	—	—	95,179
5. Schedule 5 (agriculture)........	287	232	211	214	354	361	569	496	702
6. Schedule 6 (professions).......	605	766	911	1,016	1,301	1,131	1,233	1,530	1,765
7. Schedule 7 (wages & salaries)[6] .	285	379	365	482	566	562	663	725	965
8. Schedule 8 (real estate gains)....	1,210	1,458	1,609	1,584	1,579	1,803	3,014	3,606	4,675
9. Schedule 9 (chance winnings)....	5	2	2	—[1]	2	—	4	6	—[4]
10. Withheld Taxes[2].............	17,533	19,324	19,647	23,064	25,862	28,746	31,005	48,945	51,370
Sub-Total..........	98 719	73,234	87,614	102,387	110,718	109,937	129,122	165,306	210,515
Complementary Tax on Total Income	504,635	302,455	422,229	526,542	566,749	508,838	615,670	765,987	960,447
Total..............	603,354	375,689	509,843	628,929	677 467	618,775	744,792	931,293	1,170,962

Art. 49 of the Organic Law of the National Treasury[7]	—	—	—	—	—	—	164	—	—
Extraordinary tax on incomes of more than Bs.800,000.00[8]	768	61	11,878	—	614	448	—	—	—
Fines, extraordinary tax	6	—[1]	88	—	—	—	—	—	—
Additional tax on oil and mining	14,507	1,202	6,493	32,015	43,783	56,385	34,353	54,255	68,561
Increased tax asserted by Controller of the Nation	697	41	29	8	47	63	57	22	51
Sanctions:									
Fines	4,764	1,346	1,480	1,783	2,630	1,182	1,855	3,646	3,117
Interest	336	565	816	837	1,227	1,262	1,605	1,695	2,231
Complementary tax: increases on audit	—[3]	13,458	12,268	12,122	40,662	51,755	50,858	—[3]	—[3]
General Total	624,432	392,362	542,895	675,694	766,430	729,870	833,684	990,911	1,244,922

[1] Taxes less than Bs.1,000.00.

[2] The withheld total includes taxes from the commercial-industrial, salary, professional, and chance winnings schedules.

[3] For the years 1949, 1956, and 1957 the complementary amounts are included in the respective categories.

[4] For 1957 the tax on chance winnings is included in "withheld taxes" schedule.

[5] After 1957, according to the law in force, this was separated from the third schedule.

[6] Includes only non-withheld schedular tax on wages and salaries. Nearly all of schedular tax is withheld and is covered in "withheld taxes." For breakdown of "withheld taxes" for 1957 see Table III-4.

[7] This category represents proceeds to the government from the sale of delinquent tax accounts to outside parties for collection.

[8] This tax was imposed for the year of 1945 only and applied to all income in excess of Bs.800,000. The tax collections on this account in subsequent years represent retroactive payments.

Table III-4. Amount of Withheld Taxes in 1957 (in Bs.)

Classification	Income before Exemption	Exemption (Bs.1000 per month)	Taxable Income	Amount Withheld
Wages and salaries, non-residents . . .	23,127,148		23,127,148	880,809.95
Professional, non-residents[1]	26,939		26,939	1,876.76
Insurance companies (non-resident) . .	562,318		562,318	21,340.38
Real estate commissions	16,741,898		16,741,898	417,788.05
Motion picture rentals (non-resident)	13,591,791		13,591,791	600,571.74
Wages and salaries, residents	2,646,883,613	604,216,904	2,042,666,709	20,712,584.48
Chance winnings	293,349,436		293,349,436	28,735,565.78
Total	2,994,283,143	604,216,904	2,390,066,239	51,370,537.14

[1] This withholding may have been accidental; withholding on non-resident professionals is not required now, though it was prior to 1956.

Table III-5. Allocation of Taxes Between Oil and Non-Oil Activities— Liquidations and Collections 1953-57

(Thousands of Bs.)

Activities	1953	1954	1955	1956	1957
A. Hydrocarbons					
Liquidations:					
Schedular and complementary tax	565,485	475,082	584,888	674,185	869,265
Extraordinary tax	614	448	—	—	—
Additional income tax	40,855	54,032	34,353	54,256	58,107
Total	606,954	529,562	619,241	728,441	927,372
Collections:					
Schedular and complementary tax	553,392	466,170	550,091	680,161	875,697
Extraordinary tax	614	448	—	—	—
Additional income tax	39,858	40,446	35,050	31,626	55,234
Total	593,864	507,064	585,145	711,787	930,931

Table III-5 (cont.)

Thousands of (Bs.)

Activities	1953	1954	1955	1956	1957
B. Other activities[1]					
Liquidations:					
Schedular and complementary tax	156,548	197,955	214,443	262,470	307,096
Extraordinary tax..............	—	—	—	—	—
Additional income tax..........	2,928	2,353	—	—	10,464
Total.......................	159,476	200,308	214,443	262,470	317,560
Collections:					
Schedular and complementary tax	144,987	169,704	200,964	236,636	269,946
Extraordinary tax..............	—	—	—	4	—
Additional income tax..........	1,021	1,269	—	—	10,464
Total.......................	146,008	170,973	200,964	236,640	280,410
Percentages:					
A. Hydrocarbons—Liquidations.....	80%	72%	74%	73%	74%
B. Other Activities—Liquidations...	20%	28%	26%	27%	26%
A. Hydrocarbons—Collections......	81%	74%	74%	75%	77%
B. Other Activities—Collections.....	19%	26%	26%	25%	23%
Totals:					
Liquidations in year...........	766,430	729,870	833,684	990,911	1,244,932
Collections in year............	739,872	678,037	786,109	948,427	1,211,341

[1] This table includes mining under "other activities." The additional income tax shown under "other activities" was paid by mining companies.

Table III-6. Allocation of 1957 Income Taxes Between Mineral and Non-Mineral Activities

(1957 liquidations based on 1956 incomes[1])

	Bs.
Oil and Mining Companies	
Oil companies:	
Schedular and complementary taxes	869,265,000
Additional income tax	58,107,000
Mining companies:	
Schedular and complementary taxes	29,284,000
Additional income tax	10,464,000
Total, oil and mining companies	967,120,000
Non-Mineral Activities	
Schedular and complementary taxes	277,812,000
Total, all activities	1,244,932,000
Percentage for Mineral Activities	78
Percentage for Non-Mineral Activities	22

[1] The data in the Tax Administration table on which this is based included mining activities under "other activities," so that it was simply an oil-non-oil table. The present table, on the other hand, takes account of the large payments from mining companies. Using the oil-non-oil classification of the original table gives these percentages: oil, 74 per cent; non-oil, 26 per cent.

Table III-7. Total Taxes of Taxpayers Other Than Oil Companies, Allocated Between Individuals and Juridical Persons (Corporations, etc.) (in Bs.)

(Income tax: 1957 liquidations based on 1956 incomes)

	Corporations	Individuals	Total
Schedular taxes	60,911,736	18,749,327	79,661,063
Complementary taxes	185,743,660	41,691,277	227,434,937
Additional tax (mining only)	10,464,000	—	10,464,000
Total	257,119,396	60,440,604	317,560,000

Table III-8. Number of Income Tax Declarations Received, 1956-57.

	1957[1]			1956		
	Taxable	Exempt	Total	Taxable	Exempt	Total
Caracas office.....	70,746	24,733	95,479[2]	78,390	22,200	100,590
Maracaibo office...	20,029	15,688	35,717	22,646	16,423	39,069
Total.........	90,775	40,421	131,196	101,036	38,623	139,659

[1] As to the 1957 Caracas office declarations, the following are additional classifications:

	Total	Under Bs.200,000	Over Bs.200,000
Individuals.......................	83,286	82,423	863
Juridical persons (corporations, etc.)..	11,195	10,169	1,026
Total.......................	94,481	92,592	1,889

[2] Included are 5,842 declarations from the previous year.

Table III-9. Classification of Individual Taxpayers by Family Status, for Income Tax Declarations Received in 1956

(Caracas Office only)

Status	Number
Single..	21,274
Married...	62,361
Widowed..	2,168
Divorced..	1,694
Total...	87,497
Dependents Claimed	
Wives...	55,143
Ascendants..	38,049
Descendants...	160,492
Others..	50,958
Total...	304,642

Table III-10.   Amounts of Taxable Income Classified by Schedules, 1957 Liquidations (1956 Income)[1]

Matter	Number of Liquidations	Income Declared (in Bs.)	Basic Exemptions	Net Taxable Income (in Bs.)	Tax (in Bs.)
Real property rentals....	8,398	351,705,307	122,983,867	228,721,440	5,717,158.18
Interest, etc............	4,944	252,700,977	108,688,082	144,012,888	4,320,326.95
Industrial and business income..............	26,617	1,914,250,578	281,407,656	1,632,842,918	40,792,414.02
Real estate commissions.	16	1,665,167	53,100	1,612,067	9,927.53
Hydrocarbons and mining..............	17	3,179,357,508	—	3,179,357,508	79,483,937.77
Farming..............	1,906	36,155,614	16,074,829	20,080,773	401,609.84
Resident professionals...	3,766	87,732 646	16,494,681	71,237,960	1,529,820.71
Non-resident professionals.........	8	80,504	—	80,504	5,635.38
Wages and salaries......	40,457	1,411,466,928	143,403,759	1,268,063,168	561,835.37
Real estate gains........	1,952	163,328,581	3,550,825	159,789,742	4,779,408.26
Chance winnings.......	322	8,146,095	—	8,146,095	—
Total..............	88,403	7,406,589,905	692,656,799	6,713,945,063	137,602,074.01

[1] This table does not include exempt declarations (estimated about 25,000), nearly all of which involve wage and salary recipients.   No explanation available for slight discrepancies in horizontal addition to "Net Taxable Income" column.

Table III-11. Number of Individual Taxpayers Paying Complementary Tax, Cumulated from Highest Income Class, 1957 Declarations (on 1956 Income)

Class	Number of taxpaeyrs
To Bs. 10,000	67,384
" " 14,000	58,023
" " 20,000	49,764
" " 28,000	37,098
" " 38,000	26,688
" " 50,000	17,496
" " 64,000	10,499
" " 80,000	6,349
" " 100,000	4,214
" " 140,000	2,909
" " 200,000	1,737
" " 280,000	1,006
" " 380,000	599
" " 500,000	353
" " 640,000	211
" " 800,000	131
" " 1,000,000	92
" " 1,400,000	60
" " 2,000,000	28
" " 2,800,000	10
" " 6,400,000	1

Table III-12. Cumulative Distribution, by Brackets, of Income of All Individ▪

Class	Number of taxpayers	0-10	10-14	14-20	20-28
To Bs. 10,000..........	9,361	58,184,952			
" " 14,000..........	8,259	82,590,000	19,114,502		
" " 20,000..........	12,666	126,660,000	50,664,000	36,270,042	
" " 28,000..........	10,410	104,100,000	41,640,000	62,460,000	39,695,650
" " 38,000..........	9,192	91,920,000	36,768,000	55,152,000	73,536,000
" " 50,000..........	6,997	69,970,000	27,988,000	41,982,000	55,976,000
" " 64,000..........	4,150	41,500,000	16,600,000	24,900,000	33,200,000
" " 80,000..........	2,135	21,350,000	8,540,000	12,810,000	17,080,000
" " 100,000..........	1,305	13,050,000	5,220,000	7,830,000	10,440,000
" " 140,000..........	1,172	11,720,000	4,688,000	7,032,000	9,376,000
" " 200,000..........	731	7,310,000	2,924,000	4,336,000	5,848,000
" " 280,000..........	407	4,070,000	1,628,000	2,442,000	3,256,000
" " 380,000..........	246	2,460,000	984,000	1,476,000	1,968,000
" " 500,000..........	142	1,420,000	568,000	852,000	1,136,000
" " 640,000..........	80	800,000	320,000	480,000	640,000
" " 800,000..........	39	390,000	156,000	234,000	312,000
" " 1,000,000..........	32	320,000	128,000	192,000	256,000
" " 1,400,000..........	32	320,000	128,000	192,000	256,000
" " 2,000,000..........	18	180,000	72,000	108,000	144,000
" " 2,800,000..........	9	90,000	36,000	54,000	72,000
To Bs. 6,400,000..........	1	10,000	4,000	6,000	8,000
Total	67,384	638,414,952	218,170,502	258,858,042	253,199,650
Percent		26.4	9.0	10.7	10.5

Taxpayers Paying Complementary Tax in 1957 (on 1956 Income)—in Bs.

28-38	38-50	50-64	64-80	80-100	100-140	140-200[1]
43,809,713						
69,970,000	38,337,474					
41,500,000	49,800,000	25,738,642				
21,350,000	25,620,000	29,890,000	14,819,356			
13,050,000	15,660,000	18,270,000	20,880,000	11,942,638		
11,720,000	14,064,000	16,404,000	18,752,000	23,440,000	17,228,738	
7,310,000	8,772,000	10,234,000	11,696,000	14,620,000	29,240,000	17,875,875
4,070,000	4,884,000	5,698,000	6,512,000	8,140,000	16,280,000	24,420,000
2,460,000	2,952,000	3,444,000	3,936,000	4,920,000	9,840,000	14,760,000
1,420,000	1,704,000	1,988,000	2,272,000	2,840,000	5,680,000	8,520,000
800,000	960,000	1,120,000	1,280,000	1,600,000	3,200,000	4,800,000
390,000	468,000	546,000	624,000	780,000	1,560,000	2,340,000
320,000	384,000	448,000	512,000	640,000	1,280,000	1,920,000
320,000	384,000	448,000	512,000	640,000	1,280,000	1,920,000
180,000	216,000	252,000	288,000	360,000	720,000	1,080,000
90,000	108,000	126,000	144,000	180,000	360,000	540,000
10,000	12,000	14,000	16,000	20,000	40,000	60,000
218,769,713	164,365,474	114,620,642	82,243,356	70,122,638	86,708,738	78,235,875
9.0	6.8	4.7	3.4	2.9	3.6	3.2

[1] Additional columns on following two pages.

Table III-12 (cont.)

Class	Number of taxpayers	200-280	280-380	380-500	500-640
To Bs. 10,000..........	9,361				
" " 14,000..........	8,259				
" " 20,000..........	12,666				
" " 28,000..........	10,410				
" " 38,000..........	9,192				
" " 50,000..........	6,997				
" " 64,000..........	4,150				
" " 80,000..........	2,135				
" " 100,000..........	1,305				
" " 140,000..........	1,172				
" " 200,000..........	731				
" " 280,000..........	407	14,262,041			
" " 380,000..........	246	19,680,000	10,778,326		
" " 500,000..........	142	11,360,000	14,200,000	7,455,708	
" " 640,000..........	80	6,400,000	8,000,000	9,600,000	5,067,274
" " 800,000..........	39	3,120,000	3,900,000	4,680,000	5,460,000
" " 1,000,000..........	32	2,560,000	3,200,000	3,840,000	4,480,000
" " 1,400,000..........	32	2,560,000	3,200,000	3,840,000	4,480,000
" " 2,000,000..........	18	1,440,000	1,800,000	2,160,000	2,520,000
" " 2,800,000..........	9	720,000	900,000	1,080,000	1,260,000
To Bs. 6,400,000..........	1	80,000	100,000	120,000	140,000
Total	67,384	62,182,041	46,078,326	32,775,708	23,407,274
Percent		2.6	1.9	1.4	1.0

640-800	800-1,000	1,000-1,400	1,400-2,000	2,000-2,800	2,800-6,400	Totals
						58,184,952
						101,704,502
						213,594,042
						247,895,650
						301,185,713
						304,263,474
						233,238,642
						151,459,356
						116,342,638
						134,424,738
						120,215,875
						95,662,041
						79,658,326
						61,415,708
						45,067,274
2,587,297						27,547,297
5,120,000	2,740,176					28,340,176
5,120,000	6,400,000	3,475,108				35,475,108
2,880,000	3,600,000	7,200,000	4,916,342			30,116,342
1,440,000	1,800,000	3,600,000	5,400,000	3,109,067		21,109,067
160,000	200,000	400,000	100,000	800,000	2,880,449	5,680,449
7,307,297	14,740,176	14,675,108	10,916,342	3,909,067	2,880,449	2,412,581,370
0.7	0.6	0.6	0.5	0.2	0.1	(99.8) 100%

NOTE: Income has been distributed among the brackets shown in heading, taking into consideration the total number of taxpayers and total income for every specific income class. The reasoning is that for a given total income, the amount falling in each bracket must be that which results from multiplying the figure representing the width of the bracket by the number of taxpayers in the income class, up to last bracket reached by this income group. The last bracket contains the remainder of the aggregate income of the income group.

Table III-13. Distribution, by Income Classes, of Income of All Taxpayers, Individuals and Corporations, Paying Complementary Tax in 1957 (1956 Income)[1]

Income class (in Bs.)	Number of taxpayers	Income declared (in Bs.)	Exemptions[2] (in Bs.)	Taxable income (in Bs.)	Tax (in Bs.)
To Bs. 10,000	10,004	61,365,327	60,161,596	22,685,398	104,999
" 14,000	8,505	104,647,827	85,773,016	27,903,430	134,459
" 20,000	12,976	218,874,337	74,566,992	53,229,232	520,248
" 28,000	10,699	254,799,848	178,975,086	78,360,558	1,074,895
" 38,000	9,472	310,343,045	188,578,815	122,433,108	1,948,398
" 50,000	7,294	317,632,113	154,098,346	163,798,160	2,939,361
" 64,000	4,379	246,167,429	94,785,639	151,664,956	3,033,353
" 80,000	2,370	168,302,172	50,032,533	118,385,925	2,644,339
" 100,000	1,559	139,221,658	31,568,637	107,469,892	2,677,016
" 140,000	1,509	172,857,126	28,021,096	143,983,594	4,172,392
" 200,000	1,033	170,605,978	18,370,035	150,939,167	5,201,370
" 280,000	651	154,192,159	10,232,181	142,792,582	5,729,803
" 380,000	446	144,853,766	6,821,375	135,934,609	6,079,755

" 500,000	298	129,983,055	3,793,197	124,590,177	6,181,900
" 640,000	173	97,559,689	2,178,944	94,580,740	5,122,778
" 800,000	134	96,057,453	1,194,265	94,263,185	5,601,102
" 1,000,000	98	88,555,643	977,667	87,277,974	5,691,100
" 1,400,000	128	150,264,339	1,015,778	150,648,555	10,905,155
" 2,000,000	78	132,297,784	567,322	131,430,459	10,670,930
" 2,800,000	53	126,649,692	310,634	125,339,058	11,236,222
" 3,800,000	36	114,770,866		114,770,866	11,174,040
" 5,000,000	20	83,736,799	2,526	87,734,273	9,321,728
" 6,400,000	11	63,619,268	25,000	63,594,268	7,283,850
" 8,000,000	12	87,076,683		87,076,683	10,666,030
" 10,000,000	3	27,933,554		27,933,554	3,712,012
" 14,000,000	5	59,882,088		59,882,088	8,666,997
" 20,000,000	2	30,223,427		30,223,427	4,681,191
" 28,000,000	2	44,453,008		45,453,008	7,952,778
Over " 28,000,000	12	3,174,774,729		3,177,774,729	733,711,820
Total	71,962	6,971,700,862	1,091,950,680	5,922,153,655	888,839,821

[1] Some incomes of years prior to 1956 are included.
[2] Includes business losses.

Table III-14. Distribution, by Income Classes, of Income of Individual Taxpayers Paying Complementary Tax in 1957 (1956 Income)[1]

Income class (in Bs.)	Number of taxpayers	Income declared (in Bs.)	Exemptions[2] (in Bs.)	Taxable income (in Bs.)	Tax (in Bs.)
To Bs. 10,000	9,381	58,184,952	59,359,443	19,832,386	64,959
" " 14,000	8,259	101,704,502	85,149,507	25,400,054	98,102
" " 20,000	12,666	213,594,042	73,952,299	48,473,784	444,810
" " 28,000	10,410	247,895,650	177,651,066	72,422,931	966,361
" " 38,000	9,192	301,185,713	187,782,440	113,985,158	1,786,299
" " 50,000	6,997	304,263,474	153,471,279	150,957,518	2,665,260
" " 64,000	4,150	233,238,642	94,191,945	139,065,666	2,746,352
" " 80,000	2,135	151,459,356	49,609,095	101,938,022	2,236,711
" " 100,000	1,305	116,342,638	31,397,296	84,926,372	2,057,391
" " 140,000	1,172	134,424,738	27,705,982	106,060,323	2,909,866
" " 200,000	731	120,215,875	17,784,316	101,474,136	3,419,631
" " 280,000	407	95,662,041	10,090,894	84,900,341	3,349,576
" " 380,000	246	79,658,326	6,391,138	72,061,613	3,185,625
" " 500,000	142	61,415,708	3,609,818	57,006,212	2,790,287
" " 640,000	80	45,067,274	1,992,576	42,374,692	2,259,151
" " 800,000	39	27,547,297	1,130,454	25,916,841	1,493,493
" " 1,000,000	32	28,340,176	929,786	27,110,388	1,735,927
" " 1,400,000	32	35,475,108	754,940	35,420,165	2,507,716
" " 2,000,000	18	30,116,342	469,595	29,346,745	2,359,337
" " 2,800,000	9	21,109,067	217,785	20,891,282	1,861,418
" " 6,400,000	1	5,880,449	25,000	5,855,449	672,920
Total	67,404	2,412,581,370	1,063,666,656	1,365,454,058	41,691,277

[1] Some incomes of years prior to 1956 are included.

Table III-15. Distribution, by Income Classes, of Income of All Corporations Paying Complementary Tax in 1957 (1956 Returns) [1]

Income class (in Bs.)	Number of taxpayers	Income declared (in Bs.)	Exemptions [2] (in Bs.)	Taxable income (in Bs.)	Tax (in Bs.)
To Bs. 10,000..............	623	3,180,375	802,153	2,853,032	40,040
" " 14,000..............	246	2,943,325	623,509	2,495,376	36,275
" " 20,000..............	310	5,280,295	614,693	4,755,448	75,438
" " 28,000..............	289	6,904,196	1,224,020	5,937,627	108,529
" " 38,000..............	280	9,157,332	796,375	8,447,950	162,099
" " 50,000..............	297	13,368,639	627,067	12,840,642	274,100
" " 64,000..............	229	12,928,787	593,694	12,579,290	287,001
" " 80,000..............	235	16,842,814	423,438	16,447,903	407,620
" " 100,000..............	254	22,879,020	171,341	22,543,520	619,625
" " 140,000..............	337	38,432,388	315,114	37,917,271	1,182,526
" " 200,000..............	302	50,390,103	565,719	49,465,031	1,781,739
" " 280,000..............	244	58,530,118	141,287	57,892,241	2,300,227
" " 380,000..............	200	65,195,440	430,237	63,872,996	2,894,130
" " 500,000..............	156	68,567,347	183,379	67,503,965	3,391,613
" " 640,000..............	93	52,492,415	186,366	52,206,048	2,863,628
" " 800,000..............	95	68,510,156	63,811	68,346,344	4,107,609

Continued on next page

Table III-15 (cont.)

Income class (in Bs.)	Number of taxpayers	Income declared (in Bs.)	Exemptions[2] (in Bs.)	Taxable income (in Bs.)	Tax (in Bs.)
" 1,000,000	66	60,215,467	47,881	60,167,586	3,955,174
" 1,400,000	96	114,789,231	260,638	115,228,390	8,397,439
" 2,000,000	60	102,181,442	97,727	102,083,714	8,311,592
" 2,800,000	44	105,540,625	92,849	104,447,776	9,374,005
" 3,800,000	36	114,770,866		114,770,866	11,174,040
" 5,000,000	20	83,736,799	2,526	87,734,273	9,321,727
" 6,400,000	10	57,738,619		57,738,819	6,610,929
" 8,000,000	12	67,076,683		87,076,683	10,666,829
" 10,000,000	3	27,933,554		27,933,554	3,712,012
" 14,000,000	4	59,882,088		59,882,088	8,666,997
" 20,000,000	2	30,223,427		30,223,427	4,681,190
" 28,000,000	2	44,453,008		45,453,008	7,952,778
Over" 28,000,000	12	3,174,774,729		3,177,774,729	733,711,820
Total........	4,558	4,558,919,490	8,284,024	4,556,699,597	847,148,544

[1] Some incomes of years prior to 1956 are included.
[2] Includes business losses.

Table III-16. Taxpayers Reporting Wage and Salary Income (Schedule 7) by Income Class, Income Year 1956[1]

Total wage and salary income, by income class (in Bs.)		Number of taxpayers
1,000 to	12,000	12,654
12,000 "	20,000	22,984
20,000 "	30,000	19,097
30,000 "	40,000	13,137
40,000 "	50,000	8,410
50,000 "	60,000	4,989
60,000 "	70,000	1,162
70,000 "	80,000	675
80,000 "	90,000	369
90,000 "	100,000	247
100,000 "	150,000	489
150,000 "	200,000	153
200,000 "	250,000	98
250,000 "	300,000	50
300,000 "	350,000	36
350,000 "	400,000	14
400,000 "	500,000	22
500,000 "	600,000	7
600,000 "	700,000	6
700,000 "	800,000	4
800,000 "	900,000	2
900,000 "	1,000,000	5
1,000,000 and over		2
		84,612

[1] This table includes exempt declarations. The income classes Bs.1,000 to Bs.12,000 include compensation of persons declaring for periods less than a year. The table includes residents and non-residents. As compared to the table showing amount of wages and salaries withheld on, the above table differs at least in not covering persons working only several months in the year; persons earning less than Bs.12,000 a year but more than Bs.1,000 in some months; persons who are withheld on but do not comply with requirement of filing declarations.

Table III-17. Taxpayers Reporting Business Income (Schedule 3), Classified by Income Class[1], 1956 Incomes (Caracas Office Only)

Bracket (in Bs.)	Number of taxpayers	Income (in Bs.)	Schedular exemption[2] (in Bs.)	Taxable income (in Bs.)	Schedular tax (in Bs.)
0 to 10,000	9,094	107,336,633	47,792,467	3,606,115	89,843
10,000 to 20,000	6,267	90,143,431	59,160,880	30,969,497	773,187
20,000 to 30,000	1,791	44,089,388	30,766	44,065,388	1,101,057
30,000 to 40,000	1,014	35,118,479	48,000	35,070,479	874,336
40,000 to 50,000	616	27,556,592	72,000	27,484,592	687,121
50,000 to 60,000	432	23,717,542	—	23,717,542	590,023
60,000 to 70,000	366	23,830,406	—	23,830,406	595,764
70,000 to 80,000	292	21,820,287	—	21,820,287	545,210
80,000 to 90,000	237	20,170,907	—	20,170,907	503,990
90,000 to 100,000	194	18,401,907	—	18,401,907	460,049
100,000 to 150,000	592	72,820,985	—	72,820,985	1,820,531

150,000 to 200,000	317	54,833,896	—	54,833,896	1,361,495
200,000 to 250,000	195	43,767,588	—	43,767,588	1,085,368
250,000 to 300,000	151	41,344,361	—	41,344,361	1,033,610
300,000 to 400,000	210	73,039,361	—	73,039,329	1,816,385
400,000 to 500,000	120	54,101,530	—	54,101,530	1,352,539
500,000 to 600,000	74	40,474,971	—	40,474,971	1,011,875
600,000 to 700,000	67	43,510,492	—	43,510,492	1,087,763
700,000 to 800,000	55	41,121,249	—	41,121,249	1,028,032
800,000 to 900,000	36	30,649,329	—	30,649,329	766,233
900,000 to 1,000,000	32	30,364,448	—	30,364,448	759,111
1,000,000 to 9,000,000	276	656,706,616	—	656,706,616	16,417,667
10,000,000 and over	7	132,990,126	—	132,990,126	3,324,753
Total...........	22,435	1,727,910,492	107,104,113	1,564,938,651	39,085,943

1 This table includes both individuals and corporations, though presumably there are few individuals included after the first few brackets. It does not include totally exempt declarations.

2 This represents the Bs.12,000 of exemption for the income earner. However, since the taxpayer may have applied some of this basic exemption to income in another schedule, or may have lost the exemption entirely where the total of schedule 3 income and that of other schedules exceeds Bs.19,200, the figure in this column does not automatically equal Bs.12,000 times the number of taxpayers.

Table III-18. Individual Taxpayers with Incomes Over Bs.2 Million, 1954, 1955, 1956 (Taxable Income and Income Tax)

Individual[1]	Net income (in Bs.)	Tax (in Bs.)	Effective rate (%)
Income year 1956:			
A	5,880,449	805,353	13.7
B	2,711,048	324,772	11.9
C	2,525,292	304,207	12.0
D	2,516,434	287,167	11.4
E	2,342,779	265,283	11.3
F	2,315,220	260,100	11.2
G	2,314,734	269,906	11.7
H	2,248,521	195,699	8.7
I	2,084,079	232,199	11.1
J	2,050,960	224,716	11.0
Income year 1955:			
I	3,579,077	458,401	12.8
K	3,274,548	419,300	12.8
L	3,022,404	329,376	10.9
D	2,999,282	362,452	12.1
M	2,721,940	344,693	12.7
N	2,534,073	295,023	11.6
O	2,333,602	266,449	11.4
P	2,186,465	196,528	9.0
Q	2,109,436	235,201	11.1
R	2,029,134	230,961	11.4
Income year 1954:			
S	8,163,087	1,041,901	12.8
L	5,325,429	681,061	12.8
D	3,193,606	367,879	11.5
T	2,514,098	288,828	11.5
U	2,241,278	195,829	8.7
V	2,148,891	199,374	9.3

[1] Each letter represents a given individual throughout the three years.

Table III-19. Corporate Taxpayers with Net Incomes Over Bs.6 Million, 1956 (Taxable Income and Income Tax)

Corporation	Net income (in Bs.)	Tax[1] (in Bs.)	Effective rate (%)
A— Oil	1,535,475,732	413,647,785	26.9
B— Oil	796,392,026	209,541,767	26.3
C— Oil	243,094,108	62,917,818	25.9
D— Oil	134,715,809	34,688,586	25.7
E— Oil	130,919,953	33,191,667	25.4
F— Mining	89,226,501	22,142,902	24.8
G— Oil	51,267,938	12,083,883	23.6
H— Oil	44,573,533	10,641,337	23.6
I— Oil	43,941,452	10,142,364	23.1
J— Oil	39,059,131	8,856,009	22.7
K— Electricity	36,490,256	8,157,797	22.2
M— Mining	32,618,290	7,141,726	21.9
N— Cement	23,811,609	4,792,666	20.1
O— Electricity	21,641,399	4,296,436	19.9
P— Electricity	14,074,498	2,485,387	17.6
Q— Beer	13,542,319	2,369,478	17.0
R— Cement	12,071,259	2,053,200	17.0
S— Oil	11,900,921	2,016,578	16.9
T— Oil drilling and service	11,580,911	1,947,776	16.8
U— Construction	9,434,176	1,494,715	15.8
V— Tobacco manufacture	9,289,570	1,465,794	15.8
W— Banking	9,209,808	1,449,841	15.7
X— Banking	7,862,954	1,182,526	15.0
Y— Tire	7,644,153	1,142,048	14.9
Z— Oil	7,630,047	1,139,438	14.9
AA— Oil	7,501,741	1,115,702	14.9
AB— Banking	7,121,647	1,054,438	14.8
AC— Oil	7,108,814	1,043,010	14.7
AD— Real estate development	6,927,417	1,009,452	14.6
AE— Banking	6,912,459	1,006,684	14.6
AF— Construction	6,907,494	1,005,766	14.6
AG— Construction	6,857,155	996,453	14.5
AH— Construction	6,338,223	901,377	14.2
AI— Retail tobacco	6,297,836	898,424	14.2
AJ— Retail	6,183,475	875,670	14.2

[1] These tax figures do not include additional income taxes paid by some oil and mining companies.

Table III-20. Oil and Mining Companies Reporting Payment of Additional Tax, 1955-57[1]

Company	Net income (in Bs.)	Schedular and complementary tax (in Bs.)	Additional tax (in Bs.)
Income year 1957:			
A	1,790,363,473	476,193,191	41,918,037
B	1,318,684,756	347,949,340	20,950,808
C	338,151,106	88,107,923	10,881,558
D (mining)	166,029,183	42,495,613	38,279,775
E	164,992,227	42,220,820	3,713,281
G	42,571,380	9,789,380	172,130
H	—[2]	—[2]	1,954,015
J (oil royalty co.)	3,657,366	478,771	1,238,432
L (" " ")	—[2]	—[2]	187,318
K (" " ")	2,667,452	224,246	355,563
Income year 1956:			
A	1,535,475,732	413,647,785	42,393,909
C	243,094,108	62,917,818	2,704,034
E	130,919,953	33,191,667	2,340,356
D	89,226,501	22,142,902	10,463,828
G	39,059,131	8,856,009	286,722
H	11,900,921	2,016,578	2,149,172
J	2,881,856	358,567	972,318
L	656,997	53,150	236,514
K	1,773,199	189,000	50,833
Income year 1955:			
A	1,348,735,383	372,045,281	19,012,207
C	208,838,662	54,423,899	2,466,749
E	116,692,253	29,677,915	3,949,480
H	8,302,588	1,268,262	1,471,197
I	5,270,187	720,338	171,311
J	2,437,341	293,159	732,655
K	1,630,207	183,423	61,093
L	471,219	40,160	190,750

[1] Same letter designations used for companies in Tables III-20 and III-21.

[2] Data not available.

Table III-21. Oil and Mining Companies Not Reporting Additional Tax, 1955-57[1]

Company	Net income (in Bs.)	Schedular and complementary tax (in Bs.)	Negative excess under additional tax computations[2] (in Bs.)
Income year 1957:			
M	139,608,159	35,494,569	17,441,340
N	86,272,217	21,360,017	6,472,767
O	51,265,463	12,083,227	9,008,149
F (mining)	50,166,832	12,145,482	—[3]
P	11,728,377	1,955,382	5,829,363
Q	10,683,419	1,754,815	13,466,808
R	6,172,396	873,187	11,032,003
I	—[3]	—[3]	—[3]
T	—[3]	—[3]	—[3]
Income year 1956:			
B	796,392,026	209,541,767	295,707
M	134,715,809	34,688,586	2,664,854
O	51,267,938	12,083,883	4,350,994
U	44,573,533	10,641,337	—[5]
N	43,941,452	10,142,364	12,856,301
F	32,618,290	7,141,726	—[4]
V	7,630,047	1,139,438	—[5]
R	7,501,741	1,115,702	4,825,950
Q	7,108,814	1,043,010	11,381,612
I	4,977,157	670,755	290,538
T	552,429	43,922	4,087,575
P	—[3]	—[3]	—[3]
Income year 1955:			
B	568,819,750	149,234,978	646,741
M	83,043,779	20,915,501	8,745,496
O	39,648,604	8,897,674	10,151,021
U	37,307,561	8,570,400	—[5]
D	27,717,491	7,732,339	—[4]
G	20,684,038	4,049,082	5,305,609
F	20,518,836	4,202,379	—[4]
V	15,737,755	2,858,740	—[5]
N	13,019,101	2,111,501	—[3]
Q	8,964,616	1,400,668	8,381,811
P	5,760,217	775,381	3,673,505
R	4,566,625	604,405	—[3]
T	3,724,113	470,361	2,787,773

[1] Same letter designations used for companies in Tables III-20 and III-21.

[2] One-half the amount in this column represents the reduction in payments that would have occurred if the 50-50 concept were a maximum as well as minimum limitation.

[3] Data not available.   [4] Exempt from additional tax under invested capital exception.   [5] Consolidated with Company B.

CHAPTER IV : **Income Tax:**
: **Some Technical Issues**

A. Income Tax Jurisdiction—
Territoriality Concept and Rules

Venezuela follows the territorial principle in the application of its income tax. The jurisdictional base of the tax is thus the relationship of income or expenses to a Venezuelan source or economic activity. The citizenship or the residence of the taxpayer are immaterial factors and do not have any effect, with a few minor exceptions, on the application of the tax. The statutory rule is that the tax is applicable to income obtained by virtue of economic activities realized in Venezuela, or to properties situated within the country (Art. 1). This general rule is elaborated on as follows: income proceeds from economic activities realized in Venezuela or from properties situated in the country when any of the causes that originated the income occur within the national territory, whether by reason of production from the soil or subsoil, the formation, transfer, exchange, or assignment of the use or possession of real or personal property, tangible or intangible, or by reason of services rendered by persons domiciled, resident or transient in Venezuela (Art. 1, Par. 3). The additional income tax relating to oil and mining, however, does have a somewhat broader rule, in that it encompasses income "related to operations in Venezuela" (Art. 43).

As a result of this territorial base for the income tax, income received by Venezuelan citizens, residents or corporations from sources outside Venezuela is not subject to tax. Similarly, speaking generally, expenses incurred by such persons outside of Venezuela are not deductible (except as the rule has been modified in certain specific instances discussed later); also, expenses incurred in Venezuela but relating to income arising outside Venezuela are not deductible.

A country is of course free to choose, subject to any self-imposed constitutional barriers, any jurisdictional rule it desires upon which to

154

base the scope of its income tax. Thus, some countries base their income tax on both residence (and sometimes citizenship as well) and territoriality. Under such an approach, a resident (or a citizen) is liable to income tax on income from any source regardless of its territorial connection and obtains deduction for any expense otherwise allowable. This is in effect a "world-wide" rule, reaching all of the resident's income. At the same time, in such a country a non-resident is liable for tax only under the territorial rule, so that only his income from sources within the country is taxed. In considering these matters in relation to Venezuela, consideration will first be given to deductions, then to income, and then to certain rules respecting non-residents.

TREATMENT OF DEDUCTIONS UNDER TERRITORIAL RULE

In applying the territoriality principle to deductions, the income tax states, as respects schedule 3 business income and schedule 4 oil and mining income (and, by reference, schedule 5 farming income and schedule 6 professional income), that only those costs or expenditures incurred within the country are deductible. This is a very narrow application of a territorial rule, since it looks to the place of the expense rather than its relation to Venezuelan income. Thus, strictly speaking, goods purchased and paid for outside Venezuela might not be deductible under this test though their cost obviously is related to the taxable income arising from the sale of the goods, in Venezuela, by a Venezuelan business. The statute recognizes that such a rule is too narrow, and expressly permits deduction of certain costs and expenses incurred outside Venezuela. Examples are: goods purchased abroad; expenses of moving new employees from foreign ports and the return of old employees, except when the employee is transferred between parent and subsidiary companies; transportation costs on goods purchased abroad. In addition, certain other expenses, such as interest and taxes, are deductible even if incurred outside Venezuela, if they relate to Venezuelan income. The additional income tax adopts this latter approach entirely, in lieu of the rule stressing the place where the cost or expense was incurred. It bases deductibility on the relationship of an expense to Venezuelan operations, regardless of the place where the expense was incurred.

The Venezuelan application of its territoriality concept to deductions is too strict and is not required in theory by that concept. In principle, deduction should be allowed for any expense (otherwise allowable) which is connected with and properly allocable to income taxable in

Venezuela. This is the approach taken by a number of countries having a territorial rule for non-residents. As already noted, it is, in effect, the rule applicable in Venezuela under the additional income tax. It also represents a trend in Venezuelan income tax law, as shown by the growing number of statutory allowances for certain expenses occurring abroad but nevertheless made deductible because of their relationship to Venezuelan income. It is desirable, to avoid litigation under the present rule and its inevitable stretching to prevent hardship, that the more liberal and theoretically sounder rule suggested above be adopted.

However, there is one difficulty with the rule of relationship and allocation recommended here. It is the administrative problem that is posed by expenses incurred abroad by a business with branches or activities in both Venezuela and other countries. Thus, suppose an American corporation with branches in the United States, Brazil and Venezuela incurs expenses in the United States which it claims are properly allocable to Venezuelan income. At the present stage of administrative experience, Venezuela may have difficulty in checking those expenses or the allocation. It is suggested, therefore, that the above rule be made subject to the taxpayer's proving both the expense and its allocation in accordance with rules established by the Tax Administration. One requirement might appropriately be that the claim for deduction be accompanied by the statement of a certified public accounting firm that the expense was actually incurred and that, in its opinion, the expense is connected with and properly allocable to Venezuelan activity under standard accounting principles, together with an explanation of the method of allocation followed.

POSSIBLE SHIFT TO WORLD-WIDE INCOME RULE

If the above suggestion as to deductions is adopted, Venezuela will have the territorial rule properly applied as the base for its income tax jurisdiction. The question that remains is whether a territorial rule is too limited in scope as respects the income of Venezuelan residents. Should not Venezuela tax its residents (and perhaps its citizens even if they are resident abroad) on all of their income, whether from Venezuelan or other sources? Under this approach a Venezuelan resident receiving dividends, interest or rent from foreign investments would be subject to Venezuelan tax (assuming dividends are taxable at all); a Venezuelan corporation with a branch in Colombia, say, would be liable to tax on the income of that branch; a Venezuelan corporation receiving interest or dividends from a foreign subsidiary would be subject to tax. If this approach were adopted, that is, if the territorial rule were abandoned, some recognition should be given to any foreign income tax that may be incurred on the income from sources outside Venezuela. Such recognition could appropriately take the form of an allowance of a credit for the foreign income tax paid against Venezuelan tax on the income from the foreign country, as is done by the United States and England, for example.

At present Venezuelan individuals or corporations apparently do not receive much income from abroad. In part this may be due to the low rates of the Venezuelan income tax as compared with many other tax systems and in part to investment opportunities and profits within the country. There are, however, a number of so-called base companies which have been established in Venezuela to control foreign operating subsidiaries or branches and to receive income from such foreign sources. Their location in Venezuela is generally attributable to the fact that Venezuela does not tax foreign income. In essence, these companies achieve an effect similar to that gained by Panamanian holding companies. This is so, even if the Venezuelan base company also conducts operations in Venezuela.

A country generally decides to go beyond a territorial rule and reach all the income of its residents for one or more of the following reasons: to increase its revenue; to encourage investment at home by withdrawing the incentive to invest abroad that may result from non-taxation of income from foreign investment; to achieve equity in the treatment of its residents, by reaching all income they receive regardless of sources. An added factor may also be that of administration, since the worldwide income rule makes unnecessary the determination of the question whether the income does or does not arise within the country. (The question may, however, occur in a limited and less serious form in the application of certain rules under a foreign tax credit.)

Given the present limited amount of revenue received by Venezuelan residents from sources abroad, it is not a first order of business that Venezuela now reconsider its territoriality rule as respects income. However, it would appear advisable for Venezuela ultimately to abandon that rule in favor of the world-wide income rule for residents (and perhaps citizens as well). A territorial rule is not in keeping with increased economic activity and a maturing income tax structure. If tax rates increase, and also if domestic dividends are subjected to tax, the continuation of the territorial rule leaving dividends from foreign sources tax-free may well result in an undesirable incentive to Venezuelans to invest abroad. This situation could be met by adoption of the world-wide income rule.

If Venezuela is ultimately to adopt this broader jurisdictional rule for its residents and corporations, it is appropriate that, in the meantime, by statute, regulations, or permissible interpretation it move towards that goal by increasingly asserting tax in the borderline areas of the territorial rule. Thus, for example, it is appropriate that a Venezuelan corporation accepting orders from a sales concern or salesmen elsewhere in Latin America and causing the orders to be filled by direct shipments from another country on its account, should be taxable in Venezuela. While this might be a borderline case under a strict territoriality concept that asks, Was there a Venezuelan source or activity? such questions should be resolved in favor of taxability if the ultimate goal is abandonment of territorial limitations as respects residents. In other words, in important situations where a resident has at least some Venezuelan contact with respect to the income in question, the law could well reach that income on an *ad hoc* approach even though strict application of the territorial rule might yield a different answer.

Of course, complete abandonment of the territorial rule, and even its partial abandonment in certain instances, would make the Venezuelan tax rules no longer suitable for the base company operations earlier described (and others of a similar nature). Such operations are predicated upon a territorial rule, and the countries selected as base countries are chosen on that ground. But Venezuela did not adopt its territorial rule as a lure for base company operations; accordingly, the incidental effect of their elimination under adoption of a world-wide income rule would not be a signficant factor. The issues involved should be decided on the basis of the effect on normal Venezuelan residents and corporations, wholly apart from the specialized base company situations.

FOREIGN CORPORATIONS OPERATING IN VENEZUELA

The above discussion relates only to residents (and perhaps citizens as well) and Venezuelan corporations (under Venezuelan law a "Venezuelan corporation" is a corporation organized in Venezuela, or a corporation organized outside of Venezuela but having its principal business in Venezuela or having chosen Venezuelan nationality). It does not involve non-residents, who would continue to be governed by a territorial rule. Some special problems regarding non-residents are discussed later. An intermediate situation is that of a foreign corporation having a branch in Venezuela (and not considered a Venezuelan corporation). In one sense, the corporation could be regarded as a non-resident and therefore would be taxed only on a territorial basis, on its income arising from sources in Venezuela, i.e., its activities in Venezuela. In another sense, the branch could be regarded as a "resident," and subject to tax under the world-wide rule on its income arising inside or outside Venezuela. (This statement of course refers only to the branch, not to the entire foreign corporation where that corporation has income-producing activities elsewhere. Venezuela should not tax income from those other activities.) The choice between these rules depends largely on the importance of the activities of the branch outside the country, which produce income related to the Venezuelan activity. It may be noted here that the additional income tax in effect applies this second approach. It taxes oil and mining production taxpayers, who may be branches of foreign corporations, or foreign corporations operating entirely in Venezuela, on income "related to operations" in Venezuela, thus departing from the territorial income rule.

Under present law, several rules are set forth in the regulations regarding special situations arising under the territorial rule because of the nature of the activities involved. Thus, the net income of concerns producing motion pictures outside Venezuela and leasing them in Venezuela is deemed to be 40% of gross receipts in Venezuela; the net income of international news agencies is deemed to be 15% of gross receipts; the net income of international transportation companies, 10% of gross receipts (and gross receipts here constitute 50% of receipts from service between Venezuela and other countries, plus 100% of receipts on transportation in Venezuela), and so on. Rules of this nature would continue to be needed, even under a world-wide type of tax, as to non-residents, because the territoriality concept would remain applicable to them. We have not considered these rules as respects their present operation. It is noted that complaints exist as to the rule regarding transportation companies, which is said to present difficulties and unfair results. Perhaps possible alternative rules should here be explored.

OTHER PROBLEMS OF NON-RESIDENTS

As stated above, non-residents should continue to be governed by the principle of territoriality and hence subject to tax only on income from sources in Venezuela (subject to the branch problem mentioned above). Undoubtedly, such a rule will give rise to close questions of law and fact, but these are inevitable. It is important that the Tax Administration be alert to recognize these problems and situations, and to state what, in its opinion, is the applicable rule, so that taxpayers can guide themselves accordingly. It will be necessary continually to explore troublesome situations in order to develop an appropriate rule for the determination of the source of particular items of income. For example, as respects interest on funds borrowed abroad by a Venezuelan corporation, the determination whether the interest is subject to Venezuelan tax depends, under present law, on whether the interest is obtained by virtue of economic activities realized in Venezuela or from properties situated in Venezuela. It may be desirable to adopt a specific rule for this situation under which interest paid by a Venezuelan debtor would be treated as income from a Venezuelan source and therefore subject to tax. Another specific rule could relate to the sale of shares of stock in Venezuelan corporations, where the gain from the sale could be regarded as subject to tax because of the situs of the corporation. In other words, the present general source rule could, in the interests of certainty and tax consequences desired, be buttressed by specific rules prescribing the source of particular items of income. In addition to these substantive problems, the Administration must also be vigilant to assert and collect tax in situations where income is being derived by non-residents from Venezuelan sources. Thus, scrutiny could be given to the activities of foreign concerns selling goods in Venezuela through agents, to ascertain if they are properly paying tax.

As an aid to the collection of tax from non-residents, it may be desirable to adopt a special rate structure for certain types of income going abroad, supported by withholding of tax at the source. At present, salaries of non-residents and the rentals of foreign motion picture lessors are withheld on, the former at a flat 4% rate with no complementary tax liability and the latter for both the schedular and complementary tax on a running account basis. If the suggestion earlier advanced of dropping the schedular and complementary tax structure in favor of a unitary tax at progressive rates is adopted, the following rules could be applied to non-residents.

Non-residents in general would be subject to the progressive rates. However, certain forms of income, such as salaries, wages, interest, professional fees, royalties and rents (and dividends if they are taxable; see the discussion in Chapter III) would be subject to withholding of tax at the source at a single flat rate. If, however, at the end of the year the total Venezuelan income of the non-resident resulted in a tax liability under the regular progressive rates higher than that achieved through such withholding, the non-resident would be required to file a declaration and pay the higher tax with a credit for the tax withheld. At the same time, if his liability were lower, either through the availability of deductions not recognized under withholding or because his total income fell in brackets whose rates were less than the withholding rate, he would have the option of filing a declaration and obtaining a refund. If the non-resident filed a declaration at the end of the year he could secure all the deductions properly applicable to his income and otherwise allowable by law. He would, however, receive only a single person's exemption.

The flat rate for the withholding could be fixed at the point where it would keep the need for declarations showing a higher liability at a reasonably small number, so as to achieve significant compliance even in the absence of the filing of those declarations. The flat-rate withholding would be on gross payments without regard to personal exemptions or deductions, unless the Tax Administration were able to work out a feasible procedure under which deductions could be considered. (The present withholding on motion picture rentals achieves this result through the rule that 40% of gross receipts constitutes net income.) As an enforcement measure, the payer of the income should not be allowed a tax deduction for amounts paid to non-residents unless he shows that he has withheld on those amounts in cases where withholding is required. The withholding reports would constitute information returns as to those non-residents.

B. Treatment of Certain Items of Income and Deduction

In the discussion in Chapter III above of the combination of the schedular and complementary taxes, the treatment of income and deductions was described in general. A definition of income was presented and provision made for the deduction of expenses incurred in the production of that income. The following discussion relates to certain income and deduction items.

INCOME ITEMS

Certain exclusions from income, and the treatment of capital gains, deserve special analysis.

Exclusions. The present statute provides for certain exclusions from income, some automatically and some on a discretionary basis. Some of these exclusions are desirable, such as those for gifts and inheritances; the income of charitable, educational organizations, etc.; workers' indemnifications (though indemnifications and settlements paid on dismissal could properly be taxed); and insurance proceeds (though any amounts received allocable to expenses or losses previously deducted should be included in income; the present law applies this rule only to the cost of goods sold).

But other exclusions are very doubtful. One group relates to interest income; exemption is accorded to interest on the first Bs.10,000 of savings deposits, interest on certain agricultural and industrial mortgage bonds, and interest on certain bank certificates, as well as interest from time to time on certain government bonds (see the discussion of exclusions in the summary of the present tax system). The other group relates to rents; under an act of July 10, 1958, rents on new construction after July 15, 1958, are exempt for five years, thereby broadening a former exemption granted on an area-by-area basis (exemption on this basis still is available for rents not covered by the new automatic exclusion).

Presumably, these interest and rent exclusions are intended to encourage investment in the activities involved. However, it is extremely dangerous to adopt tax incentives of this nature. One is never sure that the tax incentive—the exclusion from income, the lower rate of tax— is needed at all. The investment could well take place without the tax incentive so that the tax advantage becomes a pure windfall. This is sure to be so in a large number of cases. Consequently, much of the revenue loss from the exemption is wasted. Moreover, a tax incentive, under a progressive rate structure, gives the greatest advantage to the wealthiest taxpayers, since in their case the exclusion comes at the higher rates in the upper brackets. But these taxpayers are least in need of such tax benefits. And, of course, the exclusion is of no benefit, and therefore of no incentive, to the person not subject to tax because his income is too low. Thus, the savings deposit interest exclusion is no incentive to save to those persons not covered by an income tax. Finally, and perhaps most important, as soon as one exclusion is granted as an incentive to a particular group or activity, other groups or activities clamor and press for exclusions in their favor. Thus, an exclusion for rents from new construction could in time lead to demands for the exclusion of income from any new or essential industrial or business activity. The Bs.30,000 schedular tax exemption for agricultural activities is another example of special treatment in one place which may lead to similar exemptions in other areas. Soon the income tax, under a tax-incentive approach, can be riddled with special exclusions, exemptions, and lower rates so that it ceases to be an effective fiscal instrument. Moreover, to raise revenue at all, the rates must then be pushed higher and higher, quite unfairly, on those left subject to the tax. It is therefore suggested that the present exclusions of this character be re-examined and eliminated as far as possible.

Attention has previously been given to the present exclusion of dividends.

Capital Gains. Capital gains—gains from the sale of property—are subject to tax under the Venezuelan income tax system. Gains from the casual sale of real property are reached by schedule 8, and sales of other assets are covered by schedules 3 and 4 (and perhaps 2 in some cases). It is appropriate that an income tax should reach capital gains, and hence the basic recognition of this type of profit as taxable income is desirable in the Venezuelan law. There are, however, certain technical aspects which should be considered.

The rules for the determination of gain on casual sales of real property (schedule 8) differ from those applicable under other schedules. Thus, under schedule 8, the part of the gain allocable to the period prior to January 1, 1943, is not taxed. The allocation, however, is not based on actual January 1, 1943 values. Rather, it is made through a time pro-ration, by days, of the gain between the time the property was held by the taxpayer prior to January 1, 1943, and the period after that date. It is obvious that such a method of allocation has no correspondence to the actual facts, especially in view of the rise in values that has occurred in the past decade and even in recent years. This method of allocation simply serves to exempt part of the gain from tax if the property was held prior to January 1, 1943, even though the entire increase in value came after that date. It is also clear that it would be almost impossible administratively to substitute a calculation based on actual values on January 1, 1943. As to sales of stock and other personal property and real property sales falling under other schedules, there is no similar allocation; the entire gain is taxable even if the property had been held prior to January 1, 1943. This rule should be followed for all real property sales. By now, virtually all of the gain on the sale of almost any parcel of real estate will represent a rise in value that has actually occurred since 1943.

In computing the gain from sales of real property under schedule 8 (but not in computing any other gains), there is added to the cost price (including cost of improvements) an amount considered as interest earned, at the rate of 6% per year of the cost. The apparent theory behind this provision is that 6% is presumed to be a normal return on an investment and only the increases in value above a normal return should be considered taxable gain on a sale of the investment. This approach can perhaps be defended if there is a need to divide the gain on the sale of an unimproved asset into two components—the annual increase in value which represents the return the owner would otherwise have received if the property had been income-producing, and the increase in value occasioned by a rise in the price level, a change in the desirability of the area in which the property is located, etc. But under this approach, the assumed 6% annual return should be included in the taxpayer's ordinary income each year before being added to the cost of the property. The 6% is an assumed return and an assumed reinvestment. As to improved property on which an annual rental is being obtained, the 6% should be disregarded both as assumed income and assumed reinvestment; or at least no more should be assumed than is necessary to reach a 6% return in all. In any event, the present approach of schedule 8 is wrong, since it does not provide for taxing the 6% at all. Moreover, if capital-gain income is to be taxed essentially as other income, there is no reason to divide the gain into the two components. It would be appropriate to tax the entire gain on the sale, whether it represented either normal assumed return which was reinvested, or simply an increase in value. However, use of the presumed 6% return could be considered a modified averaging system, if the presumed return were taxed annually, leaving only the increase-in-value component to be bunched in the year of sale and then taxed. Since an averaging device for the entire gain, including as well that representing increase in value beyond the presumed annual return, is suggested below, even this aspect of the presumed-return method is not needed. Accordingly, it is suggested that the present approach be discarded.

Finally, there appear to be other minor differences between schedule 8 sales and other sales, relating to restrictions under schedule 8 rules as to the expenses of sale which may be allowed and the expenditures which may be capitalized as part of the cost. These differences should be removed.

Under the combination into one tax of the schedular and complementary taxes as recommended above, it is suggested that capital gains be treated as follows: the gain from the sale of all assets would be taxable income and fully included. The gain would be computed by subtracting from the sales price the total of the following: the cost of the asset plus any expenditures relating to it which were properly capitalized, and less any depreciation allowed or actually deducted (whichever is the greater), plus any expenses incurred on the sale of the asset. No part of the gain would be non-taxable because the asset was obtained prior to January 1, 1943. As respects property used as a residence there would be no deduction for depreciation. In view of the progressive rate structure, and to avoid taxing thereunder in the year of sale a gain that may have been attributable to several years, the taxable income from the sale could, at the taxpayer's option, be spread over the length of time the taxpayer had held the asset, or four years (perhaps three), whichever is the lesser. While this spreading or averaging does involve administrative difficulties, in that the gain would have to be pro-rated equally over this period, and the tax of the prior years increased, it is desirable as the rates become more severe. (An alternative, which does not involve recomputation of tax for prior years, would be to divide the capital gain by the number of years over which it would have been averaged, find the increase in tax in the current year on the resulting segment of the capital gain and then multiply that increase in tax by the number of years over which the capital gain would have been averaged. The result is the tax to be levied on the capital gain. Thus, if the capital gain were Bs.600,000, the number of years in the averaging were three, and the increase in tax resulting from the inclusion of Bs.200,000 in the current year were Bs.60,000, then the tax on the capital gain would be Bs.180,000.) Otherwise, there would be inequities involved by reason of the bunching of the gain in one year. Capital losses, computed in the same way, would be allowed in full. Only the net of the gains over the losses of a year would be averaged. An excess of losses over gains would not be averaged, but would be deductible in that year from other income. Any unabsorbed loss would enter in the net loss carry-over discussed elsewhere.

Special issues exist as to assets received by gift or inheritance. The recipient does not include the current value of the assets in his income. The donor or deceased is not regarded as realizing a gain or loss upon transfer of the property (by comparing what it cost him with its present value). The recipient, on a later sale of the property, uses as his cost the value at the time of the gift or inheritance. Thus, the capital gain accrued up to time of gift or death escapes income tax completely. There are inheritance and gift taxes, but at very moderate rates.

This treatment has its disadvantages. Since all property is subject to gift or inheritance tax, whether or not it has appreciated in value, the existence of those taxes is no substitute for an income tax on the appreciation. Similarly, depreciation in value should be recognized, at one time or another. The gift and inheritance taxes have a different aim: to impose a capital tax at the time the property is transmitted to new owners. Thus, if appreciated property were sold and the owner died shortly thereafter, both an income tax on the appreciation in value and an inheritance tax on the proceeds of sale would have been paid. (The proceeds of sale would be reduced, in effect, by the amount of the income tax.) Similarly, if depreciated property were sold, the owner would get the benefit of a deduction from his income. Similar results should in theory obtain if the acts are reversed, and the appreciated property is sold after it is received by inheritance. However, in this situation, it would be necessary to carry over the cost of the former owner. The present exemption of any appreciation that may have occurred prior to the gift or death, or the refusal to allow tax relief for any depreciation, is especially disturbing where the change in value has occurred shortly before death or gift, or where the recipient (donee or heir) sells the property shortly after he obtained it.

One possible solution is to require the donor to include in his income of the year of gift the total appreciation in value that has occurred prior to the date of gift and, in the case of death, to include in the decedent's last income tax return the appreciation prior to death. Similarly, accrued losses in value would be realized at those points in time. But it may be objected that these events, gift or death, should not have income tax consequences. An alternative, then, would be to carry over the donor's or decedent's cost and to treat that as the cost of the recipient. This solution involves administrative difficulties respecting record keeping, since if the asset is held for a long time by the recipient, or has been so held by the prior owner, the records may have become lost. Some would argue that the present rule is quite proper, on the grounds that the time of death is an accidental matter and should serve to fix new income tax values. This view is distinctly less appropriate as to gifts, in view of the possibility of a donor's giving property intended to be sold to a close relative, perhaps an adult son who would ultimately receive it anyway, so that the latter can make the sale instead of the donor. Income tax is thereby saved if the donee uses as his cost the market value at the time of his gift. However, if values are unstable, and if the formalities of a gift take time, this course is not likely to be followed, as the delay in consummating the gift may jeopardize the sale if values have dropped in the meantime.

As a compromise, the following may be considered: in computing the value of property for gift or inheritance tax, any appreciation in value could be included at double that amount. The asset for income tax purposes would obtain a new cost based on value at the time of gift or death, as at present. Thus, if an asset cost Bs.10,000 and had appreciated to Bs.50,000, its value for gift or inheritance tax would be Bs.50,000 plus Bs.40,000, or Bs.90,000. If the asset had been acquired by the donor or the deceased within five years of gift or death, or if it were subsequently sold by the recipient within three years of receipt, the recipient would have the option of carrying over the donor's or decedent's cost in computing capital gain or loss. A refund of gift or inheritance tax on the added appreciation would then be made in the case of gain, since the asset should then be included only at its normal value for those taxes. As respects losses, in many situations a taxpayer will dispose of the property chiefly in order to obtain his deductible loss, so that the situation is not as troublesome as it is with gains. But the problem can arise, as where death comes unexpectedly. It could be provided that a donee or heir selling property within three years of receipt could use his predecessor's cost rather than value at date of gift or death, where that cost is higher.

As indicated above, apart from the special issues caused by gift or inheritance, capital gains would be taxable as income, but would be given the benefit of an averaging device. As the economy develops and as business transactions become more complicated, new technical problems will arise in the application of the income tax to such gains. This is especially so as respects corporate transactions. Thus, suppose an individual who is engaged in a profitable business decides to incorporate that business. He forms a corporation and transfers the assets to the corporation in exchange for its shares of stock. If those assets have appreciated in value, it could be said that the difference between his cost for the assets and the value of the shares which now represent the assets, is taxable income. The corporation in turn would use the present value of the assets for its depreciation base. Likewise, suppose Corporation A merges with Corporation B and the shareholders of each receive new shares for their old stock. If their old stock had appreciated in value the difference between the cost of the old stock and the value of the new shares might be considered taxable income to the shareholders at that time. Similarly, accrued losses might be recognized for deduction from other income, at those times.

It may be thought that the imposition of a tax on such appreciation in value at the time of these and similar corporate transactions is not appropriate, as it might impede desirable business changes. Also, on the loss side, the recognition of losses at such times might encourage artificial transactions designed only to make the losses deductible without altering the taxpayer's control over the underlying assets. It would be possible, if regarded as desirable, to devise rules under which tax would not be imposed upon the occurrence of these events; instead, recognition of the gain or loss would be postponed until the stock were disposed of. Thus, in the incorporation situation there would be no tax at that time on the appreciation in value of the assets involved. The cost of the shares of stock would be determined by reference to the cost of the assets, and the corporation would use for depreciation only the same cost that the individual had been using. In the merger case, the shareholders would not then pay tax on the appreciation in value of their old shares, but instead would regard the cost of the old shares as the cost of the new shares.

But these rules, and corresponding rules for similar situations, can become complex, because the transactions to which they relate are complex. No attempt is made here to discuss the situations or rules in detail. Rather, attention is called to the problems, so that the Tax Administration and tax lawyers and accountants can be thinking about them and devising appropriate solutions as business needs warrant. Two important aspects must be kept in mind. First, a capital gain, at the time when it is taxed, and a dividend must each be taxed in full, just as is other income (subject to averaging, for capital gains). Otherwise these complicated rules on recognition of gain or loss will be subject to abuse, and income will escape tax or be taxed at preferential rates. Second, if a gain is not taxed at any particular time, it should not therefore become permanently exempt from tax. Rather, the tax on the gain should only be postponed until the new asset is sold. This postponement can be accomplished by carrying over the cost of the replaced asset. Similar considerations apply to losses.

Additional problems may exist in the corporate area: for example, the liquidation of a corporation. The fact of liquidation should involve a taxable capital gain or deductible capital loss to the shareholders, depending on the value of the assets they receive in relation to the cost of their stock. Also, contributions to the capital of a corporation, either on formation through shares issued at a premium, or later on, should not involve income to the corporation. Another illustration, in another area, where recognition of gain could be postponed is where the property of the taxpayer is taken by the Government under power of condemnation or eminent domain. Here, if the taxpayer invests the proceeds received from the Government in similar property, then the appreciation in value of the property condemned would not be taxed but instead the basis of the property condemned would be carried over to the new property. A similar rule would apply to other involuntary conversions, as where property is destroyed by fire.

DEDUCTIONS

Special problems arise with respect to certain deductions under the income tax.

Salaries. Under present law, the deductions allowable to a corporation for salaries and other payments to managers or directors are permissible only to the extent stated by the regulations. The regulations in turn state that the deduction cannot exceed 8% of the gross income (interpreted to apply individually as to each manager or director), and, in addition, if the manager or director is a shareholder, the deduction is limited to the amount normally paid by other corporations. Gross income means sales proceeds less cost of goods sold. Any amount disallowed as a deduction to the corporation under these rules is not included in the recipient's taxable income. The rules have their origin apparently in an attempt to avoid the splitting of income between a corporation and its shareholders or managers through shifting income to the latter group.

It is clear that the 8% rule-of-thumb is not workable. Thus, suppose no gross income, hence no taxable net income, exists for the corporation in the year, because of a high cost of goods sold; is the salary paid to the manager non-deductible to the corporation (which would affect its net loss carry-forward), and therefore not included in the manager's income? (Also, in a situation where dividends to the shareholders are not desired, but it is desired to reward a key high-bracket employee who is not a shareholder, the present system would seem to permit giving that employee tax-free income through paying him a salary exceeding the 8% limitation.) Aside from this aspect, it would be difficult to find a percentage figure generally appropriate. Moreover, if the manager or director is not a shareholder (or closely related to a shareholder), any such limitation is not appropriate, since, as to the employee, the salary is not a substitute for profits. As respects shareholder-employees, to be sure, some limitation is needed. Under present law, it is needed to prevent the splitting of income, by reducing the corporation's tax and increasing the shareholder's tax through high salary payments which are really distributions of profits. If a separate corporate tax is adopted and dividends are taxable to the shareholder, but not fully deductible to the corporation, it becomes necessary to distinguish between a bona fide salary and a distribution of profits disguised as a salary, to prevent the corporation's securing full deduction for what are really profit distributions. This can be done only by a comparison with salaries paid for similar work by similarly situated corporations. Hence, salaries paid to persons with an interest in profits (directly as shareholders or indirectly through close relatives who are shareholders) should be so scrutinized. If the salaries are really disguised dividends, they should be treated as such. (If the present law is kept, in reality the Tax Administration should also have the power to reach a salary disguised as a dividend paid, as when an unreasonably low salary is paid to a shareholder and a high dividend paid so as to split income by increasing corporate income and decreasing shareholder income.)

Loss Carry-overs. Under present law, the net losses of a business may be carried forward for two years under schedules 3 and 4 and three years under schedule 5 (agriculture). This carry-forward is not permitted for the complementary tax. No reason is evident for this latter denial. Under a unitary tax structure, losses should be carried forward for two years, possibly three. Also, it would be desirable to permit a loss carry-back for one or two years, so as to cushion the burden of a loss. Under the carry-back, if a tax had been paid in the preceding year, the carry-back of a current loss would result in a tax refund. If a loss carry-back is adopted, then a current loss should first be applied to the earliest carry-back year to which it is permitted to be taken, and then forward (in order) through any intervening year, on to succeeding carry-forward years until the loss is exhausted. To avoid the reopening of prior years, especially where the current loss is small in amount, it may be desirable to permit the taxpayer to carry the loss forward rather than to require him first to carry it back to earlier years.

Worthless Stock Losses. Under present law, if stock is sold at a loss, even for a nominal sales price, a deduction is allowed. But if the stock simply becomes worthless and no sale is involved, the deduction is denied. This result is inappropriate. Instead, a capital loss should be allowed when stock becomes worthless. No loss, short of a sale, should be allowed for only partially worthless stock.

Personal Expenses. Under present law, only two personal or living expenses, i.e., expenses not incurred in the production of income, are permitted as deductions, and these only for the complementary tax. The personal expenses allowed for that tax are charitable contributions if the total is in excess of Bs.5,000 and medical expenses. This general denial of personal and living expenses is appropriate. Such expenses are not directly related to the production of net income and hence deduction of them is not required in order to achieve a fair calculation of the net income subject to tax. To some extent, these personal and living expenses are recognized in the personal exemptions allowed to an individual for himself, wife and dependents. Any additional recognition becomes in effect a tax subsidy for the activity involved, as would be the case if interest and taxes on a residence could be deducted, or constitutes relief against hardship, as where a deduction is allowed for casualty losses on non-income-producing property. This latter action, of course, does not provide relief to one suffering the hardship but having so little income that he is not subject to tax.

It is therefore suggested that the statute continue not to allow deductions for personal and living expenses. This non-allowance would apply to interest and taxes not incurred in the production of income, to money set aside as savings, to money spent on education of children, and the like. An exception could be made for charitable contributions if it is desired to encourage the growth of philanthropic and similar institutions, and the present treatment could be continued. If the schedular and complementary taxes are combined, the deduction would be for purposes of the unitary tax. The present law has no provision for avoiding the sharp change in tax liability that occurs at the level of Bs.5,000 in gifts to charitable institutions. A deduction is denied for gifts totaling Bs.5,000 but is allowed in full for gifts totaling Bs.5,001. However, this approach is permissible, in view of its effect in reverse; a taxpayer giving Bs.4,500 would increase his gifts to Bs.5,001 if the additional Bs.501 in gifts would at his bracket rate save him more than Bs.501 in tax. Also, unless tax rates rise appreciably higher, there need be no maximum limitation. If it is desired to continue the present deduction for medical expenses, the deduction should be converted into one for hardship situations, both as an equity matter and to avoid administrative problems regarding small amounts. Thus, deduction should be allowed only for the amount of medical expenses in excess of a certain figure, perhaps Bs.500 or Bs.1000 per year.

C. Additional Tax

In view of the highly specialized problems involved, no detailed consideration is here given to the rules governing the computation of net income under the additional tax applicable to oil and mining production, including royalties. Thus, no analysis is made of such matters as the determination of a proper price for intercompany sales, or the proper treatment of exploration, development and drilling expenditures. Mention might here be made, however, of several technical points that seem inappropriately treated at present. As explained in the description of the tax, taxpayers with net income (after income taxes) that is not in excess of 10% of invested capital are not subject to the tax, while those with net income in excess of 10% but less than 15% of invested capital are subject to tax on half of their excess income, and hence have, in effect, a 25% rate. There is no notch provision, however, under these limits. An additional few Bs. income, by placing a taxpayer's excess just over 10% or 15% of invested capital, as the case may be, can result in a suddenly increased tax far greater than those few Bs. of income. It would seem desirable to introduce a notch provision under which, as a taxpayer passed from one step to the next step, the resulting increase in tax could not exceed the additional Bs. of income over the 10% or 15% of invested capital levels. Another problem arises from the fact that charitable contributions are not deductible under the schedular tax but are deductible under the complementary tax. Since net income for the additional tax is based upon schedular tax computations, the charitable deduction is lost under the additional tax (unless it qualifies as a normal and necessary expense). Hence, for a concern subject to the additional tax, any benefit resulting from a saving in complementary tax because of the charitable contribution is automatically lost by virtue of increased additional tax. It would seem appropriate to allow charitable contributions to be deducted in computing the net income for the additional tax.

D. Accounting Rules

The accounting rules developed under the income tax in Venezuela appear to result in a satisfactory determination of net income on an annual basis according to generally accepted principles. Thus, recognized methods of accounting, including inventory cost determinations, are permitted. Depreciation allowances for the income tax generally follow book depreciation unless the latter is clearly unreasonable. The rules regarding the keeping of books under the Commercial Code have been sufficiently modernized so as to permit the books' being kept under desired accounting systems without serious problems, though perhaps here and there accountants could suggest minor changes.

There are, however, several matters which should be mentioned. While the tax permits accrual accounting, it does not recognize install-ment-method accounting, or deferred-payment accounting. Conse-quently, on sales of assets, any gain realized must be included in full in the year of the contract, even though payment is on an installment or other deferred basis. The rules in this respect should be liberalized to permit these methods to be used for tax purposes. No reserves are permitted as deductions, even for bad debts. The additional tax, how-ever, does allow reserves for future normal and necessary outlays. Consideration should be given to allowing deductions under the income tax for reserves established by the taxpayer. However, since a deduction for reserves is subject to abuse by taxpayers, any allowance for reserves should be under the control of the Tax Administration. It should specify those reserves which it will allow as deductions, and should require a proper degree of experience and predictability of ultimate payment. Examples of possible reserves to be allowed are those for bad debts and for *utilidades* or termination pay accrued. Professional men should be permitted to use the accrual method and fiscal years.

In another area, the Tax Administration should scrutinize transac-tions between taxpayers controlled by the same interests, so as to pre-vent the improper allocation of income among the related taxpayers. Thus, if one corporation sells manufactured goods at a price below market to a controlled corporation for resale at retail (where one is a subsidiary of the other, or both are controlled by a common share-holder group) with the objective of allocating more income to the second corporation and less to the first, the Tax Administration should be able to recast the transaction and compute the income of each corporation on the basis of a fair price for the first sale. It is possible that Art. 69 now grants this power, since it states that if there are indications that the declaration is not a true exposition of the "taxable capacity" of the taxpayer the Administration may in effect redetermine the taxable income. If this interpretation is not the one to be given to this article, the power described above should be expressly granted. Thus, it could be provided that in the case of two or more organizations or businesses owned or controlled directly or indirectly by the same interests, the Tax Administration might allocate gross income and deduc-tions among those organizations or businesses, if it determined that such allocation was needed to prevent evasion or avoidance of tax or clearly to reflect the income of any of the organizations or businesses.

E. Statute of Limitations

Present law prescribes a five-year statute of limitations as respects deficiencies assessed against the taxpayer. This period commences to run from the date the declaration should have been filed. A new five-year period will be commenced by the assertion of any deficiency in tax against the taxpayer or apparently even by the official request of the Tax Administration for information concerning the taxpayer's income leading to a later recalculation of the tax. The statute of limitations on refunds is also five years.

It is apparent that the rules governing the statute of limitations on deficiencies are both too favorable and too strict for the taxpayer. As respects the beginning of the five-year period, it should commence, not on the day a declaration should have been filed, but on the day that it is actually filed. The commencement date should not, however, be earlier than the due date even when the declaration is filed earlier than the due date. A new five-year period should not be started by the assertion of a deficiency, or by a request by the Tax Administration for information. Instead, the initial five-year period should be regarded as interrupted only on the assertion of a deficiency in tax and then only to permit the later collection of deficiencies in an amount no greater than that which was asserted within the five-year period, though the grounds of deficiency may differ. Consideration should be given to permitting taxpayer and Tax Administration by agreement to extend the period for specified intervals. These agreements would, in appropriate cases, permit orderly examination of the taxpayer's situation without forcing the Administration, where the statute is about to run out, to assert deficiencies recklessly simply to prevent the expiration of the statutory period. However, the existence of such an extension device should not be seized upon by the Tax Administration as an encouragement to dilatory investigations. Consideration should also be given to providing a ten-year statute where the taxpayer has fraudulently evaded tax.

F. General

It is clear that in a brief period of time a comprehensive examination of the technical problems currently existing under an income tax is impossible. Any income tax involves a great many day-to-day technical problems, some readily apparent, some only partly perceived, and some remaining hidden until a particular situation or case suddenly brings them to light. These technical difficulties of interpretation and application range from very serious problems to minor irritations. The discussion above relates to those problems which were stressed most in discussions had with tax officials, tax lawyers, accountants, and executives. They are thus illustrative of the most serious current concerns.

It is apparent, however, that the Venezuelan income tax is moving rapidly into a period of greatly increased technical development. The expansion in amount and variety of business activities, the trend to publicly held corporations and to increased corporate activity in general, the impact of investment from abroad (bringing with it executives and their lawyers accustomed to thinking and worrying about tax technicalities), any increase in tax rates: all of these factors and others will have their impact on the tax system. More areas of uncertainty will arise requiring clarification in their tax treatment. More situations will be discovered in which the tax rules are not workable and could be altered without sacrificing revenue or equity. More situations will be seen in which the tax rules are subject to unfair manipulation and escape from tax.

It is useless to attempt to predict the technical problems of the future. Instead, it should be emphasized that successful growth of the income tax requires constant and skilled attention to technical detail by those in the Tax Administration and those outside of it who are advising taxpayers. Both groups must work together in a sincere desire to keep the system functioning properly.

CHAPTER V

: **Income Tax Administration:**
: **Description**

A. Organization

The organization of the various parts of the Government concerned with the administration of the income tax is depicted on Diagram V-1.

The organization of the Income Tax Administration itself *(Administración del Impuesto Sobre la Renta)* was revised during 1958. The chart presents the Administration as thus revised.

All three branches of Government—legislative, executive, and judicial —participate in the process of administering the income tax. The judiciary hears and decides disputes between taxpayers and the Government. This is done at two levels, the Court of Income Tax Appeals (hereafter referred to as the Tax Court), and the Federal Court. The Controller of the Nation, appointed for a 5-year term by the Congress, reports to Congress on the annual reports submitted by the various ministries of the Government. In order to comment on that part of the report of the Minister of Finance that deals with the Income Tax Administration, the Controller employs a staff to examine the declarations of taxpayers for arithmetic and legal correctness. The work of the Controller is more fully described later.

It is in the Ministry of Finance that the bulk of the work of administering the income tax takes place. The General Administration is a unit within the Ministry of Finance that acts as an overall supervisory agency of the Ministry. Its role in income tax affairs is to deal with certain matters, such as refunds, remissions of fines, etc., that according to law must be approved at the top level of administration, viz., by the Minister of Finance. Usually, the Minister of Finance delegates to the head of the General Administration these various powers of approval. The National Treasury is another unit within the Ministry. Through the receiving offices which it selects, it receives tax payments from the taxpayers. Still another unit within the Ministry, the Income

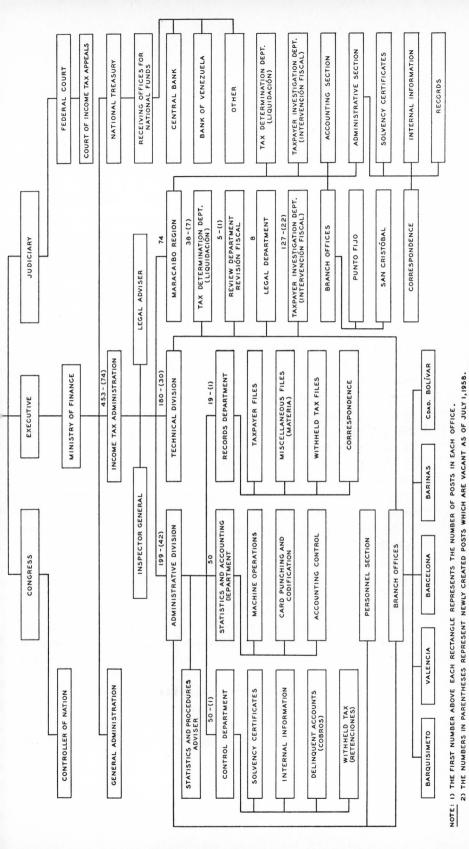

Diagram V-1. Distribution of Administrative Functions for Income Tax

NOTE: 1) THE FIRST NUMBER ABOVE EACH RECTANGLE REPRESENTS THE NUMBER OF POSTS IN EACH OFFICE.
2) THE NUMBERS IN PARENTHESES REPRESENT NEWLY CREATED POSTS WHICH ARE VACANT AS OF JULY 1, 1958.

Tax Administration, receives declarations from taxpayers, calculates and investigates the amount of tax due, issues bills, and initiates collection action to obtain payment on overdue bills.

The Income Tax Administration has at its head a general administrator. The Legal Adviser is attached to his office largely for the purpose of handling court litigation. An Inspector General and his staff of technical officials determine the income taxes due from oil companies. The everyday work of the Income Tax Administration is accomplished by the Administrative Division and the Technical Division. The 1958 revision of the organization of the Income Tax Administration was not a major one; it affected primarily the internal structure of the Administrative Division, by adding additional supervisory levels. As of August 1958, this organizational revision had not yet been completely implemented. Certain positions, such as the head of the Control Department, had not been filled, and the Withheld Tax Section of that department appeared to be under the control of the Tax Determination Department *(Liquidación)* in the Technical Division. In general, the Administrative Division does the paperwork and record keeping for the Administration. This work is described in some detail later.

The Technical Division, in its Tax Determination Department, performs one important step in the processing of every declaration: the determination of taxable income. In addition, calculation of the amount of tax due is in some cases carried through in this department, and in almost every case checked here. Details of these procedures are given later. The remainder of the Technical Division handles all problems of technical interpretation, decides whether or not to send investigators out to check a taxpayer's records, sends out these investigators in the cases selected, and processes claims for refunds as well as protests submitted by taxpayers.

The Maracaibo Region, which appears on the chart as if it were a third division of the Administration, represents almost a duplicate organization, on a smaller scale, of the Administrative and Technical Divisions located in Caracas. The Maracaibo Region receives and processes declarations in much the same way as is done in Caracas, but certain of the technical functions performed in Caracas are not duplicated in Maracaibo. There is neither a Review Department *(Revisión Fiscal)* nor a Legal Department in Maracaibo. These functions are performed on a nationwide basis in Caracas.

Of the seven branch offices located in Venezuela, two are operated by the Maracaibo Region and five by the Caracas head office. Branch offices are small, containing from one to four people. They provide information to taxpayers, receive declarations, and process and investigate the declarations in special cases.

B. *Operations*

The operations and functions described below cover the major activities performed in the process of administering the income tax.

All activities described take place within the Income Tax Administration unless otherwise noted. This description does not attempt to detail every single bit of paperwork, processing and checking that takes place. This limitation on the description is in part due to the limited time available to the Commission to learn every detail and in part to a desire not to burden this report with excessive detail.

PROCESSING OF DECLARATIONS
THROUGH THE ISSUANCE OF THE BILL

Diagram V–2 is a flow chart which shows the processing of declarations at the present time in Caracas. Slight differences in the Maracaibo procedure are pointed out in the description below.

Step 1. Declarations in triplicate are usually brought to a tax office by the taxpayer. The third copy is stamped and immediately returned to the taxpayer. The few taxpayers who file by mail are required to use registered mail, and the taxpayer's copy is returned in the same manner. Taxpayers showing income from business in schedule 3 must also file an "Annex A," a form containing detailed provision for an income statement and a balance sheet. Declarations filed by individual persons are printed on white paper, while those for corporations and other companies are on blue. The annex is on green paper. The annex was last revised at a time different from that for the white and the blue forms and is not fully integrated with them.

Taxpayers engaged in activities falling under schedules 3 (business), 4 (oil and mining) and 5 (agriculture) must file their declarations within three months after the end of the taxable year. The other taxpayers must file within two months after the end of the taxable year.

Declarations presented at branch offices are immediately transferred to Caracas, or Maracaibo, as the case may be. For each corporation declaration, a clerk uses a book containing an alphabetical listing of

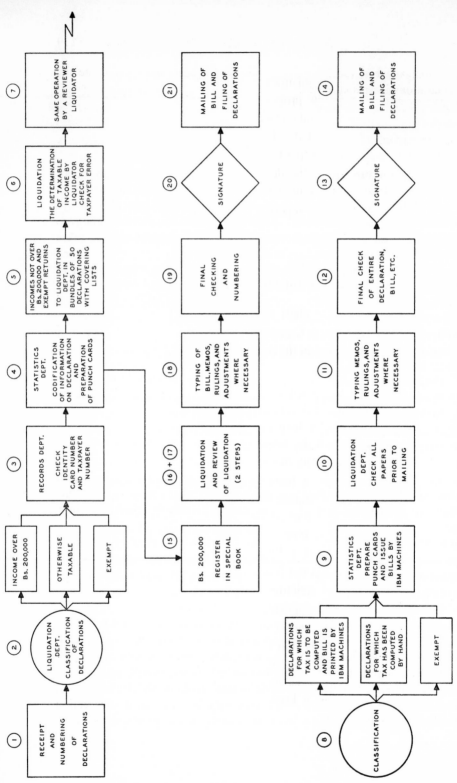

Diagram V-2. Flow Chart for Income Tax Declarations

corporations (and other companies) in order to find the taxpayer's permanent number, which is then entered on the declaration. When a list is prepared, as is done about every three years, numbers are assigned to the alphabetical list of corporate taxpayers. Numbers are assigned with a gap of 100 left between each number so that the alphabetical sequence of taxpayers is also the numerical sequence. Thereafter, new taxpayers are assigned numbers in their proper alphabetical order. Although a notation as to the year of the declaration is made in this book, it does not appear that the book is regularly examined to find out which previously listed taxpayers have failed to file for the year. A new listing, together with what are likely to be new "permanent" numbers, is prepared about every three years.

The declarations of individual taxpayers receive a number assigned in the order in which they are received. In addition, individuals are required to place on their declarations the number appearing on their Identity cards. This Identity Number is the basis now being used for the individual taxpayer files in Caracas, while Maracaibo is using for its filing system a permanent number much like the corporation number described above.

Declarations which obviously show high income are marked *"Urgente"* to assure that they go to the next processing step immediately.

In Maracaibo, before proceeding to the next step, the name on each declaration is checked against a list of taxpayers who are delinquent in the payment of their tax bills.

Step 2. The declarations of corporations and individuals are next sent to the Tax Determination Department. The Venezuelan Income Tax Administration calls this the Liquidation Department. The two names are used interchangeably in this report. In this step all that this department does is to divide all returns into three classes—those showing income over Bs.200,000 (in Maracaibo Bs.100,000 is the dividing line), those that are otherwise taxable, and those that are exempt.

This classification operation can be performed only by persons with a good understanding of the working of the income tax. The liquidators, as the technical personnel of the Liquidation Department are called, do have this understanding. It is needed because taxpayers do not on their declarations compute either their total income or their tax. They merely enumerate in the various schedules their items of income and deduction, plus family status and other information relevant to exemptions and deductions under the complementary progressive tax. Well-trained people must therefore glance at the declarations in order to determine into which category each falls.

The main reason for classification at this stage appears to be to select the higher-income declarations for rapid processing and to find the exempt declarations (non-taxable because of the nature of the taxpayers or because the tax due has already been withheld), which may be set aside and examined later after the more important declarations have been processed.

Step 3. A check on the correctness of the Identity and other numbers listed on the declaration takes place either at this point or, it appears sometimes, during Step 1. This work is done by personnel of the Records *(Archivos)* Department. In Maracaibo this step and Step 2 are simultaneously performed in the records room, which is set off by itself on a separate floor and seems to be so arranged as to offer good security against possible tampering with files.

Step 4. The declarations are now sent to the Statistics and Accounting Department, often referred to just as the Statistics Department. The first operation is codification—the translation into code numbers of several items of information appearing on the face of the declaration, i.e., the taxpayer's city of residence, state of residence, nationality, marital status, and type of corporation or other business entity. These code numbers are marked on the declaration in colored pencil.

The second operation is to punch into cards (using IBM key punch equipment) the codified information, plus the taxpayer's Identity Number (in Maracaibo, also the taxpayer's permanent number), the declaration number (assigned when the declaration was received), the taxpayer's name, the number of dependents by class, the fiscal year covered by the declaration, and the semester of the year in which the declaration was filed.

These cards, called the preliminary punch cards, are verified with IBM verifying equipment. They are then placed in an IBM accounting machine which prints in triplicate a list of the taxpayers' names, numbers and fiscal years. One copy of this list is retained by the Statistics Department, one goes to the Records Department, and one is bundled with the corresponding declarations (usually 50 in a bundle) to go back to the Liquidation Department.

It is not clear, at least during the heavy springtime filing period, that declarations in the over Bs.200,000 class go through this process of preliminary punching prior to going through the liquidation process.

In any event, as Step 15 of the flow chart shows, these declarations are immediately registered in a special book when they enter the Liquidation Department.

Step 5. Declarations are delivered to the Liquidation Department already classified into those over Bs.200,000, those otherwise taxable, and those exempt. Steps 6 to 14, now to be described, refer to returns not over Bs.200,000.

Step 6. The operation so aptly labelled "Liquidation" now takes place. First there is an arithmetic check of the figures the taxpayer entered on the declaration. Then the figures and deductions are studied to determine whether or not the taxpayer has erroneously deducted non-deductible items or otherwise presented information that requires further investigation. The net income of each schedule is entered in the appropriate space on the back of the declaration, as well as the exemptions and net taxable income. The relevant figures for the calculation of the complementary tax are also entered. For declarations under Bs.200,000 the tax is not calculated by the liquidators, since IBM equipment will do this later. (In Maracaibo, if fines are involved, the equipment seems unable to handle the calculation, so that the tax calculation is made by the liquidator, whereas the Caracas IBM equipment can handle these cases involving fines.)

The degree of complexity of the work done by the liquidators varies considerably among the declarations. For the great majority of declarations, the liquidator merely copies figures from one schedule (salaries) on to the back of the declaration. For some declarations, a fully filled out annex must be thoroughly checked (with the aid of electric calculating machines on each liquidator's desk) and studied. For others, in which real estate sales are reported in schedule 8, a very complicated series of calculations must be made to determine the taxable income. A special mimeographed form has been designed to aid the liquidator in making real estate sale calculations.

In the event that the liquidator discovers arithmetic errors made by the taxpayer or decides that certain items deducted are clearly not deductible, he will make the necessary changes and prepare a letter of explanation to go to the taxpayer with the bill. If any fines are due, an explanation of this will also be given to the taxpayer.

If the liquidator finds doubtful items, he will still ordinarily go ahead and complete the liquidation calculations, but will either write the taxpayer for further information or recommend that the taxpayer be investigated by the Income Tax Administration's field agents or investigators *(fiscales)*. If the liquidator wants technical advice on depreciation calculations or legal points, he may obtain help from others in his department, or from the technical experts elsewhere in the Technical Division.

In Caracas this department has 12 liquidators working primarily on the under Bs.200,000 declarations and 4 on the over Bs.200,000 declarations. Maracaibo has 6, all of whom work on all classes of declarations. Liquidators generally have had some accounting training, and many have had general public administration training given by the Ministry of Finance.

Step 7. Reviewers are liquidators who review all the work done by the liquidators in Step 6. Since the reviewer initials the declaration, as does the liquidator, the reviewer feels that he (or she) can fulfill his responsibility only by re-performing every operation performed by the liquidator. One reviewer stated that changes were made in as many as 20% of the declarations liquidated by inexperienced liquidators. Because reviewers need not do as much writing as the liquidators, and because the reviewers work faster, there are fewer of them—6 in Caracas (4 for under Bs.200,000) and 3 in Maracaibo.

Step 8. The liquidated declarations of the under Bs.200,000 class are now further classified into three categories. First are those on which no tax computation has been made; these are ready for automatic computation and bill printing. Second are those which for one reason or another—for example, very late declarations filed for taxable years prior to 1956, when the law was changed—had to be fully liquidated by hand through the stage of tax computations. For these, all that is needed is the bill. Third are the exempt declarations, which need little further processing. Of the declarations originally classified as exempt in Step 2, about 4% are found to be taxable when they are passed through liquidation in Steps 6 and 7.

Step 9. The liquidated declarations are now sent to the Statistics Department, where they first receive a liquidation number (marked on the back of the declaration). The declarations then go to the key punch operators. The card that is first punched is one containing the taxpayer's identifying number, the liquidation number, the declaration number, whether the declaration was filed voluntarily or involuntarily, address, time within which the bill is to be paid, e.g., 60 days (taxpayer is permitted to elect as much as 180 days), and office for receiving national funds where payment is to be made by the taxpayer. Then for each declaration one card is prepared for each schedule in which net income is reported. Each of these cards contains the liquidation and declaration numbers, city, state, schedule number, net income in that schedule, basic exemption applicable, and (for declarations that have been fully liquidated by hand) the taxable income and the tax due for that schedule. For the declarations that have not had the tax calculated, i.e., the *"mecánicas,"* the last two items are punched into the card automatically by an IBM calculating punch machine. This calculation of tax is done for each of the eight schedules as to which income is declared and is also done for the complementary tax.

Now all the cards (including the name and address card) relating to a single declaration must be brought together through the use of high-speed collating equipment. The cards are then ready to be fed into the accounting machine, which prints each taxpayer's bill in eight copies. The net income, exemption, taxable income, and tax are itemized on the bill for each schedule and for the complementary tax. The bill also has the taxpayer's name, address, and time and place for payment. The machines also prepare a buff-colored (blue in Maracaibo) card which is attached to the bill and which the taxpayer signs and returns when he receives the bill in order to acknowledge his receipt of the bill. Finally, the cards are run through the accounting machine to prepare a listing of the bills by liquidation number. The covering list together with the declarations, bills and colored cards are now sent to the Liquidation Department in bundles.

Steps 10, 11 and 12. In the Liquidation Department these bundles are opened, and those declarations are taken out which the liquidators had in Steps 6 and 7 noted for letter writing, further information, etc. For these, the necessary letters, memos, etc., are prepared and typed. The others are sent directly to reviewers who, we have been told, check not only the completeness of the file but also the accuracy of the information printed on the bill, such as the taxpayer's name and address, and time and place of payment, but not the computation of the tax. It is rare that errors are disclosed by this final check.

Step 13. The final operation performed in the Liquidation Department is the signing of the bills. The law requires all bills to be signed. In Caracas the chief of this department has delegated much of the signing chore. In Maracaibo the chief of this department signs in full hand the original of each of about 35,000 bills per year. The remaining seven copies of the bill are hand stamped by a clerk with a facsimile signature.

Step 14. The entire file is now sent to the Mailing Department for distribution. Five copies of the bill are mailed to the taxpayer with the colored receipt card. Of the other three, one is placed inside each of the two copies of the declaration which have been kept together up to now, and the third is sent to the collection section for filing. One copy of the declaration is placed in the taxpayer's file in the Records Department with his prior declarations. The other copy is sent to the Statistical Department so that additional detail may be obtained from the declaration and bill. It is then put in a file which once every six months is sent to the Examination Room of the Controller of the Nation. (In Maracaibo the mailing and filing is handled by the Records Department.)

Steps 15-21. These steps cover the processing of the over Bs.200,000 declarations and correspond to Steps 5-14 for the under Bs.200,000 group. The over Bs.200,000 (Bs.100,000 in Maracaibo) group are fully liquidated and billed without the use of IBM equipment. Experience has established that these important declarations must be the first to be billed and that hand processing for the small number of declarations involved is faster than machine processing.

COLLECTION PROCESS: PAYMENT OF BILLS
AND COLLECTION OF OVERDUE BILLS

The steps in the process of collection, including the handling of delinquent accounts, will now be described.

1. Receiving Offices. Payment of the bills issued to taxpayers must be made to one of the receiving offices for national funds established by the National Treasury agency of the Ministry of Finance (see Chart V–1). Payments may not be made at the time of filing the declaration (because the declaration has not been liquidated and no bill has been issued); nor can payment be received by the Income Tax Administration.

The National Treasury has appointed various agents as receiving offices for national funds. In Caracas, the main receiving agency is the Central Bank of Venezuela, to which payments can be made at its main office or at the small branch office it maintains for this purpose at the Centro Simón Bolívar, where the Income Tax Administration is located. The Central Bank receives the large bulk of payments, including those from the oil companies. It charges the National Treasury on the basis of its costs, which in 1957 amounted to approximately Bs.28,000—this included the cost of preparing about 90,000 punch cards. In Caracas payments may also be made at offices of the Bank of Venezuela, a private bank.

In addition, there are about 70 other offices for receiving payments throughout the country. Most of these are branches of the Bank of Venezuela. Some, in small municipalities, are business houses appointed by the National Treasury as its agents. The Bank of Venezuela and these other agents receive a commission of 3/4 of 1% of the amounts paid through them. They do not prepare punch cards, nor do they perform any function in the collection of overdue bills.

The accounts of the receiving offices are audited by the National Treasury and occasionally by the Controller of the Nation.

When the taxpayer goes to a receiving office with his five copies of the bill he usually pays in cash. Checks are accepted, but apparently only under rigid rules. The amount of the check must be the exact amount of the bill; the difference cannot be made up in cash. If checks are made out in the wrong name, e.g., to the Ministry of Finance, they are either rejected or must be approved in four stages by the Ministry of Finance before the banks will accept them.

Of the five copies of the bill presented by the taxpayer, the original is returned to him duly stamped, one is kept by the receiving agency, one goes to the National Treasury, and two to the Income Tax Administration.

2. Accounting for Payment. The two copies of paid bills sent to the Income Tax Administration, either in Caracas or Maracaibo, are processed by the Accounting Department, as the Statistics and Accounting Department is sometimes called. The green copy is used to record payments received by each receiving office for control purposes, and the pink copy goes to the key punch operators, who prepare a punch card showing the amount of payment, date, and liquidation number. This card may be called the payment card. The Central Bank prepares these cards for all payments received by it, and delivers cards and copies of the bills to the Accounting Department 24 hours after payments are received. The pink copy of the bill may eventually find its way to the taxpayer's file.

The payment cards are first run through an accounting machine for the preparation of a daily (or so) list of payments and then are automatically run against the billing cards originally prepared in Step 9.

The unpaid billing cards are taken out for running against the next batch of payment cards. Payment cards, as well as billing cards, are maintained for each calendar year corresponding to the year in which the taxes under the declarations were due to be paid. If a taxpayer files in 1958 the declaration he should have filed in 1955, the billing and payment cards will be kept with the 1958 cards. Since payments are always coming in for prior years as well as the current one, there must be a run of payment cards against billing cards for each year for which payments are still being made.

Once in six months the outstanding unpaid billing cards for each year are run through an IBM accounting machine in order to print a list, by years, of unpaid bills. These lists are sent to the Delinquent Accounts (Cobros) Section. About once a year in Maracaibo all the unpaid bill cards are re-arranged into taxpayer order, and also apparently by years, and a list is automatically printed which shows all the bills outstanding against each taxpayer in alphabetical order. In Caracas, because of the change to the Identity Number system about two years ago, it is not yet possible to prepare the list Maracaibo prepares. Instead, two lists have to be prepared, one cumulating the years prior to the change and one for the subsequent years to date. This is done in Caracas once a year and the resulting information is printed on account cards, one for each delinquent taxpayer, all of which are sent to the Delinquent Accounts Section.

In Caracas plans are being made—in fact, a new delinquent account bill form has already been delivered in large quantity—for a system whereby monthly bills can be sent to taxpayers whose accounts are in arrears. The bill will contain a cumulative total of the amount due and will be automatically printed by machine from cards. The system is likely to take some time to perfect.

3. Delinquent Accounts. The Delinquent Accounts (Cobros) Section receives all of the above information—daily payment registers, annual cumulative delinquent taxpayer account lists on cards, and semiannual non-cumulative delinquent taxpayer lists by years.

This section has the function of trying to collect overdue accounts from delinquent taxpayers. At present it can do this only through the use of notices mailed to taxpayers. The effectiveness of this section depends upon the speed with which it can process paper, and the eventual cooperation it receives in the form of collections made through legal processes instituted by private lawyers appointed by the Ministry of Finance to collect the larger and older delinquent accounts.

On the matter of the paperwork—sending notices out to taxpayers promptly—it appears in Caracas that the system is about to bog down. In Maracaibo, though there are cumbersome aspects to the system, it seems to function without undue delay in the issuance of notices. It is difficult, if not impossible, to obtain an accurate picture of the amount of delinquent accounts in view of the way the figures are compiled. Thus, amounts currently in litigation are included in delinquent payments. Estimates furnished indicate that the percentage of total tax due for a current year that is unpaid at the end of the year is about 15% for the Caracas office and 10% for the Maracaibo office. After a year or so, these figures drop to about 8% and 5% respectively. The oil companies are not considered in these estimates.

One of the main problems in the paperwork is finding out, on the day it is desired to send a cumulative arrears notice to a delinquent taxpayer, whether or not the taxpayer has recently made a payment on account of any of his outstanding bills. This requires checking through a large amount of information, much more so in Caracas than in Maracaibo. In neither office does there appear to be any kind of system for a daily posting of payments received to taxpayer accounts maintained on a cumulative basis. This problem of checking for recent payments arises not only when the first notice is sent to a delinquent taxpayer but again and again when the second and third notices are sent.

Since information in the Delinquent Accounts Section is not on punch cards, all notices are prepared in the section by typewriter. Though the notice shows the total tax due for prior years, it does not include or make reference to the interest that is also due for late payment. After the bills are paid, new bills for the interest are prepared and sent out. These have been troublesome to collect.

Once these three notices have been sent to a delinquent taxpayer, it is then possible to institute legal action. The Delinquent Accounts Section has no staff or power to take any step other than to mail notices or recommend "upstairs" that a lawyer be hired to take legal collection measures. Not all accounts for which three notices have been sent are recommended for legal action. It seems to be expected that payments are going to be made late by people who want to do so, so that there is no use pressing them until a year or more has passed. Then, provided the delinquent account is more than about Bs.2,000, it becomes suitable for a legal collection recommendation.

The Delinquent Accounts Section regularly prepares a list of accounts recommended for legal collection. This list is sent to the head of the

Income Tax Administration, who turns it over to the General Administration of the Ministry of Finance. The signature and approval of the Minister of Finance is next obtained, as well as an approval from the Controller of the Nation. The list, to the extent now approved, comes back to the General Administration for assignment to one or more private lawyers on a commission fee basis.

ENFORCEMENT THROUGH COMPARISON, AUDIT,
AND EXAMINATION OF DECLARATIONS AND OTHER RECORDS

The operations and functions now to be described are all means of checking the veracity of statements made by taxpayers on their declarations or of determining whether or not a declaration has been filed by those obligated to do so.

1. Information Section. At the present time the Information Section receives a considerable amount of information primarily from official sources. Red cards reporting the details of real estate sales are prepared by the official notaries as part of the process of recording a real estate transaction. These cards contain the Identity Numbers of the parties and are useful for checking purposes. Similar information relating to mortgage loans (blue cards) and mortgage discharges (brown cards) also comes in regularly.

Municipalities furnish information as to all business and commercial licenses issued, property taxes paid by owners of real property, building permits granted, and lists of rental information. Much of the information from the municipalities does not include Identity Numbers and is submitted in a form that requires the Information Section to prepare a yellow card for each item of information received on a list or on a card of an unsuitable size.

Banks furnish information as to those to whom they pay interest on savings accounts. The commercial courts furnish a list of the people involved in the creation of new corporations. The Hippodrome (race track) furnishes information showing the prizes paid to owners of horses, trainers, and jockeys.

Other information comes to the section or is dug out by the section. Other officials investigating taxpayer records will sometimes make a note as to an income item and send the information on to the section. Personnel in the section used to go through the annex form (submitted with declarations of business income) in order to pick out information as to those to whom interest or commissions were paid. Other information is taken from the forms submitted in connection with withheld income tax.

About 500,000 yellow cards are prepared each year from the information that comes to the section. These cards and the red, blue, etc., cards are filed alphabetically. Officials investigating a taxpayer's declaration may come in to the Information Section to check the cards on file. About two persons in Caracas are engaged in going through the files to select cards containing items of substantial amount and check them against declarations on file. If an amount is not reported in the declaration, a note is sent to the liquidators for further action. If no declaration at all is found, a letter notifying the taxpayer to file one is sent. If the declaration is not submitted, the name and information are turned over to the Taxpayer Investigation Department. The work of systematically checking the information on file against declarations is almost hopelessly behind. Now being matched are cards that are about five years old, and these are being checked because of the five-year statute of limitations.

By far the most important use of the card file appears to be as a check-point in the consideration of applications for certificates of solvency, which are described more fully later. Once cards are checked they are removed from the active file to a dead file. Information about a taxpayer is usually not placed in the file containing his declarations.

2. Tax Determination Department (Liquidación). The work of the liquidators has already been discussed. Their function is to examine the correctness of the declarations from the point of view of the information contained therein. They will correct obvious incorrect entries, such as salaries paid by an individual businessman to himself. They will also seek further factual information where the declaration is incomplete or contains entries that are not readily understandable. Such corrections as the liquidator can make himself or from further information supplied by the taxpayer are made in the Liquidation Department. But where the matter appears to be too complicated or to involve a suspicion of false reporting or to involve large sums, the liquidators will prepare a memorandum outlining the situation and send it on to the Review Department *(Revisión Fiscal)*. Liquidators do not deal directly with taxpayers, except when liquidators have occasion to correspond with taxpayers, or they come into the office to discuss a point.

3. Review Department (Revisión Fiscal). This department now has the function of deciding whether or not a field investigator from the Taxpayer Investigation Department *(Intervención Fiscal)* should be sent out to examine the taxpayer's records. The cases for which a decision whether or not to investigate has to be made arise primarily from the memoranda submitted by the liquidators. There are, however, other sources, such as applications for solvency certificates, which are recommended for field investigation.

In order to make its decision, the Review Department calls for the taxpayer's complete file of declarations. After examination of these and the memorandum which brought the matter to it for decision, the department may or may not forward the case to the Taxpayer Investigation Department. If the case is sent there for investigation, the field agent *(fiscal)* who investigates it must submit to the Review Department a report of his findings and recommendations, if any, for additional tax. If the report is approved, the field agent shows it to the taxpayer, has him sign it (the signature does not represent agreement but merely receipt), and then turns the matter over to the Liquidation Department for billing.

The Review Department appears to have two or three technical officials and expects two more to be added.

During 1957 the Review Department handled 31 individual and 121 corporation cases in the over Bs.200,000 category, and 171 and 281, respectively, in the under Bs.200,000 group. Of these, one statement that was prepared reported only 21 cases as being sent for investigation. An orally obtained estimate was that almost 40% of the cases sent to Review were forwarded to Investigation.

4. Taxpayer Investigation Department (Intervención Fiscal). This department has the field agents or investigators *(fiscales)* who are sent out to investigate the accounting facts of taxpayers. As of the end of July, 1958, there were about 33 field agents working out of Caracas, 6 in the branch offices controlled directly by Caracas, 4 in Maracaibo, and 3 in its branch offices—a total of 46. Current plans call for raising this number to about 110. In the Caracas office, all 33 agents are supervised by the head of the department. They are not divided into groups, nor does the head yet have an assistant to help in supervisory work.

Most of the cases assigned to this department for investigation come from the Liquidation Department through the Review Department. Some cases come from the Legal Department, which handles refund claims and sometimes asks for an investigation prior to deciding the claim. Other cases arise as a result of solvency certificate applications, sometimes even at the taxpayer's request in order to hasten the issuance of the certificate. Recently a number of cases have come from the Delinquent Accounts Section, which, having no field men of its own, has asked that certain delinquent taxpayers be checked as to whether or not they had the ability to pay.

Not all cases assigned for investigation are investigated, since the investigation capacity is not that large. The more important and the easier cases tend to be handled first, though efforts are apparently being made to change this latter aspect and to consider more complex cases. In 1957, in Caracas there were 168 cases assigned, 153 investigations completed and 153 started. In Maracaibo most of the investigation work of 1957 was concentrated on nine large taxpayers; in addition, several agents were borrowed from Caracas to go out on the streets and discover taxpayers who were not filing. These two activities in Maracaibo brought in about 1200 additional declarations, sometimes as many as 5 from one taxpayer. About one-fourth of the additional declarations arose from the investigation of persons dealing with or working for the nine large taxpayers investigated.

Field agents are not given uniform training, though they all have some accounting background. Consequently, different agents have different techniques of investigating taxpayers. Some check collateral records of banks, suppliers, purchasers, etc. Some concentrate on finding out whether employees of the taxpayer who is being investigated have filed declarations, etc. Agents in their reports recommend what fine if any should be imposed. Though the Tax Administration may impose fines of from 10% to 200% of the increase in tax, it is rare that more than 10% is imposed.

Cases are assigned to the department by means of memoranda. Declarations are not seen until asked for. Agents get the permission of the department head prior to asking for declarations for years other than the one assigned for investigation. Formerly a list of cases selected for investigation had to be sent to the head of the Income Tax Administration and the list approved before investigation could commence. At present this list appears to be a routine notification.

Agents proceed into the field on their own. Other than the reports they must make at the end of an investigation, they do not appear to be supervised on their field activities. Agents do not generally communicate the results of their findings to the taxpayer, nor do they discuss technical points with the taxpayer. The results of investigation are known to the taxpayer only when presented to him just prior to billing any additional tax.

5. *Inspector General.* The Inspector General and his staff of about 16 field agents deal only with the declarations and examination of the oil and mining companies, and also royalty holders, as respects all their income taxes. Apparently the better agents are assigned to this office in view of the importance attached to the declarations which it considers.

6. *Controller of the Nation.* A copy of every declaration, bill, paid bill, and additional assessment made as the result of investigation goes to the Examination Room of the Controller of the Nation. This Room maintains a set of taxpayer files which duplicate the files of the Income Tax Administration, except that the Room is about two years behind in its filing. A card index of taxpayers is also maintained, and each taxpayer is assigned a permanent number by the Room.

The Examination Room must also examine the records of other government agencies. It has 48 examiners. Of these, 6 are qualified to examine income tax declarations, but ordinarily only 2 of these devote full time to this work. It was stated that about 180,000 declarations were examined each year. The examiners look for errors in computation and in law. About 3 or 4 examinations a year are made at the premises of the taxpayer. About 200 objections are found each year. Objections are brought to the attention of the Income Tax Administration, which calls in the taxpayer to see if there is disagreement. In the arithmetic cases, there is no problem. In the others, if a dispute arises, the Controller brings the case to the Tax Court. The additional taxes assessed as a result of the Controller's activities amounted to about Bs.150,000 in the past year. No refunds arise from this activity, because the examiners ignore errors in favor of the Government.

The Room does not attempt to establish a duplicate payment register and does not systematically audit the payment and collection records of the Income Tax Administration. However, it does look through the delinquent account lists furnished by the Administration and calls to the attention of the Minister of Finance those overdue accounts that are very large and old.

WITHHELD TAX *(Retenciones)*

The Withheld Tax Section is at the present time largely a filing unit for the forms that must be submitted in connection with the withholding of income tax from certain payments. The great majority of forms consist of the 100,000 or so submitted for the 1% wage and salary withholding. About 8,000 of these, covering 85,000 employees, are filed each month. The information on these forms is not currently being matched against a list of declarations filed. The form filed each month is identical throughout the year, with no reconciliation at year-end. Employers are not required to furnish employees with statements of the amounts of tax withheld unless employees ask for these.

The same form used for employee withholding is used for the 2½% that must be withheld from commissions paid to real estate brokers. About 1200 of these, covering 300 brokers, are filed in a year. The 4% withholding from salaries paid to non-residents is reported on a different form, and about 2,500 of these are filed each year. About 100 motion picture distributors are required to withhold both schedular and complementary tax from payments made to foreign producers. Each company designs its own form, subject to Tax Administration approval. The forms vary widely in size and content. Withholding on certain premiums paid to foreign insurance companies is handled in a similar manner. Finally, 10% withholding is required on chance gains. There are only 6 withholding agents for this tax. They are lottery pools and the Hippodrome "5 y 6" horse race betting pool. Winnings on TV quiz programs have not yet been pursued.

In general, it does not appear that withholding tax records are seriously used to aid in the enforcement of regular income tax collections; nor does it appear that much checking is done to determine whether or not withholding agents are withholding the correct amounts of tax, or, if they are, whether all withheld taxes are paid over to the National Treasury.

CERTIFICATES OF SOLVENCY

Certificates of solvency issued by the Income Tax Administration are required of any person (with a few exceptions) who wishes to leave the country, whether permanently or temporarily, and are also required in order to dissolve corporations, enter into contracts (over Bs.10,000 in value) with any level of government, assume public office if the salary is over Bs.1,000 a month, and obtain patents, trademarks, business licenses, construction permits, etc. As respects persons leaving the country, certificates are not required from tourists and persons in transit, foreign diplomatic personnel, and minors.

To obtain the certificate that he must show for the above actions, the taxpayer must satisfy the Tax Administration that his income tax obligations have been met for all prior years and the current year. The regular taxpayer can satisfy the Tax Administration by exhibiting his copy of the paid tax bill last due from him. If the current tax bill has not been issued to him yet, he shows his copy of the declaration he filed. If a taxpayer cannot produce these documents, he generally must wait for the Tax Administration to check its records—mainly the delinquent accounts and the Information Section files. In some cases the Administration may wish to send a field agent out to examine the taxpayer's records. Persons who have not previously filed but who expect to need certificates will often file declarations for the preceding 5 years well before they apply for the certificate.

The procedure for getting a certificate involves submitting a one-page application form, presentation and checking of documents, checking files, and issuance of the certificate. The "Solvencia" section does all the work. Officials in the section have been delegated the power to sign certificates, which in proper cases may be obtained very rapidly. If a taxpayer has paid his tax for the current year (and all prior years), his certificate will be valid for the balance of the year. If his current tax is not yet paid (as where a bill has not been issued or all installments are not yet due), the certificate will be valid only for a short period such as 30 days.

The number of certificates issued annually is about 165,000. Of these about 110,000 are issued in Caracas, 22,000 in Maracaibo, and the balance in five other cities. A taxpayer may of course receive several certificates during the year. Some are also issued by the branch offices in cases where speed is necessary. In such cases, and also in some other cases, the applicant furnishes a guarantor who agrees to pay any tax obligations that the applicant is found to have had at the time the certificate is issued.

Both in Maracaibo and in Caracas it was reported that since the certificate system was firmly implanted in the 1955 revision of the law, there has been a marked increase in the number of declarations, promptness of payment, and payment of delinquent accounts.

APPEALS

After the declaration made by the taxpayer has been investigated by an agent, he is presented with a statement of findings *(acta)*. This is in writing and is made up of one or more *reparos*. A *reparo* is a statement of the agent's claim that an additional amount of tax is owing from the taxpayer. This is usually the first time that the taxpayer is aware of the claim against him and the supporting reasons. There is no procedure available under which the taxpayer can obtain administrative consideration of this statement without his first going to the Tax Court (Tribunal of Appeals). Normally, the Administration will issue a bill *(planilla)* for the additional amount of tax, and the taxpayer must, if he disputes it, appeal in 10 days to the Tax Court. The notice of appeal must be accompanied by payment of the tax or the posting of a bond. A bond is usually used, since it avoids refund delays that would exist if the taxpayer had paid his tax and then won his case. At this point, the Tax Administration has 30 days in which to reconsider the asserted claim. The task of making this reconsideration falls on the Legal Department, with the final decision being made by the Administrator General. Informally, taxpayers may attempt to talk with any of the top officials they can interest in the matter.

If the Tax Administration does not change its position, the matter proceeds through the Tax Court. This is a Court of three members appointed by the Federal Court (the Supreme Court) for a five-year term (the general judicial term in Venezuela), from a list submitted to it by the National Executive. Two members must be lawyers and one an accountant. These are full-time positions. The Court hears only income tax matters. The Court follows a procedure set forth in the law under which it receives a statement of the taxpayer's views and any Tax Administration views in addition to those in the agent's statement, and hears oral argument. It may receive the testimony of witnesses. The burden rests upon the taxpayer to show that the agent's statement is incorrect. An appeal may be taken from decisions of the Tax Court to the Federal Court, but as a prerequisite the taxpayer must pay the tax found due by the Tax Court. The Tax Court decides about 70 cases a year, and a few appeals are taken to the Federal Court.

As respects the administrative proceedings, the Inspector General, who has jurisdiction over the oil and mining companies, informally applies a different procedure. He consults frequently with the agents during their investigations and considers their statements before issuance. When an agent's statement is issued, the Inspector General grants the taxpayer involved an opportunity to discuss the statement with him and to present arguments and data in opposition to the claims asserted in the statement. The Inspector General may then make recommendations to the Administrator General regarding a modification of the statement, and if these are accepted the bill will be issued in accordance with the modified statement. The judicial steps then follow.

REFUNDS

The granting of a refund to a taxpayer (other than those refunds arising from the payment of tax pursuant to an appeal to the Tax Court) is a matter of grace rather than a matter of right. Power to grant refunds is given to the Minister of Finance and applications for refund are addressed to him. The Legal Department of the Income Tax Administration acts for the Minister's account in processing refund items. Refund items approved by the Legal Department are forwarded by the head of the Income Tax Administration to the Minister. A special budget appropriation made for refund items, including customs duties, is administered by the General Administration of the Ministry of Finance by delegation from the Minister. In the mechanics of processing a refund item, the Legal Department applies to approved items a rubber stamp which cites the delegation order from the Minister authorizing signing by the Director General of the General Administration and which stamps his name also. Thus all the Director General need do is sign.

Refund claims may arise from errors discovered by the Administration or by the taxpayer. The errors may be simple ones of arithmetic or payment of the same bill twice, or more complicated ones relating to omission of deductible sums or inclusion of non-taxable sums. In all cases the Legal Department does the processing.

If the matter is discovered by an official in the Administration, say in the course of investigation or review, the matter is checked by the Legal Department. If a refund is due, the General Administrator of the Income Tax Department sends the taxpayer a letter informing him of the facts and asking him to address a refund application to the Minister of Finance. No refund form is used. After the claim is submitted and approved, the Income Tax Administration sends the taxpayer a memorandum, which, with the approved claim, authorizes the taxpayer to get his money from an agency of the National Treasury. If the taxpayer made the original error and if he collects from the Bank of Venezuela, then the Bank charges him a commission of from 6% to 8%. If he goes to the Central Bank or if the Administration was at fault, no commission is charged to the taxpayer.

If it is the taxpayer who discovers the basis for a refund claim, the first step is application to the Minister. The remaining procedure is the same. Where there is any complication or doubt, the Legal Department will generally send out a field agent from its own department or from the Taxpayer Investigation Department.

As many as 1000 refund claims are processed by the Legal Department each year. Of these about 225 are granted. The speed with which
they are granted, and perhaps the fact of granting, may depend in part
on how the budget appropriation for refunds stands at any given
moment.

LEGAL DEPARTMENT

In addition to the processing of refunds, the Legal Department handles
a number of other items for the Minister's accounts, such as remissions
of fines, exemptions of certain credit bonds, etc. Other matters handled
by the Legal Department are: requests from taxpayers or from Administration officials for interpretations of the law, taxpayer requests to
change a fiscal year or to extend the dates for filing or payment beyond
those permitted in the law, and reconsiderations following taxpayer
appeals to the Tax Court.

On interpretation matters brought to the Legal Department, rulings
are usually issued. Rulings that deal with new subject matters are signed
by the General Administrator and are published in the Income Tax
Bulletin, currently a semi-annual publication. Rulings that cite prior
rulings as authority are signed by the head of the Technical Division
and are published if they represent a new interpretation or clarification
of an old ruling.

The staff of the Legal Department consists of the head and 6 tech-
nically trained officials. The head and his assistant are lawyers, as is
the head of the Technical Division. The others have accounting training and in-service technical training.

COST OF ADMINISTRATION

The percentage figure that indicates the cost of administering the
income tax in relation to the entire income tax revenue collected is currently estimated by the Tax Administration as 0.9%, with respect to
taxes totalling Bs.1.3 billion. However, this percentage comparison is
not very informative in view of the very large amounts of revenue
collected from the oil and mining companies. Thus, for 1957 about 75%
of the total income tax revenues of Bs.1.25 billion comes from about
twenty or so corporations with about 40% from one corporation, and
60% from the three largest corporations. Very little in the way of cost
to the Tax Administration is involved in collecting taxes from these few
taxpayers. A more realistic figure would be that relating costs of ad-

ministration to the revenue from the non-mineral area. The revenue from taxpayers other than oil or mining companies that can be estimated for the year 1958-1959 may be taken as about Bs.280 million. The budget figure for the Tax Administration in 1958-1959 is Bs.11,622,471. To this should be added the following: other Ministry of Finance activities related to the income tax, estimated at Bs.200,000 for the National Treasury and Bs.100,000 for other activities; amounts paid to the Bank of Venezuela for its services in receiving tax payments, ¾ of 1% of the collections, estimated at Bs.7,381,852 (the 1957 figure); amounts expended by the Central Bank of Venezuela in its collection work, estimated at Bs.30,000; the cost of maintaining the Tax Court, estimated at about Bs.150,000 and amounts spent by the Controller in his examination of income tax declarations and documents, estimated at Bs.300,000. There should then be subtracted the amount expended in collecting tax from the oil and mining companies, estimated at about Bs.700,000. The total costs are thus about Bs.19,084,000. The cost of administration for the non-oil and mining company sector is thus about 6.8%.

C. General Comments

Foreign observers who are privileged to have an intimate, even if brief, look at Venezuela's system for the administration of the income tax are bound to form some general impressions based on their own prior experience as well as what they have observed in Venezuela. The first impression one gets is that of a well-equipped Income Tax Administration with a nucleus of able and devoted officials. Certainly the Income Tax Administration compares favorably with at least some state tax administrations of comparable size in the United States. Comments made by persons in private life in Venezuela indicate that the Income Tax Administration operates rather more efficiently and with more integrity than do many other government agencies. There was no charge of dishonesty with respect to the functioning of the income tax system; the same statement could not be made as to certain other sections of the revenue structure.

On the other side of the ledger one might comment upon what appears to be a general lack of adequate supervision of the many functions performed in the Tax Administration. To some extent this may be due to temporary conditions in the political sphere; to a more relaxed approach to the relationships within large organizations of people; and to a shortage of persons of supervisory calibre. But to some extent it may also be due to a lack of sufficient co-ordinated attention to planning for the future, and to the need for some changes in law, organization, and technique. One has the impression of an organization with considerable esprit de corps, a recognition of the demands made upon it by the technical nature of the work and its importance, and a serious desire to do a creditable job. The maintenance of this attitude, despite obvious political handicaps in the past, is very encouraging. At the same time, the organization does reflect the lack of emphasis in recent years on specialized training and on high standards of recruitment. It is at the point where any continuation of this trend will become dangerous to the morale and functioning of the organization. Fortunately, by the same token, it is at the stage where attention to these matters and to operating procedures in general will yield significant results.

The recommendations presented hereafter are by no means all original. Many of them have already been advanced or considered by one or more Administration officials. In any event, it seems reasonable to predict that within a relatively short period of time the Income Tax Administration can become a model for other government agencies and for other countries of the world. Even more important, it can become the efficient and equitable organization that Venezuela will need to finance its national goals.

Many of the suggestions set out here are interrelated with each other and are to be viewed accordingly. As a whole, the suggestions on administration are applicable even if the structure of the income tax law is not changed. Although the administrative suggestions have been coordinated with those relating to the substantive law, it is feasible to act upon many administrative matters immediately.

Declarations and Payment

REDESIGN OF DECLARATION FORM

Revision of the declaration form is an essential first step. This will simplify the task of the taxpayer and will also facilitate the processing of the declaration form by the Administration. Taxpayers should be required to file only one copy with the Administration. (The copy now sent to the Controller will not be needed if the suggestions offered below regarding the Controller's work are adopted.) The copy retained by the taxpayer need not be stamped by the Administration except at the taxpayer's request.

Declaration forms should be redesigned with simplification and convenience in mind. If, as suggested elsewhere in this report, the schedular system is abolished, the design of the general declaration form (as well as the special form for salary and wage income only) can easily be such as to encourage and in some cases require the taxpayer himself to compute his net taxable income and to calculate the tax due. The forms will still require that the various types of income be reported separately on the form. Thus, there would be separate spaces on the form for reporting rent, interest, dividends (if made taxable as discussed in Chapter III), salaries, and sales of real and personal property. The reporting of income of individuals from business, agriculture, and oil might each be on individual slip sheets to be included only with the declaration of those taxpayers having such income. The net result of the computations on each slip sheet would be carried over to a single line of the basic declaration, so that it would be in place for the computation of net taxable income from all sources. Since apparently about 60 per cent of the declarations filed report only salary and wage income, a special short form can be designed solely for taxpayers in this category.

The corporation declarations will need to be coordinated with forms such as the present "annex" that may also have to be filed with the declaration. The declaration form and the blank spaces provided in it should be of a size to suit ordinary filing equipment and typewriters. Corporations, which will continue to be assigned permanent numbers, should be required to put their number on the face of the declaration just as individuals list their Identity Numbers. Permission could be granted to all taxpayers to omit reporting the céntimos for income and deduction items. All figures would thus be in bolívares only.

The face (the first page) of the declaration form should contain all the information that is to be transcribed for statistical purposes, e.g., gross income, net taxable income, tax due, number and type of dependency exemptions, etc. Check boxes on the face of the declaration form should require the taxpayer to indicate whether or not he has submitted a declaration for each of the past five years. This is already a requirement on the application for a solvency certificate. The taxpayer should also write in his principal and subsidiary occupations; a descriptive list of occupations could appear in the instruction sheet.

The redesign of declaration forms can largely be done by present staff, provided the qualified people can be relieved of other duties. Because of the importance of avoiding errors in the redesigning process, it will be helpful if the contemplated designs are thoroughly checked and discussed by an ad hoc forms committee that might well include two outside lawyers and accountants. As a further precaution, and perhaps as a general policy, for the first few years only enough forms should be printed to last for one year. This will permit annual reconsideration to be given to design problems without the expense or delay that would be involved if the Administration had a three-year stock of forms already on hand. Annually printed forms can also be imprinted with the year, to aid in filing of declarations.

PAYMENT

The payment process can to a considerable extent be coordinated with the process of submitting the declaration. Under present procedures, as a consequence both of the time required for liquidation and then of the further time in which payment is permitted, actual payment occurs at a date considerably later than the filing of the declaration. The result is far too great an interval between the receipt of income and the payment of the tax due on that income. It is suggested, therefore, that taxpayers with incomes of say Bs.20,000 or more be required to pay the full amount of tax, as calculated by them, at the time of filing the declaration. Or the rule might be that payment at the time of declaration would be required of all taxpayers without salary income and of all those with salary income in excess of an amount coordinated with the retention obtained under the withholding tax. Cashiers of the Central Bank or of other receiving offices of the National Treasury can be physically located in the same room where declarations are submitted. Eventually, consideration should be given to making the Income Tax Administration itself a receiving agency of the National Treasury. For some time it may be essential to authorize receiving offices in outlying districts to receive the payment as well as the declaration. The general audit of receiving agencies ought to be sufficient to prevent defalcations. The taxpayer himself will be given a receipt for his payment.

During the year of transition to the principle of payment in full with the declaration, it may be advisable to allow taxpayers owing more than a certain amount of tax to pay in two installments. If this arrangement is adopted while income tax rates are still relatively low, the transition problem should not be serious. (The adoption of a pay-as-you-go system is discussed later in this chapter.)

The mailing in of declarations together with payment by check can be encouraged to develop side by side with an anticipated increase in the use of checks generally. Correspondingly, the Administration may formulate plans for automatically mailing blank declaration forms to registered taxpayers. Meanwhile, declaration forms might be made more readily accessible in public places such as post offices.

Whether taxpayers file and pay by mail or in person, they should be provided with receipts, essential for obtaining a solvency certificate.

Instructions and Tax Table

The instructions provided to the taxpayer with the declaration forms would explain and illustrate how income is to be summarized, how deductions and exemptions are to be taken into account, and how the tax can be determined. A tax table can be provided on the instruction sheet, so that the computation of the tax by the taxpayer can be simplified.

For enforcement purposes, consideration may be given to requiring all taxpayers with over Bs.100,000 of income to submit a balance sheet of assets and liabilities with their declarations. Property would be listed at cost. Depreciation would not be taken into account except for assets also listed in an "annex" type of form for business purposes. The balance sheet would include holdings of corporate and government securities, but would exclude minor household items.

Processing of Declarations

Many changes in the processing of declarations will be brought about if the schedular system is eliminated and if a significant number of declarations are fully paid at the time of filing the declaration. No attempt will be made here to outline a complete processing guide. Consultants who are expert both in taxation and in the use of files, as well as those expert in the capabilities of mechanical equipment, might well be employed in planning new procedures. Specific steps in the procedures adopted will of course depend on the kinds of mechanical and electronic equipment utilized.

Fully-paid, part-paid, and unpaid declarations would of course be separated upon reception. A further separation would be required for those declarations where the tax was not computed by the taxpayer. These would receive first priority in processing, so that bills could be issued promptly.

In order that maximum useful information for statistical and control purposes may be placed on a single punch card for each declaration, consideration should be given to reducing the number of identifying numbers now used. Perhaps liquidation numbers could be eliminated. Whether or not the Identity Number should continue to be used for individuals as the basis of the filing system for their declarations should be reconsidered. If, because of the common-name problem, these numbers must be used, then their use must be expanded and perfected.

One change that may require an amendment to the law is that taxpayers who do not report on a calendar year basis should be required to select fiscal years that end on the last day of a month. Thus, there would be only twelve possible fiscal years that could be used for reporting purposes. This would simplify codification, payment, and punch card operations. Taxpayers who begin business on other than the first day of the month should be permitted, without prior approval, to make their first taxable year end at the end of any month not more than one year after the beginning date. Thereafter, changes in the fiscal year would require Administration approval. If a change in the taxable year results in a short taxable year (a period of less than 12 months), then the income of the short taxable year should be placed on an annual basis in the computation of the tax for that year. The net income would be multiplied by 12 and the result divided by the number of months in the short year; the tax is then that proportion of the tax on this latter net income as the number of months in the short year is of 12. Alternatively, the tax computation may be made by taking the actual income for a period of 12 months, beginning with the short year, and the tax would be that proportion of the tax which the net income for the short year bears to the net income of the 12 months. In this latter case, the tax due should in any event not be considered as less than the tax computed on the actual income of the short year. Also, the income for the portion of the 12 months falling in the succeeding taxable year after the short year would of course be used in computing the tax for that succeeding taxable year.

Codification of information as to taxpayer's occupation will be useful for statistical analyses of incomes and will aid in identifying classes of taxpayers that may need further checking.

Checks on Whether Declarations Are Filed

At the present time there is no effective system for finding out whether or not persons obligated to file declarations have done so. Such a system can be developed from information already on hand and from information that can be readily obtained. The system involves building up a list of potential taxpayers. The idea is to make not a list of all persons, but a selected list of persons likely to be obligated to declare their incomes.

The list would be country-wide in scope, and each name, address, and Identity Number would be placed on a punch card. The list would be constantly changing as a result of additions and deletions (death, leaving the country, etc.). The sources of information for compiling and adding to the list would be varied. The ingenuity of experienced tax officials can be relied upon to select profitable information leads, e.g., lists of professional men licensed to practice law, medicine, dentistry, engineering, etc., lists of persons belonging to associations and clubs, lists of those who have business licenses, etc. Much of the information now coming to the Information Section may be usefully checked against this master list of potential taxpayers. The master list is of course of limited use if it is not kept up to date by constantly feeding information into it and adding and removing names.

Periodically, once or twice a year, this list should be run against the punch cards for declarations already filed. Those on the list who have not filed must be contacted. The punch cards themselves can be used automatically to print a self-mailing notice to the potential taxpayer requiring him to file or explain why he need not file.

Similarly, this year's taxpayer list could be run against the prior year's list and perhaps also the list of the year before that.

Intelligent preparation of a master list plus effective follow-up action should make it unnecessary for many field agents to spend their time "walking the streets" to check businesses to see if they filed declarations or to concentrate in their investigations of big companies on ascertaining whether those dealing with the companies had filed declarations. Occasional spot checking by the agents would be sufficient. Moreover, the system might sow the seeds for its own eventual elimination or at least reduction to a spot check system.

Liquidation, Billing and Payment

The liquidation function as now performed would be significantly altered as a result of the elimination of the schedular taxes and the requirement that the larger taxpayers themselves compute the tax due and pay the tax when they file their declarations. Those declarations that were accompanied by payment would be sent at once to the Taxpayer Investigation Department for the selection and examination process described later.

The function of what is now the Liquidation Department would be to check and prepare for machine computation and billing those declarations that were not accompanied by full payment of the tax as computed by the taxpayer. These declarations would for the most part be simple ones, often, if not always, on the new short salary form. The only item requiring checking would ordinarily be claims for dependency exemptions. Clerical help can be trained to do this work. Experienced liquidators would become a part of the office examination staff of the Taxpayer Investigation Department and would devote their time only to the more important declarations.

All this work of processing declarations unaccompanied by payment would be done by a declarations processing section (this could be called liquidation) in the Administrative Division. Computation of the tax and issuance of bills would be done by machine. These machine operations, especially the punching of cards (generally a bottleneck in the process), would be considerably simplified by the elimination of the separate rate structure of the schedular system. There appears to be no need to check the machine-prepared bills prior to mailing them out, and the requirement for signing the bills should be completely eliminated. The necessary safeguards can be built into the design of the procedure and effective, continual supervision of it. In fact, there is no reason why the bills should not be systematically fed from the printing machine to a machine which places them in envelopes ready for mailing. The bill itself might well be a printed punch card. In the rare case of arithmetical error, the taxpayer would have 10 days to return his bill for correction.

The taxpayer would get only the one copy of the bill, which would be so perforated that a part of it could be torn off at the time of payment to serve as his receipt. The receipt portion would be validated by a special sealed numbering machine, to prevent unauthorized validation of receipts. The importance of this will appear in connection with the solvency certificate procedure.

Taxpayers receiving bills, i.e., those not required to pay on submission of their declarations, would be required to pay in full within 10 days. The present colored card requiring the taxpayer to acknowledge receipt of the bill can probably be eliminated in favor of a rapid follow-up system for bills remaining unpaid for more than 15 days after the due date (10 days plus mailing time).

Payment and validation of receipts can be made through the present receiving offices of the National Treasury. The provision of special equipment for this purpose should be the responsibility of the Administration. Special provision for the issuance of hand-prepared numbered receipts may have to be made for the smaller outlying receiving offices.

Preparation of the unpaid declarations for billing should be able to be done rapidly enough to eliminate entirely the need for the preliminary punching operation now performed (Step 4 of the description given in Chapter V).

Collection of Delinquent Accounts

The problem of delinquent accounts would be greatly reduced by an improved withholding system and by the requirement for payment in full with the declaration or payment within 10 days for those who are billed. Nevertheless, there will always be some taxpayers who do not pay their bills.

The first essential in the collection of these accounts is that a given taxpayer's total account should be available upon a moment's notice. A corollary of this is that notices demanding payment should be sent to the taxpayer within 15 to 30 days after the due date. Various systems can be used to accomplish these ends. One is for the machines to print monthly an alphabetical list of cumulative amounts due. This list would be kept up to date by daily entries of payments received. If the delinquent account problem became of sufficient magnitude, automatic bookkeeping and posting equipment might be profitably used. If the delinquency problem is greatly reduced, it may well pay to maintain individual delinquent account cards by hand with a daily posting to them and with a filing system that automatically "ages" the cards each day, so that appropriate collection steps are flagged and taken promptly.

When the typing for the first demand notice is done, it may well be sensible to type first, second, and third notices simultaneously. Each would be a different color and contain appropriately different wording. The second and third notices would automatically be sent to the taxpayer unless payment was made.

Interest on overdue accounts could be handled by adding it to the demand notice, using 30 days after the date of the notice for purposes of calculation. If the bill were paid within the 30-day period the interest stated would still have to be paid; the interest for the extra days would simply be an additional penalty for delinquency. Some thought might also be given to printing an interest table which shows the amount due for a variety of round sums for a variety of fixed periods. The period and the sum closest to those on the bill would automatically show the amount of interest due. This table could be printed on the back of the demand notice or could accompany it. All receiving offices would be asked to collect interest in addition to the amount shown on the notice if payment were made after the interest date used in the notice.

The paperwork problems connected with delinquent accounts can certainly be worked out without great difficulty. The larger problem is that of actually collecting the money from those who ignore all three notices. The more effectively this problem is pursued, the simpler the paperwork problems are likely to become, because taxpayers will not delay so much when they know the Administration is determined to collect promptly.

It is proposed, first of all, that the Delinquent Accounts Section be given a small group of men whose function, for which they would be specially trained, would be to make collections by visiting the delinquent taxpayers. These men would also determine whether the taxpayer had the capacity to pay and, in appropriate cases, could recommend installment payments. Only after such visits were unsuccessful should it be necessary to resort to legal measures. Secondly, it is proposed that the Administration utilize its powers to garnishee the wages or other payments being made to delinquent taxpayers. Another power that should be utilized is that of attaching liens against property owned by the taxpayer, so that he may not sell or mortgage it without first paying his overdue tax bills with interest. (Apparently, these powers exist, but are not utilized. If such powers do not exist, they should be granted to the Tax Administration.) Initially, if it seemed necessary, the exercise of these powers might require some sort of judicial approval. But, to the extent that judicial approval is required, the judges should recognize the importance to the nation of having its taxes collected effectively. They therefore should act promptly in handling these matters and in assisting the Tax Administration in collecting its delinquent accounts.

Thirdly, some consideration should be given to the gradual ending of the system of turning over large overdue accounts to private lawyers on a commission basis. Smaller accounts are not being enforced for collection at all under the present system. On larger accounts where the taxpayer has the money, it hardly seems necessary to pay commissions. To the extent that legal action is necessary, the Tax Administration should develop its own legal personnel.

Investigation through Information

The function of the information gathering and processing system developed below is to check the veracity of declarations that are filed. Some of the information would, as already mentioned, be used in the maintenance of a master list of potential taxpayers. The same information may well be used again in connection with checking declarations once filed.

The problems involved in developing and using an information system as a tool for office investigation of declarations are to gather useful information and to bring that information together with the declarations at some point.

The gathering system should attempt to bring in as much useful information as possible without bringing in too much useless information.

To this end the supplier of information, e.g., banks supplying interest information, should in the first instance not be required to report small amounts. The dividing line between reported and non-reported information may be changed from time to time either on the basis of experience or of prevention of tax evasion practices. Types of information to be gathered include: sales of real estate, salaries, dividends (if made taxable), interest, sales of shares and other securities, etc. Real estate sales and salaries should probably all be reported, while other items would require reporting only above a minimum prescribed amount.

A rather general scheme for requiring information returns on prescribed forms may also be introduced. The requirement might be that an information slip or return be submitted by business concerns for each person to whom more than Bs.2,000 is paid during the calendar year. Each slip would include name, address and Identity Number of the recipient, and total payments for the year. For most business concerns that would be affected, this information can be readily prepared from the regular books of account, once a year.

Larger business concerns filing information returns and larger government offices furnishing information may be induced to furnish as much as possible of the information on standard punch cards when the Administration's information processing system is able profitably to handle punch card information. In the future it may be feasible to work out a system for putting all information on punch cards, so that machine matching of information and declarations may be accomplished. At the present time it does not appear that punch cards for the information returns will serve any purpose other than to put the cards in either alphabetical or Identity Number order. This operation may be worth doing by machine. If all suppliers of information were furnished with cards of a size that could be machine processed, the key punch operation might consist only of the punching of the Identity Number in the card, where this had not already been done by the supplier of the information. This operation could be done with the most simple types of punching devices.

Whether or not all or some of the information is on punch cards, it is essential that a well-maintained filing system be provided at least for the information returns reporting the larger payments. If it can be worked out, even though hand labor is required, it would seem useful to get the information into the taxpayer's individual file. It may be worth redesigning the files containing taxpayer declarations, so that information cards or slips can be readily inserted.

The aim of the recommendation above is to promote the regular processing of information as it flows into the office, rather than to bring the information files into use primarily only when solvency certificates are applied for, which is the aim of the system now in force. Thus, information coming in would be filed with the declarations. Where the individual has filed no declaration, the information perhaps ought still to be in the declarations file, but in a folder of a different color to signify that for this individual there is no declaration in the folder.

The clerks who file the information would not ordinarily also have the task of comparing the information with the declarations. That work should be separately and systematically organized so that each declaration file is examined by a qualified person at least once in three years or, if feasible, once each year. It is important that there be coordination between the processing of information and the audit work described below.

Investigation through Office Examination and Field Audit

The proposed organization chart (Chart VI-1) that appears later in this chapter establishes at a high level the position of the "Inspector Nacional de Fiscalización." He would be the head of a new Examination and Audit Division, which would be on a par with the Administrative and Technical Divisions. It is apparent from this proposal that we recommend a thorough reorganization and strengthening of the functions of examination of declarations in the tax office and of audit of taxpayer records in the field. It is clear that at least the field audit function is now largely performed in an inadequate, haphazard fashion. This shortcoming is due partly to the manner in which taxpayers are selected for field audit, partly to the lack of a large enough staff of trained field agents, and partly to an inadequate system of supervision.

SELECTION OF DECLARATIONS ABOVE BS.100,000

It may be supposed that during the processing of declarations they can be separated into those showing net incomes above and below, say, Bs.100,000. (This sorting process will be simplified if, on the face of the return, there is a particular line showing total net income. Clerks will then be able to sort very rapidly when the declarations first come into the office.) All declarations above Bs.100,000 (a figure that probably should be changed from time to time) should be screened by the most experienced field agents. Also, all corporation declarations, and declarations under Bs.100,000 showing business income, should be screened by these agents. Their function at this point is to select declarations that appear to require either an office examination or a field audit. These agents are the ones most likely to develop the best criteria for selection. Moreover, their rapid glance at the declaration may give them enough information to enable them to attach to a selected declaration a list of the specific points to be looked into. This work will be helped by the use of a checklist form for the selectors. The agents assigned to this activity should be among the most experienced and capable in the Administration. Their task is highly important since an intelligent selection at this point will set the stage for an effective field audit system.

Some declarations will automatically be selected for field audit every year, e.g., those with net incomes over Bs.500,000. Some, e.g., those over Bs.200,000, may be selected once every three years. Returns with gross incomes over a certain figure should also be selected.

SELECTION OF DECLARATIONS UNDER BS.100,000

Declarations in this group could be screened for selection by the persons who are now the better and experienced liquidators. It is to be expected that most of the declarations selected by them would be for office examination, though some would be selected for field audit. Criteria for selection would have to be developed over time.

RANDOM SELECTION

A limited amount of random selection ought to be done every year in order to secure a desirable compliance effect. General knowledge among taxpayers that any one of their declarations may be selected for examination or audit will prevent at least some of them from relying merely on a declaration that looks good. Another and important reason for random selection on a fairly large scale once every few years is to analyze statistically the degree of compliance of various taxpayer groups. Of course, careful coding of the taxpayers selected will be needed, and also of the results of each audit. A study of the results of such a program should provide valuable guides as to selection criteria and as to the need for special enforcement devices among some groups of taxpayers. It will also suggest ways to improve the declaration forms and the instructions to taxpayers to prevent errors by taxpayers.

OFFICE EXAMINATION

An office examination would be somewhat similar to what liquidators now do when they make changes in a declaration. Office examiners would carefully check the declarations assigned to them. Frequently, if not always, the selector would have attached a slip on which he specified the points to be checked. Specifically, the office examiner might be directed to compare the declaration with those for prior years. Even where not so directed, examiners should be permitted so to compare if they consider it advisable. After examination of the declaration and other information, the examiner should be permitted to correspond with the taxpayer and, if convenient and useful, to ask him to come to the office with some or all of his records. Ordinarily, office examiners would be dealing with taxpayers on questions relating to their dependents, or other problems not concerning business, or concerning only small business. Report forms would be prepared for each examination stating the errors found, changes made, and whether or not the taxpayer agreed. The examiner would discuss his findings with the taxpayer or would write to him. The great majority of office examination cases are likely to end in an agreement signed by the taxpayer. Care should also be taken in the examination process to inform the taxpayer of any errors found to be in his favor.

Personnel of the office examination section would be largely those persons now doing liquidation work. They would be divided into groups of from 10 to 15, each group having a chief who would control the flow of work and be available for consultation with the examiners in his group.

FIELD AUDIT

The field audit section would have one group of field agents who would specialize in the audit of oil companies. The other groups might each cover the whole range of non-oil audit work. The present segregation of the field agents of the oil group in a completely distinct unit makes it impossible for the general field audit section to benefit from the training and experience of those oil-company examiners. While the continued assignment of specially skilled agents to this work is appropriate, placing this group in the Audit Division should tend to raise the general level of performance. It may be desirable to have one or two groups that specialize in the audit of taxpayers outside of Caracas.

Some of these men would live in the areas where they work; others would be based in Caracas and Maracaibo and travel to the interior regularly.

At the present time additional, better-trained men need to be added for field audit work. Existing staff might well be provided with further training, such as for example, a series of conferences in which experienced agents would describe how they conduct an audit. Practicing outside accountants and teachers of accounting might also be used. Consideration might also be given to the short-term hiring of experienced Spanish-speaking agents from other countries having well developed field audit practices. In any event, field agents must learn what to look for and where to find it in the taxpayer's records without wasting time. They must learn when it is worthwhile to check banks and others who deal with the taxpayer.

Group supervisors, each in charge of a group of 10 to 15 agents, would be responsible for assigning cases to their field agents. They would see to it that most of a field agent's time was spent in taxpayers' offices. This can in part be supervised by knowing where the agent is supposed to be and by once in a while checking by phone or otherwise.

Agents would discuss their cases both with their group supervisor and with the taxpayer in order to seek agreement on as many items as possible. To prevent possible collusion between the taxpayer and the agent a system of post-audit review of cases should be instituted. This would be somewhat like the work now done by the Review Department *(Revisión Fiscal)*. One important difference is that review work would be done *after* agreement was reached with the taxpayer and an additional tax had been imposed. Sufficient control can still be maintained in this fashion because of the knowledge that review will take place and because flagrant cases could, if necessary, be reopened.

OVER-ALL SCHEDULING OF WORK

Examination and audit work must be kept current. One of the purposes of the selection system is to assure that the number of declarations selected each year is approximately the number that can be handled effectively during the year. It is the responsibility of the head of the Examination and Audit Division to see that selection work is coordinated with the audit capacity of the division. Naturally, there will be some selected declarations that have not been audited by the end of the year. These should be re-examined and only the most important ones kept for audit. These will be considered part of the following year's selection and will be taken into account in deciding how many more to select for that year. When a taxpayer is to be examined for a particular year, the agent should at the same time usually check the declarations of the taxpayer for several years past if they have not previously been examined.

SPECIAL INVESTIGATIONS

At the present time there are no agents who specialize in the handling of cases involving fraudulent reporting, that is, deliberate falsification of the declaration or of records. Work of this type is highly specialized and requires people who are not only good accountants, but also detectives. It is time that the Administration began to devote some of its efforts to this type of case. If a few cases a year were developed and maximum fines imposed, together with some publicity, the compliance effect and deterrent effect would be substantial.

Several persons might be assigned to this work. The cases they would study would probably have arisen as a result of a field agent's audit. The field agent would report the evidence giving rise to his suspicion of fraud, and the special investigator would take over the case. Techniques of special investigation might have to be studied in other countries, though Venezuela might well develop its own, if a few able men are assigned to this work and do some experimenting.

Certificates of Solvency—Expansion of the System

The purpose of the present solvency certificate system is to get taxpayers to submit their declarations and pay their bills. The reason why the system is necessary in Venezuela, as in several other countries, is that no other effective sanction exists in the income tax law. Sanctions that might theoretically exist in general penal laws are not applied to income tax cases. Moreover, the tax laws themselves do not carry criminal sanctions. The sanction that the solvency system imposes is that of preventing the taxpayer from doing something he wants to do, such as enter into a contract with a governmental agency, obtain a license to operate a business, get permission to travel abroad or to reside abroad. The taxpayer is prevented from doing what he wants to do unless he can show a valid solvency certificate. In effect, for example, all the sanctions used to prevent people from operating a business without a license, etc., are indirectly incorporated into the income tax law through the solvency system. It seems that this type of sanction is quite acceptable to Venezuelan social and political philosophy, while direct sanctions, such as jail sentences for tax violations, are not acceptable. We recognize these views and therefore recommend that ways be found to make the solvency system more effective in its results and simpler in its operation.

Perhaps the guiding principle in the design of a solvency system is that it should as nearly as possible require certificates of only those persons who are obligated to declare their income and to pay tax. One refinement is that, if possible, certificates ought not to be required of persons whose income tax is fully paid through a withholding system. Of course, it is not possible to design a system that will impinge only upon persons required to pay taxes, since they cannot all be identified in advance. Therefore, the system must seek to single out those groups in the community that are likely to consist predominantly of taxpayers. The chief characteristic of such a group is that its members are engaged in economic activities likely to produce more than the exempt amount of income. Businessmen of almost all kinds constitute a likely group. So too do purchasers of homes above a certain price. Buyers of expensive cars may constitute such a group, whereas all buyers of cars would be too broad a group. Members of the legal, medical, engineering, and accounting professions are likely groups. A careful student of Venezuela's economy should be able to single out a number of groups each of which is likely to consist predominantly of taxpayers. There is no particular need for each group to consist of persons mutually exclusive of persons in any other group. If a person is in more than one group, he merely has to show his certificate more than once.

It is one thing to choose the groups, but it is quite another to find an annual (or more frequent) occasion when each member of each group must show his certificate under penalty of no longer being permitted to function in the group. The present law has seized upon already existing occasions for certain groups—the time of leaving the country, the act of getting business licenses, patents and trademarks, etc. To the extent that already existing occasions can be found for groups selected as above suggested, they are of course the easiest to use. But for some groups, e.g., lawyers, it may be difficult to find an annual occasion or act that involves all lawyers, so that each will be asked to show his certificate at least once a year. A suit in court would seem to be the logical occasion for lawyers, but by no means all lawyers go to court once each year. Probably almost all lawyers have some dealings on behalf of their clients with one or more government agencies each year. Would it be too burdensome to ask a lawyer to show his certificate every time he deals with a government official? An alternative would be to create an artificial occasion, that is, one not now existing. Such an occasion would arise if lawyers were required to renew annually their licenses to practice law. It may be left to a representative group of lawyers to find an already existing occasion or to create an occasion for this purpose. A similar procedure should be followed for other professions and groups where needed.

There are further questions that need to be dealt with in the design of a certificate system: How often should a certificate be issued and for how long should it be valid? In what form should it be issued? Should it be issued automatically as part of the process of receipting for payment, or should it be issued only upon specific application? How handle the problem of issuing certificates to persons who need them but are not taxable? Should one form of certificate be valid for all occasions when a certificate must be shown? Still further questions are likely to arise in practice.

Our tentative thinking as to a system that would answer many of these questions is that the tax receipt itself should serve as the basic certificate of solvency. The receipt might be issued to different taxpayers in slightly different forms, if certificates were issued by machine in some payment-receiving offices and by hand in others. But these differences ought to cause no problem. Certificates could be valid for a period of 18 months from the last day of the taxpayer's taxable year. This date would have to appear on the receipt. The 18-month validity period would provide sufficient leeway or margin for those taxpayers who filed declarations at the end of the 2-month period after their taxable year and who were not billed until one month or so later.

If a person not liable for tax needed a certificate, he would have to submit an application certifying that he was not liable for tax and owed no unpaid bills. The application could require relevant data pertinent to demonstrating this status. The application would have to be co-signed by a guarantor. Such an application could be submitted to any receiving office for national funds, and the office should issue the certificate immediately as long as the guarantor was reasonably known to be reliable. The application would thereafter be checked against the Administration's files. If necessary, the Administration would immediately proceed against the guarantor for any tax due, plus a substantial penalty, e.g., Bs.1,000, for the false application. If a person could not obtain a guarantor, he would have to wait until his application were checked. Prompt handling would have to be given these latter applications.

For persons leaving the country a special validation stamp for this purpose would have to appear on the certificate. Those leaving temporarily would be permitted to offer a guarantor as a substitute for filing and paying, since presumably their taxable years would not yet have closed. Those leaving permanently would be required to file a declaration and pay the tax due before receiving the validation stamp. In this latter situation, present procedures for ascertaining whether such persons have received taxable income prior to their departure should be strengthened. Thus, persons having *transeunte* visas should be required to appear in person for their certificates. Care should be taken by consuls abroad that tourist visas (for which a solvency certificate is not required) are not issued to persons intending to engage in business activities. Perhaps tourist visas could initially be issued for a limited period only, say two weeks, renewable in person in Venezuela by the tourist if he stays longer and shows he is only present as a tourist.

Similarly, the certificate of a corporation that is about to dissolve would have to be especially validated for this dissolution purpose in order to assure that the final tax due had been paid. Also, the administrator of a decedent's estate should be required to obtain a certificate as respects the decedent's income taxes, and this certificate would likewise have to be specially validated.

Taxpayers would get their receipts by paying in person at any receiving office or would get them by registered mail if they paid by mail. Tight control would have to be maintained over the receiving offices, so that no receipt serving as a certificate could be issued without either an application or a payment. The application or the bill, as the case might be, would have the same number as the certificate. It would be a relatively simple matter to audit the numbers so that all of them would be accounted for.

Two problems come to mind that have not been dealt with above and that are to some extent taken care of by the existing solvency system. What about the taxpayer who has an old unpaid bill, say for a year in which he did not need a certificate, and what about the taxpayer who leaves unpaid a bill for an additional amount of tax that resulted from audit? These persons would have obtained, under the procedure described above, one of the automatically issued receipt-type certificates, especially if they had paid their tax at the time of filing a declaration. They might have been detected had they been billed, in which case the bill would include unpaid taxes. But suppose they were not detected. One way to approach the problem, though not a complete solution, is to require taxpayers to certify on their declarations that they have no unpaid tax bills. If they report the bills, then of course no certificate-type receipt is issued until all are paid. If they certify falsely, a substantial non-discretionary penalty could be imposed. The fact that these two types of cases are not dealt with by an effective solvency sanction does not destroy the usefulness of the system, but merely proves what was known from the beginning, that it is not possible to design a perfect solvency system. The problems respecting unpaid bills for prior years will considerably lessen in importance when the Tax Administration institutes the procedures earlier described for collecting delinquent accounts and when the present backlog of delinquent accounts is significantly reduced. These steps would thus facilitate the transition to the certificate system above suggested.

Where a taxpayer has properly declared his income but is financially unable to pay the tax, procedures should be devised under which a solvency certificate could be granted if the taxpayer needed one. Before granting the certificate, the Tax Administration would have to be satisfied as to the taxpayer's financial condition and suitable arrangements made regarding the ultimate payment of the tax, such as in installments, consistent with the taxpayer's financial condition.

An effective solvency system will only insure the filing of declarations and the payment of the tax based on the information contained in the declaration. It does not insure that the information contained in the declaration is correct. Hence, it is still necessary, even under an effective solvency system, for declarations to be carefully audited in accordance with the procedure previously described.

Withholding of Tax

At the present time, withholding of tax at the source on salaries and wages is used only for the 1% tax under schedule 7. The withholding is on a monthly basis.

It is suggested that withholding of tax on wages and salaries be made into a more effective collection device for a larger portion of the tax on employment income. This is difficult to do under the present schedular tax and complementary tax in view of their differing exemptions. However, more effective collection through withholding would be possible under the unitary tax recommended in Chapter III above. The personal exemptions under that tax would be on an annual basis.

Consequently, for withholding purposes these exemptions would be pro-rated on a daily, weekly or monthly basis, according to the method by which a particular employer pays his employees. The employee would have to notify the employer of his family status and the number of exemptions to which he was entitled. The employer would consult tables furnished by the Tax Administration which would indicate the amount of tax to be withheld. The tables would take account of the rate of tax, the pro-rated exemptions for the various family statuses, and an earned income credit if one were granted under the tax law.

No adjustment would be made from payroll period to payroll period to keep the withheld tax in accordance with the exact tax liability to date of the employee. Thus, if an employee did not work during one month, the pro-rated monthly exemption not utilized in that month would not be added to that for another month. Instead, discrepancies between withheld tax and actual tax liability for the full year would be adjusted by the Tax Administration on the basis of an annual declaration filed by the employee. The adjustment would be made by a refund to the taxpayer or by additional payment by the taxpayer.

This withholding should be designed to cover the tax liabilities of by far the larger number of lower-wage and lower-salary employees who are subject to tax. This can be accomplished by fixing the withholding rates to collect tax through the first two brackets of income, or through only the first bracket if that bracket is sufficiently wide. These rates would be built into the withholding tables discussed above. The year-end adjustments would take care of any discrepancies resulting from variations in the levels of a taxpayer's wages or salary throughout the year.

The employer would be required to furnish each employee at the end of the year (or earlier termination of employment) with two copies of a statement showing the amount of compensation paid, the exemptions claimed, and the tax withheld. The employee would attach one copy to his tax declaration. The employer would also send a copy to the Tax Administration. The employer would be required to pay, monthly, any amounts collected and also to make quarterly returns showing the total number of employees involved, wages paid, and amounts withheld. If thought desirable, especially in situations where the employer's payroll period was on a weekly basis, the payment of withheld amounts might be required twice monthly so that funds would be held no more than 15 days. Only an annual return would be required if the employer had posted a compliance bond. The employer would not be required to list each employee on these returns, since this function would be served by the Administration copies of the withholding statement given each employee at the end of the year.

As discussed earlier, a simple distinct type of declaration should be devised to be used by taxpayers having only wage or salary income. It is possible that the withholding statement given to the employee by the employer could be so arranged as itself to constitute a declaration form to be used by the employee. The employee would only have to add to this statement the names of his dependents and perhaps another item or two of information, and send it in as his declaration. A special summary form might be needed for employees having more than one employer; or perhaps the statement form could be worded to meet this situation without complicating it.

This withholding system would result in refunds' being due to a number of taxpayers. This situation does not exist today under the limited and monthly withholding utilized. It would be imperative that the Tax Administration send these refunds to taxpayers as promptly as possible. This matter is discussed below under refund procedure.

The procedure of withholding tax has application to other items in addition to wages and salaries. At present withholding is used for commissions paid to real estate brokers, at the rate of 2½% under schedule 3. This withholding should be continued but at rates similar to those to be used under withholding for wages and salaries. Withholding is also applied at a 10% rate to betting pools and to other fortuitous gains or chance winnings. In Chapter III it is suggested that this withholding continue as, in effect, a special tax on these chance winnings. In addition, the amount of chance winnings actually received by a person should be included in his taxable income, as suggested in Chapter III. It may be desirable to institute withholding (in addition to the 10% withholding) on such amounts, at rates in accordance with the progressive income tax rate schedule as applied to the amount of winnings received by the person, in order to insure collection of the income tax on those winnings. The application of withholding to non-residents is discussed in Chapter III.

It would be desirable to work toward the withholding of tax on interest, and also on dividends if these are made taxable as discussed in Chapter III.

Pay-as-you-go System

As a consequence of an effective withholding system, most employees would be current in their income tax payments and would have little or no tax liability at the end of the year. Meanwhile, individuals with other sources of income, employees with higher salaries, and corporations would not have paid their tax liabilities until at least March of the following year. It is desirable that these taxpayers should also be on a reasonably current basis. This could be accomplished through (a) a declaration of estimated tax that will be due on the current year's estimated income, this declaration to be filed early in the current year, and (b) installment payments of this estimated tax during the current year. The estimated tax could, if necessary, be based on the preceding year's income. Final adjustment would be made when the usual declaration was filed in March (assuming a calendar year taxpayer) of the succeeding year. The current payment of estimated tax on the current year's income would in effect correspond to the withholding of tax on salaries and wages. Any excess of the payment of estimated tax over the final tax due could be refunded or could be applied as a credit against the first installment of estimated tax for the succeeding year. Individuals could be required to file the declaration of estimated tax in March along with the final declaration for the preceding year. One installment of the estimated tax could be paid at that time and other installments paid in June, September and December (or January of the next year). As respects corporations, either the above procedure could be followed, or instead only a modified pay-as-you-go system adopted. Under this modified system, a corporation would file a declaration of estimated tax in September (assuming a calendar year corporation), and pay one-quarter of the estimated tax at that time and another one-quarter in December. The payment of the balance of the tax due could be made when the final declaration is filed in March of the succeeding year, at which time the payment would of course be based on the final figures for the year. The corporation could be required either to pay this entire balance at that time, or perhaps to pay it in two installments, one in March and one in June. This latter approach would result in effect in four installments for corporations, as for individuals, but with a corporation's payments commencing six months later than an individual's payments.

It may not be feasible to attempt such an estimated tax system immediately. However, if income tax rates rise, it would certainly be desirable to adopt that system, both to provide equity among taxpayers (the withheld taxpayers would then basically pay no sooner than other taxpayers) and to prevent taxpayers whose income may decline, or who do not budget carefully, from incurring a burdensome debt to the Government through their failure to save for tax payments. The transition to an estimated tax system can most readily be made when tax rates are still relatively low.

Appeals by Taxpayers

Several changes are advisable in the present system, with respect to appeals by taxpayers.

ADMINISTRATIVE CONSIDERATION

As described earlier, a taxpayer usually does not know the details of any claim asserted against him as the result of an investigation until he is presented with the agent's statement *(acta)*. Thereafter, if he contests the assertion, he must first appeal to the Tax Court (Tribunal of Appeals), and at that point he can obtain from the Tax Administration reconsideration of the claim within the thirty-day period allowed for that action. It is clear that this is not a satisfactory procedure. No tax administration can always be right, especially when it acts without hearing the taxpayer's arguments and facts. The present system inevitably results in the assertion of a number of claims not well founded because the taxpayer's views have not been obtained. Also, if the taxpayer agrees with some of the claims but not with others, he must appeal as to all, since they are contained in one statement. Consequently, payment is generally postponed on the agreed claims, since a bond is posted for the entire statement. A bond is commonly used, as it avoids refund delays if the taxpayer succeeds in winning his case. In fact, as we have seen in Chapter V, in order to overcome these disadvantages of the present system, the Inspector General does follow informally, for oil and mining companies, a procedure that permits discussion by the taxpayer of the issues, before the bill for additional amounts of tax *(planilla)* is finally issued. The experience under this informal procedure indicates the desirability of instituting a regular and orderly procedure for administrative appeals.

Accordingly, it is suggested that once a statement is issued, the taxpayer be permitted to discuss the statement before the final bill is issued. A special group of experienced personnel, legal and technical, should be established for this purpose. The proceedings should be informal and of the conference type. The taxpayer should be required to file a protest in writing, summarizing his arguments and any factual data he desires to present. This protest would then be the subject of one or more conferences. The field agent familiar with the case could be permitted to attend. But he, and the other officials, would have to recognize that the purpose of the procedure is not to defend his statement but to achieve the correct result in the light of all of the information available. There would be no time limit fixed for the decision. This group should be located in the Technical Division, so that the persons hearing the taxpayer's views would not previously have passed on the issues. For this reason, the group should not be located in the Audit Division. The final decision on the taxpayer's appeal could be made by the head of the Technical Division on recommendation of the head of the appeals group. The most important cases would then be submitted to the Administrator General. Perhaps the less important uses could be determined finally by the head of the appeals group without further consideration by the head of the Technical Division.

An Interministerial Committee has been established by the Ministry of Finance and the Ministry of Mines and Hydrocarbons to determine price issues in the oil area. This committee should continue to have jurisdiction over this matter because of its technical experience.

JUDICIAL CONSIDERATION

After the Tax Administration has considered the taxpayer's protest, the taxpayer, if unsuccessful, should then be allowed to litigate his case before the Tax Court (Tribunal of Appeals) as under present law. He should, as today, be required to pay the tax or post a bond. The thirty-day period now permitted for administrative reconsideration would not be needed in view of the appeal procedure afforded prior to issuance of the final bill for additional tax. However, if at any time the lawyers defending the case for the Tax Administration before the Court concluded that the Administration was in error, they should so advise the Court and thereby permit the matter to be concluded.

No major changes are here suggested in the judicial procedure before the Court, since it appears to be working satisfactorily. Since the Tribunal is a court and since the issues before it are legal issues, turning essentially on the interpretation of the statute and regulations and the application of prior jurisprudence, it is desirable that all three members of the Tribunal be lawyers. Further, as the investigative activity of the Tax Administration increases, it is likely that more cases will come before the Court. The Court should therefore constantly be considering the number of cases on its docket and the length of time it takes to decide a case, so that decisions may not be delayed because of the volume of cases. At some point it may be necessary to increase the number of members or to have them sit in panels of less than three.

At the present time the Court does not publish its decisions in any regular form. Mimeographed copies of the decisions are available at the Court's office. A few important decisions, as so viewed by the Tax Administration, are published in its Bulletin, which is currently issued twice a year. The latest collection of tax jurisprudence was published in 1955 and contains summaries of decisions prior to 1954. There is really no effective way for a lawyer to know what decisions have been rendered by the Court and whether he has all of its opinions. The Court should therefore arrange, itself or through the Tax Administration, to have all of its decisions published regularly in permanent form.

Refunds

The procedure for handling taxpayer refund claims can largely parallel that applicable to audits in general. A form should be provided for such refund claims. They should be submitted, for statistical and record purposes, to the Administrative Division. Thereafter, the refund claim should be submitted to the Audit Division for consideration on the merits. This division, if it decides favorably, should settle the matter, subject only to review by the Technical Division if the claim exceeds a certain amount, and to a final review of the largest claims by the Minister or Administrator General. If the claim is denied, the taxpayer should be permitted to protest the decision to the Technical Division, as in the case of audit statements. Thereafter, he should be allowed to litigate the matter in the Tax Court (Tribunal of Appeals). In order to prevent undue delay in the consideration of refund claims, the taxpayer should be permitted to bring his action in the Tax Court within one year after the refund claim was filed if no administrative decision has been made within that time. However, he would not be required to do so, but could instead await further administrative developments.

If the withholding system on wages and salaries develops as suggested above, a number of cases of overwithholding will result, and refunds will be due at the end of the year. The employee's copy of the withholding statement, submitted by the employee as a declaration, could readily be made to serve automatically as a refund claim. That is, the statement from the employer, given to the employee, would be sent by the employee to the Tax Administration, and it would show whether tax had been underwithheld or overwithheld. In the latter event the statement (declaration) would constitute a refund claim. Refunds of this character would be handled by the Collection Office and usually paid without further inquiry so that there would be as little delay as possible. Only refunds above a certain amount should involve office scrutiny of the declaration to see whether the declaration should be investigated before the refund was paid. The other refunds would require nothing but checking for arithmetical or other obvious errors appearing on the face of the form. Although interest should be paid on refunds generally, no interest should be paid on these withholding tax refunds if the refund were made within 45 or 60 days from the date the declaration was filed. Interest would run from the later date.

Since all refunds properly due the taxpayer are a just debt owing to him, their payment should not depend on a budget appropriation's being available at the time of refund. This budget aspect should be worked out so that as soon as the refund is ascertained it can be promptly paid.

Interest today is not paid on refunds. Consideration should be given to the payment of interest on refunds, perhaps at a rate of ¼% to ½% per month, from the time the tax refunded had been paid by the taxpayer (or from the date above described in the case of withheld tax refunds).

Penalties

The present penalties, speaking generally, are as follows: a late declaration involves a fine of Bs.25 plus, if a tax is due, an amount ranging from 10% to 100% of the tax, at the discretion of the Administration. If the tax based on the declaration is increased on audit by more than 10% of that amount, a fine may be imposed ranging from 10% to 200% of the increase in the amount of tax, again at the Administration's discretion. This latter fine is not applicable if the increase in the amount of tax results from differences in the rate of amortization used or from errors by the taxpayer in the classification of income among the schedules, or when the additional amount is based exclusively on information furnished by the taxpayer in his declaration. Certain specific fines apply to refusals to submit documents and other acts of non-compliance with administrative requests. In actual practice, fines of more than 10% appear to be very rare, even in cases involving deliberate misconduct or even fraud. The amount of the fine is initially suggested by the agent, and then reviewed by the head of the Investigation Department and then by the Review Department. Thereafter, the taxpayer may ask the

Minister for reconsideration. Any fine initially fixed at over 10% usually gets reduced to that figure in this process, or may even disappear. Fines imposed are not subject to an appeal to the Tax Court (Tribunal of Appeals).

Any unpaid tax draws interest at the rate of 1% per month from the date the tax payment is due.

The present system of penalties, based on a range of 10% to 100% and 200% of the amount of tax involved, is unsatisfactory because it involves too much administrative discretion. The pressure of the various forces inevitably involved will keep fines to a minimum under this method. A gradation of penalties that would be largely automatic in application should be used instead. The following penalties are therefore suggested as an illustration of a possible penalty structure. These penalties would be in addition to the 1% per month interest for non-payment of tax.

   1. Failure to file declaration on time:

      (a) Flat sum of Bs.25.00;
      (b) Plus 5% a month of the tax due, to a maximum of 25%;
      (c) Plus 5% a month (after the first 5 months) up to a maximum of 100%.

The fines under 1(a) and 1(b) above would be automatic, but with respect to the fine under 1(c), the taxpayer could be permitted to show reasonable cause for delay in filing to prevent application of the fine. The taxpayer would have to take the initiative in this respect; the Administration would be required to impose the fine in the first instance. Extensions of the time for filing could be permitted up to 90 days if application were made before the due date for filing, but interest would begin to run on the original due date.

   2. Late payment of tax amounts admitted to be due:

      (a) 5% of the amount of tax—an automatic fine to be paid even though an extension of time to file a declaration is granted;
      (b) Plus 10% of the amount of tax if the delay is due to the taxpayer's negligence;
      (c) Plus 50% (instead of 10%) if the taxpayer conceals assets in an attempt to defeat collection.

These penalties would be added to those involved in a failure to file a declaration on time if both failure to file and failure to pay were involved.

All late filing and late payment penalties, as well as interest, can be avoided where the taxpayer obtains an extension of time for filing and also pays, before the due date, an amount of tax that turns out to be at least the amount due. Any excess payment would be promptly refunded after filing takes place. Any underpayment would be subject to interest and late payment penalties, but only as to the amount of underpayment.

In practice the automatic 5% fine under 2(a) above would most often be applicable when the delay is short, one month or perhaps two, while the 10% fine under 2(b) above is most likely to be initially applied in all other cases. Under 2(b) above, however, a taxpayer would be entitled to protest to the Administrative Division on the ground that he was not negligent. In appropriate cases the head of collection activities would reduce the fine to the automatic 5% fine. The taxpayer could appeal the negligence issue to the Tax Court, but he would bear the burden of proof.

The 50% fine under 2(c) above, applicable in concealment cases, is most likely to arise in connection with collection action taken in cases where payment is long overdue. The fine would be imposed by the head of collection activities on recommendation of a collection agent. The taxpayer could appeal the concealment issue to the Tax Court, but he would bear the burden of proof.

3. Increase in tax due to failure to report items of income or due to disallowed deductions:

   (a) 10% of the increase in tax found to be due. This would be an automatic fine, except for the reasons that at present exonerate a taxpayer (differences in amortization rate and increase in tax occasioned solely by data on declaration). The fact that the increase resulted by matching information reports against the taxpayer's declaration should not bar this fine, nor should such an excuse as forgetting to report the item;

   (b) Plus 50% of the increase in tax, if the increase is due to fraud on the part of the taxpayer. This penalty should always be asserted if fraud is found; the taxpayer could litigate this fine in the Tax Court by showing an absence of fraud, but he would bear the burden of proof. This fine would initially be imposed by a group supervisor in the Examination and Audit Division on the recommendation of a field agent;

(c) Plus 200% of the increase in tax (instead of 50%) if the Tax Administration finds a willful and flagrant attempt to evade tax and if it files a petition with the Tax Court asserting the fine and then sustains the burden of proof. The guilt here involved would in effect be tantamount to the criminal guilt that would be found if a penal sanction were used. The assertion of this fine would be the responsibility of the Inspector Nacional de Fiscalización. Since the imposition of this fine would be by the Tax Court, a court of record, publicity might be given to the Court's decision in appropriate cases.

4. Other fines:

Fines for failure to present documents, fines imposed on withholding agents, and the like, may remain as under present law. However, as withholding of taxes will become more important under the suggestions made earlier, the enforcement provisions applicable to withholding agents should be carefully watched, and should be strengthened if this is necessary.

The non-automatic fines could be reviewed by the Appeals Group in the Technical Division, and thereafter litigated by the taxpayer in the Tax Court. Petitions for "grace" to the Administrator General or the Minister to reduce any automatic fine should not be permitted.

The 1% a month interest requirement would remain. However, the Administration would be permitted to ignore interest amounting to less than Bs.10 or 15. The interest would run from the time the taxpayer's declaration was originally due, and not from the date a claim for an additional amount of tax was asserted.

Technical Division

The various suggestions made above require some recasting of the work of the Technical Division. This division should essentially be a group of skilled technical experts, legal and accounting, charged with the tasks of interpreting the statute and regulations and dealing with the complex technical problems arising at the administrative level. Thus, it would consider taxpayer requests for rulings, provide interpretations at the request of the other tax offices, consider the appeals from taxpayers, with respect to the audits or refund denials made by the Audit Division, and represent the Administration before the Tax Court. Perhaps a more appropriate name can be found for this Division; Appellate and Interpretive Division may be a possibility.

The Technical Division would also be responsible for making interpretive and technical material available to lawyers, accountants, etc., who are interested in tax matters. It should therefore have supervision over the issuance of the Bulletin, and should see that it contains all of the important rulings issued by the division as a result of taxpayers' requests or otherwise. It should keep up-to-date the published compilations of administrative doctrine, and should cooperate with the Tax Court to see that all Court decisions in tax cases are published regularly.

At a different level, it could be given responsibility for the general information to be made available to the public, in the form, for example, of simplified newspaper articles and pamphlets explaining the tax law, and more technical summaries and material to be distributed to legal, accounting, and business associations. It would conduct studies with respect to simplification of tax forms, the development of simple tax accounting systems for various types of taxpayers, especially small business and farm activities, and like matters.

The activities of this division are highly important. As a tax system develops it tends to become more complicated from a technical standpoint. It is therefore necessary that the Tax Administration possess skilled legal and accounting experts who can furnish technical leadership to the rest of the Administration and to lawyers, accountants, and others on the outside involved in tax work. These skilled technicians must keep abreast of technical developments. They must recognize when official interpretations are necessary to clarify problems or when changes in the regulations or law are required. They should indicate to the Audit Division the points involved in new administrative or judicial doctrine, or in new statutory or regulatory provisions, which should be considered by the field agents. Unless this technical leadership and guidance is thus furnished, the Administration will not be able to keep its tax rules sufficiently developed to cope with the problems created by the rapidly developing business world in Venezuela. It would be desirable for the Technical Division to employ a group of able young lawyers and give them intensive training in tax law so that they would be competent to assist in carrying out these responsibilities of the Division. The aim should be to make it a mark of prestige for a young lawyer to work for the Tax Administration.

Field Offices

As described earlier, the Caracas headquarters controls 5 branch offices and the Maracaibo office controls 2 branch offices. The Maracaibo office performs for its area many of the functions performed for the rest of the country by the Caracas office, such as liquidation, investigation, and statistical preparations. The declarations processed in Maracaibo are about 35,000 in number as compared with 101,500 for Caracas. The income tax amounts involved are much smaller for the Maracaibo office, however, as the larger taxpayers, including the oil companies, file with the Caracas office. Thus, as respects liquidations under the complementary tax, the Maracaibo office total for 1955 was Bs.14.3 million and the Caracas total Bs.601 million.

Two main problems are posed under this organizational form; one is the existence of the Maracaibo office and the second is the existence of branch offices generally.

As respects the Maracaibo office, it would be desirable to shift its Administrative Division functions, such as liquidation, collection, and statistical work, to Caracas. These tasks can be handled more efficiently on a centralized basis, especially in view of the machine operations involved. As improvements and changes occur in these tasks they can more readily be carried out if all of this work has been centralized. The keeping and publishing of separate statistical data for the Maracaibo region serves no useful function. In fact, the separation usually makes it much more difficult to interpret existing data, since tables are often presented only for the Caracas headquarters office, though not clearly designated as such.

The transfer of these functions from Maracaibo to Caracas should occur when it is clear that the Caracas office has its own problems under control and is therefore ready to accommodate the additional work. Any improvements and changes in the Caracas office, however, should be designed on the assumption that this transfer from Maracaibo to Caracas will occur. When the transition period arrives, the Maracaibo filing system will have to be coordinated with that of Caracas before actual transfer; thus, Identity Numbers will have to be added to the Maracaibo files.

While all Administrative Division functions should be centralized in Caracas, it is desirable to have some of the investigation activities carried out on a decentralized basis. Consequently, branch offices responsible directly to Caracas should be maintained in the various main cities, with each office having two or more agents. These agents would confine their activities to conducting the investigations of cases sent to them by Caracas and to answering questions presented to them by local taxpayers in connection with the filing of declarations and similar problems. There would be no need, under the procedures earlier suggested, for these agents to handle liquidations. Their investigatory work would be supplemented from time to time by visiting groups of agents sent from Caracas to handle the additional investigations required in the particular area. In each city this branch tax office should be located near a tax-receiving agency. As the annual investigatory work increased in any branch office, the number of agents permanently stationed there would likewise be increased. There should be at least two or possibly three agents in each branch office, so that they could confer with each other on their work. While it is desirable for the branch office personnel to assist taxpayers in filing declarations and in other ways to handle their questions concerning tax matters, the main function of these agents should be to conduct investigations. Special solvency certificate situations in which more than the suggested tax receipt would be needed, as in the case of persons leaving the country, could be handled in these branch offices if adequate communications between them and Caracas can be developed. The applications could be filed in the appropriate branch office if the taxpayer desired, and the requisite check made by Caracas when it received the notification of the application.

Organization

The organizational arrangement in Diagram VI-1 presents a suggested basic organization designed to provide more supervision and control than now exists. The chart does not attempt to show every section and branch, but it does indicate in which of the three main divisions the various important functions would be performed. The chart is based upon the suggestions made above.

The Administrator General's office has been strengthened in this proposed reorganization, by the addition of a Deputy Administrator and an Assistant Administrator. The Deputy is to be a person capable of running the Administration in the absence of the Administrator. The Assistant is to be an all-round technical man who will work with the division heads and section heads on planning problems. He will be a clearing house and a coordinator for plans made throughout the Administration. He will be available to do necessary research on new devices,

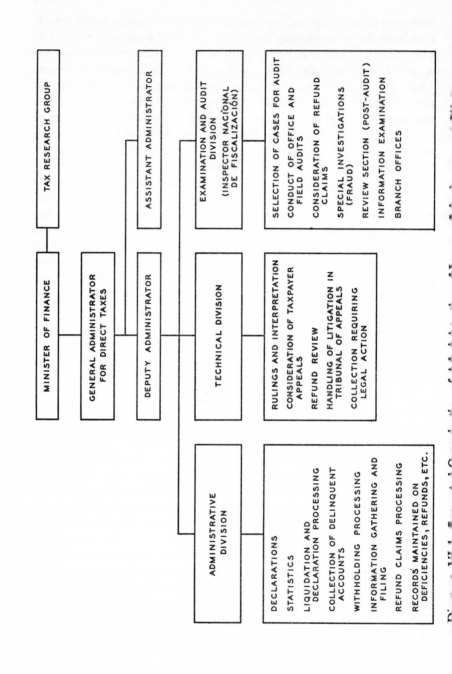

techniques, and ideas. He will of course deal with the Deputy and the Administrator in the formation and implementation of plans. It is quite proper that all unit, branch, section, and division heads should be regularly devoting a reasonable part of their time to short-range and long-range planning for the area of their responsibility. The planning functions to be performed at the top level are primarily those of stimulating, coordinating, and perfecting plans.

The supervisory functions of the Administrator and his Deputy will be aided by the formulation of a system of regular reports going to them from all unit, branch, section, and division heads. Such matters as personnel changes, daily record of payments, monthly statement of declarations filed, audits made, status of delinquent accounts, etc., should all be reported in writing. Regular weekly and monthly meetings should be held to discuss reports and current problems. The Administrator and his Deputy should concentrate on overall aspects of administration and supervision. They should not be drawn into the details or disposition of particular cases, except in the rare case involving highly important problems.

The main functional change suggested on the diagram is the centralization of all examination and audit responsibility in a new strengthened Examination and Audit Division whose work has already been described. The importance of this division is underscored by placing it on the same level as the other two main divisions.

The Technical Division has had some functions added and some removed, in this proposed reorganization, so that it is in a better position to render the substantial legal and technical services that the Administration and the taxpayers are requiring in increasing amounts. The functions listed have been described elsewhere.

The Administrative Division has not been significantly altered structurally in this proposal. Functionally it will handle more aspects of declaration processing than formerly, because the work of the Liquidation Department has been partly given to the Administration Division and partly to the Examination and Audit Division. A refund processing function has been added because of an expected increase in refund activity from the proposed new type of withholding tax and because of the establishment of a more formal procedure for the filing of all refund claims.

As the number of taxpayers doubles and trebles, and as they become more densely located in scattered cities, it will be necessary to consider the desirability of decentralization of at least the audit function, and possibly even of taxpayer's files once declarations are processed.

As the Administration demonstrates its capability of solving its own problems, it may wish to consider incorporating within its own organization the receiving of tax payments.

It is elsewhere recommended that the Tax Administration be given the responsibility for the administration of inheritance and gift taxes. For this reason Chart VI-1 refers to the General Administrator for Direct Taxes. However, it is not necessary to have one Deputy Administrator for income taxes and another for inheritance and gift taxes. Any separation or specialization necessary respecting these taxes can be handled within the operating divisions themselves.

A Tax Research Group that would advise the Minister of Finance on economic policy and legal aspects of taxation is needed in the Ministry. It is doubtful that it should be located in the Tax Administration, if for no other reason than the fact that there are many other taxes in addition to income, inheritance and gift taxes that require economic and legal research. Nevertheless, when serious discussions of tax policy take place, the Administrator and some of his staff should certainly take part, in order that the administrative viewpoint may be given adequate consideration. It is useless to recommend tax laws that cannot be administered successfully. Also, changes in tax law or policy necessitated by administrative experience must be brought to the attention of the top policy makers.

Controller of the Nation

The activities of the Controller of the Nation in the tax field have been described above. A copy of every declaration, paid bill, and additional assessment is sent to the Controller, and his staff examines this material. The resulting extensive duplication of papers, files, and work is obvious. Yet this extensive duplication does not appear to produce any significant benefits. The additional taxes assessed in 1957 from this work amounted only to some Bs.150,000. Probably the salaries paid to officials in the Controller's office engaged in this work exceeded this figure, let alone the cost of paper and materials. The taxpayer is also subject to inconvenience under this system, since it is responsible for the requirement that there be a third copy of his declaration.

It would seem clear that at least the enormous duplication of paper work involved should be eliminated, at a saving both to Government and taxpayers. This could readily be accomplished without at the same time ending the examination activity of the Controller. Just as a business does not make a copy of every one of its documents for the independent certified public accounting firm that audits its books, it is likewise not necessary that the Tax Administration provide a copy of all its documents to enable the Controller to check its activities. The Controller could have space in the Tax Administration offices assigned to his staff, and they could there conduct their examinations. It would also seem sufficient that a spot check of the declarations be made, rather than an examination of every declaration. Thus, the Controller's staff could make a random selection of cases to be checked plus a selection taken from high income declarations. If it is thought that actual location of the examiners in the Tax Administration office is not desirable, these declarations so selected for examination could be photographed and sent to the Controller.

While these changes in themselves would be highly beneficial in removing the duplication of papers and files now required, it is doubtful that the examination by the Controller should be continued at all. It is unlikely that this examination in itself serves to maintain the standards of tax administration desired. The level of performance of the Tax Administration would not be likely to fall if the examination by the Controller's office were eliminated. All that this examination would accomplish in practice would be to uncover some of the errors any large organization is bound to make. But in the interest of overall efficiency, checks and rechecks must end sometime. The fact that the examination yielded only Bs.150,000 in 1957 indicates that the process of checking can end at the Tax Administration agency.

Miscellaneous

Following are some additional administrative matters on which suggestions are made.

TRAINING

At the present time a generalized training course in public administration is offered to Ministry of Finance employees. Formerly, prior to about 1954, a special course for field agents and liquidators was provided. It is essential to improvement in personnel performance that appropriate training be given to the tax employees. This training should be directly related to their particular work. Thus, field agents should be given special training in auditing and tax law. If necessary, instructors from outside the Tax Administration should be especially engaged for this purpose. This initial intensive training should be supplemented from time to time, as when a change in tax law occurs.

Several of the personnel charged with, or being groomed for, responsible positions should visit other countries to observe tax administration elsewhere. Such training abroad, however, should be in connection with carefully designed training courses, such as the United Nations-Harvard Law School International Program in Taxation course, or other U. N.-supervised work. Otherwise, much of the travel abroad will be of relatively little value. Moreover, the Tax Research Group recommended above cannot be adequately staffed until graduate training in economics in Venezuelan universities is undertaken still more intensively. Meanwhile, prospective members of that group should receive two or three years of training in universities abroad in which public finance is covered intensively in a department of economics.

Related to this training is the development of internal-procedures manuals describing and governing the office procedures to be followed. These manuals will be helpful in guiding new employees, in initiating changes in procedures, and in controlling the work of employees in general.

FILING SYSTEM AND MACHINE OPERATIONS

The Tax Administration appears to be facing difficulties in devising adequate filing systems for its documents. Related to this problem is the processing of documents through machine operations and making the most efficient use of machine operations. It would be helpful if assistance from experts in these special fields could be obtained. Any expert so engaged should be carefully briefed by, and consult with, persons familiar with the substantive tax rules and the tax processes involved, so that the expert is acquainted with the relationship of the filing and machine operations to the substantive and procedural tax aspects of those operations. Tax accountants with some training in filing and machine operations may well be the most useful experts for this work.

STATISTICAL MATERIAL

While considerable statistical material is now published annually in the *Memoria* of the Ministry of Finance, a good deal of useful information that could readily be presented is not made available. For example, the *Memoria* does not contain data (a) on income distribution by brackets showing the total taxable income, in each bracket, of all tax-payers in and above the bracket, (b) on the amount of income by types of income, (c) on the breakdown of types of income by individuals and corporations separately, (d) on the breakdown of the different taxes paid by the oil and mining companies, (e) on a breakdown of the dependents claimed by taxpayers by status and bracket of taxpayer, and so on. Additional statistical information of this character would be helpful in interpreting the results of the system, in analyzing proposed changes, and in relating the tax picture to the national income picture. The Tax Research Group recommended above could be helpful in determining what statistical data should be compiled and made available. It could also work with other Governmental agencies in coordinating the preparation and presentation of statistical data, and in providing adequate training in statistical methods for those working on this activity in the Tax Administration.

PERCENTAGE OF INCREASED-TAX POOL

At present, 10% (a) of the delinquent taxes collected, (b) of the additional amount of taxes obtained as a result of investigations and (c) of the fines collected, is placed in a pool. Disbursements are then made each year from the pool for the year to all field agents, liquidators, lawyers and other technical personnel, and all chiefs of sections, in proportion to salary; but the distribution to any one person is limited to two months' salary. In practice, the pool has always been large enough to allow this maximum of two months' salary to be distributed. In effect, the pool constitutes an additional salary for those it covers. It is so carried in gross in the Budget. In the year 1957 the 10% figure came to Bs.3,687,262; the Budget-amount for the disbursements for the year 1958-59 is a little over one million bolivars.

This pool system should be discontinued, and a direct increase in salaries substituted. The existence of the pool probably does not act as a direct motivation to an agent to assert additional amounts of taxes, or impose fines, since he does not share directly in the taxes and fines he obtains, and since the pool in practice has been considerably larger than the maximum permitted to be distributed. However, these aspects of the pool system are not generally known to many taxpayers and their tax advisors, though they may know of the pool, or may know that agents somehow share in the increased taxes and fines they collect. The consequence is that many taxpayers believe that the tax agents stand to gain personally by asserting claims for additional amounts of tax and even believe that the agents assert such tax on those grounds. This belief in turn produces a feeling that the Tax Administration is biased and unfair. Obviously, this attitude interferes with proper compliance with the tax laws, and lessens the respect that taxpayers should have for the Tax Administration and its personnel. Complete elimination of the pool system would end these suspicions. This recommendation becomes all the more important as effective steps are taken to reduce delinquency in tax payments. At the present time a figure of 10% of the delinquent accounts currently collected is somewhat above the maximum distribution permitted from the pool. But in the future, as tax delinquency declines under improved administration, the maximum distribution from the pool will be achieved only from the assertion of fines and deficiencies, so that there will, in this sense, be a basis for taxpayer suspicion as to the effect of the pool system.

If it is not possible to substitute a direct increase in salaries for the present bonus now being obtained through the device of the pool, then a bonus system could be continued but with a different base. Thus, the bonus pool could be 1% of the national revenue, with the bonus to particular employee limited to two months' salary as at present. Since the bonus pool would not be confined, as it is at present, in effect, to additional amounts obtained from taxpayers and since the percentage figure established would be large enough in relation to the national revenue to readily provide an excess in the pool over actual bonuses paid, the element of possible anti-taxpayer bias or unfairness would thus be eliminated. If a bonus pool is continued, then all employees of the Tax Administration should participate. Whatever a person's particular function may be, he contributes to the overall success of the Tax Administration if he performs that function competently.

INFORMATION TO PUBLIC

It is desirable that the general public be instructed as to the main substantive aspects of the tax system, the methods of administration, and their responsibilities under the tax system. This can be accomplished by adequate, simple, and clear instructions accompanying the declarations, by general articles in newspapers and magazines, by radio and television programs, by general information made available to high school and university students, by somewhat more technical articles and materials distributed to business groups and professional associations, and so on. In addition, arrangements should be made to provide assistance to taxpayers at the time of the year when their declarations must be filed. For this last purpose tax personnel can be temporarily assigned at filing time to special offices and locations in the larger cities convenient to taxpayers, and the public can be informed of their availability. Large employers, unions, and other groups can acquaint employees and members with their tax filing obligations and have special personnel available to provide guidance. It is important that the top officials in Government, both in the executive and the legislative branches, impress on the public the importance of complying fully with the tax laws. These officials should recognize that the Tax Administration is making real progress towards providing the country with an effective and orderly agency for the collection of revenue. As the Tax Administration puts its house in order, so to speak, so that it is in a position to enforce compliance, it is vital that the public be made to understand the serious civic duty in a democracy of paying the taxes imposed by law.

ACCOUNTANTS AND LAWYERS

Efforts should be made to educate accountants and lawyers generally as to the significant aspects of the tax system. A good deal of this can be accomplished by special tax courses in law schools and business schools in which the technical aspects of taxation are fully dealt with. Thus, a full-time competent Professor of Tax Law on the faculties of the law schools could both educate the coming generation of lawyers on the importance of tax law and create an interest in the law schools in the continual improvement of the tax laws. As a related matter, the Tax Administration should encourage and cooperate with efforts to raise the status and skills of public accountants and to encourage business to obtain outside accounting audits. Further, as a method of encouraging discussions and exchange of information on tax matters among lawyers, accountants, professors, and administrators, it would be helpful to form an organization interested in the subject of taxation, such as a Venezuelan Tax Association. This association could hold meetings devoted to discussions of tax subjects and publish a periodical containing articles on tax policy and technical tax issues.

CHAPTER VII : **Inheritance and Gift Taxes**

A. Description

The present inheritance and gift taxes are levied under a law enacted originally in 1936, modified slightly in 1939, and left almost unchanged since that time. The inheritance tax is of the succession type. Each recipient of property from the deceased is taxed according to the amount of property he receives and his relationship to the decedent. Inheritances received by a person from different decedents are separately taxed. The same rates, exemptions, and provisions apply to gifts *(donaciones)*. Each gift is also separately taxed, whether given by the same donor or different donors.

As respects inheritances, the tax is imposed on the value of the inheritance at the time of death, taking into account debts of the decedent chargeable to the inheritance. One return is made for the entire estate of the decedent. There are provisions in the law for valuing life estates and remainders, estates for a term, conditional bequests, and the like. The tax applies to all property located in Venezuela, and also to personal property located outside of Venezuela owned by Venezuelan citizens and inherited by or given to persons domiciled in Venezuela. However, if the latter property is subject to a foreign tax it is not taxed by Venezuela. Property going to the Government, including states and municipalities, to hospitals, or to charitable institutions is exempt from tax; property going to artistic, scientific, literary or cultural organizations may be exempted in the discretion of the National Executive. Life insurance proceeds of policies paid for by the deceased are exempt. Farm or cattle-raising land the value of which is not in excess of Bs.50,000 is exempt, provided that the total inheritance is not higher than this figure. The community property character of property is recognized under this tax, so that, for example, when the husband dies his wife's share of community property is not a taxable inheritance.

If the inheritance, plus the property already owned by the recipient,

242

does not exceed Bs.60,000, then the inheritance is reduced for tax purposes by percentages that vary with relationship, age and capacity to work. The percentage reductions in general are: spouse, 20%; child under 14 years, 20%; child 14 to 21 years, 10%; persons over 60 years, 25%; incapacitated persons, 25%-30%; any recipient, for wife, each son under 21 years, each unwed daughter, and each relative being supported, 5%. If a person falls in several categories, he obtains the percentage of the highest category plus 50% of the next highest percentage. The National Executive has authority to reduce the tax further on elderly or incapacitated persons.

If the tax comes to less than Bs.5.00, then no tax is levied. In the case of a wife or children, for example, this constitutes an exemption of Bs.1,250, considering the rate and percentage reductions above described. If a person receives a taxed inheritance and dies within five years, transmitting property in the direct line, the property is reduced in taxable amount by 10% for each year yet remaining between his death and five years from the date of his inheritance of the property.

The rates of inheritance and gift taxes are presented in Table VII-1.

These taxes are administered by the Indirect Tax Administration of the Ministry of Finance *(Dirección de la Renta Interna)*. No declaration form is prescribed for these taxes. The heirs or donor present a written statement to the tax official, who then determines the tax. Judicial administration of an estate cannot be completed without a tax settlement, though it is not clear how fully this requirement is observed or how promptly the courts notify the tax officials of pending estates.

In 1956 the inheritance and gift taxes assessed amounted to Bs.10,022,500 almost all of which represented inheritance tax. The 1958-1959 budget figure is Bs.13,500,000. In 1956 there were 3,227 taxable inheritance tax returns closed and 48 taxable gift tax returns. There were 31 exempt gift tax returns, 122 inheritance tax returns showing no net assets, 1,535 exempt inheritance tax returns involving agricultural property, and 491 inheritance tax returns in which the 5-year statute of limitations had run.

B. Recommendations

GENERAL RECOMMENDATIONS

It is recognized in the Ministry of Finance that both the substantive and administrative provisions of the inheritance and gift taxes are in need

Table VII-1. Rates of Venezuelan Inheritance and Gift Taxes

(In percentages)

Relationship	Bs.1 15,000	Bs.15,000 50,000	Bs.50,000 100,000	Bs.100,000 250,000	Bs.250,000 500,000	Bs.500,000 1,000,000	Bs.1,000,000 4,000,000	Over Bs.4,000,000
Ascendants, descendants, and spouse..........	½	1½	3	4½	5½	8	10½	13
Brothers and sisters, nephews, nieces and adopted children..........	1½	4½	6½	8½	10½	13½	15½	20
Collaterals of the third and fourth degree..........	4	8½	11	13	16	18½	20½	25
Other relatives and strangers..........	7½	10	13	16	18½	21	25	30

of extensive revision. There are about 35 agents *(fiscales)* handling these taxes, but their general training and performance are not regarded as adequate to the task.

At the outset, those concerned with the revision must decide what kinds of taxes are desired on inheritances and gifts. Generally, taxes of this nature fall into two classes—those levied on the decedent or donor and those levied on the recipient. If the tax is levied on the decedent it is termed an estate tax. Under such a tax there is usually a flat exemption, and estates above this amount are taxed at progressive rates depending on the size of the estate. No account is generally taken of the degree of relationship of the beneficiaries of the estate to the decedent or of their own personal situation, though sometimes a special deduction is granted for the portion of the estate going to a wife, in non-community property cases. The tax is essentially, therefore, on the net wealth of the decedent considered as a unit. The estate tax is usually, though not always, coupled with a gift tax levied on donors. When no gift tax exists, the estate tax may include all transfers made within a period of years, for example, five years, prior to death. A gift tax is generally applied at cumulative rates to all gifts made during the donor's lifetime, with annual exemptions to exclude small gifts and perhaps an overall exemption. The rates of gift tax are related to those of the estate tax. The gift tax could also be combined with the estate tax in one unitary transfer tax. In that event the transfer of the estate would simply be the last gift; only one rate structure and one tax would be needed. There would thus not be a separate bracket progression for the gift tax and another for the estate tax.

If the death tax is levied on the recipient it is termed a succession tax. Here several variations are possible. The tax may apply separately to inheritances and gifts from each decedent and donor. Or the tax may be a cumulative tax, with each succeeding inheritance or gift received being taxed at a bracket rate determined by the combined total of prior gifts to that donee and the current inheritance or gift. Indeed, it would seem that unless some cumulation is built into a succession-gift tax, it can hardly be effective. Lack of such cumulation is a weakness in the present gift tax in Venezuela. Since the tax-rate schedule applies separately to each gift, a contemplated large gift can be transformed into a series of smaller gifts with consequent reduction of tax. Cumulation of gifts and inheritance passing to a given child from his parents would more realistically reach the transmission of property within a family. Further, cumulation of all inheritances and gifts received by an individual, whether from one or more donors or decedents, would realistically measure the accession to wealth of any particular individual.

There are no clear guideposts pointing to a choice between the two classes of taxes, estate tax and succession tax. Either can be made to serve the main functions of both taxes, namely, to provide revenue and to check undue accumulations of wealth. Both types of tax will develop technical difficulties and complexities. The trend seems to be toward the estate type of tax, perhaps because it may be somewhat simpler of administration.

Whichever type of tax is used, certain observations are in order respecting rates and exemptions. Since the essential problem under this tax, once the assets involved are known, is that of valuation, and since valuations can often be troublesome and difficult, the coverage of the tax should not be too broad. For these reasons exemptions should be set at a level that will eliminate returns yielding little revenue. A sacrifice of revenue through substantial exemptions can be offset by using a substantial initial rate (first-bracket rate) and also by the concentration of effective administration on the larger estates that will be possible if the smaller estates are exempted. At the other end of the scale the maximum rates should rise above the maximum income tax rates. As between a transfer tax and the income tax, the former can stand higher rates with less adverse effect on the economy. Further, if a significant restraint on the undue concentration of wealth is desired, high rates in the upper estate brackets are needed. Since an estate tax is applied to the wealth of a decedent as a whole, while the succession tax applies to that wealth as divided among the various recipients, the exemptions under a succession tax must be lower and the rates must be higher than those under an estate tax if the same amount of revenue is to be produced under both taxes.

If the succession type of tax is chosen, the question arises whether the rates should vary according to the relationship of the recipient to the decedent or donor. It is doubtful that gradations of this nature as conventionally applied are very useful. The usual pattern is the one now being followed in Venezuela: children, spouses, and parents are placed in the lowest category of rates. But since most wealth is left to the spouse and children, that category covers most of the transfers. The existence of the other categories, however, probably tends to keep the rates in the first category somewhat lower than they would otherwise be. Higher rates in this first category will of necessity lead to rates in the other categories that may loom too large.

The usual defense of these categories is that an inheritance going to a distant relative or a friend is more of a windfall than that received by a close relative. But the degree of expectation held by a distant relative or a friend depends on whether any close relatives are living. If there are no close relatives the inheritance is not unexpected (a windfall) by the one who receives it. Put the other way, if one of two children dies, the other could be regarded as receiving a windfall in the same sense as does a distant relative who succeeds to property because there are no closer relatives. A similar analysis applies to the argument that a son, for example, should be taxed at a lower rate because it is presumed he helped the father accumulate the inheritance which is left to the son. But, presumably, if the father leaves the property to a friend and not the son, it may well be because the friend had been more helpful to the father during his lifetime than the son. Moreover, it is arguable that the categories should be based, not on the degree of family relationship to the decedent, but on the age relationship involved. These transfer taxes are essentially taxes on capital irregularly applied according to the interval between successive deaths. Hence, property passing to persons closely related in age to the decedent should be more lightly taxed than property passing to much younger persons, since the property going to the elderly will soon be taxed again. By this reasoning, parents should be in the lowest tax category, brothers in an intermediate category, children in the next category, and grandchildren in the last and heaviest taxed category. But such a classification, essentially based on the age of the recipient, though quite rational in this view, is not likely to be accepted as fair by most people; it is too contrary to conventional beliefs. And, since little rational defense can be offered for the existing classifications, perhaps there should be no classification at all of heirs or other recipients.

The exemption should be a flat Bs. figure per taxpayer. This exemption should not vanish if the property involved exceeds this figure. There seems little value in retaining the percentage reduction approach of present law, with its minor percentage variations by classes of taxpayer and with the reduction vanishing when the value of the property passes a certain point. It would also not be necessary to continue the minimum exemption of Bs.5 in tax. Also, it does not seem desirable to continue the special exemption for agricultural land. The basic exemption for all taxpayers, under the suggestion made above, would cover average property holdings, and it is not appropriate to draw distinctions between different kinds of property under these taxes. In addition to this flat, or overall, exemption for the recipient, a small annual exemption could also be applied to eliminate application of the tax to small gifts during the year.

TECHNICAL RECOMMENDATIONS

A few observations may be made as to some of the technical aspects of the inheritance and gift taxes.

Administration. At present the inheritance and gift taxes are administered by the Indirect Tax Administration of the Ministry of Finance, a division which has jurisdiction over stamp taxes, the liquor tax, the cigarette tax and the like. Administration of the inheritance and gift taxes should be transferred to the Income Tax Administration, for they are obviously much more closely related to the income tax than to excise taxes. The technical problems are similar to those under the income tax, and there are substantive interrelationships. Information obtained under the income tax will aid in checking the inheritance and gift taxes, and vice versa. The administrative and judicial procedures suggested in Chapter VI above for the income tax can be readily applied to these two taxes.

Valuation of Property. Under present law there appears to be no clear statement of the standard of valuation to be used for the inheritance tax. One provision does state that the Minister can grant a reduction in value on items which the taxpayer would have difficulty in disposing of. Such a provision in itself indicates a confusion as to standards, since the marketability of an asset is itself a factor that determines its value; hence the reference to "reduction in value" is misleading. Value should be based on fair market or commercial value. As respects an estate or inheritance tax, the value would be that on the date of death. It may be appropriate, however, in order to grant relief where property declines rapidly in value after death, to permit use of a value one year after death, if the taxpayer so chooses. In this event, he would have to use that later value for all assets involved. In the alternative the permission to use a lower value after death could be in the discretion of the Tax Administration under rules prescribed in the law. In this case, relief should not be granted for a decline in the value of an asset if another asset had increased in value in the same period (assuming the increase in value is not attributable to activities of the heirs). Relief also would not be granted where the decline in value is due to activities of the heirs.

Definition of a Gift. Apparently under present law, if a person sells property to a relative for an amount clearly less than its current value, the difference is not regarded as a gift; instead, the transaction is treated as a sale. Normally, of course, such a transaction would not occur between parties dealing at arms-length in the commercial world. Such a "sale" could occur between members of a family, but only because the seller is really making a gift of part of the property. Therefore, the difference between the sales price and the higher commercial value of the property should be treated as a gift and so taxed. Thus, a useful definition of "gift" for a gift tax is the amount by which the market value of property transferred exceeds the amount of consideration (in money or property having market value) received in return. Such a definition would reach family gifts disguised as sales. If the transaction is not between members of a family or other relatives but instead occurs in the commercial world, then a gift should not be found to exist despite differences in value (perhaps one party drove a better bargain) unless upon examination of the facts a donative intention is discovered.

This discussion of the definition of a gift indicates that the concept of a taxable transfer for the purposes of the gift tax should not be limited to the concept of a gift in the Civil Code. Instead, the concept of a taxable transfer should cover traditional Civil Code gifts and also other transfers appropriate for taxation under a gift tax. The situation of a transfer which is part sale and part gift is one illustration, which could be met as suggested above by a definition covering transfers for an inadequate consideration. The case of a debt forgiven gratuitously is another illustration, and such forgiveness should be included under the definition of a taxable transfer for the purpose of the gift tax.

The discussion of a sale at a price lower than current value assumes that the seller-donor at least actually received the sales price stated. But apparently the gift tax is evaded today by transactions disguised as sales in which no proceeds at all are transferred to the "seller"; the sale is entirely fictitious. The sales price is generally fixed in relation to the "seller's" cost so as to eliminate income tax on the transaction. But if the transaction involves significant amounts, it should not be too difficult to check this type of avoidance. "Sales" between family members should be carefully investigated. Once such a "sale" is found the financial position of the buyer should be fully studied to see if he really could have possessed the cash necessary to buy the property. An examination of his prior income tax returns would here be helpful. The position of the "seller" could also be checked to see whether his assets and income reflect possession of the alleged sale proceeds. Intelligent and careful administration, proceeding from coordinated enforcement of income and gift taxes, could thus meet evasion through fictitious sales. In the same fashion, coordinated administration of these taxes would aid in disclosing assets held by a decedent and not reported for inheritance tax purposes.

Foreign Property. Present law taxes the inheritance or gift of personal property located outside Venezuela if the decedent or donor is a Venezuelan citizen (whether or not domiciled in Venezuela) and the heir or donee is domiciled in Venezuela (whether or not a Venezuelan citizen). The tax is not imposed, however, if a foreign tax is paid. Such a provision is appropriate if the Venezuelan tax rate is likely to be less than the rates of tax in countries where the property may be located. If, however, the Venezuelan rate may be higher, the provision is inadvisable. It would appear desirable to apply the Venezuelan tax to the foreign property, but then allow a credit of any foreign tax paid on the property, against the Venezuelan tax on that property (computed at the average rate of Venezuelan tax on property in Venezuela and outside). It would also seem appropriate to apply the Venezuelan tax to foreign real property as well as personal property.

Bearer Shares. In an effort to prevent evasion of tax through bearer shares, present law imposes inheritance tax on a corporation that issues bearer shares to a stockholder whose capital contribution to the corporation exceeds 50% of the property he owns at that time. The tax is computed as if the stockholder had died at that time leaving the stock to his apparent heirs. The technical details of this provision are complicated and it is not clear that it reaches all avenues of escape. Mention has been made above, in discussion of the income tax, of the various ways to cope with the bearer-share problem. If these devices are effective this inheritance tax provision could be dropped. If not, the provision should be retained and strengthened.

CHAPTER VIII : Indirect Taxation: Liquor,
: Tobacco, and Gasoline Taxes

A. Indirect Taxation

REVENUE FROM INDIRECT TAXES IN VENEZUELA

Indirect taxes are collected from business firms, and are presumed to be shifted to consumers by an increase in prices. The major indirect tax revenues for the fiscal year 1957-58 and the figures in the budget for 1958-59 are shown in Table VIII-1.

The indirect taxes are administered by two services of the Ministerio de Hacienda, namely, the Customs Administration *(Dirección de Aduanas),* and the Indirect Tax Administration *(Dirección de la Renta Interna).* The latter is divided into sections dealing with taxes on liquor, on cigarettes and matches and the stamp and gross receipts taxes. Enforcement of the indirect taxes, in the sense of inspection and control, is in the hands of an Inspector General of the Ministry, aided by Inspectors General for Customs, for Liquor, for Revenue Stamps (including gross receipts), and for the Inheritance Tax. The tax on inheritances, although a direct tax under usual classifications, is administered by the Indirect Tax Administration. The administrative and enforcement organizations for customs and for internal indirect taxes are distinct from those for the income tax. When the latter tax was established in 1943, a completely new administrative organization was established.

The tax on petroleum products is collected by the Ministry of Mines and Hydrocarbons.

The indirect taxes can be classed into two major groups, those imposed on the importation of goods, and those applied to internal production, sale, or use of goods.

The Venezuelan import levies consist of two general types, the customs duties, imposed, with minor exceptions, on the basis of weight, and the so-called consular fees, collected at the time of importation on

251

the basis of value. The latter are taxes, not fees, despite the legal designation, since the yield greatly exceeds the costs of the activities of the consular service. They produce a sum equal to about one-third of the revenue of the customs duties.

The internal or domestic levies apply to liquor, cigarettes, matches, petroleum products (including gasoline), the use of motor vehicles and the gross receipts of all business firms (the cinco por mil—5 per 1000—tax). There are also miscellaneous stamp taxes.

Table VIII-1. Indirect Tax Revenues

Tax	Revenue, fiscal year 1957-58 (millions of Bs.)	Revenue, budget estimate, fiscal year 1958-59 (millions of Bs.)
On imports:		
Customs duties[1]	546.8	530.3
Consular fees.................	150.8	154.0
Total on imports..............	697.6	684.3
Internal:		
Liquor[2].........................	126.1	126.0
Cigarettes[2]......................	94.8	95.0
Matches.........................	2.5	2.4
Petroleum products[2]...............	25.5	24.5
Gross receipts (cinco por mil)........	117.0	—[3]
Other stamp duties.................	22.2	62.0
Motor vehicle licenses	13.7	15.5
Total, internal.................	401.8	325.4
Total.......................	1,099.4	1,009.7

[1] Including penalties of Bs.3.8 million and export fees of Bs.0.3 million for 1957-58, and Bs. 4.1 million and Bs. 0.2 million respectively for 1958-59.

[2] Excluding customs duties on these articles, which are included with revenue from customs duties.

[3] Omitted from the budget, on assumption the tax would be repealed.

SOURCES: 1958-59 Budget, and information supplied by Ministerio de Hacienda.

THE ROLE OF INDIRECT TAXATION IN VENEZUELA

The historic role of indirect taxation, in Venezuela as in other countries, can easily be explained in terms of economic, political and administrative considerations. Direct taxation, with liability for payment directly imposed upon large numbers of individuals, was long regarded as impossible of satisfactory administration, whereas revenues could easily be raised by collecting taxes from importers or sellers of goods. Only with the gradual improvement in levels of education, record keeping, government administrative standards, and public acceptance of responsibility for financial support of government was it feasible to rely heavily upon direct taxes. Moreover, indirect taxes have continued to play a major role in most tax systems. As total expenditure and tax levels have risen sharply, popular opposition to further income tax increases has forced governments of many countries to accept continued use of indirect levies—a factor, however, of limited significance in Venezuela. Closely related is the argument that excessively high income taxes retard economic development. Indirect taxes have also frequently been retained on the grounds that they provide an effective means of extracting some contribution from the great mass of the population not subject to income taxes—an argument which has lost most of its validity as withholding systems for income taxation have been developed. Certain excise taxes, such as those on liquor, tobacco, and petroleum products, have been retained on the principle that the use of the commodities represents a suitable measure of ability to pay or reflects enjoyment of certain government provided facilities, such as highways, directly benefiting those paying the taxes.

In the field of customs duties, protection aspects have played a major role in retention of the levies.

Despite continued use, however, indirect taxation in all countries is generally regarded as inferior to direct taxes, and particularly to the income tax. Only the latter can adjust the burden in the light of tax-paying ability of various individuals as determined by their incomes, numbers of dependents, and other personal considerations. Shifting of indirect taxes by business firms may be difficult, especially if various firms are affected in unequal fashion. A portion of the tax may then rest unequally upon the owners of various business establishments. Moreover, to the extent to which the taxes are shifted, their burden rests on consumption expenditures of the lowest income classes as well as those of the wealthy, and is distributed frequently in a regressive fashion.

Many indirect taxes interfere with the most efficient functioning of the economy by favoring some methods of production or types of consumption over others. Taxes imposed upon particular commodities discriminate against the persons who have particularly high preferences for the taxed items. Collection costs are often substantial, and the taxes may involve administrative machinery and compliance activity duplicating those of the income tax.

With specific reference to Venezuela, the case against extensive use of indirect taxation is particularly strong. Unlike most countries, Venezuela has an important source of tax revenue in its natural resources. Moreover, the present income tax can be expanded to yield substantially greater revenue, at tax rates far lower than those typical of most countries. Fortunately, there exists in Venezuela widespread support of the principle that most revenues should come from direct taxation. Such support comes even from groups whose counterparts are frequently hostile to greater reliance on income taxes in other countries. A typical Venezuelan point of view is reflected in the 1958 "Declaración Económica" of La Federación Venezolana de Cámaras y Asociaciones de Comercio y Producción:

"El sistema impositivo debe orientarse según principios de justicia tributaria y, en tal sentido, es recomendable la sustitución paulatina de los impuestos indirectos que gravan desproporcionalmente a los más necesitados por impuestos directos, acordes con la capacidad de pagos de los contribuyentes."

B. The Taxation of Liquor

Venezuela applies internal taxes to the production and to the sale of liquor, including wine and beer, in addition to the customs duties on these articles.

PRODUCTION AND IMPORTATION TAXES

Domestic and imported liquors are subject to different levies:

1. Taxes on the sale by the producer of domestic liquor are as follows:

   a. On liquor of higher alcoholic content, such as whisky, rum, gin, etc., a tax is levied either upon the alcohol itself or on the liquor, and it varies with the alcoholic content, as follows:

Tax rate on *los alcoholes* (Bs. per litre)	Alcoholic content in terms of "proof spirits" 100° = 50% alcohol	Tax rate on *las bebidas alcohólicas* (Bs. per litre)
	15° or less	.75
	15° - 30°	1.50
	30° - 50°	2.50
	Over 30° but subject to aging process (rum, primarily)	2.00
3.00	50° - 75°	—
4.00	Over 75°	—

b. On beer: Bs.0.3 per litre.
c. On wine:
   less than 14% alcohol (standard table wines): Bs.0.1 per lit.
   more than 14% alcohol (dessert wine, sherry): Bs.0.5 per lit.

2. Taxes on imported liquor, in addition to the duties, are:

   a. Aguardiente and rum   Bs.4.00 per lit.
   b. Liqueurs   Bs.4.50 per lit.
   c. Brandy, whisky, and other liquor   Bs.6.80 per lit.
   d. Beer   Bs.1.00 per lit.
   e. Wine
      of less than 14% alcohol   Bs.0.25 per lit.
      of more than 14% alcohol   Bs.1.00 per lit.
   f. Cider, of less than 7% alcohol   Bs.0.25 per lit.

3. The duty on imported whisky and related liquors is Bs.3 per Kg.; on brandy and gin, 5; on liqueurs, 4; on cognac, 3; on beer, 1.10; on red wine of less than 14% alcohol, 1; of more than 14%, 2; on white wine of less than 18% alcohol in casks, 1; in bottles, 2; over 18%, 3.

RETAIL LICENSE TAXES

Apart from the levies on the sale and importation of liquor, license taxes are imposed upon wholesalers and retailers of liquor, under the following schedule:

1. Liquor wholesalers pay an annual tax of Bs.240, which enables them to sell up to 500 litres of liquor, per month, with an additional charge of Bs.25 for each additional 500 litres or fraction thereof per month.

2. Liquor retailers selling package goods (not drinks) pay a license tax of Bs.240, which permits them to sell 250 litres per month, with an additional tax of Bs.25 for each additional 500 litres or fraction.

3. Bars and similar establishments selling drinks pay Bs.480 per year for sale up to 250 litres per month. For each additional 500 litres sold, they must pay Bs.50.

4. Temporary establishments pay Bs.100, for permission to sell up to 250 litres.

These charges are of course relatively moderate; the system of charges on dealers is designed not so much to produce revenue as to facilitate and aid in the financing of the liquor control system. On this basis, and not on revenue grounds, it may be defended.

ADMINISTRATION

The tax on imported products is paid in conjunction with the customs duties, the bottles being sealed as evidence of payment. Domestic liquor tax is paid on the basis of a declaration. Manufacturers are subject to strict regulation. Enforcement of the domestic taxes is in the hands of the Inspector Fiscal General de Licores. There are 14 regional offices, each under an administrator, with a liquor inspector who has direct charge of enforcement. In the Caracas office there are about 40 sub-inspectors. In a few states, including Zulia, the regional office has no inspection of its own, but relies on the National Guard to enforce the tax.

In addition, for the country as a whole, there are about 400 "celadores" or agents who assist in enforcement of liquor regulations. Bars are inspected at frequent intervals (several times a year) partly to check on their sales, partly to insure proper conduct of the establishments. There are over 2,800 bars in Caracas alone. Control is also exercised over transport of liquor.

Despite the rigid control measures, some illicit production and sale occurs, the magnitude of which is difficult to estimate, but it is probably not a large proportion of total consumption.

TAX YIELD AND TAX BURDEN

The internal taxes yield about Bs.126 million annually, while the customs duties on liquor produce perhaps Bs.25 million.

The burden of these levies on consumers is influenced, of course, by the extent to which the products are imported.

1. Beer is produced domestically, except for negligible imports. The effective levy is therefore the domestic one; for usual brands, the tax constitutes about 15% of retail selling price.

2. Wine is largely imported. The customs duty constitutes typically from 25 to 30% of the retail price, and the very low internal tax, only about 8%, brings the total to perhaps 33%, on the average, for the combined burden for table wines. On domestic wines, the tax would scarcely average more than 5% of retail prices.

3. Rum and aguardiente are domestically produced in large part. The tax ranges from around 50% of retail price on the cheaper brands to 20% on the better brands, which are of course more expensive, per litre.

4. Other liquor is largely imported, whisky and cognac being the most important in total. On good grade imported whisky, the domestic tax is about 25% of the selling price, and the duty is about 11%, for a total of slightly over one-third. On cheaper whisky, the tax is of course a greater percentage of selling price.

All of these levies are relatively moderate by comparison with those in other countries, and particularly the United States, in which well over half of the selling price of liquors of higher alcoholic content consists of tax. In terms of the generally accepted principle that the consumption of these commodities is a suitable basis for special taxation, the present taxes may be defended, and a case made for even higher levies—perhaps as much as 50% more—if large sums of additional revenue are required.

There are no obvious features of liquor taxation which appear to warrant drastic revision. The specific nature of the rates, of course, in a sense discriminates against the user of cheaper brands, but this can be defended on the grounds of a general social policy of discouraging excessive drinking. The light taxes on wine and beer correspond with the treatment of these beverages in other countries. Administration of the tax might be improved by removing the task of inspection from the National Guard, in Zulia and the adjoining area, and giving it to professionally trained liquor-tax inspectors.

C. Tobacco Taxes

Venezuela taxes cigarettes, but not other tobacco products. The tax treatment of cigarettes differs for imported and domestic articles.

IMPORTED TOBACCO

In addition to the customs duty (Bs.12 per kilo), imported cigarettes are subject to a special tax of Bs.20.00 per kilo, which is collected at customs. Payment is evidenced by a seal applied to the packages. The duty and tax together amount to about Bs.0.03 per cigarette, or 30% of the retail price on a brand selling for Bs.2. In recent years about 40% of the volume (60% by value) of cigarettes sold has been imported. Imported cigarettes, which are standard American and British brands, sell for from Bs.2 to Bs.2½ per package of 20, or roughly double the price of typical domestic brands.

DOMESTIC TOBACCO

The tax on domestic cigarettes is Bs.15 per kilo, or Bs.0.015 per cigarette. The domestic tax is collected through sale, by the government, of special cigarette paper, with which all domestic cigarettes must be made. Because of the heavy outlay of money involved, the companies buy supplies for only a day or so at a time. The domestic cigarettes sell for from Bs.0.62½ to Bs.1.50 per package, and thus the tax accounts for from 25% to 50% of the retail price. Most domestic cigarettes differ substantially in composition from imported cigarettes, but one brand, Kent, is now made to American specifications under license.

In contrast to the situation in earlier years, little difficulty is now encountered with smuggling, although small amounts are brought in illegally by travellers, ship crews, etc.

The yield of the tax is now Bs.95 million per year, about equally divided between domestic and imported cigarettes. In addition, about Bs.12 million is produced by the customs duties on the imported items.

Domestic cigarette manufacturers are urging increased protection, present levels being regarded as inadequate to dampen smokers' preferences for foreign brands. They point out that the combined customs duty and tax on imported cigarettes does not constitute, on the average, a higher percentage of the retail price of cigarettes than does the tax on domestic brands, since the domestic brands are so much cheaper. In time, undoubtedly more foreign brands will be made in Venezuela; the chief limiting factor has been lack of output of the types of tobacco necessary. As such output is increased, the need for protection will fall, since production costs are apparently little greater than in the United States.

The uniform specific-rate structure discriminates against the cheaper brands of cigarettes. The most expensive domestic brand sells for more than twice the price of the cheapest domestic brand, yet the tax is the same, per package. Accordingly, it is argued, the tax checks the development and sale of the cheaper brands, and is unfair to persons in the lower income groups who smoke the cheaper brands. The tax that they bear, per Bs. spent on cigarettes, is much greater than that borne by the wealthy person smoking expensive brands. This argument has some merit. It would be possible to provide a bracket system, for the tax, with 2 to 4 brackets, the rate being adjusted in terms of retail selling price. Thus, if the tax on brands selling for Bs.1.25 or more was Bs.0.30 per package, the tax on those selling for less than Bs.0.75 might be Bs.0.15.

The Venezuelan cigarette taxes are relatively light compared with those of most countries, averaging around 30% of the selling price, whereas in the United States, Federal and state taxes combined account for nearly 50% of the retail selling price. In some countries the figure is over 75%. While the case that is commonly made for cigarette taxation rests upon a somewhat flimsy basis of popular notions about the non-necessity of smoking, still, such levies are less objectionable than most other indirect taxes. An increase in the rates, on both domestic and imported, may be regarded as a tolerable, though not strongly recommended, form of tax increase, if more revenue from indirect taxes is regarded as essential.

THE TAX ON MATCHES

A levy of minor importance is the tax on matches, Bs.0.01 per box up to 40 matches and Bs.0.005 for every 20 matches beyond this number. This is the easiest of all taxes to collect, since all matches in Venezuela are manufactured by one firm under government concession. Importation or manufacture by other firms is banned. In addition, the producer pays a royalty to the government of about Bs.70,000 a year. The tax yields Bs.2.5 million annually. This levy is scarcely worth the trouble; it is a curious carryover from earlier years.

D. *National Taxes on Petroleum Products and Motor Vehicle Use*

Venezuela imposes three taxes on the use of motor vehicles: a national tax on domestic consumption of petroleum products, a national license fee on motor vehicles, and a tax on motor vehicles imposed by municipalities.

TAXES ON PETROLEUM PRODUCTS

The national government collects from the refineries a relatively moderate tax on petroleum products, as follows:

		Bs. per litre
1.	Gasoline, standard grades	.0099425
2.	Gasoline, super grade	.019885
3.	White gasoline, lighter fluid, etc.	.0099425
4.	Kerosene	.00026
5.	Lubricating oil, in barrels	.10061
6.	Lubricating oil, in cases	.1109
7.	Fuel and diesel oil	.00123
8.	Solvents, etc.	.040560

These rates are one half the import duties on these products. The import duties are based on kilograms, and the conversion to litres produces the unusual figures shown in the table. It would be preferable to base the customs duties on litres, using rates not running to more than two decimal points (e.g., in line 1 above, Bs.0.01 per litre).

The taxes on petroleum products are collected monthly by the Ministry of Mines and Hydrocarbons, on the basis of declarations filed by the oil refining companies. The tax is based upon sales made during the period by the refineries to dealers in Venezuela.

The taxes yield about Bs.27 million annually, of which about Bs.19 million comes from standard grades of gasoline, and Bs.4 million from the super grade. The tax on gasoline constitutes about 7% of the selling price of standard gasoline used by cheaper cars, and about 9.5% of the price of super gasoline used by cars requiring high octane fuel.

This is a very light burden compared with the gasoline taxes of most countries, especially in the United States, where the tax (Federal and state together) on standard grade gasoline is about 9 times as high as the Venezuelan tax, and 30% or more of the retail price.[1] Gasoline is very cheap in Venezuela, the regular grade being scarcely half the United States price; it is one of the very few commodities which, at cur-

---

[1] This computation uses the median state rate (10 states) of 6 cents per gallon.

rent exchange rates, is cheaper in Venezuela than in the United States.

The basic philosophy, long accepted in the United States and Canada, that highway users should bear a large part of highway costs through gasoline taxes, has never been seriously considered in Venezuela. The government is spending more than Bs.800 million a year on highway construction, an item treated as a regular government expenditure, and many times greater than the yield of all levies on motor vehicle users. Nevertheless, the principle of making vehicle users pay a large part of road costs has considerable merit. The benefits from road construction accrue in large measure to the persons directly using the roads for personal or business purposes. It is the desire on the part of these persons to use roads that makes their construction necessary. There is, therefore, substantial justification for requiring these persons to pay most of the cost. In the first place, the assessment of the road costs against the users increases efficiency in the use of resources, by providing a guide to annual expenditures on highways, and by discouraging excessive use of crowded roads. If commercial operators do not pay for the roads, they are essentially being subsidized by taxpayers in general. Efficient resource utilization requires that marginal costs for which particular recipients of services are responsible be assessed against the recipients and be reflected in the prices which they charge for their services.

In the second place, considerations of equity suggest that the road users be made to pay a substantial portion of road costs. Car owners who benefit particularly from road building consist in large measure of persons in the middle and upper income groups, who can afford to pay for road usage. Greater reliance upon highway user taxes would release some of the income tax revenue for education and public health.

A special problem exists in Caracas, where vehicle traffic, especially in rush hours, has reached the point of serious traffic congestion. Additional car usage in Caracas gives rise to real costs to society, in the form of lost time for other drivers, higher accident rates, and need for expensive construction of additional expressways. Higher motor vehicle user taxes would force motorists in Caracas to contribute to society a sum reflecting the real costs to society for which they are responsible.[2]

[2] It would appear that the only adequate solution to the traffic problem in Caracas is the building of some form of off-street rapid transit system. Caracas provides an extreme example of the inability of an expressway system to meet rush hour traffic needs. As population and car ownership grow in Caracas the next decade, chaos is almost certain to ensue if improved transit facilities are not provided.

It is true, of course, that road development aids industrial growth of the country. But this is no argument against the gasoline and motor vehicle taxes. The benefits to society from road building accrue primarily through the direct gains to individuals using the roads. These individuals can be made to pay, without interfering with development of the highway system.

Limited use has been made of the toll principle. It could be expanded on main routes. But it is not suited for light-traffic roads, or for travel in the Caracas area. Collection costs on many roads would be excessive. The tax on gasoline is a far simpler and more economical method of collecting the sums necessary for highway finance.

It has been argued that all persons should be able to buy gasoline cheaply because petroleum is the country's most important product. But this is not a logical argument against heavier gasoline taxation. It is little more than a slogan, one which can interfere seriously with a sound program of highway finance, and, ultimately, with highway development. As demands by education and other government functions increase, funds available for needed highway construction will become inadequate. In time, only by the use of a higher gasoline tax will acceptable levels of highway construction be possible.

Thus, in order to provide greater equity in the financing of highways and to assure the government of adequate funds for highway construction in the years ahead, the tax on regular grades of gasoline should be increased to Bs.0.05 per litre, and on super grade to Bs.0.09 per litre, a change that could increase the yield of the gasoline taxes to nearly Bs.100 million a year. The petroleum companies should be permitted to increase prices by the amount of the tax; that is, the retail price inclusive of tax would be allowed to rise, from present levels, by Bs.0.04 per litre on standard grades and Bs.0.07 per litre on super grades. The government would need to give wide publicity to the fact that the price had risen because of the tax increase. In fact, a system of separate quotation of the gas tax from the price of the product has substantial merit.

GENERAL MOTOR VEHICLE LICENSE FEES

The national government issues the annual motor vehicle licenses, for a flat fee of Bs.20 for initial purchase, and Bs.15 for renewal. All vehicles—cars, trucks and buses—are assessed the same amount. The total yield (including sums from drivers' licenses) is Bs.14 million a year. These are relatively light charges, but they are supplemented by substantial municipal taxes on automobiles. These municipal taxes are heavier on large vehicles than on small cars. An increase in the national license tax on automobiles is not desirable so long as the high-rate municipal taxes are employed, but the national government could justifiably place a heavier charge on trucks and buses, which are treated very leniently.

CHAPTER IX : Customs Duties and Consular Fees

For many years customs duties provided the bulk of revenues of the national government of Venezuela. With the increased importance of oil royalties and income taxes, the relative importance of customs duties has fallen, but in the 1957-58 fiscal year, the duties proper yielded Bs.542 million. In addition, a total of Bs.3.8 million was collected in customs penalties, and Bs.0.3 million from export levies. In addition the so-called consular fees, which are actually import duties, yielded Bs.154 million.

A. Customs Duties and the Consumer

The customs duties are based upon weight, without regard to the value of the commodities, except in a very limited number of cases, such as watches, furs, fountain pens and nylon stockings, in which the specific duty is supplemented by an ad valorem rate. In a few instances, such as automobiles, radios, and refrigerators, a schedule of rates for various weight classes is provided, with higher rates per kilogram on the heavier types, in an effort to make a rough approximation to value, but in a haphazard way.

The rate schedule consists of 10 rate classes, with rates ranging from Bs.0.05 per kilo in the first to Bs.50 per kilo in the tenth. There are many variations from the standard rates, produced by adding or subtracting specified percentages from the standard figure. Thus, for example, bacon is subject to a rate of the fifth class (Bs.1.00) plus 20%, or Bs.1.20 per kilogram. Since January 1, 1959, these rate variants have been stated directly, in place of the cumbersome system of standard figure plus or minus a percentage.

The schedule contains 474 items, plus a number of sub-items, which bring the total number of separate classifications to well over 1000. This is comparable to the number in other specific-rate systems; there are 1163 items (plus sub-groups) in the Swiss specific-rate tariff schedule, for example.

PROTECTIVE VERSUS REVENUE AIMS

Customs duties in Venezuela have for many years had both protective and revenue aims. Some rates are designed solely for protection, others solely for revenue, and many for both, in varying degree. The trend in recent years has been to provide more and more protection, in conformity with the general policy of attempting to build up domestic industry and agriculture. On the basis of the relative importance of the two goals, the various duties may be classed into several groups.

In the first place, a number of duties are designed to be, and are in fact, completely prohibitive, the rates being so high—often several times the retail selling price of the goods—that importation is quite impossible. These duties are for the most part on items whose demand can be completely supplied from domestic sources, and where the industry is regarded as significant to the economy. Coffee, with a rate of Bs.16 per kilo, is a good example, as is sugar. Clothing and wooden furniture are likewise very highly protected; the duty on men's undershirts is currently 2½ times the retail selling price of the articles in Caracas. Other examples include margarine, corn, and some soaps.

Secondly, a number of the rates provide substantial protection but are not prohibitive, and thus imports do come into the country (typically because domestic production is inadequate to meet demand at current prices). Considerable revenue is obtained from these duties. Automobiles provide a good example. A fairly high tariff (on typical present-day cars, Bs.1.40 per kilo, and thus about Bs.2,500.00 on a cheaper American car) has been established to encourage car assembly in Venezuela; still, more than half the cars used in the country are imported in assembled form. As a consequence, large sums of money are yielded by this customs class. A similar situation exists with cigarettes, on which the protection is, relatively, much less. A large portion (over half), in terms of value, of all cigarettes are imported, in large part because of a strong preference on the part of many smokers for foreign types of cigarettes. The domestic industry is capable of supplying a much larger part of total consumption than it now is doing.

Thirdly, a number of products are subject to moderate rates, with revenue considerations dominant, and protection only secondary, or nonexistent. This group includes a number of food items, such as bacon, ham, and canned fish, refrigerators, radios, phonographs, watches, table lamps, and a wide variety of other goods. Typically, the duty on these items, expressed as a percentage of retail price, ranges from 5 to 25%. This portion of the tariff is essentially a selective sales tax system of fairly wide scope, the rates being adjusted in some rough degree in terms of "luxury" characteristics.

Finally, the tariff schedules contain a number of rates which are low or nominal, including such items as machinery of various types, books, wheat and flour, steel, most tools, fertilizer, car parts for assembly of cars, and the like. This category consists in general of articles not produced in Venezuela at all, the importation of which is desired to aid industrial and agricultural development or is needed to meet domestic requirements for basic staples. Importation of wheat and flour is permitted, however, only by license, which in general is granted only to the extent necessary to meet the deficit of current domestic output below demand, at current prices. Some of the rates are entirely nominal, e.g., Bs.0.001 per kilo, and are kept only for statistical reasons and to provide a basis from which an increase can be made in the event protection of domestic industry is later desired.

Outright exemptions by law are relatively limited, confined to certain specified types of machinery and tools, farm equipment, scientific books, purebred livestock, and the like. As noted below, however, many importations are in practice freed from duty by exonerations granted in specific cases.

Outright prohibition of imports is confined by law to a few items, such as matches and salt (subject to monopoly production, under government contract, in the first case, and produced largely by the government, in the second), and gambling machines. In practice, as noted, certain other imports are barred by the license system.

Rates and classifications are not subject to frequent change. In 1943 significant reductions were made in flour, machinery, and other items. The signing of the reciprocal trade agreement treaty with the United States later resulted in extensive reductions. In recent years, while no general increases have occurred, many individual rates have been raised in response to demands of domestic producers for protection. Thus in May, 1958, duties on cotton cloth were sharply increased, largely to check dumping from Europe, and in July of 1958 the duty on various jewelry products was increased to aid domestic producers.

Tariffs affect consumers in two ways. In the first place, to the extent to which commodities are imported and the duties are reflected in higher domestic prices, the consumers may be considered to bear the burden of the duty directly, so long as the duties do not affect exchange rates, as will be assumed, given the circumstances of the Venezuelan foreign exchange situation. Any attempt to trace this direct burden of the duty among consumers in a precise fashion is impossible, for several reasons. First, no data on duty collections by commodity are available; figures can merely be estimated from data on imports and duty rates. Secondly, many of the duties apply to machinery, materials, etc., used in production, and the burden on these imports becomes diffused among the production of various consumer goods. Thirdly, knowledge of consumer spending by income class is inadequate.

The second, or indirect burden, is that of the protective effects of the duties in holding up domestic prices. Protective duties make consumers pay more for domestic output than the cost of the products in world markets. Protection, if effective, supports domestic industries which are more costly and less efficient than those of other countries. Venezuela may be willing to pay the price, in order to gain industrial diversification, but the price is real. It is impossible to trace the indirect burden; only general statements can be made.

THE SIGNIFICANCE OF CUSTOMS DUTIES
RELATIVE TO RETAIL PRICES

To obtain a detailed picture of the importance of customs duties relative to retail prices, and therefore to gain some idea of the effect of the duties on consumers, a sample study was made for the present report. Retail prices were obtained from representative stores in Caracas. For each commodity, a typical brand or quality was chosen. Food price figures consist of an average of the prices of supermarkets and typical small grocery stores. Too much significance must not be attached to the precise figures, because of the wide variety of prices and qualities in some fields, but they give a rough indication of the importance of the tariffs. The consular fee was not included; likewise, no adjustment was made for the weight of the packing materials. These adjustments would raise the figures slightly. Commodities frequently imported are included, as well as those not imported because of the prohibitive duty.

The retail prices used include, of course, the amount of the tariff, if any, which is shifted forward to the consumer. Hence if the percentage is 100 per cent or more, obviously no imports of the article are occurring.[1] For example, the duty is twice the present price of sugar. Under

---

[1] The duty could be expressed as a percentage of an adjusted retail price, that is, the actual price minus an amount equal to the duty. Under this method of expression, the percentages would be much higher. Thus for example with olive oil, the duty is 40 per cent of the retail price including duty element, but would be 66⅔ per cent of the price less the duty element.

these conditions, all of the sugar sold in Venezuela must be domestic sugar.

Where an article is given twice, once as "domestic," once as "imported," the "imported" line merely shows what the duty would amount to if the article were imported. In fact, in such cases, the article is not imported.

This information is presented in Table IX–1.

CUSTOMS YIELD BY COMMODITY

It is most unfortunate that the government does not compile data of customs duty collections by commodity class. (Steps should be taken to do so immediately). Consequently, only rough estimates can be made of the yield of customs duties by commodities. These estimates are made on the basis of data published by the Minister of Development showing imports by commodity class for 1957. Large items include cigarettes (Bs.32 million), automobiles and other motor vehicles (Bs.34 million), whisky and other liquor (Bs.28 million), radios, television sets, and other electrical appliances and equipment (Bs.15 million), household fats and oils, textile products (despite prohibitive duties on many items), paper products, glass and bottles, basic steel products (despite very low rates), metal furniture and cleaning compounds and various organic chemicals. Substantial sums, in total, are gained from duties on a tremendous variety of articles subject to low rates. Two special features should be noted. One is the substantial portion of the total burden resting on a wide variety of producers' goods of all types, including many chemicals. Another is the importance, in many individual instances, of the yield of the "not otherwise specified," or catchall, categories in the general classes.

Food Consumption. The direct impact of the duties on food consumption is moderate. Most of the basic staples are domestically produced, either because of natural advantages, as in the case of tropical fruits and coffee, or because of protection, which checks importation of, for example, margarine. Meat and fish, corn (used widely for bread), fruits and vegetables, butter and margarine, coffee and sugar are largely of domestic origin.

The most important food import, in monetary terms, is canned and powdered milk, the domestic supplies of which are quite inadequate. While the tariff is moderate, the total impact on consumers would be substantial if all imports paid duty. But actually, under present policies,

Table IX-1. Customs Duties: Per Cent of Retail Prices, July, 1958

Commodity	Duty Bs. per kilo	Duty as a percentage of retail price
Foods:		
Beef...	.001	.5
Ham, Danish....................................	1.20	11
Bacon, Danish..................................	1.20	12
Chicken...	1.20	14
Pork..	.001	.5
Fish, fresh......................................	2.00	36
Tuna, U.S.......................................	2.00	19
Salmon, pink Alaska............................	2.00	26
Cheese..	1.00	18
Butter...	2.20	28
Margarine.......................................	8.00	155
Hydrogenated fats, cooking......................	1.20	25
Olive oil..	4.00	40
Cooking oil.....................................	4.00	92
Powdered milk[1]................................	.50	14
Canned milk....................................	.50	23
Sugar...	2.00	200
Flour, wheat....................................	.04	4
Flour, corn.....................................	2.00	74
Corn..	1.20	200
Rice..	.23	12
Black beans.....................................	.30	25
Baking powder..................................	1.20	14
Tea...	3.00	14
Cocoa...	16.00	16
Coffee..	16.00	211
Instant coffee...................................	16.00	75
Candy (chocolate bar)..........................	4.50	45
Macaroni..	2.00	66
Potatoes..	.18	10
Fresh fruit:		
oranges.....................................	1.20	85
bananas.....................................	1.00	152
avocados....................................	1.00	49
tomatoes....................................	1.00	60
apples......................................	.10	4

[1] Most imported duty free.

Table IX-1 (cont.)

Commodity	Duty Bs. per kilo	Duty as a percentage of retail price
Peaches, canned...................................	1.20	27
Peas, canned......................................	1.20	38
Baby food..	.10	3
Pepsi-Cola..	.40	40
Beer (domestic)...................................	1.10	55
Wine (Chianti, Italy).............................	1.00	27
Household supplies:		
Soap, laundry..................................	2.00	100
Soap, toilet....................................	4.00	37
Detergents.....................................	2.00	60
Toilet paper....................................	1.00	45
Pharmaceuticals:		
Tooth paste, small.............................	2.00	15
Tooth brush...................................	.20	2
Shampoo......................................	2.00	7
Milk of Magnesia..............................	2.00	10
Aspirin..	2.00	8
Vitamins......................................	2.00	2
Appliances:		
Radio, small...................................	1.00	2
Radio-phonograph.............................	2.00	8
TV set, portable...............................	1.00	2
TV set, cabinet model..........................	2.00	8
Phonograph, portable...........................	1.00	3
Typewriter, portable...........................	.10	0.2
Refrigerator, small.............................	.20	2
Refrigerator, large.............................	.30	2
Furniture and related items:		
Bath tubs, steel................................	.20	3
Table lamps....................................	1.50	10
Mattress, high quality..........................	8.00	121
Baby bed and mattress..........................	8.00	85
Upholstered furniture, suite......................	4.00	66
Dining room table..............................	4.00	75
Chair, dining room, wooden.....................	4.00	25

Commodity	Duty Bs. per kilo	Duty as a percentage of retail price
Clothing and textiles:		
Wool suits, men's.............................	50.00	51
Cotton shirts, men's...........................	50.00	151
Underwear, men's..............................	50.00	250
Cotton dresses, women's........................	50.00	31
Sheets, cotton.................................	15.00	47
Blankets, cotton...............................	25.00	114
Stockings, nylon...............................	95.00 plus 25% ad valorem	84
Slip, nylon....................................	100.00	105
Dress shoes, men's............................	32.00	83
Work shoes, men's.............................	.40	2
Dress shoes, women's..........................	32.00	69
Dress fabrics, cotton...........................	12.00	34
Dress fabrics, synthetic........................	32.00	69
Drapery fabrics, cotton.........................	12.00	9
Pedal pushers.................................	50.00	46
Jewelry, leather goods, etc.:		
Wallets, cowhide..............................	32.00	26
Clock, travel-alarm............................	1.00 plus 10% ad valorem	11
Costume jewelry...............................	12.00	9
Handbags.....................................	24.00	65
Earrings......................................	12.00	14
Film, Kodachrome, 36 exp......................	.50	negl.
Automobiles and related items:		
Automobile, cheaper U.S. model.................	1.40	23
Lubricating oil................................	.20	4
Tire, 670 x 15 tubeless.........................	1.00	8
Cement.......................................	.02	2

NOTE: For items that are covered by trade agreements, the trade agreement figure has been used.

the bulk of the imports are made duty free under special exoneration. But there is no assurance that this policy will be continued. The other major import, wheat flour, is subject to very low duty, but importation is permitted only to meet the deficits of domestic output relative to demand. Domestic prices of wheat are therefore higher than they would be with free importation.

Beans and related products and potatoes are imported in some quantity, but are subject to moderate rates relative to retail prices. Most consumption of these articles is from domestic sources. On the other hand, cheese, canned and dried fish, ham and bacon, and prepared meat, which are imported in substantial quantities, are subjected to relatively higher rates, but are used primarily by consumers in higher income levels.

Removal of some of the low-rate non-protective food tariffs is recommended.

Beer, Wine and Liquor. Virtually all beer is domestically produced, under substantial protection. On the other hand, most wine is imported, although the total consumption is not great even though the customs duty is moderate. Whisky, however, bears a substantial duty, as do related liquor items, and the yield of the duties on these items is substantial. This treatment can be justified in terms of usual sumptuary principles.

Cigarettes. Cigarettes are subjected to considerable duty, which results in moderate protection. Nevertheless, a large proportion of all cigarettes are imported, even though these sell at prices typically more than twice the domestic brands. Thus the yield from the duty is substantial. Potential domestic output is greater than current sales, and more protection is urgently sought by the producers. The present duty is probably distributed much less regressively than cigarette taxes generally, because the lower-income groups primarily use the cheap domestic brands. On the whole, the duty may be regarded as acceptable.

Textiles. The textile industry has been accorded high protection. For a number of years clothing has been heavily protected, and protection has been gradually extended to cloth, particularly by rates imposed in May of 1958. Some clothing articles are imported despite the tariff, but these are primarily articles used in the higher-income groups. While Venezuela produces most of its clothing and in the future will produce most of its cloth, it does not produce a large portion of the necessary yarns, especially synthetic. Yarn therefore does not receive high protection, but the amount of duty is considerable, and thus all consumers are burdened with some textile duty in this form. But the cost to the consumer of the textile duties is primarily indirect, in the form of higher costs for domestic goods than the prices for which the goods could be obtained abroad.

Furniture. Like textiles, wooden and upholstered furniture has been strongly protected, and thus very little is imported; the direct costs are negligible, but the indirect costs are tremendous. On the average, furniture costs perhaps twice as much as it would if it could be imported.

Automobiles. The government has sought to encourage automobile assembly in Venezuela by charging a relatively high duty on assembled cars, while providing a nominal one on parts for assembly. Two of the large United States companies assemble half or more of the cars which they sell in Venezuela, whereas the third, and also all European companies, import all cars in assembled form despite the protection. Thus the total direct duty burden on the users of cars is substantial; a fourth or more of the selling price of a typical car will consist of duty. The burden distribution produced is comparable to that of a luxury excise tax on cars, and is much less objectionable than the burden pattern on most foodstuffs and other items. Tires, except those on new cars, which bear a moderate duty, cannot be imported. Substantial lubricating oil is imported at a low duty.

Household and personal supplies. Soap is primarily produced domestically, behind considerable protection, and thus the burden is indirect. The same is true of detergents. Articles such as cosmetics, jewelry, perfume and the like, are partially imported, partially produced domestically; duties are relatively high per kilo, but are not too significant relative to retail price, and the overall burden on the typical family is small. The same is true of most other items in this general class. Most drugs and medicines are subject to very low duties.

Building materials. Venezuela imports large quantities of building materials, and relatively little protection has been applied. Most basic steel for building and other purposes is subject to only a nominal amount of duty; some special types pay higher, but still not heavy, duty. Consequently, despite the large quantity of imports of steel, total duty collections from it are moderate. Over 90% of the cement, which is subject to a low duty, is of domestic origin. The bulk of the lumber imported for building is free of duty. Floor tile is subject to considerable duty, partly for protective reasons; nevertheless, considerable amounts come in, the duty adding of course to building costs. Paint is now strongly protected, but enough (including ingredients) is imported to yield some revenue (perhaps Bs.2 million). But most of the cost to the consumer is indirect.

Household Appliances. The great bulk of all appliances, television sets, radios, lamps, etc., are imported. Almost all of them, except some kitchen items, are subject to moderate rates; the revenue yield is significant but not great, and the burden on consumers, relative to retail prices, is light.

Expenditures on these items are small in the lower income groups, and thus substantially higher levies for revenue purposes could be justified. Much the same conditions exist with films and cameras, sporting goods, and toys. For all of these items, the specific basis of the tariff is particularly unsatisfactory.

Producers' Goods. A considerable portion of all customs revenue, perhaps a half or more, is collected on the importation of producers' goods, even though many such goods are not taxed, and almost all have moderate rates. The volume of their imports is so great that the total revenue mounts up. The burden of these levies is ultimately reflected in the prices of the final goods produced, and thus is spread very widely over necessities and luxuries, probably burdening the consumers as a whole in a manner regressive relative to income.

Summary. As the tariff now stands, the primary direct burdens on the consumer in the lower income levels arise from the taxation of certain food products (even though most of the basic foods are domestically produced or pay little duty), and from the taxation of producers' goods. In the higher income groups, expenditures on cigarettes, liquor, automobiles, appliances and other "luxury" items give rise to relatively greater duty burdens. The greatest indirect burdens are on textile and furniture expenditures. On the whole, the duties would be more acceptable if the burden on foods were cut, if that on articles such as automobiles, appliances, jewelry, and similar items were increased, and if most producers' goods were freed from duty.

RELATIVE PRICES IN VENEZUELA AND THE UNITED STATES

A sample study was made, for the present report, of prices of a number of items in Caracas, compared with prices of identical items in Champaign, Illinois.[2] The brands and quality of items selected were those most widely consumed in Caracas; selection of items was made after careful analysis of the family-expenditure studies available in Venezuela. Conversion was made at the exchange rate of 3.32 bolivars to one dollar. An attempt was made to insure identical products in all cases, although this goal may not have been fully attained. Prices, of course, vary, in different shops, but the figures selected are believed to be typical. The data are presented in Table IX-2.

B. *The System of Import Licenses and Exonerations*

The tariff system is supplemented by the use of import licenses, whereby importation of certain articles is specifically prohibited without a special license. The most important articles treated in this manner are wheat and flour, automobile tires, dried and salted meats, powdered milk, onions, rice, tapioca, wool cloth, fibre sacks, and a few other items. Some of these, such as wheat, are low-tariff items, while others such as tires have moderate duties.

The licensing device is used primarily to insure that all of the domestic output of the commodity will be absorbed at current prices before any importation into the country is permitted, yet to permit necessary importation at nominal or moderate tariff rates. The alternative, given the general protection policies followed, would be that of setting a tariff high enough to stimulate domestic output and curtail imports to the desired amount. This alternative is less attractive than the licensing system, with respect to basic commodities of such a character that the government seeks to aid domestic production, while domestic output is inadequate. For those commodities, the present licensing system has considerable merit, given the general premise of the policy of protection. Since the imported articles are cheaper, typically, than the domestic output, some system of allocation of domestic output among various purchasers is necessary. Frequently this is done by a formula which permits a firm to import a certain number of units for each unit pur-

[2] This is a not untypical city in the United States and was selected because the author of this comparison resides there.

Table IX-2. Comparison of Prices of Certain Items, in Caracas, Venezuela and Champaign, Illinois, U.S.A., July, 1958

	Unit	Price Caracas ($)	Price U.S.A. ($)	Caracas U.S.A. %
Food items:				
Beef, rolled roast..............	1#	.99	.89	111
Ham, canned.................	1#	1.38	1.00	138
Bacon, sliced.................	1#	1.33	.75	177
Pork chops...................	1#	.96	.79	122
Chicken......................	1#	1.15	.40	287
Fish, fresh...................	1#	.75	.39	192
Cheese......................	1#	.61	.69	90
Eggs—domestic...............	1 doz.	1.05	.60	175
Eggs—imported...............	1 doz.	.75	.60	125
Butter......................	1#	1.07	.74	144
Margarine...................	1#	.70	.35	200
Hydrogenated fats.............	3#	2.02	.95	213
Fresh milk...................	qt.	.30	.20	150
Canned milk, evaporated........	14½ oz.	.27	.15	180
Tuna........................	7 oz.	.50	.35	169
Salmon, pink Alaska	1# can	.90	.49	184
Sugar.......................	1#	.14	.10	140
Flour, wheat..................	1#	.14	.11	127
Rice........................	1#	.24	.14	171
Baking powder................	8 oz.	.48	.15	320
Tea.........................	¼#	.68	.49	139
Cocoa......................	8 oz.	.74	.35	211
Coffee......................	1#	.98	.98	100
Nescafe and instant coffee.......	8 oz.	1.43	1.10	130
Candy, milk chocolate bar.......	4 oz.	.42	.30	140
Salt.........................	1#	.10	.10	100
Marmalade...................	1#	.53	.39	136
Bread, wheat.................	1 loaf	.30	.20	150
Potatoes.....................	1#	.24	.08	300
Fresh fruit:				
oranges...................	1 doz.	.32	.30	107
bananas...................	1#	.09	.15	60
tomatoes, field..............	1#	.27	.10	270
apples[1].....................	1#	.34	.15	227
Canned peaches...............	15 oz.	.50	.30	166
Canned peas.................	16 oz.	.45	.17	265
Baby food...................	4¾ oz.	.14	.09	156

[1] Imported in Caracas.

	Unit	Price Caracas ($)	Price U.S.A. ($)	Caracas U.S.A. %
Miscellaneous non-foods:				
Detergents....................	17 oz.	.53	.30	177
Toilet soap...................	bar	.27	.09	300
Kleenex......................	box of 200	.23	.16	144
Tooth brush..................	1	.60	.30	200
Tooth paste..................	4.2 oz.	.89	.49	182
Aspirin......................	100	.90	.62	145
Vitamins.....................	100	3.61	3.55	102
Electrical appliances:				
Radio, small cabinet.....................		24.00	16.00	150
TV—portable 17″.......................		180.00	147.00	122
TV—cabinet 21″.......................		331.00	199.00	166
Radio-phonograph cabinet................		226.00	139.00	162
Radio-phonograph portable..............		120.00	47.00	255
Refrigerator, stripped model:				
8.2 cu. ft...........................		271.00	170.00	159
12.9 cu. ft...........................		391.00	210.00	186
Furniture:				
Upholstered suite, sofa and chair...........		313.00	200.00	156
Dining room table......................		72.00	40.00	180
Dining room chairs, each.................		30.00	15.00	200
Baby bed and mattress...................		108.00	50.00	216
Mattress..............................		66.00	35.00	189
Table lamp............................		21.00	15.00	140
Clothing:				
Men's wool suit, lightweight..............		58.70	35.00	167
" cotton shirts......................		5.65	2.98	190
" " undershirts..................		1.58	1.00	158
" dress shoes......................		16.26	11.00	148
Women's cotton dresses..................		25.00	10.00	250
" nylon half slips.................		3.23	1.98	163
" " stockings.................		2.86	1.00	286
" shoes, loafers..................		8.96	3.00	299
Children's pedal pushers.................		3.84	1.98	194
Yardgoods—cotton......................		1.18	.69	171
" —synthetic.....................		2.33	1.08	216
" —cotton barkcloth..............		5.95	2.98	200
Handbags.............................		7.45	4.50	166
Costume jewelry.......................		2.25	1.98	114

Table IX-2 (cont.)

	Unit	Price Caracas ($)	Price U.S.A. ($)	Caracas U.S.A. %
Miscellaneous items:				
Typewriter, Smith Corona portable.........		108.00	72.00	150
Steel bath tub, 5 ft......................		126.00	85.00	148
Cement, per bag 94 lbs...................		1.30	1.25	104
Tire, 670 x 15 tubeless nylon, black.........		38.25	25.00	153
Oil, 1 qt................................		.75	.45	166
Paint, 1 gallon outside white..............		6.55	5.85	112
City bus fares.................	1	.08	.167	48
Automobile, standard				
lower priced make...........	1	3600.00	2200.00	164
Taxi fare....................	3 miles	.90	.75	120
Haircut, men's...............	1	.66	1.75	38
Gasoline, regular (medium grade).	1 gal.	.15	.31	48
Gasoline, super...............	1 gal.	.20	.35	58
Cigarettes, U.S...............	pkg.	.66	.25	260
Cigarettes, Venezuelan, U.S......	pkg.	.33	.25	130

chased in the country. Thus, in the case of powdered milk, each supplier is permitted to import 5 kilos for each 1 kilo purchased in the country, since domestic output is about 17 per cent of the total domestic needs.

Closely related are the exonerations which free from duty specific imports, particularly of machinery and raw materials. The term *exoneration* is distinguished from the term *exemption* in that it means freeing from tax certain imports of particular business firms under specific authorization, rather than the blanket exclusion from tax of all importations of a commodity. Exoneration is permitted upon specific application, under a lengthy procedure which involves concurrence in the request by the Ministries of Finance (CEFA) and Development. Most of the work of investigation is done by the Ministry of Development. Typically, when a new manufacturing industry is established in the country, the firm will seek exoneration on the machinery which it wishes to bring in. After operation commences, the firm may seek exoneration for importation of its raw materials. Typically, in order to foster industrial development in the country, the government will grant these requests, so long as there are no domestic producers of the machinery or materials, or if the latter cannot meet the demand. In 1956, for example, exonerations granted to industry covered Bs.85 million worth of imports.

The exonerations are established in several ways. Particularly for machinery, or materials which are not domestically produced at all, the firm will receive exonerations from duty on all imports of the specified items during the period. When there is some domestic production, firms may be permitted to import a certain quantity of the article duty-free for each unit of quantity acquired from domestic sources. Such a rule, for example, is provided for tallow used in making soap.

The exoneration system facilitates the provision of assistance to new industries without blanket removal of tariffs from the materials and equipment which they need for production, some of which may be used for very different purposes by other firms.[3]

Both the license and exoneration systems are open to some criticism. In the first place, the process for the granting of licenses and exonerations is rather complex, and, as a result, is relatively slow. Exonerations are granted for 6-month periods only, and a period of from 1 to 5 months (on the average about 3 months) is required to obtain a permit. The delay is of course largely due to the fact that more than one government agency is involved. Firms using raw materials for which exonerations are obtained must constantly prepare forms well in anticipation of the time they are required. The delay is particularly serious when a firm's production and selling plans are contingent upon obtaining permits. The government must, of course, exercise care in the granting of permits, in order to prevent evasion of duties, as not infrequently occurs. For example, in some instances firms that were not, in fact, engaged in manufacturing have succeeded in getting exonerations and then have sold the products. Also, the importance of the exoneration device in the overall protection system necessitates a review of their granting by agencies of government concerned with economic development. The government is clearly aware of the difficulties arising from the delays, and has taken steps to speed the operation of the system. However, it would appear that more fundamental changes are desirable. Specifically, two modifications should be seriously considered:

1. The complete exemption, rather than exoneration, from duty, for a number of basic materials not produced within the country. A large

---

[3] It is argued by some that the fact that the duties are in the law, although rendered ineffective by continual exoneration, puts Venezuela in a stronger bargaining position when reciprocal tariff negotiations are undertaken. However, this argument is of doubtful value.

number of items are subjected to duty, most of the imports of which are granted exoneration. The government has been too unwilling to grant general exemptions; if domestic industry later develops in these fields, protection can be established when desired.

2. The granting of permits for longer periods of time than 6 months, perhaps for an indefinite period, with respect to articles commonly used for industrial purposes, and not domestically produced. This is essentially an alternative to the first suggestion, one which would avoid most of the nuisance of the present system, yet retain the tariffs as at present. Some commodities may more appropriately be handled under the second approach, others under the first. In addition, all possible steps should be undertaken to speed the process of handling applications. These two alternatives, of course, are not suitable as substitutes for the import license system used to insure protection of domestic industries not capable of meeting the entire demand; in these cases continued use of the present system is necessary.

A second objection relates to policies in the granting of exoneration. For the most part business firms offer few complaints; in general the decisions of the government are regarded as reasonable and firms obtain favorable decisions whenever the case is at all good. In some instances, however, firms maintain that exonerations are denied in order to protect domestic producers who are not capable of providing an adequate supply of goods of acceptable quality. In other words, protection is provided too soon, and firms must import despite the duty. A number of specific examples have been cited to us by business firms. In part, the difficulty apparently arises from the lack on the part of the Ministry of Development of an adequate field force to investigate actual production possibilities of the protected firms. In other cases, firms object to a refusal to grant exoneration on items of production which have low tariffs when the refusal is based on the grounds that the low rate makes exoneration unnecessary. The total annual amount of duties may still be substantial, for certain firms.

A third criticism of the system relates to the large element of discretion on the part of the officials involved, which, under previous governments, has paved the way for the making of bribes to obtain licenses or speed the process of granting them. On the basis of statements of responsible persons, it would appear that in past periods permits could be obtained within a reasonable period of time only if outright payments were made to officials involved. Higher standards of political morality lessen the danger of recurrence of such action, but the dangers can also be reduced by revision of the system to reduce the number of cases in which exonerations are required.

C. Customs Administration and Operation

The Customs Administration *(Dirección de Aduanas),* a division of Ministerio de Hacienda, is headed by a director who has general charge of operation. A Tariff Board *(Junta de Arancel)* now functions in the the general jurisdiction of the Inspector General of Customs, who is sub-important capacity of determining the appropriate classification of a new commodity, or in case of disputes. Enforcement of the duties is under the general jurisdiction of the Inspector General of Customs, who is subordinate to the Inspector General of Finance.

In each port, one basic organization is employed. The operations are in charge of an administrator, who reports to the Inspector General. Under the administrator are three officials, the inspector *(Interventor),* the warehouse superintendent *(Guardalmacén),* and the assessor *(Liqui-dador).* The inspector examines the imported goods, approves or alters the classification listed by the shipper, and determines fines for misclassification. The warehouse superintendent has physical custody of the goods in the warehouse, and delivers them to the importer upon presentation of the appropriate papers. The assessor determines the amount of duty payable, together with other sums, such as storage and transfer charges. Payment is made to the branches of the Bank of Venezuela (a private banking system, which collects many government revenues under contract). In addition to inspecting goods at the time of importation, the Inspector General's office maintains a force of investigators who check business firms to determine if customs duties have been paid.

The port of La Guaira, through which the bulk of the country's imports come, has seven inspectors and seven warehouse superintendents. In 1957, 50% (by value) of all imports by ship came through La Guaira, 21% through Maracaibo, 10% through Puerto Cabello, 9% through Puerto La Cruz, and 10% through smaller ports.

One peculiarity of the Venezuelan customs administration is the compensation of the customs officials in each port with a portion of fines assessed, in addition to their base pay. For example, the base pay of an inspector is Bs.1,400 a month. But in addition he receives a portion of all fines collected, up to a maximum income of about Bs.4,600 a month. The administrator of the customs service in the port receives up to Bs.5,000 a month, and the storekeeper up to Bs.3,600; both of them share in the penalties assessed.

The fines take three major forms. Desk fines are applied for minor violations in the filling out of consular invoices (typically Bs.10). Fines equal to double the duty are assessed in the event of misclassification, the chief source of error. Finally, heavy penalties may be assessed in the event of suspected fraud.

CUSTOMS PROCEDURE

The basic procedure in the collection of customs can be outlined briefly. The firm exporting to Venezuela by ship must first obtain consular invoice forms, and fill them in in septuplicate. The precise customs tariff description of the appropriate classification must be given, together with other information, including value and weight. Any error, in Spanish or otherwise, will result in a penalty. The invoices are then mailed, together with the bill of lading, to the consignee.

The goods, upon arrival, are placed in a customs warehouse (except for a limited amount of direct loading of bulk goods onto trucks). The importer, or, more commonly, his customs broker, presents the invoices to the customs officer, together with the bill of lading. The inspector checks the goods, or more commonly, a sample of them, and, after assessing fines, if any, for misclassification, approves the invoices. The invoices are then given to the assessor for determination of duties. Since this usually takes two days, importers are allowed to obtain their goods immediately following inspection, by establishing bond, or, in La Guaira, by making a provisional payment equal to the estimated duties. Upon final ascertainment of duty by the assessor, the transaction is completed.

Any action of the inspector with respect to classification and fines is subject to review by Ministerio de Hacienda; frequently inspectors are overruled, goods reclassified, and fines are decreased or eliminated. Meanwhile, during appeal, the assessed duty must be paid or a bond posted.

Air and Parcel Post Shipments. Shipments by air freight or express and by parcel post receive special treatment. Shipments by air do not require a consular invoice or classification by the shippers, but only a commercial description. All air shipments are examined and classified by the inspectors, upon arrival. This procedure eliminates the danger of fines for misclassification; but classification by the inspectors requires great vigilance on the part of the importer and his customs broker to insure that an acceptable classification is made. Firms often complain that the inspectors do not relate the goods to the tariff schedules properly.

In earlier years, the handling of air freight through customs was faster than that of freight arriving by ship. But the lack of adequate space at Maiquetía and the trucking of all air freight to Caracas for examination have slowed down the process, decreasing in some instances the chief advantage of shipment by air. Air freight transport has become of considerable importance in recent years for certain types of merchandise shipments. In 1957, imports by ship totalled 3.7 billion kilograms, worth Bs.5.1 billion, while those by air totalled .02 billion kilograms, worth Bs.0.9 billion.

Parcel post likewise does not require a consular invoice, classification being made by the inspectors in the parcel post customs service. A 2 per cent surcharge is added, presumably to offset the lighter packing required. Frequent complaints are heard of slow handling of parcel post, but part of the trouble obviously rests with agencies other than the customs administration.

Evasion. Evasion takes two forms: outright smuggling, and deliberate misclassification or underreporting of weight of shipments. Smuggling was once a major problem for Venezuela, even as late as 15 years ago. But improvements in coastal patrols have reduced this to a minimum. Small-scale smuggling occurs in the form of bringing in individual articles for the traveller's own use, or for friends, in excess of allowances.

Without question, some deliberate misclassification occurs, sometimes involving mislabelling of goods. Likewise, some firms deliberately understate weight. These practices are rare among larger established firms, but are not uncommon with small fly-by-night importers. More complete inspection and weighing, with more trained personnel and equipment for scientific analysis when necessary, will help to prevent this type of evasion.

THE CLASSIFICATION PROBLEM[4]

The greatest difficulties in the operation of the Venezuelan customs system center around classification for customs purposes, coupled with

[4] This problem is said to have been considerably mitigated by the adoption, on January 1, 1959, of a new *Arancel de Aduanas,* which uses the uniform Central American customs nomenclature, derived from the Uniform Classification for International Trade of the United Nations. See *Gaceta Oficial,* Nov. 5, 1958, No. 574 (Extraordinary). The basic problems of classification remain, however, and in 1959 the General Office of Customs has been attacking them by intensive training of the customs inspectors in classification.

extensive application of fines. Much of the difficulty arises from the large number of classes of commodities. The definition of a class is often cryptic or unclear. As a consequence, importers and inspectors may easily differ on the classification of a particular article. Furthermore, uniformity of treatment by inspectors is difficult to obtain. Importers often complain that different classifications will be applied by various inspectors, even in the same port. Much of the trouble occurs with chemical products, with industrial equipment of complex forms, and similar items. Products which constitute combinations of two or more articles frequently give rise to classification difficulties. The problems should not be exaggerated; firms importing extensively usually exercise great care in classification, sometimes by sending a person to the country of origin who is quite familiar with the Venezuelan tariff. But the problem is nevertheless serious.

Some of the difficulty lies with customs personnel and methods. Customs inspectors have not in all cases been well trained, many have been political appointments, and the numbers, especially in La Guaira, are inadequate. Furthermore, the system of paying the inspectors a portion of fines assessed may make them overzealous in application of fines in some instances. Cases of outright bribery to obtain favorable treatment in the past are rumored. Excessive application of penalties when no fraud is intended is in part a carryover from earlier years when smuggling was common. Moreover, vigilance on the part of inspectors is necessitated by the fact that some firms will deliberately seek to evade duty by misclassification or underweighing. Facilities in the ports do not permit frequent weighing (only a small number of suspicious items are reweighed), and the inspectors' offices lack men trained in chemical analysis.

The process of appeal from the inspector's decision is also open to improvement. The appeal may take several months, and doubt as to the outcome may interfere with the development of business operations. Especially in La Guaira and Maracaibo attention should be given to the possibility of providing for rehearing by a responsible authority at the port, with only the most difficult questions being referred to the Tariff Board in Caracas. Some firms are reluctant to appeal the decision of the inspector for fear of incurring his ill will.

Much of the difficulty in classification centers around change—the development of new products and modifications in old ones. When a new product is developed, or a new material substituted for an old one, doubt frequently exists about the tax status, since there is likely to be no reference to the commodity in the tariff schedule. The importer will frequently submit the product to the Tariff Board for a decision, but this may take several months, and delay business plans. It is often possible to obtain an informal ruling more quickly, however.

Frequently, a new product, being unspecified in any category, will be classed in the "not otherwise specified" group which usually (but not always) bears a higher rate than related enumerated items. Since changes in the classification are difficult to obtain, the firm may find it impossible to import the item profitably, or may seek complete exoneration. The result is to increase materially the number of exoneration applications. Some firms protest that too frequently new items will be classified on the basis of the ingredients of the article rather than the use to which it will be put, a practice which usually results in a much higher rate.[5]

Changes in the nature of products frequently render the old classifications obsolete, and the original purpose is defeated. Thus the continued increase in the weight of automobiles has rendered the classification unsatisfactory, since almost all cars are now in the upper two rate brackets.

The solution to the classification problem is not an easy one to find. Improved personnel selection and training methods and increased personnel would improve operation. The issuance to all inspectors of a monthly bulletin summarizing recent rulings and interpretations of the customs tariff would bring greater uniformity of action on the part of inspectors.

Abolition of the system of paying fines to the inspectors and other officials might also increase efficiency of operation. But more fundamentally, a general revision of the customs classification schedules is needed. In the first place, as noted above, a wide variety of articles now subject to low or moderate rates should be exempted from customs duties. This is particularly true in the chemicals and machinery field, where much of the present difficulty lies. Secondly, increased use of the ad valorem basis, as recommended in Section E of this chapter, below, would lessen the number of separate classes. Finally, careful rewording of many sections, with more explicit definitions and provision for new articles related to those now in the tariff, classified on the basis of use, would greatly reduce the amount of ambiguity and doubt.[6] Furthermore, tariff classifications must be more frequently and carefully adapted to changing conditions.

---

[5] Thus nylon safety belts were classified as "nylon articles, not specified," dutiable at a prohibitive rate, instead of as "protective devices," dutiable at a low rate.

[6] See footnote 4, above.

THE PROBLEM OF DELAY

A chronic complaint against customs operations in all countries is that they delay the delivery of merchandise. These complaints seem to be no more frequent or severe in Venezuela than in most countries, and many firms experience no particular problems. The worst trouble comes in the December-January period, when the Christmas and first-of-the-year rushes swamp both the warehouses and the customs officials. A few firms complain of more general delays (especially in Puerto Cabello), and particularly of inability to get rush service on items for which speed is urgent.

There is obviously room for some improvement. Much of the difficulty lies in La Guaira, largely because this port handles such a great volume of traffic, which has grown tremendously in recent years. Warehouse facilities, despite rapid expansion, are inadequate, and are a source both of delay and of weather damage, since many goods must be stored outside. Further expansion is necessary, and is planned.[7] A more fundamental reform, suggested by persons familiar with customs operation, would involve a reorganization of the operation of the service in La Guaira (and ultimately in other larger ports as well), whereby each warehouse in the port would have its own sub-administrator responsible to the general administrator, its own inspector, and its own warehouse superintendent. This would not only increase the number of responsible personnel, but also, by decentralizing operations, would save time and waste motion, and allow more adequate inspection. To the office of the general administrator of customs service in the port could be attached a representative of the Tariff Board, who would deal with cases of appeal from an inspector's decision. Major cases only would then be referred to the Board in Caracas.

One source of nuisance to many firms in the past has been the delay in receipt of invoices from the shipper, which sometimes results in the application of heavy warehouse storage charges when goods are held beyond the 6-day free time. This is a criticism of the mail service rather than customs, and of the banks, which it is reported, are slow in handling drafts.

One peculiar problem arises from the fact that a consignee, once customs obligations have been met, can obtain delivery of the goods

---

[7] Handling of some types of merchandise would have been facilitated had the railroad between La Guaira and Caracas been retained and modernized and connected with factories and warehouses in the latter city.

from the customs warehouse even though he has not paid his vendors for the goods. The consignee is required to post bond in such a case, but this provides inadequate protection in practice for the foreign exporter, primarily because of the long delay before he can receive his money (from one to two years) in case of default on the bond. The money placed in bond should be held in a special trust fund and paid immediately to the foreign exporter, rather than going into the national treasury, upon default. Under the present procedure, the exporter can obtain his money only after authorization has been made for payment through normal budgetary channels. The problem does not arise with responsible importers, but unfortunately there is a fringe of wildcat firms which will defraud their suppliers at the slightest opportunity.

Long delays also occur when the consignee refuses the merchandise and it is sold at auction. Any balance over duties and charges due the exporter can be obtained by the latter only after a very long delay.

THE WEIGHT BASIS OF THE TARIFF

The Venezuelan tariff, like that of several other countries, is based (with a few minor exceptions) upon weight; that is, almost all the tariff rates are specific, being applied uniformly per kilogram of the commodity regardless of value. This procedure was adopted for purposes of simplification, to avoid the problems of valuation which arise with an ad valorem duty, particularly when there is dumping, or deliberate undervaluation. These problems become especially acute when the rate is high; hence there may be some instances where a weight basis should be used for a part of the tax, to avoid the extreme pressures toward price wars or evasion through undervaluation that a very high ad valorem rate might induce. In general, however, the weight basis is to be avoided. It is objectionable on several counts. In the first place, the weight of the packing enters into the base of the duty, the tariffs being on gross weight, with a few exceptions. This practice discriminates, in a sense, against goods with heavy packing relative to the weight of the article. Adjustments could be made to a net weight basis, or at least a rough approximation of a net weight basis, without altering the general use of specific rates.

A much more serious effect of the use of the weight basis arises from the lack of correlation of weight and value, and the corresponding discrimination against relatively inexpensive articles compared with expensive ones in the same rate class. With many articles, the cheaper items will weigh as much as the more expensive ones; at least, weight will not increase in proportion to value. As a consequence, the duty will constitute a much higher percentage of the selling price of the less expensive article, and thus the distribution of burden among income classes in the economy becomes regressive. In addition, this treatment lessens use of the cheaper goods.

The results are fantastic in some classes, such as those covering a broad range of equipment and machinery. Small items may be far more complex and expensive than the larger ones, yet the duty will be much heavier on the latter.

In a few cases an attempt has been made to compensate by setting up classes by weight, and applying higher rates to heavy articles, under the assumption that value increases faster than weight. But this is a very crude sort of adjustment, and may create more inequities than it resolves.

Thirdly, the weight basis inevitably results in a larger number of customs rate schedules than an ad valorem type, as efforts are made to differentiate between various types of items in a general class.

Finally, specific rates suffer from the disadvantage that the burden of the duty, and also the degree of protection, vary inversely with the general price level. The increase in the general level of prices over the past fifteen years has reduced the impact and the protective influence of the duties.

These difficulties can be solved in only one way, namely, by shifting to an ad valorem basis those imports for which value per unit of weight varies widely in a particular commodity class. Major categories for which such treatment is desirable include automobiles, parts and accessories, electrical appliances of all types, radios and television sets, film, drugs and pharmaceutical items, records, and such industrial machinery and equipment as is subject to duty.[8] These commodities, for the most part, have easily established prices, and therefore the fundamental objection to the ad valorem basis, the valuation problem, is not serious. As pointed out in the next section, Venezuela already utilizes a general ad valorem customs duty on all goods, in the guise of a consular fee, which has given rise to little difficulty. The same principle can easily be extended to many of the customs duties.

---

[8] The weight basis is extremely unsatisfactory with textiles, and its use has led to a complicated textile tariff structure. But since the textile and clothing duties are now essentially prohibitive, the type of base in use does not make much difference. Valuation problems with an ad valorem duty on clothing are often troublesome.

D. The Consular Fees

The system of consular fees employed by Venezuela is unusual because of the height of the fees and the significant contribution to government revenue, Bs.150 million per year. The schedule is based on the value of the shipments, as follows:

Value of shipment (in Bs.)	Rate
under 10,000	2 per cent (minimum fee Bs.0.5)
between 10,000 and 20,000	2½ per cent
between 20,000 and 30,000	3 per cent
over 30,000	3½ per cent

All invoices of shipments from one distributor to one importer on one ship are cumulated for determination of the rate.

The rate applies to the value figure shown on the invoice, which represents the wholesale value of the goods at the port of exportation, including internal transport costs, but not including ocean freight. In general the Venezuelan government does not question the validity of the figures as shown on the invoices, beyond some spot checks of importers. The relatively low rate probably does not give strong enough incentive for deliberate understatement of price, which is difficult to conceal in any case except in transactions between controlled companies.

The fees are paid in Venezuela at the time of importation, but theoretically they are payments for the rather nominal services of the consular officials in the country of export, primarily the stamping of invoices. The consular fees must be regarded as a tax levy, not true fees, since their yield far exceeds the cost of the work of the consular offices.

The peculiar "progressive" rate schedule makes little sense of any kind, and has been widely criticized for many years. For example, in 1944, La Comisión de Estudios de Legislación Fiscal urged that the fees be made proportional.[9]

There are no exemptions or exonerations of any consequence, and thus the system constitutes essentially a uniform-rate tax (apart from the lower rate on small shipments) on all imports, including those specifically exempted or exonerated from customs duties proper. The effect is much the same as that of a universal, single-stage, sales tax confined to imported goods and to articles made from them. While many articles

---

[9] Appendix 10, p. 256, to the Report.

used by the lowest income groups in Venezuela are domestically produced, some are imported (a portion of the flour used, for example), and thus some burden is placed on persons in these groups. If, however, as may well be the case, the percentage of income spent on imported goods is greater in the higher income levels than in the lower, the consular-fee system may be progressive. But it is of course haphazard in its incidence on consumption of various commodities. It contributes some additional protection to that provided by the customs duties themselves.

Two specific recommendations can be made with respect to these fees:

1. The rates should be made proportional, since the present system has no logical basis.

2. The levy should be designated as a tariff, not as a consular fee. Much of the opposition at present can be attributed to the label of "consular fee," because the height of the charge is so great relative to the work performed by the consular offices.

With the levy renamed as a tax, it would be possible to exempt from it a few major categories of goods, such as flour, the taxation of which is particularly undesirable. Even with this change, however, the case for continued reliance on the levy is not a particularly strong one.

Air shipments should be subjected to the levy if it is retained.

E. Recommendations

The following recommendations are made for changes in tariff schedules and customs procedure, in light of the foregoing discussion.

1. Exemption from tariff of a wide range of articles which are not domestically produced, but which are now subject to low or moderate duties. Protection has no immediate relevance for such items; if anyone in Venezuela wishes to commence production of them in the future, protection can then be provided, if such a policy is regarded as desirable. Many of the items involved are used in production; taxes on them retard economic development and increase production costs. The burden of distribution among final consumers of the products is haphazard, and conforms to no particular pattern for which a logical case can be made. Essentially these levies constitute a type of nonuniform sales tax indirectly burdening the lower-income groups in a regressive and unequal fashion.

Outright exemption of these goods (or provision of the nominal .001 rate) would eliminate the need for a large portion of the exonerations now provided, and would greatly simplify the work of the Ministry of Development in handling applications for exoneration, as well as the work of importing firms. Basically, the tariff now covers far too many items. There is no point in applying low-rate duties on a specific basis to hundreds of different types of items that do not compete with the domestic production.

Selection of the specific items for exemption is a task that cannot be done within the confines of the present study; it is an appropriate task for the Ministry of Development, in conjunction with the Ministry of Finance. However, it can be said at once that commodities for which exemption is particularly appropriate include various food items not produced in Venezuela, paper of various types, industrial machinery of all forms except the particular types of items for which protection is desired, and chemicals of all forms including acids, caustic soda, and the like, except where protection is sought.

2. On a specified list of articles which may be regarded as luxuries, the transfer of the tariff to an ad valorem basis, the ad valorem rates to be applied to the wholesale selling price in Venezuela, that is, to the price at which the importer sells the merchandise to a dealer. In the case of importation by a retail dealer, the taxable price would be defined as the price for which the goods would have sold had they been sold to a retailer. In practice this rule would be applied by providing a schedule of discounts from the retail price for determining taxable price, representing the typical retail margin in the industry. This procedure, which is very troublesome in a general type of levy, should cause little difficulty when confined to a relatively few categories of specified commodities having fairly standard prices.

If the imported commodity of this type is also produced in Venezuela, the domestic product should be subject to an excise tax applied to sale by the manufacturer or wholesaler. If no protection were sought, this rate would be the same as that on imported goods. If protection were sought, the rate on the domestic article would be less than the import duty; existing trade agreements do, of course, limit the degree to which this technique can be applied.

The revised system would insure the collection of a certain amount of money from levies which in a rough way would measure taxable capacity, and in any event would not burden the lower income groups, as does the present tariff system. The replacement of the specific rates by the ad valorem rates would not only provide a much more equitable treatment of various consumption purchases by eliminating the discrimination against the high-weight, low-value items, but would also greatly simplify the tariff classifications of these items and the tasks of the importers, without creating serious valuation problems.

The following articles and rates are suggested as suitable for this form of tax, in the light of relative customs burdens and excise tax burdens found in other countries. The change would at least double the present customs yield from these articles. Again, any such recommendations may imply renegotiation of existing trade agreements.

Type of commodity	Rate domestic %	Rate imported %	Estimated yield (millions of Bs.)
Automobiles, parts and accessories[10]......	10	30	60
Television sets.........................	20	20	16
Radios and phonographs.................	20	20	4
Watches and clocks.....................	20	20	4
Cameras and film.......................	20	20	4
Electric appliances and lamps............	10	10	10
Total.........................			98

[10] Including motorcycles and small delivery trucks, and tires. No duty would be applied to parts brought in for assembly in Venezuela.

Some objections can, of course, be advanced against this type of excise tax system, particularly on the basis of discrimination against the users of certain products compared with others. But if it is considered desirable to raise some revenue from indirect taxation, this method is far superior to the present clumsy and inequitable customs duties on these articles. It is important, for administrative reasons, that the list be kept short.

3. Rewriting of the remainder of the tariff schedules, consisting largely of protective items, to provide more precise definitions, and more satisfactory means of handling new products, to avoid the present tendency to place new products in high-rate "not specified" classes. With many commodities, the number of sub-classes is far too great; those tariffs designed to be primarily protective do not need such refinements, since the rates can simply be set sufficiently high to block importation of all varieties, without specifying a wide variety of rates for

different species of the article. On the other hand, the use of the ad valorem basis for various luxury articles noted above will in itself allow a substantial reduction in the number of tariff classes and reduce classification problems.

4. Reduction in the use of the exoneration system by outright exemption of various categories of producers' goods, not domestically produced, for which exoneration is usually granted. Meanwhile, for certain basic materials, exoneration permits should be granted for an indefinite period, subject to revocation. Likewise, every effort should be made to speed up the process of granting import licenses and exonerations, consistent with the prevention of fraud.

5. Redesignation of the so-called consular fees as a general ad valorem duty, with the rate put on a proportional basis regardless of the size of the invoices. Possibly, exemption of a few basic goods, such as flour, consumed in large quantities by those in the lower income groups should be considered. The entire consular-fee system is open to serious question, but if a substantial sum of money is to be collected from the import form of indirect taxation, a general ad valorem duty is preferable to the helterskelter weight-based duties whose elimination is recommended in (2) above.

6. With respect to customs procedure, the following changes are desirable to improve the efficiency of operation:

a. Elimination of the system of granting a portion of fines assessed to customs inspectors and other personnel; but this change should be accompanied by appropriate increases in base pay. This obsolete method of payment results in misplaced emphasis on the part of inspectors, and is contrary to universally accepted principles of public administration; moreover, it causes a general loss in confidence on the part of business firms in the integrity of the customs service. At the same time every step should be taken to eliminate any suspicion of bribery of customs officials. It is impossible to assess the extent of this practice, but the existence of widespread suspicion that it has occurred in the past is obviously unfortunate, even if actual cases are rare.

b. Increase in the number of trained and qualified inspectors in the larger ports, and possible reorganization to make each customs warehouse a complete entity for customs operations.

c. Stationing in La Guaira of a representative of the Tariff Board, to reconsider, upon request, classifications made by the inspectors, in order to speed the process of review and lessen the number of cases going to the Board in Caracas.

d. Sharp curtailment in the assessment of fines when no intent to defraud is evidenced.

e. Increase in the physical facilities in La Guaira.

f. Treatment as a trust fund of money placed in bond by an importer to get his merchandise before settlement with the exporter, with immediate release of the money to the exporter upon default on the bond by the importer.

g. Preparation of a monthly bulletin for circulation to all inspectors and other interested parties summarizing recent rulings and interpretations of the Tariff Board.

h. Simplification of the consular invoices, which call for far too much detail, especially in requiring statement of the precise customs definition of the class.

i. Codification of the customs regulations.

j. Extension of the consular fees to air shipments, if the consular fee is retained.

7. Collection of data on customs duty yield by commodity class.

CHAPTER X : **The Tax on Gross Receipts**
: **(Cinco por Mil)[1] and Stamp Taxes**

A. Tax on Gross Receipts

The only tax of general scope levied on domestic transactions by the national government of Venezuela is the one on gross receipts, generally known as the *cinco por mil* tax. This tax applies to the gross receipts of all business firms at the rate of .5 per cent (5 per 1000), as imposed by the Fiscal Stamp Law *(Ley de Timbre Fiscal)*. It is a relatively new levy, imposed in 1956 to replace (a) most of a great variety of stamp taxes on documents, and (b) equally objectionable sealed paper taxes of the states under which various documents could be prepared only on special paper purchased from the state governments. These stamp taxes and sealed-paper taxes were carryovers from earlier decades. They are very unsatisfactory forms of tax, and the cinco por mil, unpopular though it is, is universally regarded as preferable to the taxes which it replaced. Some stamp taxes are still employed, but they are of minor consequence, applying to passports, diplomas, etc.[2]

STRUCTURE OF THE TAX

The present tax applies to all fields of production and distribution, and to the service industries, including banks and insurance companies. Persons in the liberal professions are subject if they establish partnerships, clinics, etc., but not when in independent practice. Contractors are subject, but not on the charge for materials if labor and materials are contracted for separately. The tax is a levy on businesses, as such, and does not apply to isolated transactions between individuals.

---

[1] Section A of this chapter, written in June, 1958, uses the present tense in describing the tax on gross receipts. Subsequently, the tax was repealed (as of Oct. 1, 1958).

[2] See the concluding section of this chapter, below.

Exemptions by law are quite limited. They are confined to various governmental, non-profit, and cooperative enterprises. In addition, firms with quarterly gross receipts of less than Bs.20,000 are exempt from tax on the first Bs.12,000 of gross receipts. This exemption is increased for firms engaged in farming, cattle raising, and fishing; they pay no tax on the first Bs.20,000 of their quarterly receipts if their total receipts do not exceed Bs.30,000. Moreover, these firms are allowed a percentage deduction from tax equal to the percentage of profits reinvested in expansion of the enterprise. This tax-relief measure is designed to encourage expansion of agriculture; for example, if a cattle ranch reinvests 25 per cent of its net profit in expansion, it pays the cinco por mil on only 75 per cent of its gross receipts. In practice, therefore, the typical farm or ranch incurs no liability at all, under the cinco por mil tax.

The government is authorized to grant complete exemption to firms engaged in production and processing of farm products, and to exempt from tax for one or two quarters firms suffering serious losses from fire or other disaster.

The tax applies at a uniform rate of .5 per cent. While the government has the power to raise or lower the rate by 40 per cent, it has not done so. The measure of the tax liability is gross receipts, in a cash sense—the actual sum of money taken in during the period, including sums received from the sale of capital assets (except upon liquidation of the business). Insurance companies pay on gross premiums and interest and other receipts while banks pay on gross income. Receipts consisting of the acquisition of additional money capital are not subject to tax. Receipts from exports are taxable, at a price representing the value at the place of exportation; tax in this case accrues at the time of export rather than at the time of receipt of cash for the sale of the articles.

The tax is collected from smaller firms by means of stamps. Each establishment must keep a stamp book, in which revenue stamps must be affixed quarterly for the correct amount. The stamps are purchased from the government and must be cancelled as they are applied to the book. A statement of gross receipts must also be entered in the book quarterly when stamps are applied. As a result of the great nuisance of stamps to larger firms, such firms are permitted to obtain authorization to pay on the basis of quarterly returns. Most larger firms now pay by the use of returns, and more money is collected in this form than by the stamps. In 1957-1958, Bs.61 million were collected by returns and Bs.56 million by stamps, for a total of Bs.117 million.

SHIFTING

The law contains no reference to the shifting of the tax. Therefore, it is by no means clear where the burden of the tax is supposed to rest. Probably the tax is intended to be one on business enterprises, rather than on consumers. However, many firms initially attempted to invoice the tax separately from the price of the goods, and thus to shift it directly. This policy encountered strong opposition from dealers and other purchasers, who simply refused to pay the amount and thus forced sellers to stop the practice. However, since the tax becomes an expense of doing business, it presumably tends to be shifted to consumers over a period of time. The process of shifting may be a slow one, in view of the low tax rate, the tendency of firms to treat the tax as a deduction from sales instead of as a general expense, and the existence of controls on the prices of a few basic articles (milk and gasoline, for example). The tax, of course, applies to each transaction through which a good passes, and thus the overall burden on each final consumer product is higher than simply ½ of 1 per cent.

PROBLEMS IN OPERATION

A tax which applies to the gross receipts of all business firms is in many respects a relatively simple levy. Nevertheless, various problems have arisen.

1. Receipts vs. sales. The tax is imposed upon receipts of money rather than sales. Initially a number of larger firms sought to use the sales basis (even though tax on credit sales would thus be paid at an earlier date), since typical accounting systems provide this information more readily than figures of cash receipts. Others feared that the cash basis would subject to tax such receipts as advances of funds by parent companies. However, in general, the government has required the use of the receipts basis except on export transactions.

2. Sales of capital assets. There have been questions relating to the exact tax status of sums received from the sale of capital assets, as, for example, from a parent to a subsidiary firm. Such transactions are typically taxable.

3. Insurance companies. Receipts of insurance companies are subject to tax, and problems have arisen as to exact tax base, especially in the case of reinsurance.

4. International transport companies, subject to special income tax treatment. In general, receipts from freight or passenger charges collected from transactions of this character made in Venezuela are taxable. Private companies complain of the exemption from tax of the government-owned air and steamship lines.

5. The stamp system. This system is a source of general nuisance, which is in part overcome by allowing larger firms to pay on the basis of returns. It is very doubtful if the stamp technique contributes anything toward effective collection. In any event, the use of the return method could well be extended to far more firms than at present.

For firms paying by the use of returns, the requirement that a special book be kept in which a record is made of tax liability and payments is a nuisance and of no value for administrative purposes; in fact, it may well detract from effective enforcement.

ENFORCEMENT

The enforcement of the tax rests with the Inspector General of Revenue Stamps and his staff of inspectors. Each of the 14 regional offices is under the direction of an administrator of revenue stamp taxes (*Administrador de la Renta de Timbre Fiscal*), and includes one or more inspectors of revenue stamps, who inspect business firms. The number of inspectors varies from one in small regions to 30 in Caracas. An attempt is made to inspect each firm once or twice a year. Frequently, inspectors merely walk from store to store, checking stamp books, and in some instances comparing reported figures with those in the firm's books. Larger firms paying by return are visited, about once a year on the average, and a brief check is made of the reported amount against the books of the firm. In general, however, there is no real audit, in the sense of determination of the validity of the sales figure reported by the firm. In part this is due to the lack of an adequate staff trained in accounting. The inspectors were largely taken over from the old stamp tax administration. The widespread belief that the tax is temporary has precluded a systematic recruitment and training program.

Some fines are assessed, mainly for failure of the firm to keep stamp books. A relatively high percentage of the potential revenue is no doubt collected, in part because so much comes from the larger firms, which are not likely to attempt deliberate violation of the law. Most of the evasion is by firms that stay in business only a few months, and by other small firms which either do not pay at all, or understate sales. Many payors who should withhold the tax no doubt fail to do so: for instance, many debtors paying interest to creditors outside Venezuela. Under a low-rate tax of this type collected from large numbers of small firms lacking adequate record systems, any complete enforcement program would be intolerably costly, if not impossible. As with other indirect taxes, inspectors receive a portion of fines collected, up to a fixed amount per month.

EVALUATION OF THE TAX

The cinco por mil levy is probably the most unpopular segment of the tax system. The basic argument raised against the tax is that it constitutes an antiquated, unnecessary, and in many ways objectionable supplement to the income tax, raising revenue which could easily be obtained by increases in the income tax.

Specifically, the primary objections include the following:

1. The tax is inevitably subject to considerable evasion on the part of smaller firms, with consequent inequity, loss of revenue, and decline in tax morality. Even limited enforcement requires a staff which duplicates that of the income tax; if this personnel were added to income tax enforcement (with adequate training), more effective overall tax enforcement could be obtained.

2. The tax is cumulative in its operation, applying to the receipts from each transaction through which a good passes from initial production to final sale to the consumer. This results in a cumulative burden on the final consumer in excess of the nominal rate of the tax, one which is unequal, in a haphazard pattern, on various products, because of the different number of sales through which they pass on the way from initial manufacture to final consumption.

At the same time, the tax is discriminatory against nonintegrated business firms, favoring those firms which combine a number of stages. Incentive is thus given toward further vertical integration. Obviously the effects cannot be too serious so long as the rate is only .5 per cent, but even this rate may exercise some influence.

3. Complete and immediate shifting of the tax may be difficult, because the low rate may encourage some firms to leave prices unchanged, and also because of the uneven burden on firms in various distribution channels. To the extent to which shifting does not occur, the tax discriminates against firms with low profit margins relative to gross receipts. This is so because the tax constitutes a higher percentage of net profit in such cases. Similarly, the tax discriminates against firms with rapid

turnover relative to the amount of capital investment; for these firms, the tax constitutes a relatively high percentage of the return on capital.

4. To the extent to which the tax shifts, it causes higher prices of basic necessities as well as other goods. This results in an unjustifiable burden on the large numbers of persons in Venezuela at bare subsistence levels, and checks increases in the standards of living of the lower income groups.

5. Finally, one of the greatest dangers from continuing the tax is the possibility that in time it might develop into a high-rate turnover tax, a sales tax of the worst type. The present tax is comparable to the sales tax of other countries, differing only in that the rate is very low. If the tax is retained and revenue needs increase, there is a danger that the rate might be increased—to 1, 2, or higher percentages. This happened in France and in Germany, directly after World War I. The next stage is that, under the higher tax rate, the discrimination against the non-integrated firms—the smaller independent retailers and wholesalers—becomes intolerable. Efforts are made then to meet this problem by varying the rates on different transactions. The structure of the tax becomes extremely complex. The tax becomes extremely difficult to administer effectively, yet the inequities and the interference with efficient functioning of the economy are not completely eliminated. If Venezuela is ultimately to have a sales tax, the form of the tax should be chosen in the light of the relative merits of various forms of sales taxation, rather than being determined by the historical accident that a general gross receipts tax has already been in use.

Elimination of the cinco por mil tax would not reduce the total tax revenue of the national government by the amount that is now being yielded by the tax. The cinco por mil tax is deductible in computing business net income for the income tax. Accordingly, repeal of the cinco por mil tax would automatically increase the amount of net income subject to the income tax, to the extent that the repeal of the tax did not lead to reductions in prices charged by the firms.

Moreover, a large part of the cinco por mil tax is paid by the petroleum companies. It is paid chiefly on their exports of oil. Some of these companies are below the 50-50 line, with respect to their ordinary taxes (royalty tax, ordinary income tax, customs duties, cinco por mil tax), and are therefore paying, in addition, the "additional income tax" to bring their total tax and royalty payments up to 50 per cent of their pre-tax income. For such companies, repeal of the cinco por mil would lead automatically to an equal increase in the additional income tax. To this extent, therefore, repeal of the cinco por mil tax would cause the government no loss of revenue at all.

In the light of these considerations, we recommend that the cinco por mil tax be repealed at once. The revenue lost by repeal can be obtained more equitably and with less administrative trouble by an increase in the income tax.

B. Stamp Taxes

The budget for 1959-60 includes under direct taxes a line entitled "Income from Stamp Taxes" (*Renta de Timbre Fiscal*), estimated at Bs.32,400,000. The greater part of this amount, about Bs.20 million, will come from collections from taxpayers who failed to pay their gross receipts tax *(cinco por mil)* on time. As noted at the beginning of this chapter, that tax was repealed as of October 1, 1958. The remainder, about Bs.12 million, will be received from the sale of stamps, or stamped paper, for use on various occasions, usually involving formal petitions, statements, registrations, certificates, or licenses.[3] For example: a personal identity card (*Cédula de Identidad Personal*) must carry a Bs.2 stamp; a license to carry firearms, Bs.50 in stamps; passports, Bs.12 on issuance and Bs.2 on renewal; certificates of registration of a patent or a trademark, Bs.20; doctoral diploma at the University, Bs.50. Stamped paper (*papel sellado*) must be used for formal petitions or statements to the government (excluding tax returns, and a few other items). It must also be employed for certain court documents, notarized documents, certified copies of records supplied by the government, documents concerning patents, and so on. The paper is sold by the government at 50 centimos per sheet.

These stamp duties are characteristic of an earlier age of taxation, when governments were restricted to taxes that could be readily enforced, especially when the individual was in need of some formal action by the State, and could therefore be forced to pay a "fee" or a "tax" before the government would act. They are bothersome to the business firm, and to individuals, and should not be counted on as an important source of revenue.

To the extent that the government is put to some expense in certifying the formal nature of this or that document, the stamp duties are justified

---

[3] See Ley de Timbre Fiscal, taking effect January 1, 1959, *Gaceta Oficial*, Dec. 19, 1958.

as being fees, rather than taxes. Indeed, they are regarded by the Venezuelan tax administrator as being fees (*tasas*), not taxes (*impuestos*).

The current rates seem moderate; they are probably somewhat too high, especially in some cases, to be regarded as "fees," but for the time being they do not need to be reduced. No attempt should be made to increase them, or extend their scope.

The revenue under the heading, *Renta de Timbre Fiscal,* will of course decline in future years, as delinquent accounts under the repealed *cinco por mil* are cleared up. The revenue will probably stabilize at about Bs.15 million a year: a reduction of Bs.17 million from the estimate for 1959-60.

CHAPTER XI : A Possible General Sales Tax

Most of the nations of the western world employ two major taxes: the income tax and the general sales tax. The general sales tax is imposed upon the sales of all or a wide variety of commodities. The tax is intended to be borne by the ultimate consumers. In some countries, such as Germany, the sales tax is the greatest single source of revenue, while in others it is second only to the income tax. In the United States the sales tax, although not used by the Federal government, is the largest source of state revenue. It is a major revenue source in Canada at both Dominion and provincial levels, in Brazil at Federal and state levels, and in Uruguay, Chile, and Argentina, together with many European countries.

The Case For and Against the Tax in Venezuela

Venezuela has never used a sales tax, although the cinco por mil levy was in essence a small-scale tax of this type. It differed from the usual sales tax by virtue of the low rate and because it was considered to be a business license tax, not intended to be shifted to consumers.

The primary argument for a sales tax is its ability to yield relatively large sums of money at low rates, simply because it strikes all (or most) consumer expenditures. The sales tax thus has a much broader base than an income tax, so long as the latter has such high exemptions that the typical lower income family is exempt. Are there any advantages, however, in raising revenue from a sales tax rather than by means of lower exemptions and higher rates under an income tax? One is the practical political advantage of avoiding the public reaction to a sharp increase in income taxes. Secondly, the sales tax will reach many persons who, for administrative reasons, cannot be taxed directly on their incomes. Thirdly, if revenue needs increase, the income tax rates might reach a level at which they would curtail investment seriously and inter-

303

fere with economic development, whereas the sales tax will directly reduce consumption more than investment. However, it must be kept in
mind that consumption may be a more important factor controlling the
level of investment than the height of the tax on earnings from business
enterprise.

On the other hand, there are serious objections to a sales tax. In the
first place, purely on equity grounds, the tax conforms much less with
accepted principles of distribution of burden among individuals than
does an income tax. If food is taxable, a serious burden is placed on
the lower income classes, and the overall burden of the tax is almost
certain to be regressive relative to income. Even with food exempt, a
considerable burden remains on poorer persons. In a society with large
numbers of persons in the low income classes, enjoying only a subsistence minimum, it is unfortunate to use a form of tax which does not
free them from fiscal burden. Even in other income classes, the sales
tax burden is distributed in a haphazard and somewhat inequitable
fashion, overburdening those families which, for one reason or another,
find it necessary to spend relatively high percentages of their incomes.
Thus, large families are overburdened relative to smaller ones with the
same income, though they have less tax capacity.

Secondly, a sales tax directly increases the cost of living, and thus
tends to generate wage increases, which strengthen inflationary tend-
encies. At the same time there results a very unequal final distribution
of the tax burden, since some persons will be able to shift the tax to a
greater extent than others.

Thirdly, even in a non-inflationary period, it is difficult to insure that
complete and exact shifting of the tax by business firms will occur. If
the tax cannot be shifted, it will constitute a very non-uniform and inequitable burden upon the owners of various types of businesses. At the
same time there is constant danger that the tax will result in some price
increases in excess of the amount of the tax, and place an unnecessary
burden upon the consumer.

Finally, the tax requires an administrative organization which duplicates that of the income tax, and creates various compliance problems
for the firms subject to tax. Effective enforcement, especially with small
firms, is difficult, yet if the tax is to yield significant revenue, the rate
must be so high that evasion creates serious inequity. As explained
below, the type of sales tax which is most suitable for the Venezuelan
economy, the wholesale sales tax, raises problems of ascertaining a
suitable taxable sales price with certain types of transactions.

In light of these considerations, the introduction of a sales tax in

Venezuela is not recommended at this time. Income tax rates are very low, and exemptions are so high that many families pay no tax at all. If additional revenues are needed, readjustments of the income tax to increase payments from present taxpayers and to bring additional families within the scope of the tax will produce a far more acceptable pattern of distribution of burden and fewer administrative problems than the adding of a sales tax to the tax structure. Not until income tax rates reach several times the present levels is there any danger of adverse effects on economic development. A sales tax may do far more to retard development by checking the increase in consumption in the lower income levels, which is necessary to absorb the output of expanding industry. The case against sales taxation is strengthened by the existence in Venezuela of large numbers of persons in the lower income levels. In a country such as Norway, with a rather uniform income distribution, and few extremely poor or extremely wealthy persons, the burden of distribution of a sales tax may be acceptable in terms of usual standards. But in the present-day Venezuelan economy, with its sharp nonuniformity in distribution, a general commodity tax is particularly objectionable.

The Wholesale Sales Tax as the Least Objectionable Form

While a sales tax is not now recommended, it is recognized that growing revenue needs and possible future opposition to income tax increases may ultimately lead to the use of a sales tax. Accordingly, it is desirable to consider briefly the relative merits of various principal forms, since the world abounds with unfortunate types of sales tax installed with little consideration of relative merits of the alternatives and then adhered to, despite serious defects, because they yield so much money that the governments are reluctant to tamper with them.

There are five major alternatives:

TRANSACTIONS TAX, OR TURNOVER TAX

The turnover tax applies to each transaction through which a commodity passes on the way from initial production of raw materials to final sale to the ultimate consumer. The only advantage is that this type of sales tax can raise a given sum of money at a lower tax rate.

On the other hand, the turnover tax has serious disadvantages which in general make it the most objectionable of all forms of sales tax. Because it applies to each transaction through which a commodity passes, it induces vertical integration of business firms both in production and distribution channels. By the same token, it discriminates against the non-integrated firms, the independent wholesalers and producers of parts and materials. Thus the tax checks the development of specialization in industry, and causes integration and monopoly influence to be carried further than is warranted by economic conditions.

In practice, the pressure on the non-integrated firms has typically led to demands for revision of the tax. This revision, in Germany, Belgium, and elsewhere, has taken the form of adjustments in rates on various transactions in an effort to lessen the competitive disadvantages of the non-integrated firms. But, without exception, these adjustments have not only failed to accomplish fully the desired results, but have also created new inequities and have seriously complicated the operation of the taxes. Whenever varied rates are applied to different transactions, the problems of delimitation of the various transactions become tremendous.

Finally, the turnover tax results in widely varying burdens on the final consumption of various products, since the number of stages through which different goods pass on the way from initial production to final consumption differs widely. This variation, unfortunately, bears no relation to "luxury" as against "necessity" characteristics.

In general, any of the other forms of sales taxation will function in a tolerable fashion; the turnover tax is to be avoided under all circumstances.

RETAIL SALES TAX

In many respects, the retail form of sales tax, under which the tax is collected only on the final sale to the consumer, is the most satisfactory type. Only this form insures complete uniformity of the ratio of tax to consumption expenditures on various goods (assuming complete shifting), since the tax is imposed directly upon the final sale price. Only the retail tax can be quoted separately from the price of the good, to the final consumer. It can thus be made clearly evident to the consumer. It avoids the "pyramiding" of tax that occurs under other forms of sales tax when dealers apply fixed percentage markups to purchase prices which include the tax. The retail sales tax permits the lowest tax rate of any acceptable form of sales tax, to raise a given sum of money, since retail margins are included within the base of the tax. Under a low rate, the incentive to evade is somewhat less. The retail tax can be applied to actual selling prices in all cases, without causing inequity. The troublesome adjustments in prices for tax purposes that are necessary on some transactions under a wholesale or manufacturers' sales tax are avoided. Finally, rumored changes in tax rates do not cause dealers to stock up on inventories, or delay purchases, as under the other kinds of sales tax.

On the other hand, retail trade in Venezuela is carried on by a large number of very small shops and stands. Administration of the retail sales tax would therefore be extremely difficult. Substantial evasion would be inevitable. A retail sales tax will function effectively only in an economy in which the great bulk of retail sales are made through stores large enough so that adequate records are kept.

WHOLESALE SALES TAX

The evils of the turnover tax can be avoided as well as the problems of collection from a very large number of small retailers by placing the sales tax upon the sale to the retailer, rather than upon the sale by the retailer to the consumer. Such a sales tax is known as a wholesale sales tax. It is collected from all firms selling to retailers, whether they be wholesalers, manufacturers, or importers. In the case of a few large retailers who import directly, the tax would be collected at the time of importation. This type of tax is collected from a relatively small number of firms. Most of these firms are large enough to have adequate record systems, which will permit audit of returns. The wholesale sales tax is used successfully in Switzerland, Australia, and other countries.

The wholesale sales tax does, to be sure, have some disadvantages compared to the retail tax. A somewhat higher rate would be required. The tax would necessarily be hidden in the prices of the goods. Some "pyramiding" would occur. Some problems of determination of taxable price would arise, particularly on imports by retailers and on purchase of goods by large retailers at relatively low prices. But on the whole, use of the wholesale tax is preferable, given the conditions of the present-day Venezuelan economy.

MANUFACTURERS' SALES TAX

An alternative to the wholesale sales tax is the manufacturers' sales tax, as used in Canada, the Argentine, Uruguay, and elsewhere. This tax is applied to the sales of finished products by the manufacturer. In many respects the two taxes are similar. But for a country which relies heavily on imports, the wholesale tax is preferable. The imported goods, not being manufactured within the country, must be taxed at the time of importation under a manufacturers' tax. As a consequence, problems of ascertaining the taxable price are more troublesome. Under the wholesale tax, the tax rate is applied to an actual domestic selling price, that of sale by the importer to a dealer (except in the case of imports directly by retailers). Fewer debatable questions therefore arise about the appropriate taxable price. This consideration was the primary factor leading Australia, for example, to adopt the wholesale tax rather than the manufacturers' sales tax.

VALUE ADDED TAX

The value added tax as employed in France applies to each transaction through which a good passes, down through the wholesale level, but only to the value added by each seller. "Value added" is the difference between selling price and cost of goods sold.[1] This form of tax avoids the evils of the turnover tax, but offers only one advantage over the wholesale tax. It spreads the impact of the tax over a larger number of firms, and thus perhaps lessens the incentive to evade. The value added tax is more complicated, especially if exemptions are granted.

THE STRUCTURE OF A WHOLESALE SALES TAX

A few major points on the structure of the wholesale sales tax are sketched below.

Technique of Operation. The wholesale sales tax requires licensing of all firms selling at wholesale (that is, selling for resale by others, including all manufacturers). Sales from one licensed firm to another are exempt from tax, the license number of the purchaser being entered upon the sales invoice. Sales by a licensed firm to an unlicensed buyer, and thus to a retailer or a final consumer, are taxable. A firm doing extensive wholesale and retail business (not a common situation) would be required to keep the two types of activities separate for tax purposes. If a retailer made a few wholesale sales, these transactions would be regarded as retail sales and the tax would be applied, as usual, to the purchase by the retailer.

---

[1] Under the French version of the tax, the firm calculates tax on its total sales and then deducts the amount of tax that has already been paid by its vendors, on goods purchased.

When a licensed firm bought taxable goods tax free for use in the firm—for example, purchase of an automobile by a business firm—it would be required to pay tax on the purchase.

Importation by licensed firms would be tax free. Importation by re-tailers or individual consumers would be subject to tax, collected at time of importation upon the wholesale price. If this system created serious problems, an alternative could be used, as follows. The rela-tively few large retailers doing extensive importing could be licensed, and the tax could be applied to all of their retail sales at a rate reflecting the basic tax rate, reduced by the typical retail margin. This system, as employed in Switzerland, is not entirely equitable, but works with reasonable success.

Coverage. If a sales tax is to be productive of revenue and feasible of administration, coverage should be broad, and exemptions held to a minimum. As indicated above, goods purchased by wholesalers or manufacturers for resale, or by manufacturers for use in manufacturing, would be tax free under the licensing system, to prevent multiple appli-cation of the tax. Beyond this, there is strong justification for exempting industrial machinery and equipment, industrial fuel, and goods directly consumed in industrial processing, in order to minimize tax burden on economic development and to avoid a cumulative burden of the tax on finished products. It is not feasible, however, to exempt all goods used by business firms, because so many of these items are also purchased for consumption purposes.

Likewise, a good case, from an equity standpoint, can be made for exempting food, because the expenditures of the lower income groups concentrate so heavily on food products. In Venezuela, food exemption would probably cut the yield of the tax nearly in half, and thus a sub-stantially greater rate would be needed to gain the same amount of revenue. The decision would have to be made in terms of a balance of equity, administrative, and revenue considerations. One alternative is the exemption of a few products which form the basic diet of the low income groups—corn and corn products, bread and flour, fresh meat and vegetables, beans and milk.

There is substantial merit in limiting exemptions to industrial ma-chinery, fuel, and related items, and food. If any effort is made to ex-clude other items used by the lower income groups, such as various articles of clothing, soap, etc., the administration of the tax becomes seriously complicated. Vendors also find it difficult to comply with the law. A choice must be made between a relatively limited selective excise system, or a general sales tax system; if the latter is selected for revenue reasons, then it must be kept relatively broad in scope if it is to operate successfully.

A common error in sales tax laws is to exempt cigarettes, liquor and other items subject to excise. This policy complicates administration, and gains nothing in terms of general tax policy.

A wholesale sales tax must almost of necessity be confined to tangible goods. Consumer services, such as laundry and hair cutting, can easily be brought within the scope of a retail tax, but they obviously cannot be reached by a tax restricted to large-scale wholesale and manufacturing establishments.

Just as exemptions must be kept to a minimum for successful operation, so is uniformity of rate desirable. A multiple-rate system, although more feasible under a wholesale tax than a retail tax, complicates operation, particularly by creating many lines of demarcation. However, if it is regarded as desirable to single out a relatively few products for higher taxation, this can be done, either by collecting a supplementary excise, or by using a higher sales tax rate on these articles.

The Problem of Taxable Price. In usual wholesale transactions, the tax can be applied to the actual selling price, net of cash, quantity, and other discounts, or, in total, to the sales figures of the period (net of returns, etc.). But when goods are imported by retailers, a problem arises, which has already been discussed above. Another problem is that of the large retailer who can buy from manufacturers at prices substantially lower than those charged to small retailers by typical wholesalers in the field. Any attempt to "uplift" the taxable price in such cases, as attempted in Great Britain, is a source of great nuisance. Since there are only a very small number of such large retailers, and since most of them also are likely to be importing in large quantities, the same solution as that suggested for imports can be used, namely, the licensing of these large retailers by special permission, and application of the tax to their sales, reduced by the typical margin figure.

Administration. Effective operation of a sales tax requires the establishment of an adequate administrative procedure and organization. Several features are of particular importance:

1. Collection of the tax on the basis of returns filed, preferably on a quarterly basis. The stamp system (as under the repealed "cinco por mil") tends to detract from effective enforcement by ineffective utilization of inspectors' time and effort. Returns should be simple, requiring

merely information on total sales, exempt sales, if any, and taxable sales.

2. Provision of adequate information to taxpaying firms, particularly at the time of establishment of the tax.

3. Registration of all taxpaying firms (manufacturers and wholesalers). This is necessary both for enforcement and for operation of a system which prevents multiple collection of tax on the same articles.

4. An extensive inspection and audit program, involving actual check upon the validity of reported sales by analysis of the firms' books, purchase invoices and the like. Most manufacturers and wholesalers will not seek to evade tax, but a few will, if not checked, and some unintentional misstatement of tax due is inevitable unless a careful audit is made. Inspectors must have a knowledge of accounting procedures, and be well trained for the task. The routine check used under the cinco por mil levy is inadequate for effective operation of a sales tax.

Tax Yield. It is impossible to predict with any degree of accuracy the possible yield of a wholesale sales tax in Venezuela. With all food taxable, the probable total base for the tax can be estimated to be around Bs.6 billion and with food exempt, around Bs.4 billion. Thus a 10 per cent tax with food subject to tax might yield 600 million bolivars; with food exempt, 400 million bolivars. These figures are only very rough estimates.

Study of Other Taxes

In the event of the establishment of a sales tax in Venezuela, careful analysis should be made of the sales tax systems which have proven to be most satisfactory elsewhere. In the light of the general economic structure of Venezuela, the system which appears to be most suitable is that of Switzerland, despite substantial differences in the economies of the two countries. Of the South American countries, the Argentine system is probably the most satisfactory, but it is unnecessarily complex in some respects, and is less suited to the Venezuelan economy than the wholesale type of tax.

The text of the Swiss law is to be found in the publication, *Impôt Fédéral sur le Chiffre d'Affaires,* Berne: Editions de la Feuille officielle suisse du commerce. A detailed commentary on the tax is that of H. Herold, *Praxis der Umsatzsteuerrechts,* Basel: Verlag für Recht und Gesellschaft, 1953.

Descriptions of other sales taxes are to be found in the following:

Argentine: Reig, E. J., *El Impuesto a las Ventas*. 4th ed., Buenos Aires: Ediciones Contabilidad Moderna, 1954.

Uruguay: Peirano Facio, J. C., *El Impuesto a las Ventas*. Montevideo: Facultad de Derecho y Ciencias Sociales, 1955.

Brazil: Gomes de Souza, R., *O Impôsto Sôbre Vendas e Consignações No Sistema Tributário Brasileiro*. Rio de Janeiro: Ediçoes Financeiras S. A., 1956.

United States: Oster, C. V., *State Retail Sales Taxation*. Columbus: State University of Ohio, 1957.

Canada: Due, J. F., *The General Manufacturers Sales Tax in Canada*, and *Canadian Provincial Retail Sales Taxes*. Toronto: Canadian Tax Foundation, 1951, 1953.

Australia: Irving, H. R., *Irving's Commonwealth Sales Tax Law and Practise*. Sydney: Norwood Press, 1950.

France: Lauré, M., *La Taxe sur la Valeur Ajoutée*. Paris: Receuil Sirey, 1952.

Germany: Zierold Pritsch, D., *Die Umsatzsteuersysteme*. Bonn: 1952; and *Die Optimale Umsatzsteuer*, Koln: Otto Schmidt, 1954 and 1956.

General: Due, J. F., *Sales Taxation*. London: Routledge and Kegan Paul, 1957.

Organization for European Economic Cooperation, *The Influence of Sales Taxes on Productivity*. Paris, 1958.

CHAPTER XII : State and Municipal Finance

A. Relative Financial Importance of National, State and Municipal Governments

The present Venezuelan system of government has been described as a mixture of French and United States systems—involving a high degree of centralization on the one hand and a considerable degree of local autonomy on the other. The bulk of government spending, and hence decisions over the allocation of public funds, is in the hands of the national government. The national government also provides, through the constitutional grants and supporting grants, about 90 per cent of the revenues of the state and territorial governments. The districts and municipalities[1] raise most of their revenues through local taxes and charges, although a small amount is provided by state grants.

Our rough estimate for 1958-59 puts total government expenditures—national, state and municipal—at Bs.6,000 million, of which national

		Millions of bolivars
Estimated national government expenditures		
Total budget, 1958-59...................................	5,813	
Deduct constitutional and supporting grants to states........	513	5,300
Estimated state-territorial government expenditures		
Total...	570	
Deduct grants to districts and municipalities...............	40	530
Estimated district-municipal expenditures....................		170
Total..		6,000

[1] For convenience, the collective term "municipalities" will be used to designate districts and municipalities proper; "states" will designate the national regional entities: twenty states and two territories. In addition, there is the Federal District which includes the City of Caracas.

expenditures, ex grants to state and territorial government, will constitute about 88 per cent; state-territorial expenditures, ex grants to localities, about 9 per cent; and district-municipal expenditures about 3 per cent. (Here the Federal District is included with the states rather than with the districts-municipalities.) These estimates—as they are listed on the preceding page—while subject to some margin of error, indicate the relative importance of the three levels of government. The state and municipal governments play a small role indeed in Venezuelan government.

By contrast, in the United States the states and local governments spend more than the national government for purposes other than defense.[2] The figures for 1957 were as follows:

		Billions of dollars
Federal expenditures..		$80.6
Less: expenditures on defense.............................	45.8	
grants to states and local governments................	3.9	30.9
State expenditures..	24.2	
Less: net grants to localities...............................	7.3	16.9
Local government expenditures...............................		30.7
Total state and local government expenditures..............		$47.6

SOURCE: United States Bureau of the Census, *Summary of Governmental Finances* 1957.

In size and population Venezuela is comparable to the larger states of the United States. Its revenue structure, however, is much simpler than that of most of the larger U.S. states and their local governments, and the state and municipal governments play a much less important role than in U.S. states.

Per capita state and municipal expenditures of each state in Venezuela are shown in Table XII-1.

B. Governmental Structure and Financial Control

The system briefly described below is the present system; because the country's governmental structure is in transition as a result of recent political changes, the existing patterns may change in many respects.

[2] Defense is budgeted as Bs.552 million in the 1958-59 Venezuelan national budget, about 9 per cent of total governmental expenditures.

Table XII-1. Per Capita Expenditures of States, 1956-57 Fiscal Year, and Districts and Municipalities, 1956

(Amounts in bolivars)

	States	Districts and Municipalities	Total
Distrito Federal..........................	—	204	204
Anzoátegui.............................	54	32	86
Apure.................................	78	28	106
Aragua................................	86	46	132
Barinas...............................	85	13	98
Bolívar...............................	67	33	100
Carabobo..............................	53	58	111
Cojedes...............................	126	17	143
Falcón................................	54	17	71
Guárico...............................	61	22	83
Lara..................................	52	21	73
Mérida................................	58	11	69
Miranda...............................	58	83	141
Monagas...............................	62	18	80
Nueva Esparta..........................	165	21	186
Portuguesa.............................	61	18	79
Sucre.................................	48	10	58
Táchira...............................	57	21	78
Trujillo...............................	55	19	74
Yaracuy...............................	77	14	91
Zulia.................................	49	38	87
Federal Territories			
Amazonas.........................	253	10	263
Delta Amacuro.....................	148	9	157
Weighted average.......................	86	30	116

SOURCE: Data compiled by Dirección de Estadística, Ministerio de Fomento.

THE STATES

The Constitution (Art. 15[3]) provides that the states shall administer their constitutional grants and taxes and other revenues which may be established by their legislative assemblies, and thus apparently contemplates that budgets shall be reviewed by the legislative assemblies. Since in the past several years legislative assemblies have had no meaningful existence, the work of preparing budgets has been entirely the responsibility of the governors, whose appointment is one of the President's constitutional powers.

The Constitution also empowers the President to "establish standards for the utilization of the revenues of the States, of the Federal District, and of the Federal Territories, and coordinate the budgets of receipts and expenditures of said entities with that of the Nation." (Art. 108.) The state budgets for the first full fiscal year (1958-59) under the new regime appear not to have been much affected by this provision. The budgets are being reviewed in the Ministry of the Interior, but only with respect to form and technical details. There have been no considerable revisions of any state's budget, and the degree of control exercised is so slight that several governors interviewed have been unaware that the national government has any voice in controlling the allocation of their budgets. Nonetheless, the wording of the Constitution gives the national government almost complete authority over the state budgets. Wisely handled, this power can be an instrument of effective planning and integration, without undue influence by the national government over the affairs of the states; however, the authority also can be used to concentrate control in the central government.

State taxing powers are severely restricted. The Constitution specifies that the states cannot impose import, export or transit taxes on national or foreign goods, or on matters within the competence of the national or municipal governments (*materias de la competencia nacional o municipal*), or on consumption goods before they enter into circulation within state territory. Also, the states are prohibited from taxing goods produced outside their territory more heavily than goods produced inside, and from contracting foreign loans (Art. 16). We are advised by counsel that although there is some question concerning the meaning of the above wording, it probably implies that the states cannot impose taxes or charges which the Constitution attributes to the nation or to the municipalities; further, that the national power extends to those taxes, contributions, charges and other revenues which are not expressly attributed to the states or the municipalities.

The prohibition against taxing goods produced outside state territory more heavily than goods produced inside implies the power to levy a non-discriminatory tax on sales of goods after they have gone into circulation within the state, although, as our authority says, the Constitution is not clear on this point. This appears to be the only major tax which the states can levy, with the possible exception of a tax on rural real estate. The states are prohibited from imposing income taxes and specific excises on such items as liquor and tobacco, which are imposed by the national government, and urban real estate taxes, which are reserved to the municipalities. A former source of revenue, the stamp tax, has been taken over by the national government.

The only taxes now imposed by the states are very minor ones on raffles and sales of lottery tickets of other states, and the anomalous unconstitutional tax on imports imposed by the State of Zulia.

Probably owing to the lack of state taxing powers there is no tradition of self-help; governors in need of money look to Caracas rather than to their own local resources and are doubtless judged by their constituencies in part on their ability to obtain national funds.

Roughly 91 per cent of the 1956-57 revenue of the states and territories, excluding the Federal District, was made up of grants from the national treasury—including the constitutional grant *(situado constitucional),* supplementary grants, payments from the autonomous institutes and a share of the proceeds of the national racetrack *(hipódromo nacional).* The percentage probably will be larger in 1958-59, because of the considerable increase in the amounts of grants projected in the 1958-59 national budget.

The constitutional grants to the states, which in each year must aggregate between 12½ and 25 per cent of the estimated total receipts of the national government, are distributed: 30 per cent in equal parts and 70 per cent according to population.[3] The Constitution provides also that "the amount shall be precisely determined each year at the Convention of Governors."

In theory, therefore, the amount of the constitutional grant is a matter for negotiation between the governors and the national authorities. In practice, the amount has been held to a minimum; the total amount budgeted for 1958-59 is only Bs.512 million, about 12½ per cent of the total budgeted revenues of approximately Bs.4,000 million. However, the constitutional grant proper is only Bs.389 million, less than 10 per cent of budgeted revenues. The rest is accounted for by supplementary grants *(aportes)* for specific purposes, divided into Bs.93 million allocated for payment of previously contracted obligations and Bs.30 million for cancellation of contracts for public works projects.

In addition, the government is allocating considerable funds for emergency works, for raising salaries of state school teachers, and for other purposes. It appears that the amounts of additional grants depend somewhat on the vigor of the governors and their influence in the Ministries of Interior Relations, Public Works, Education, and others with money to dispense. There are many ways of getting things done; for instance, beginning construction on a stretch of road and asking the national government to finish it or supply funds for finishing it; or building a school

[3] Constitution, Art. 127.

and asking the national government for funds to operate it. Some governors spend considerable time in Caracas negotiating for additional funds; one or two, on the other hand, have said that they have few dealings with national authorities.

The system whereby nationally appointed governors have a large degree of independence in making up and administering budgets financed largely by national funds is of course extra-constitutional, and will be changed when constitutional procedures are resumed, and legislative assemblies elected.

DISTRICTS AND MUNICIPALITIES

The Constitution recognizes the division of the states into districts, and the division of the districts into municipalities (Art. 3). It provides that the municipal authority will be constituted in each district by a municipal council, "autonomous in that which concerns the fiscal, economic and administrative regime of the municipality, without restrictions other than those established by this Constitution." (Art. 18.) Municipal organizations outside the Federal District are reported to be largely uniform, in spite of the fact that the state legislative assemblies can specify the organization and procedures which appear most suitable.[4] The municipal power is exercised by the district municipal councils, and, under them, the *juntas comunales* which exercise jurisdiction over some municipalities, typically those (*municipios foráneos*) outside the principal urban area of the district, which is governed directly by the district municipal council.

Although the *juntas comunales* perform some of the functions of the district municipal councils, they have no corporate status, and so far as we could determine do not ordinarily pass ordinances or fix tax rates. In some cases, they collect taxes and spend money. In a few instances observed by our Commission, municipalities appear to be largely self-governing; for instance, the municipality of Córdoba in the District of San Cristóbal, Táchira, imposes and collects its own taxes, makes up its own budget, and enjoys a considerable degree of independence from the district government.

Under the dictatorships, the municipal councils and communal juntas have come to be appointed by the governors of the states (the juntas are appointed either directly or by the municipal councils). The system of control from the top is further strengthened by the fact that police ad-

---

[4] Dr. Arturo Cardozo, *Hacienda y Servicios Municipales,* Maracaibo, 1945.

ministration is in charge of prefects, at the district level, and sub-prefects, at the municipal level, appointed by the governors.

By tradition and under the Constitution, however, districts and their municipal councils are regarded as being autonomous rather than, as are local governments in the United States, subordinate jurisdictions of state government. Thus the Organic Law of Municipal Power of the State of Mérida states that "the Municipalities are autonomous and independent of the National Power and of the State, in all that concerns their fiscal, economic, and administrative regime . . . " (Chapter 1).

Most of the governors interviewed said that they exercised no authority over municipal governments, although one governor said the districts and municipalities in his state are continuously supervised through the prefects and sub-prefects, and that local government budgets are reviewed by the state.

Ordinances relating to revenue generally are passed and administered by the municipal councils; for example, the law of the State of Miranda (Organic Code of Municipal Power, 1954) imposes the following obligations on the municipal councils (Chapter I, Art. 10):

To collect and administer directly all the municipal revenues of the district.

To formulate the revenue ordinances, and fix annually the general budget of disbursements and receipts of the municipalities.

Another source of authority lies in the power of the President of the Municipal Council to appoint and remove municipal employees and fix their salaries (Chapter II, Art. 11 [3]). The right to authorize expenditures is reserved to the municipal councils, and is specifically denied to the prefects (Chapter III, Art. 48).

Respecting municipal taxing powers, the Constitution provides that the municipalities can impose "patentes" on industry, commerce and vehicles, taxes on urban real estate and public spectacles, and charges for municipal public services. Their revenues also include proceeds from the rent, sale or exploitation of common lands. Agricultural products are subject only to taxes on retail sales.

C. *Functions of State and Municipal Governments*

The major functions of the state and municipal governments and the Federal District, with the amounts spent on each function in a recent year, are shown by Tables XII–2, XII–4 and XII–6. About a third of total state expenditure was in the categories of education and culture, and public health and social assistance. This figure does not include expenditures on related public works, such as school buildings; public works were about 36 per cent of the total.

The most important categories of municipal expenditure include sanitation, education, and public works; the latter includes school buildings, water supply and sewerage systems, streets and so on.

There is no clear demarcation among the three levels of government responsibility for many functions, notably education, sanitation and health, and construction of roads, aqueducts, and other public works. Nevertheless, as Tables XII–2 and XII–4 show, state and municipal governments tend to concentrate on particular functions, although the aggregate data presented here conceal many variations among the individual states and municipalities.

There is undoubtedly a tendency on the part of the state governments to concentrate their efforts on providing services to municipalities other than the larger cities. This accounts for some of the apparent duplication in services between the state and municipal governments. Conversely, municipal expenditure tends to be concentrated in the large cities. The seven cities outside the national-capital metropolitan area with populations estimated to exceed 50,000 account for 21 per cent of total population and 34 per cent of municipal expenditures outside the capital area.

Table XII-2. Expenditures of Venezuelan States, 1956-57 Fiscal Year (Excluding Federal District)

Items	Amounts (millions of bolivars)
Legislative power	1.9
Executive power	28.3
Defense[1]	1.0
Security and internal order[2]	17.1
Revenue collection and administration	2.0
Education and culture	45.9
Public health and social assistance	42.9
Agriculture	3.7
Other public services	10.4
Employees pensions and benefits, welfare payments[3]	12.3
Total current expenditures	165.5
Public works	114.0
Other	
Grants to districts and municipalities	26.8

Table XII-2 (cont.)

Items	Amounts (millons of bolivars)
Ecclesiastical grants..	1.3
Prior budgets..	6.2
Not classified and miscellaneous...........................	3.9
	38.2
Total..	317.4

1 Military recruitment for Armed Forces.
2 Police.
3 Welfare payments include grants to charitable institutions and help to needy persons.

NOTE: Figures may not add to totals because of rounding.
SOURCE: Compiled by Dirección de Estadistica, Ministerio de Fomento.

Table XII-3.   Revenues of Venezuelan States, 1956-57 Fiscal Year (Excluding Federal District)

Revenues	Amounts (millions of bolivars)
National treasury[1]..	278.3
Taxes[2]...	7.5
Public domain and lottery proceeds[3].......................	13.3
Charges[4]..	0.2
Other..	8.6
Total revenues....................................	307.9

1 Constitutional grants, supplementary grants, payments from the autonomous institutes and the National Treasury.
2 Mainly taxes on public spectacles and lottery tickets of other states.
3 Sale and rent of public lands, and state lotteries.
4 Charges for electric plants, garbage collection, hospital services, and other items.

SOURCE: Compiled by Dirección de Estadistica, Ministerio de Fomento.

Table XII-4. Expenditures of Venezuelan Municipalities, 1956

Functions	Amounts (millions of bolivars)	
	Federal District	Other municipalities
Current expenditures		
Legislative....................................	1.3	9.0
Judicial.......................................	—	.3
General administration (Jefatura Civil)............	3.7	2.8
Revenue administration.........................	3.7	9.6
Education.....................................	8.6	6.8
Police..	17.2	16.7
Sanitation....................................	23.7	11.1
Public lighting................................	—	7.5
Health.......................................	—	4.1
Gardens and plazas............................	—	2.4
Cemeteries...................................	—	1.0
Aqueducts....................................	—	1.9
Public markets................................	—	1.3
Slaughter houses..............................	—	1.8
Total current expenditures....................	58.2	76.3
Public works and development....................	37.6	23.0
Other		
Contingencies.................................	4.5	5.7
Cancellations and debt payments.................	49.6	4.1
Miscellaneous and not classified.................	25.2[1]	38.3
Total, other.................................	79.3	48.1
Total..	175.1	147.4

[1] Includes several items classified as current expenditures in "other municipalities" column.

SOURCE: Compiled by Dirección de Estadistica, Ministerio de Fomento.

Table XII-5. Revenues of Venezuelan Municipalities, 1956

	Amounts (millions of bolivars)	
	Federal District	Other municipalities
Taxes		
Industry and commerce.............................	30.0	25.3
Motor vehicles....................................	19.3	18.3
Real estate rentals.................................	24.5	12.6
Livestock slaughtering.............................	—	8.9
Peddlers...	—	0.3
Public spectacles..................................	4.3	6.3
Gasoline pumps....................................	—	.4
Total...	78.1	72.1
Charges		
Markets...	—[1]	4.8
Cemeteries..	0.6	0.8
Aqueducts...	—	3.4
Rents of municipal property........................	—	7.4
Total...	0.6	16.4
State grants..	31.3[2]	15.1
Other		
Reimbursements...................................	3.1	1.1
Weights and measures, scales.......................	1.0	2.8
Loans...	21.5	3.1
Not otherwise classified............................	38.4	41.2
Total...	64.0	48.2
Grand total..	174.0	151.8

[1] Bs.2,772.
[2] National grants.

SOURCE: Compiled by Dirección de Estadística, Ministerio de Fomento.

Table XII-6. Venezuelan Federal District Budget, July-December, 1958[1]

Expenditures   (millions of bolivars)

Municipal Council (legislative)	1.4
Administration, general	2.2
Revenue administration	2.4
Security and public order	17.8
Education and culture	7.5
Other public services	20.1
Employment, pensions and benefits, welfare payments	0.9
Public Welfare Board	27.1
Miscellaneous	2.6
	82.0
Public works	50.1
Previous budgets, budget "rectifications"	47.7
	179.9

Receipts

From National Treasury

Constitutional grant	19.1	
Special emergency grant	80.0	
National racetrack	1.3	100.4

Taxes

Real estate	14.5	
Public spectacles	2.3	
Industry and commerce	17.0	
Advertising	.3	
Vehicles	8.5	
Construction permits	.2	
Percentage of autobus receipts	1.3	44.0

Charges for goods and services, fees

Real estate valuation fee	.3	
Sale of municipal lands	1.0	
Municipal gazette	.1	
"Teleférico" (cable cars)	1.3	
Parking meters	.8	
Sanitation services	1.6	
Cemeteries	.5	
Weights and measures	1.1	
Fees for documents	.5	7.2

Other

Fines	.7
Lottery proceeds	9.2

Table XII-6 (cont.)

	(millions of bolivars)	
Reimbursements and miscellaneous.........................	2.8	12.7
Total receipts...		163.9
Resources on hand, June 30, 1958.......................		16.0
Total available resources............................		179.9

1 The Federal District budget was revised sharply upward for the last half of the 1958 budget period (calendar year). This table presents expenditure and revenue data in greater detail than is afforded by Tables XII-4 and XII-5. Expenditures and revenues of this half-year budget were nearly at the level of the full-year budget of 1956.

NOTE: Figures may not add to totals because of rounding.

D. *State Revenues*

State revenue sources are shown by Table XII–3. The states, as previously noted, depend on the national treasury for about 90 per cent of their revenue. They collect minor amounts from miscellaneous taxes on sporting events and the sale of tickets of lotteries of other states, and from the sale and rental of state lands. Several states operate lotteries. Small amounts are collected in a few instances from miscellaneous charges. Of particular note is Zulia's unconstitutional tax on imports.

DEVELOPMENT OF STATE TAXING POWERS

It appears that at present the states may be regarded as essentially spending arms of the national government. If they are to develop any considerable measure of independence, it would seem that they must also develop independent revenue-raising powers. But here they are severely restricted, both by the Constitution in ways previously discussed, and by economic considerations. Even assuming that constitutional barriers were removed, there are few feasible tax sources which the states can effectively administer.

The main sources of state revenues in the United States are corporate and personal income taxes, general retail sales taxes, special excises on motor fuel, alcoholic beverages, cigarettes and certain other commodities, and taxes on utility services. Many cities and a few states impose taxes on gross receipts or gross income somewhat similar to the Venezuelan national government *cinco por mil;* a few have elaborate schedules for classifying taxpayers, though none so elaborate as those found in the *patentes* imposed by such Venezuelan jurisdictions as the Federal District and Valencia.

We believe that none of these sources is particularly well suited to the Venezuelan states at the present time. Retail sales taxes, popular in the states of the U.S., would be difficult to administer in Venezuela because of the large numbers of small firms and street peddlers who keep no books and cannot easily be held accountable. Specific or general sales taxes, if they are to be used, can be imposed much more efficiently at the wholesale level by the national government than at the retail level by the state governments.

A retail sales tax exempting food (food, at least, should be exempted for reasons of equity), and possibly other necessities, would be even more difficult to administer effectively than the present clumsy system of *patentes* on industry and commerce. Under the *patentes,* once a firm's classification is established, it is subject to a single rate on all sales, or a flat-sum under the flat-sum *patentes.* A retail sales tax with exemptions, however, inevitably necessitates distinguishing between taxable and nontaxable sales by the same merchant. The more numerous the exemptions, the greater is the administrative task.

Personal and corporation income taxes are also much better administered at the national than the state level. However, once a broader-based income tax, such as is discussed in this report, is established, the states might impose a supplement tax on the national income tax. The supplement can be either a percentage of national tax assessed on residents of the state, or a percentage of taxable income as defined for national income tax purposes, reported by residents of the state. In either case, it would be possible for the national government to do most of the administrative work, under contract with the states.

The supplement income tax, imposed by one governmental unit and collected by another, is used in several European countries. It has not been tried in the United States, although several states base their own income taxes on the federal income tax base, with minor modifications. One state, Alaska, imposes a tax which is a percentage of federal income tax assessed; and another, Utah, allows the taxpayer to pay either (a) a tax, computed by using the state's own rates and exemptions, or (b) a specified percentage of federal income tax.

A supplement income tax in Venezuela would require a constitutional amendment. To prevent such a tax from impinging too heavily on national taxing powers, a maximum rate equivalent to, say, ten to twenty per cent of the national rate should be established. The states might impose rates below the maximum but could not exceed it.

Another possible state tax, which would take some time to develop, is a tax on agricultural land holdings; these now pay no tax at all. Such a tax would encourage the productive use of land which is now allowed to lie idle, to the detriment of the country. To prevent hardship to small subsistence farmers, exemptions could be granted, either by excluding holdings with a capital (or rental) value below a specified minimum, or by giving all holders a basic exemption, as under income tax.

Two obstacles, in addition to a possible constitutional barrier, now stand in the way of agricultural land taxation: (1) the fact that most of the country has not been surveyed, so that the size of holdings cannot as yet be established; (2) the fact that before the tax was imposed, capital (or rental) values would have to be determined.

It has been urged that agricultural land taxation be undertaken only as a system of general agricultural reform, covering land holdings, land-use policies, improvement of rural living conditions, and so on. We concur in the thought that agricultural taxation should be included in any land reform program, but would point out that there is already a sufficiently strong case for taxing larger holdings, as soon as the necessary machinery can be set up.

In any event, a program of land reform can be formulated and carried out only with precise knowledge of the size and value of land holdings. For all these purposes, surveys and appraisals should be undertaken as soon as possible.

THE ZULIA TAX ON CONSUMPTION

This tax is admittedly contrary to the clause of the Constitution prohibiting state taxes on foreign imports. The base of the tax is the amount of customs duties applicable to goods entering through the Port of Maracaibo. Fabricated goods pay a rate of 7 per cent of applicable customs duties; primary goods for fabrication pay a rate of 3 per cent. Firms or individuals subject to the tax are classified as major and minor. A major firm is one which pays a consecutive monthly tax of more than Bs.200; such firms are thereby exempted from the municipal patente. The minor firms pay the 7 per cent tax which the law imposes, but can offset the amount of the payments against the amount of the municipal patente. (Presumably the same provision applies to minor firms subject to the 3 per cent rate.)

The tax yields about Bs.2.7 million (estimate in 1958 budget), and is estimated to cost the District of Maracaibo some Bs.2 million a year in yield of the municipal patente, much to the indignation of city officials.

Although the tax is unconstitutional, taxpayers have as yet been unable to devise legal means of prohibiting its collection. We have not studied the technicalities involved, but do not consider that any intrinsic merit of the tax warrants amending the Constitution to legalize it.

BLOCK GRANTS TO STATES

The grants from the national government, which are the chief source of state revenues, are mainly unconditional block grants, that is, they are not earmarked for specific programs and are not conditional upon the states' spending any specified amounts from their own tax or other local resources. The constitutional grant is distributed 30 per cent equally among the states and 70 per cent on the basis of population. This formula favors the states with the smaller populations. To be sure, some of the low income states, as Bolívar and Apure, are large geographically and perhaps need larger grants on that account. But other states, as Cojedes and Nueva Esparta, are very small both in size and in population, as shown by Table XII–7. Under the formula, these states get relatively large shares of the national constitutional grants.

The distorting effect of the formulas is made particularly apparent by comparing Cojedes and Nueva Esparta, whose per capita constitutional grants are Bs.146 and Bs.115 respectively, with two of the poorest states, Mérida and Táchira, whose constitutional grants are Bs.75 and Bs.61, respectively.

The part of the formula by which 30 per cent of the constitutional grant is distributed equally among the states has nothing to recommend it and ought to be eliminated.

Population is probably the best single basis of distributing general-purpose grants, particularly so long as the states have little revenue other than grants. Equal per capita grants tend to equalize per capita income distribution among the states because they have the effect of transferring purchasing power from states with higher per capita wealth and income to the poorer states.

One reason for departing from equal per capita grants arises when the cost of a unit of input—a day's wage, for instance—differs from one part of the country to another, owing in part, perhaps, to differences in the cost of living. Then a unit of output—a certain amount of education, for example—will cost less in the low-cost area, and the grant per capita could be correspondingly less.

Table XII-7. Data Relating to Constitutional Grants to States (Area and Estimated Population, 1958)

State	Area Km²	Population Total (thousands)	Population Per Km²	Constitutional Grants, 1958-9 per capita
Federal District............	1,930	1,204	624	36
Anzoátegui...............	43,300	349	8	52
Apure...................	76,500	106	1	92
Aragua..................	7,014	245	35	64
Barinas.................	35,200	96	3	99
Bolívar.................	238,000	162	1	73
Carabobo...............	4,650	291	63	63
Cojedes.................	14,800	54	4	146
Falcón.................	24,800	276	11	70
Guárico................	64,986	190	3	73
Lara...................	19,800	390	20	65
Mérida.................	11,300	221	20	75
Miranda................	7,950	318	40	64
Monagas...............	28,900	234	8	63
Nueva Esparta..........	1,150	80	70	115
Portuguesa.............	15,200	160	11	71
Sucre..................	11,800	365	31	63
Táchira................	11,100	356	32	61
Trujillo................	7,400	277	37	75
Yaracuy................	7,100	134	19	92
Zulia..................	63,100	838	13	40
Amazon Territory........	175,750	26	0.1	210
Amacuro Delta Territory...	40,200	38	1	177

SOURCES: Area and population data, *Octavo Censo General de Población, Principales Resultados Nacionales,* Ministerio de Fomento, 1957. Amounts of constitutional grants, *Dirección General de Presupuesto, Ministerio de Hacienda.*

Another reason for not using a strictly equal per capita grant arises from differences in amount of services per capita that must be rendered, from one state to another. An under-developed, thinly populated state may need higher-than-average expenditure per capita on roads. A state with a high proportion of children in its population will have a higher-than-average expenditure on education, per capita.

These special cases can be taken care of by supplementary grants earmarked for particular purposes, such as road building, health programs, education, agricultural development, and so on. (As already noted above, the state governors can frequently obtain special assistance of various kinds by negotiating with Caracas.)

E. Municipal Revenues

The municipalities (districts) impose a considerable number of taxes and charges, in addition to receiving grants from the states. Most of these taxes and charges are of minor importance. The principal revenue items, which in municipalities outside the Federal District accounted for more than half of total receipts in 1956, are the state grants, taxes (*patentes*) on industry and commerce, taxes on real estate rents, vehicle taxes, and taxes on public spectacles.

The Federal District is in the special position, comparable with that of the District of Columbia in the United States, of having the attributes both of a state, with governor and national grant, and of a municipality, with a Municipal Council and the usual variety of municipal taxing powers.

MUNICIPAL PATENTES ON INDUSTRY AND COMMERCE

These taxes, which are the oldest municipal revenue sources, take two main forms: (1) a per millage of gross sales or gross revenues, the rate depending on the type of business, and (2) a system of flat-sum taxes, the amount depending upon the "class" of the particular firm.

The taxes on gross sales or revenues employ an elaborate system of classification and a wide range of rates—the rates imposed by the Federal District range from 5 per mill on coffee, cocoa, salt and leather merchants and several other categories, to 15 per mill on jewelry, gift and luxury stores and other categories, to 40 per mill on house rental agents. In addition, there are a number of flat-sum levies, for instance, an annual levy of Bs.1,000 on bowling establishments.

Table XII–8 compares representative rates on retail establishments in the Federal District and Valencia.

The other, more primitive, form of the patente is that employing a number of business classes, each with a fixed rate of tax. This form is found, for example, in Ciudad Bolívar (Distrito Heres), Maracaibo, and San Cristóbal. Administration of this type of patente requires a classification board, which in Ciudad Bolívar includes, among others, a member of the Municipal Council, a member of the chamber of commerce, a merchant, and the prefect. There are no definite criteria of classifica-

Table XII-8. Representative Rates of Patentes in Federal District and Valencia

Item	Federal District	Valencia
	Rate—Per thousand on sales unless otherwise stated	
Food...	1½	2 (Bs.360)[3]
Furniture stores...........................	5[1]	4 (Bs.240)[3]
Drug stores...............................	5	3½
Agricultural implements....................	2	2
Automobile dealers.......................	10	4
Shoe stores...............................	5	2½
Electrical apparatus......................	6	4 (Bs.1000)[3]
Stationery stores.........................	3	3
Liquors..................................	—[2]	6 (Bs.480)[3]
Jewelry stores............................	15	6
Barber shops, two chairs..................	Bs.60	Bs.90
each additional chair...................	Bs.30	Bs.30
Electric utilities.........................	10[1]	10[1]

[1] Statute specifies gross receipts.

[2] Minimum—Bs.200: maximum—Bs.10,000.

[3] Minimum tax payable.

tion, the determination being based mainly on the amount of the tax which the board feels a particular business is able to pay. The Municipal Council is studying the problem of classification with a view of establishing more definite criteria.

These local patentes are subject to all the objections raised against the *cinco por mil* discussed in Chapter X of this report, plus still others.

The elaborate classifications complicate administration and make the application of the tax extremely uncertain. Taxpayers complain that categories are not well defined or not defined at all. The terminology is often vague; some of the laws imposing the patentes still use obsolete Spanish words.

New firms frequently have trouble determining the classification into which they fall. Firms selling articles falling under several categories are often taxed at the highest applicable rate, which may put them at a competitive disadvantage. Some smaller cities do not even make copies of the law available to taxpayers.

The flat-sum patentes often have little relation to any logical criteria of business volume or profitability. The patentes imposing percentage levies on gross receipts often discriminate sharply among different types of business with little apparent reason.

These defects make possible arbitrary classifications which may be changed from year to year; the rates, particularly the flat-sum rates, are often pushed up sharply and then, after bargaining or payments of bribes, reduced. It is reported that a large manufacturer in one of the smaller cities was suddenly assessed for Bs.100,000 on the basis of the volume of his imports (presumably an invalid basis). The firm protested and a compromise was reached after long negotiation; city officials admitted that the increase was imposed because of the municipality's need for more money.

As with other taxes imposed at the local level, enforcement procedures are ineffective. Most firms interviewed report that they have not been inspected by tax officials; where inspections are made, they are superficial. Many small firms, it is alleged, do not bother to pay the tax at all, preferring to settle for a fine if their evasion is discovered.

The tax can significantly affect business decisions by inducing business firms to locate in communities with low rates, or in rural communities which do not impose the tax at all. Business practices respecting places of billing also are affected; some firms report changing the place of billing to take advantage of lower tax rates. Thus the taxes impose a great amount of nuisance for relatively small revenues. There is a strong case for eliminating the patente entirely.

If the tax is retained, we recommend several changes:

1. Eliminating the tax from manufacturing and wholesaling firms, to reduce the pyramiding effect of the tax and the incentive to arrange factory locations, business billings, and other business procedures so as to avoid tax.

2. Revising and codifying the laws, preferably through a national "model" law which could be adapted by the taxing municipalities, using their own rates.

3. Eliminating the flat-sum taxes, except where justified by peculiar circumstances.

4. Simplifying the rate structure, with no more than two basic rates, one a general rate and the other a rate for business with very low markups. The latter might be imposed on gross income or cost of goods sold.

THE URBAN REAL ESTATE TAX

The most important potential revenue source for municipal governments in Venezuela is the urban real estate tax.

The urban real estate tax in Venezuela differs from that imposed in the United States by the local governments and a few state governments. First, the Venezuelan tax resembles the British local "rates" in being based primarily on rental values; in the United States, the real estate tax is based on capital values. Second, the rates of tax are very low, compared with those found in the United States (or Great Britain). Third, many Venezuelan municipalities (but not the Federal District or Maracaibo) tax only those properties that are being rented for a money income, whereas the tax in the United States typically applies to all real estate, whether rented or occupied by the owner.

Finally, the real estate tax in Venezuela is regarded as a kind of payment, or fee, for urban services rendered by the municipalities; so far as we could ascertain, the real estate tax is nowhere in Venezuela applied to agricultural land. (No such distinction is made in the United States.) Again, the Federal District exempts residences that are not supplied by it with city services such as paved streets, garbage collection, and lighting.

In the Federal District, properties consisting of land and building (that is, not vacant land) are taxed at 6½ per cent on the rent received, in the case of rented properties, and on imputed rentals calculated for owner-occupied properties. There are two principal exemptions: (1) the usual exemption for charitable, religious, and other public-purpose property; and (2) homesteads.[5] The Maracaibo tax is much the same, except that the rate is 6 per cent. The imputed rent on owner-occupied properties is computed as a percentage of the appraised capital value, less an exemption of Bs.50,000.

The Federal District and Maracaibo tax land without buildings at the rate of $\frac{9}{10}$ of 1 per cent of capital value; the rate is higher than the rate on properties with buildings, when both are viewed as taxes on capital value.

Where only money rents are taxed, the base of the tax in the cases that we have observed is simply gross rents. However, various other

---

[5] The homestead is a special legal status accorded to certain properties for the purpose of assuring that the benefit of the property will accrue to the property owner or his designee. The principal protection is that the property cannot be seized for the debts of the owner. Only properties valued at Bs.60,000 or less in Caracas, Bs.40,000 or less in a state capital or a seaport, or Bs.20,000 or less in any other place, are eligible. Another condition of eligibility is that there has been no lien against the property for thirty years. Homestead status is obtained by application to a competent Court. Once the status is established, the property cannot be alienated or mortgaged without the permission of the beneficiaries. The status endures until the last member of the family for whom the homestead was set up dies, or until the right to enjoy it has been forfeited.

levies may be made on properties not rented for money; for instance, in Ciudad Bolívar (Distrito Heres) a charge *(derecho de frente)* is imposed at the rate of Bs.1 per linear meter of street front on properties not subject to the money rent tax.

Money rents are often ascertainable from the records of the rent control offices, so that determining the base of the tax is no great problem where only money rents are taxed. A means of avoidance reported in one jurisdiction involves fathers renting property to sons at figures below the market; the jurisdiction had no legal remedy for this practice.

Where the tax applies to imputed as well as to money rents, the difficult job of estimating equivalent money rental values must be undertaken.

In the Federal District the rent is estimated at 12 per cent of the original acquisition cost.

Administration of the real estate rental tax seems to be generally poor. None of the municipal offices have the necessary tools for adequate enforcement, such as tax maps to locate properties and to make sure that all are accounted for, and modern techniques of appraisal. A recent survey undertaken in Maracaibo with the assistance of a professional management firm revealed that only 10 per cent of the potential tax was actually being collected. Now the city is engaged in mapping all properties, and developing land value formulas and procedures for appraising values of improvements. Federal District authorities also intend to prepare a tax map.

Delinquency is also a problem. In the Federal District it is estimated that at least 20 per cent of taxes due are never collected. One bar to collection is that tax liabilities lapse after three years unless the municipality can prove that it has made an attempt at collection in the meantime.

A real estate tax applied only to rented properties is grossly discriminatory and has no particular justification under present conditions, whatever may have been its justification in the past. If a real estate tax is used at all, it should apply to all properties, other than those devoted to charitable, religious, or other public purposes. Exemptions for low-value residences may be justified as removing some of the regressive effect of the tax, but it is doubtful if the exemption should go as high as the Maracaibo figure of Bs.50,000. The loopholes afforded by such exemptions are enlarged, of course, by under-valuation of properties. For instance, if properties are valued for tax purposes at 40 per cent of full market value, the effect of a Bs.50,000 legal exemption is to exempt properties of up to Bs.125,000 full market value.

With an exemption for low-value homes, there is no apparent justification for further homestead exemptions such as those granted in the Federal District.

Should the tax continue to be imposed on rents, or is capital value a preferable base?

Since the ratio of rents to capital value is likely to differ among different types of property, the impact of a tax on actual or estimated market rents will be somewhat different from that of a tax on capital value. In New York City, for instance, ratios of gross rents to capital values of inferior properties are typically higher than those of high-grade properties. Compared with a capital value tax, a tax on gross rents would be relatively higher on inferior properties and lower on high-grade properties. Since average incomes of owners and tenants of inferior properties probably tend to be lower than average incomes of owners and tenants of high-grade properties, the gross rents tax may tend to be more regressive than the capital value tax.

A building in a good or improving neighborhood ordinarily will be valued higher, relative to rents, than a similar building in a less desirable or declining neighborhood. The rental tax discriminates relatively against the building with the higher ratio of gross rental to capital value.

The rental tax has the advantage of eliminating the necessity of determining the capital value of rented properties; the tax base is simply the rental figure. Of course, where rental values of owner-occupied properties are computed from capital value figures, as in Maracaibo and the Federal District, the computation of rents becomes a meaningless, if minor, extra step.

We believe that the rental tax is easier to apply equitably. First, as noted above, the tax base on rented properties is determined by the market (or by rent controls), eliminating the necessity of administrative assessment. Second, on an owner-occupied property, it is easier to estimate rental values than capital values, because data on rental values of similar spaces are ordinarily more plentiful than are sales data on comparable properties. Third, the rental tax has the advantages of tradition and familiarity in Venezuela, whereas the capital value tax would require a new approach and a new system of administration.

We believe that administrators should attempt to estimate rents directly, rather than computing them as an arbitrary percentage of some capital value figure. The practice in the Federal District of using acquisition cost as the measure of capital value for the purpose of computing rents is highly inequitable, because of rapidly rising real estate values. The effective rate of the rental tax on an owner-occupied property depends upon the time of acquisition; the more recently the property was acquired, the higher is likely to be the effective rate of the tax. The practice has nothing to commend it but simplicity, and is tolerable only as long as the tax rate is very low.

Possibilities of Increased Use of Real Estate Tax. The real estate tax, in our opinion, is the only state or municipal tax source capable of yielding substantial increased revenues. Total proceeds from this tax in 1956 were Bs.37.4 million, of which the Federal District accounted for approximately Bs.24.8 million (66 per cent) and all other municipalities approximately Bs.12.6 million (34 per cent). The figures are somewhat higher in 1958; the Federal District 1958 budget estimate was Bs.29 million, and the other municipalities are probably in the range of Bs.15-20 million. As previously mentioned, Maracaibo is vigorously improving the administration of its real estate tax, and projects an increase in yield of 900 per cent, from Bs.1.3 million to Bs.13 million. The increase is nearly equal to total 1956 collections by all municipalities outside the Federal District.

The per capita average collections by the Federal District are approximately Bs.25 per year; Maracaibo collections after administrative reform, if they come up to expectations, will amount to about Bs.30 (based on 1958 population estimate).

Let us assume that the per capita value of urban property in the rest of the country, outside Maracaibo and the Federal District, averages one-third that in the Federal District, and that approximately 2.5 million persons live in such urban areas. If real estate were taxed at the same rate on capital value as in the Federal District, the per capita amount would be approximately Bs.8, and the aggregate amount approximately Bs.20 million, which is nearly double the amount actually collected.

The rate on capital value on owner-occupied property in the Federal District amounts to 0.78 per cent of acquisition cost (6.5 per cent rate on 12 per cent imputed rent). If we assume that acquisition cost averages 50 per cent of current market values, the actual rate on current market value comes to 0.39 per cent. By comparison, rates on full value in the District of Columbia, the capital district of the U.S.A., are more than three times as much, about 1.25 per cent. The New York City rate on current market value, approximately 3.3 per cent, is approximately eight times as much.

If the Federal District raised its rates to three times the present level, putting them in the neighborhood of the rates of the District of Columbia, the yield would be about Bs.75 per capita annually, or an aggregate of approximately Bs.87 million, at the present level of administration. Probably 25 per cent of the potential present real estate tax is now escaping through delinquency or evasion, so it would be possible, at Washington rates and with improved administration, to reach a figure approaching Bs.110 million annually.

By the same chain of reasoning, Maracaibo should be able to reach a figure approaching Bs.40 million annually, and the rest of the country should be able to achieve a figure of Bs.50 million annually. The total is Bs.200 million, approximately five times the present yield of the tax (about Bs.160 million more than is now being raised). This figure amounts to about 45 per cent of the total estimated municipal government revenues of 1958.

SPECIAL ASSESSMENTS FOR PUBLIC IMPROVEMENTS

Special assessments are levies on owners of property directly benefited by public improvements, such as street paving or repaving, water and sewer mains. The principle might be applied, but in the U.S.A. it usually is not, to such value-creating improvements as public schools and parks.

Owners of benefited property may be assessed part or all of the cost of the improvement. In principle, the amount of the assessment is payable at the time of completion of the improvement; in practice, owners may pay assessments over periods of several years.

Special assessments were widely used in the United States during the 1920's, but fell into disfavor during the depression of the 1930's, when the collapse of the real estate market made it difficult to collect assessments that were still owing for improvements which had been constructed during prosperous years. In the period following World War II, many local governments have turned again to the special assessment for substantial revenues.

Venezuelan governments at all levels are empowered to use the special assessment device by a provision in the 1947 *Ley de Expropiacion por Causa de Utilidad Pública o Social.* The law provides that where real estate values are increased by public works construction, such as opening or widening of streets, avenues, plazas, parks, or gardens, or roads, or irrigation or drainage projects, owing to the proximity of the real estate to such construction, the owners of the real estate shall pay three-fourths of the value increment *(plusvalia),* which the public or private agency that has constructed the works will collect in conformity with the law.

To establish value increases, the law provides for an appraisal before the project is started, and one after it has been completed. The contribution required of each owner may be paid immediately or in ten annual installments; in the latter case, 25 per cent is added to the original charge.

So far as we can determine, no use has been made of this provision. However, the Federal District and possibly other municipalities have employed the alternative device, also used in U.S.A., of requiring developers of new areas to pay the costs of streets, access roads, and sewer and water mains.

DIFFERENTIAL REAL ESTATE TAX RATES ON LAND AND BUILDINGS

If more revenues are demanded from the urban real estate tax, should land and buildings be burdened equally, or should the rate on land be higher than on buildings?

The argument for a higher rate on urban land values than on building values, to raise a given amount of money, is based on the premise that a land-value tax will not deter building construction. Urban land is a natural resource, whose supply cannot be increased or decreased. In urban uses, a piece of land derives its value from its location with reference to the concentration of economic activity. Land at the center of economic activity typically is most highly valued, and values decrease progressively as one moves away from the center.

Urban land can be heavily taxed without affecting its supply, since the tax does not affect the source of its production, that is, its location. Taxes on buildings, on the other hand, in effect add to construction costs; the higher the value of an improvement, the heavier will be the tax. A substantial tax will reduce the incentive to invest in building construction, and thus will reduce the supply of residential and commercial building space.

Moreover, a higher tax on land values will enable the municipality to capture for public purposes some of the increase in land values which typically occurs as cities grow and land is put to more intensive use. The phenomenal increases in land values in Caracas in recent years illustrate this point.

As the tax system now stands, the only way of recapturing these land value increments characteristic of city growth is through the income tax on capital gains, and through the special assessments for public improvements. Income tax rates have been too low to be of much consequence, and, in any case, income from the capital gains tax is not available to municipalities, except through the uncertain medium of federal grants to states. Special assessments have not been used at all.

There are two chief arguments against the principle of taxing the value of land more heavily than that of buildings. The first is an argument of equity. Substantial increases in taxes on land would reduce land values below the values which otherwise would prevail, and perhaps below values prevailing at the time the tax was announced. This being the case, persons who have bought land anticipating that no such tax would be imposed will suffer losses, either absolute or relative, by reason of the tax.

If real estate taxes generally are raised, however, all property owners who have purchased with no anticipation of increases are bound to suffer losses. So the question is really one of whether the losses should be concentrated more heavily upon landholders as such (as would be the case under a higher tax on land), or divided more equally among all real estate owners (as would be the case if land and building values were taxed at equal rates).

The second argument against a differential land tax is the difficulty of administration. The tax requires that land and buildings be appraised separately. This poses problems in the case of land already improved, where it is difficult to separate out the value of land from the total value of the property. This separation can be done more or less satisfactorily, however, by the following procedure which is used by New York State municipalities and many others in the U.S.A. The land component of an improved parcel is appraised at the figure for which the land would sell unimproved (*sin construcción*). The building is valued at its cost, adjusted to current price levels, less depreciation.

Another administrative difficulty is in distinguishing between the value of land as such, which results from its location, and the value added by improvements other than construction, such as grading, planting, and so on. Such refinements, however, do not have to be taken into account where the amounts are small. If, as on the mountainsides of suburban Caracas, the expenditure required to prepare land for construction is so great that development could be seriously impaired by a heavy land-value tax, the value of such improvements could be separated out and taxed at the rate applicable to buildings.

The principle of the differentiated tax has been used for a considerable time in several of the Australian states, the prairie provinces of Canada, and at least one American city, Pittsburgh.

Should Venezuela undertake to tax land more heavily than buildings? The fact that real estate rates are still so low makes the idea more feasible than it would be if rates were already relatively high. As and if the tax burden on real estate is gradually increased, the bulk of the increase can be put on land. If the increases are gradual and assessment is competently done, there need be no major disturbance of land values.

We believe that the theoretical case for a differentiated tax, in a country with rapidly increasing urbanization, is so strong that it merits careful consideration. The principle of a differentiated tax on land has already been established; land without construction is taxed differently from houses and other buildings in the Federal District and elsewhere.

The differentiated tax would probably require adoption of capital value as a base in place of rentals. Conceptually, it is more difficult to separate the rent on a property into the land component and the building component, than it is to separate the capital values on the same building, in the manner described above. A methodical assessment program such as that now underway in Maracaibo will provide separate appraisals of land and building values, which would make possible the imposition of a differentiated tax.

RECOMMENDATIONS RESPECTING REAL ESTATE TAXATION

1. The tax on urban real estate should be left to the municipalities. Taxes on agricultural land should be reserved to the states, or possibly to the national government, in connection with a general land reform program.

2. The municipal tax should apply to all real estate, allowing only the conventional exemptions for property devoted to charitable, religious and other public welfare purposes and small properties of a value of less than, say, Bs.20,000.

3. Governments at all levels should employ the power they now have under the law to impose special assessments for the purpose of recovering the cost of public improvements, such as street paving, water and sewer mains, and the like, which enhance the value of land.

4. A policy should be adopted of basing future real estate tax increases largely on land. This will necessitate a policy of differentiating between land and buildings, for tax purposes, and basing the tax conceptually on capital value instead of rents. It is suggested that the rate on land be twice that on buildings.

5. If the previous recommendation is not followed, and different rates are not applied to land and buildings (except for the special tax on unoccupied land), the real estate tax should be based consistently on rents.

Emphasis should be placed on determining directly rental values on owner-occupied properties, instead of computing them from measures of capital value, as is now done in Maracaibo and the Federal District. Capital value should of course be one of the factors taken into account when determining rental value.

TAX ON VEHICLES

The municipal tax on automobiles is often based on weight, and that of trucks on cargo-carrying capacity. For instance, the Valencia tax on automobiles goes from Bs.100 on automobiles of less than 1,000 kilograms to Bs.300 on automobiles exceeding 2,000 kilograms; a standard Chevrolet would pay Bs.120. On cargo-carrying trucks, the tax goes from Bs.180 on trucks under 2,000 kilograms capacity, to Bs.2,460 on trucks of capacity between 20,000 and 50,000 kilograms. The Federal District rates are somewhat higher—from Bs.140 to Bs.352 on automobiles, e.g., Bs.172 on a Chevrolet; and from Bs.248 to Bs.3,268 on trucks. The Maracaibo tax is Bs.200 per year on automobiles (no differentiation for weight), and from Bs.240 to Bs.560 per year on trucks.

But many localities impose lower taxes, and thereby create difficulty for the others. Thus in San Cristóbal, the annual rate on all motor vehicles is only Bs.20. Such discrepancies give rise to the well-known problem of tax avoidance on the part of the residents of the municipalities of higher rates. Enforcement is principally through the national motor vehicle license plates; to obtain a plate an applicant must produce receipts showing payment of his municipal tax for the preceding four quarters. Consequently, many persons register their automobiles in municipalities where rates are lowest. The number of cars registered in the State of Nueva Esparta, for instance, is reported to be nearly ten times as many as the number actually resident there.

Considering the enormous discrepancy between taxes paid by highway users and the costs of roadway building and maintenance, there seems to be no good reason for continuing to tolerate the low rates imposed by many communities (including many that are most in need of local roads), at the expense of other municipalities.

Two measures are therefore recommended to attack the problem of inter-municipal competition. (1) Make the rates uniform throughout the nation. (2) Base the automobile rate on value, rather than on weight. Concerning the last recommendation, it is not difficult to prepare a list of standard values, for various makes and models, which would take into account the approximate original selling price of the model and its accumulated depreciation. Similar lists of standard prices of various makes and models, prepared for the use of secondhand car dealers in the U.S.A., are used by U.S.A. local tax officials in determining the value of automobiles for purposes of personal property taxation.

Serious consideration should be given to taxing luxury automobiles at proportionately higher rates than other cars. For instance, a schedule of rates, which would also favor lower-valued cars over new standard models (Fords, Chevrolets, Plymouths), might be as follows:

Value in Bs.	Rate (Per cent)
0 -10,000	.75
10,000-15,000	1.50
Over 15,000	3.00

These are bracket rates, not average rates. For example, the tax on a car worth Bs.11,000 would be .75 per cent of the first Bs.10,000, or Bs.75, plus 1.50 per cent of the excess above Bs.10,000, that is, plus 1.50 per cent of Bs.1,000, which is Bs.15, giving a total tax of Bs.75 + 15 = Bs.90.

A local tax based on values has several advantages. First, it is more equitable than a tax based solely on weight, which is a poor index of value or economic status. Second, it makes possible a system of proportionately higher taxes on higher-valued automobiles, as illustrated by the above schedule. Third, it overcomes at least in part an objection to the proposal for nation-wide uniform tax rates on automobiles—that they would discriminate against the poorer communities. The problem is not so much that of discriminating against poorer communities, but of discriminating against poorer people, and this would be met by lower taxes on lower-valued cars.

Trucks pose a different problem, since the wear and tear on a road is closely related to truck weight. Therefore, the case for differentiation by value is less strong than for private automobiles. However, we recommend that the tax on trucks also be made uniform nationally. The level of the rates will depend upon national policy regarding transportation; if it is desired to cheapen commodity transportation by truck, rates will be somewhat lower than if they are based on cost-of-service (that is, use of roads) or benefit principles of taxation. We have not studied this problem and are not prepared to make recommendations thereon.

Other types of vehicle tax preference, for instance, on farm trucks doing no commercial hauling, may be desired.

Assuming that the proceeds of the vehicle patentes or their replacement are to be retained by the municipalities, there is still the question of whether they should continue to administer this tax.

There would seem to be no reason why they cannot administer the tax, if the national government rigorously enforces its requirement that applicants for license plates must present municipal tax receipts for the preceding four quarters *(trimestres)*. With uniform rates there would be no incentive to avoid the tax by registering motor vehicles in states other than those of owners' residence.

Administration would be simplified if the national government simply collected the tax along with the fee for license plates, and remitted the proceeds to the individual municipalities. That is, the national government would act as the agent of the municipalities in collecting the tax. Such arrangements are not uncommon among state and local governments in the United States. Several objections have been raised against the idea, however. (1) Municipalities would be reluctant to turn over the task of fund-collecting to the national government, for fear that the latter might ultimately claim the tax for itself. (2) The mechanics of payment by the national government are so cumbersome as to offset any administrative advantages that might accrue from the rest of the procedure. However, this problem can easily be solved with adequate protection to everyone concerned, if the national government is willing to modify its procedures to take care of such payments. (3) The payment of the tax would have to be in one lump sum, instead of quarterly, which might pose a cash problem for some taxpayers. (4) If the tax were based on values which changed from year to year, the business of imposing the tax would become so complicated that the national machinery would break down. It is true that existing national machinery might break down, but it is also true that methods and procedures utilizing data-processing machinery could readily handle the work involved, and more efficiently than it could be done at the municipal level.

RECOMMENDATIONS RESPECTING MUNICIPAL VEHICLE TAXES

1. Rates should be made uniform throughout the nation.

2. Passenger cars should be taxed according to value instead of weight. Serious consideration should be given to higher rates on more valuable cars.

3. Trucks should continue to be taxed according to weight; rates should be set in accordance with national transportation policy.

4. If possible, an arrangement should be worked out whereby the

national government would collect the municipal vehicle taxes and remit them to municipalities.[6]

NEED FOR BETTER TAX ADMINISTRATION

We observe everywhere a deplorable lack of good administration of local taxes. However, this shortcoming is the result of historical circumstance rather than lack of ability or understanding. Under dictatorships, local governments have been grossly neglected; no opportunity or incentive existed for high levels of performance. The consequences are still being felt. For example, the few figures we have been able to obtain indicate that a large proportion—in many cases probably more than half—of potential tax revenues is not collected. Maracaibo, as has been noted, discovered that it was assessing only one-tenth of real estate taxes due. Federal District officials estimate that 20 per cent of municipal taxes billed are never collected. Of the *patentes,* more than 25 per cent due in the second quarter of 1958 were delinquent. Nearly Bs.50 million now owed will soon become uncollectible, under a provision of the law whereby taxes three or more years overdue are cancelled if no attempt at collection can be proved. In San Cristóbal, only a third of the taxes due were collected in the last quarter of 1957.

Ability to enforce revenue laws is one of the first essentials of effective local government. Unless revenue administration can be improved, it is questionable whether more authority and responsibility can be or should be delegated to the municipalities.

There are two difficulties. The first is a lack of proper tools of administration. As has been noted, no municipality to our knowledge uses a tax map to locate properties for purposes of the real estate tax and to make sure that all properties are covered (Maracaibo is now preparing such a map). Only Maracaibo, so far as we are aware, is undertaking a systematic assessment of the value of its properties. Enforcement of the *patentes,* from the testimony of taxpayers and from our observation, is most primitive. Taxpayers are rarely inspected, and when inspections do occur they are likely to be ineffective. The level of education required of inspectors, nowhere more than primary school, so far as we could ascertain, is not sufficient. The larger jurisdictions claim that their inspectors receive intensive training, but we have no evidence

[6] In June, 1959, a revision of the tax was about to be enacted that would make the annual license rates uniform throughout the country, using weight as a tax base. In addition, a once-for-all ad valorem tax, ranging from 2% to 20%, would be imposed at the time of initial registration.

from taxpayers that inspectors are able to do a competent job on any but the simplest problems. There is no such thing as a scientific audit program employing modern techniques of statistical sampling.

The second difficulty is a lack of energy in collecting taxes which are known to be due, coupled with a general resistance to paying taxes.

Finally, the deficiencies of the present laws, particularly those relating to the *patentes,* promote bad administration because they are difficult to enforce.

RECOMMENDATIONS RESPECTING TAX ADMINISTRATION

The national government should undertake a vigorous program to improve revenue administration at the local level by the following measures.

1. Draft, and encourage the municipalities to adopt, model laws for real estate taxes, *patentes,* and other local taxes.

2. Devise model forms and procedures for administering various taxes, covering such phases as records, assessment, audit, and methods of proceeding against delinquents.

3. Conduct training sessions for tax administrators in the various states. Encourage regional and national conferences of administrators to discuss common problems.

4. Create a permanent central unit charged with the responsibility of improving local revenue administration. In addition to the measures listed above, such a unit would provide consultative services for municipalities requesting them, and carry on a field program of visiting municipal tax offices to inspect records, make suggestions and discuss problems.

5. Explore the idea of making grants conditional upon greater local efforts to raise revenues.

STATE GRANTS TO MUNICIPALITIES

The grants by states to municipalities are in effect a further distribution of the constitutional grant from the national government to the states. The distribution of the grant is not uniform, either as to the overall percentages of the national grants which are handed down to the municipalities or as to the formulas by which they are allocated. Some municipalities get substantial proportions of their total revenues from the states; San Cristóbal's state grant in 1958-59 is estimated at 16 per cent of its total revenue. Other representative figures are Valencia—6 per cent, Ciudad Bolívar (Distrito Heres)—4 per cent, Mérida—6 per cent, Maracaibo—nothing.

On the average, the states in 1956-57 distributed 9.3 per cent of their receipts from the national treasury to the municipalities, but the percentage for individual states was as low as 3.4 for Yaracuy and as high as 16 for Táchira.

If the poorer municipalities in Venezuela are to show much local initiative in education, public health, or indeed any field of public service, they will have to be aided substantially by grants. Yet the states, dependent almost entirely on grants themselves, are not a likely source of further aid to the municipalities. Accordingly, grants will also have to come from the national government. These grants to the municipalities might be routed through the states, by increasing the grants to the states, and requiring, or persuading, the states to pass the money on to the municipalities. The other way is for the national government to make grants directly to the municipalities. This second method might well prove the better, if reasonable formulas for distributing the grant among the many municipalities of Venezuela can be devised. Grant programs can economize by concentrating on the needs of poorer communities, and leaving the richer communities to meet their own needs. This policy is practicable only if the richer communities have adequate taxes and other revenue-raising powers.

Formulas which take into account the needs and the financial capacity of local jurisdictions are frequently found in the United States and elsewhere.

a. Need may be measured by population, number of school children, number of older persons in the population, and so on. Occasionally, several factors are combined to form a single index of need.

b. Financial capacity may be measured by income per capita, value of taxable property, the proceeds of a standard hypothetical tax upon a specified tax base, or otherwise.

Such grants frequently stipulate that the recipient government spend at least a minimal amount on the program or programs for which the grant is made.

Such grants may be made either for general purposes, or for specific programs. The New York State school grant affords a good illustration of the application of this type of formula to a specific program.

a. Need is determined by the number of school children in daily attendance in the school district. The basic grant is $330 per school child. This is the amount deemed necessary for a minimum or "foundation" program.[7]

b. Financial capacity is determined by the amount of taxable real estate in the school district. From the aggregate basic amount of $330 per school child is subtracted an "adjustment" equal to $6.75 per $1,000 of taxable real estate in the district. The remainder is the amount of the actual grant.

Thus if a school district had 1,000 pupils and taxable real estate of $30 million, the amount of its grant would be $330,000 less an "adjustment" of $202,500 or $127,500.

Each district is required to spend at least the minimal or "foundation" amount on its educational program to qualify for the full amount of the grant under the formula. If a district spends less, its grant is reduced by the amount of the deficiency.

Matching or percentage grants, under which the grantor government pays a specified percentage of the cost of a specific program, are common in the United States. The most common purpose of such grants is to stimulate recipients to develop programs for which the grants are made. One objection to this type of grant is that it may cause the recipient government to spend too much on programs subsidized by grants, at the expense of other programs. Another objection is that the percentage-type grant is likely to be conducive to waste, because the recipient government bears only part of the cost of any expenditure item.

Percentage grants are usually not well adapted to the purpose of giving special help to the poorer communities; in fact, they often favor the richer communities. There appears to be no great use for them in Venezuela at the present time. One possible aim is to induce municipalities to make greater use of local taxes. So far as we could learn, no formal arrangements for matching grants now exist in Venezuela, although the principle has been employed in the past in rural road-building programs. Of course, informal arrangements for cooperation on particular projects are often worked out between state governors and the national government, but the state governments ordinarily finance their shares by funds from their constitutional grants, which of course also come from the national government.

---

[7] $330 is the basic amount for elementary school children. More is allowed for secondary school children, and for special needs, and for handicapped children.

F. Venezuela's Problem of Greater
Centralization vs. Decentralization

Venezuela faces the alternatives of continuing the trend toward centralized control which has grown up under dictatorships, or reversing the trend and strengthening the states and municipalities.

ALTERNATIVES OF POLICIES RESPECTING DECENTRALIZATION

Decentralization involves delegating more decision-making power to state and municipal governments, concerning (1) the purposes for which government funds are to be spent, and (2) the amounts to be spent.

Decentralization can be achieved either by giving states and municipalities larger proportions of funds raised by the national government, as by increasing the amounts of the constitutional grants, or by giving states and municipalities more taxing powers, to be used or not, as they desire, and for purposes they choose themselves.

Greater centralization, on the other hand, involves concentrating more decision-making power in the hands of the national government. It can decrease the proportion of national revenues distributed to states and municipalities, or, alternatively, require that grants be spent as the national government directs—for instance, it may make grants specifically for schools, roads and other particular objects. Also, the national government can require that states and municipalities themselves raise more money from local sources and spend it for purposes specified by the national government.

RESPONSIBILITY FOR RAISING REVENUE

Our examination of state and municipal revenue sources leads to the conclusion that the national government must continue to raise the bulk of the nation's public revenues. The main possibilities of substantial increases of local revenues lie in (1) better administration and (2) expanded use of the real estate tax. Some revenues should be sacrificed to improve the equity of the existing system, notably by repealing or improving the business and commercial *patentes*.

In any case, the potential revenues are small, compared with needs. The most optimistic estimate of the real estate potential puts increased revenues at only Bs.160 million, and even this potential depends on conditions, including improved administration and public acceptance, that will require considerable time to bring about.

RESPONSIBILITY FOR SPENDING REVENUE

With a return to democratic constitutional government, with popularly elected state and local legislatures, there are strong arguments for granting greater spending powers to the states and municipalities. The principal arguments as we see them are as follows:

1. Certain local needs, as for schools, local roads, water supply, police and fire protection, and so on, can be better met by decisions of local officials, than by national government officials working from Caracas.

2. In a country as large as Venezuela, especially one with a deficient communications system, central government authorities cannot have the same familiarity with local government problems as have local officials.

3. A responsible electorate can be built up only by citizen experience with and participation in government. The best and indeed the only way to gain such experience, so far as most citizens are concerned, is at the local and state government level.

4. Because the country is so large and heterogeneous, needs vary widely from state to state. National policies, unless very wisely formulated and administered, will not be sufficiently flexible to take account of varying needs.

5. Giving the states and municipalities more financial power enables them to experiment with and develop new governmental services and administrative procedures, to meet their peculiar needs. Many decision-making centers afford a wider opportunity for experimentation than does one. This has been demonstrated in the United States, where individual state and local governments have pioneered with many services and techniques which have later been adopted generally.

6. In so far as state and local governments are given more revenue-raising power, the citizens have some discretion over the proportion of local income to be used for public and private purposes. There is thus a greater opportunity for satisfying local preferences than is the case where the decision-making power is concentrated at the national level.

On the other hand, there are a number of arguments for increasing, or at least not decreasing, the existing degree of centralized control over government spending:

1. State, and more especially district and municipal, governments have not the trained personnel with which to make and administer decisions respecting technical governmental services, including roads, water supply, sanitary facilities, schools, and the like. The country cannot afford to wait upon the lengthy trial and error process by which state and local government administrative skill developed in the United States. Moreover, many state and local jurisdictions are too small to maintain highly trained bureaucracies.

2. Concerning citizen participation, United States experience has been that, in many communities, local and state government affairs arouse less interest than do national affairs, as evidenced by the fact that the proportion of citizens voting in local and state elections is ordinarily much smaller than in national elections. Policies regarding most services ordinarily are dictated by the professional administrators, rather than being debated and decided by citizens.

3. Although a wider distribution of powers may promote desirable experimentation in some communities, it may have the opposite effect in others. A lethargic population under unwise leadership may impede progress or undertake foolish or impracticable schemes. The country's financial situation requires the most careful central planning to repair past mistakes and to assure continued development; perhaps there is no margin with which to gamble on successful experimentation at the local level.

4. So far as revenue-raising powers are concerned, most taxes can be more effectively administered at the national rather than the state or local level. Moreover, uniform national rates avoid the dangers of tax competition among the states and localities.

5. The disparity of resources among the states and the territories argues for a policy of more equal distribution of resources between the richer and poorer areas; such policies can be effected only by the central government. However, this is not an argument against state and municipal government spending as such, since the redistribution can be carried out by a system of national taxes and grants.

With only a short period for observation in the country, we do not pretend to be able to evaluate the arguments for and against decentralization in the context of Venezuelan governmental traditions and culture. We list the arguments because we believe that they should be carefully weighed in arriving at decisions concerning the nation's future course. Coming from the United States, we are predisposed toward a system of strong state and local government; an observer from France, with an area more nearly comparable with that of Venezuela's, might well recommend greater centralization, along the lines of the French system.

There is no evidence that centralization thus far has contributed to efficiency of government. But past performance is not a good guide; the national government under the recent dictatorship wasted large sums. What it will do under a constitutional system, and improved public administration and planning, is another matter.

In any case the proportion of public funds spent by states and municipalities is so small, relative to national expenditures, that the responsibilities of states and localities can be greatly expanded by means of national grants with no considerable decrease in national direct expenditures. Starting from present expenditure levels, state and local expenditures could be increased by 50 per cent, with only a 7 per cent decrease in national direct expenditures. This implies that the national government will continue to be the dominant power in the foreseeable future, even assuming the utmost effort to push responsibilities to the lower governmental levels.

COOPERATION AMONG THE THREE LEVELS OF GOVERNMENT

In our trips around the country, and in conversations with numerous state and local officials, we have been impressed by two things: first, by the apparent competence and understanding of the great majority of state and local public officials with whom we have had the opportunity of meeting, and second, the fact that their lists of things most badly needed in their communities—schools, improved water supply and sanitation, health and medical facilities, rural roads, and measures to increase farm productivity—are obviously of the highest priority for furthering the economic and political development of the country.

We have been impressed also with the degree of overlapping of responsibility among the three levels of government for the functions mentioned above. There is no systematic procedure, so far as we can determine, for allocating responsibilities for education; each level "does what it can."

It appears to us that the first requisite is more cooperation, and more systematic cooperation, among the three levels of government, under an arrangement which would give a larger role and more responsibility to the states and municipalities.

The instruments of improved cooperation include the following:

1. Establishment of a commission of national, state and municipal

officials to study the governmental structure, the development of operating relationships among national, state and municipal governments, and allocation of functions among them. The commission should be furnished with a professional staff.

2. Establishment, by the national government, of a consulting service and clearing house for states and municipalities, with responsibilities for studying state and municipal government problems, developing administrative techniques, holding conferences and training sessions for public officials and serving as an exchange for information. There are several such service organizations in the U.S.A., including the American Municipal Association, the International City Managers Association, and the Council of State Governments, and many organizations which serve particular professional groups, such as health officers, accountants and comptrollers, tax administrators, and so on. The improvement of municipal tax administration, suggested in a preceding section, would be part of the responsibility of such a center.

3. Establishment, at the national level, of a local government commission, removed from any place in the government where political pressure might impair its activities. This local government commission would be an operating body, in contrast to the commission recommended above. It would have charge of administering the grants to municipalities envisaged in the recommendations earlier in this chapter. And its powers in this field of local finance could be expanded, perhaps to the point of having something to do with administering grants to the states, if it proved successful in its first task. It could certainly assist municipalities in technical problems of administration, including tax administration, planning and accounting.

These three recommendations can be implemented only by trained specialists in various fields, of which Venezuela is in short supply. The situation justifies an intensive training program, perhaps under the joint sponsorship of the national government and the University, drawing upon the persons now available in Venezuela, upon United Nations assistance, and upon experts from other countries. Selected career personnel should be sent abroad for advanced training.

SPECIAL PROBLEM OF THE FEDERAL DISTRICT

The Federal District has been subject to special financial pressures in 1958, and is seeking ways to increase its revenue. Under the former government of Venezuela, a huge public works program was concentrated largely in the Caracas area, and concentrated, too, in time, the work being rushed toward completion at extraordinary speed. The aftermath has been an unusual degree of unemployment, at the same time that the Federal District has been left with a depleted treasury.

The national government has recently given the District a special emergency grant of Bs.80 million, yet there seems to be a need for further tax revenue.

In our view, the need can be met without inventing new taxes; indeed, such new taxes as we have heard suggested, or that we have been able to think of, do not seem promising, either in revenue yield or in administrative aspects. A tax on the ownership of television sets would, indeed, according to certain consumer studies that we have seen, rest almost wholly on well-to-do families of the Caracas area, and on bars or other businesses that make use of them; but the task of locating all the sets, given the possibility of indoor aerials, is formidable compared with the revenue possibilities. The task of collection would not be easy either.

There lies ready at hand a fiscal instrument that should give Caracas all that it needs for the time being: the real estate tax. It has been pointed out above that the present tax in Caracas, 6.5 per cent of rental, is equivalent to little more than $\frac{1}{3}$ of 1 per cent of current capital value, for owner-occupied houses. The tax yields nearly Bs.30 million a year, and, with better enforcement, it could easily yield about Bs.35 million or even Bs.40 million. At a rate of 13 per cent, and with stricter enforcement, especially in collecting the taxes that the taxpayer admits are due, the yield could be about Bs.75 million, an increase of Bs.40 million over the current yield.

The increase in tax rate should apply to both land and buildings; the differential rate on land, suggested above, could wait until the present crisis is surmounted.

It is inadvisable to drain off into the administration of new, untried taxes, whose problems we cannot even forecast, the limited amount of tax-administration talent that the District now possesses. Concentration on the real estate tax will buy more revenue per man-hour. A special effort should be made to see that all properties in existence are on the tax rolls (if not exempt by law); that the assessed rentals are close to market values; and that taxes due are collected promptly. Some of the major steps recommended above, such as the building up of a tax map, will take some time, but meanwhile there is much to be done.

CHAPTER XIII : **The Tax System**
: **and Economic Stability**

A. The Aim: A Tax System
Sensitive to Economic Disturbances

Under traditional public finance doctrine of two or three decades ago, there was nothing good to be said for a tax system that was sensitive to fluctuations in business, a tax system the revenue from which moved up and down with business. An unstable tax system, as it was called, was an inconvenience, if not a peril, to the government. But this point of view failed to consider the effect of a stable-yield tax system on the private sector of the economy. In a boom period, when inflation threatens, and the government should be drawing more and more purchasing power away from the private sector of the economy in order to restrain an undue bidding for labor and capital, a tax system whose yield does not rise automatically under those conditions is not helpful in checking inflation. Likewise, when unemployment develops during a recession, a tax system that continues to extract from the pockets of business men and consumers just as much money as it did during full employment is not helping place the private sector in a position where it can resume buying at the normal rate.

The viewpoint taken here is the one that is now generally accepted in economic analysis, namely, that a national tax system should be sensitive to fluctuations in prices and employment. This implies that in boom times the national government should have an excess of revenues over expenditures, and in depressions, an automatic deficit. This point of view further implies that the government will set aside its boom period surpluses, in one form or another, and will draw upon those reserves (or take some equivalent action) in periods of reduced economic activity. "Reserves," in this context, does not include reserves of foreign exchange; changes in those reserves may well be moving in an opposite direction from that of changes in a domestic money reserve held by the Treasury, as shown in Chapter II above, in the section on Budget Surpluses and Deficits.

354

Under this approach, which favors a cycle-sensitive tax system, added responsibilities attach to the Ministry of Finance. Moreover, the Ministry and the Central Bank must agree on a policy, to be implemented by close technical cooperation. In the paragraphs to follow, it is assumed that the Ministry of Finance will possess an economic advisory staff, in the form of a tax research division, as recommended in Chapter VI above, and perhaps also a research division devoted to the study of business fluctuations and their effects on tax revenues, expenditure, and the public debt. It also assumes cooperation of these groups with the research staff of the Central Bank.

It is worth emphasizing here that the research essential to a sound fiscal policy cannot proceed far unless there is an expansion in scope and still further improvement in quality of the statistics-gathering function of other government agencies, particularly the Bureau of Statistics. Venezuela already has a better statistics-gathering service than many countries, yet the demands for data in a modern, rapidly developing economy are so great that present efforts and expenditures in this field could profitably be increased quite markedly.

The policy recommended here, based on a sensitive tax system, has little value unless it is followed in periods of inflation as well as depression. But for simplicity in exposition, the analysis below will be cast in terms of a hypothetical depression, with reminders of the corresponding policy required when the economy is in a period of boom.

Finally, we shall see that in Venezuela there is one important type of economic fluctuation where the newer rule (a sensitive tax system is desirable) does not apply. If the fluctuation in question is one simply in the profits of foreign-owned petroleum companies operating in Venezuela, a tax system that is sensitive to a fall in those profits is not a stabilizing force for the Venezuelan economy.

B. *How Sensitive Is the Present Tax System?*

We first attempt to ascertain how sensitive Venezuela's present tax system is to fluctuations in business. A useful measure of sensitivity is the number of bolivars by which the government's current revenues would automatically fall in the event that national income fell by 100 bolivars. National income, in this context, might mean either national income produced within the territorial area of Venezuela, or national income received by the residents of Venezuela. For Venezuela, the difference is important. National income produced includes the profits of the foreign-owned petroleum companies operating in Venezuela. National income received includes only about half those profits, this being the share that accrues to the government under the so-called fifty-fifty policy. Each measuring rod has its advantages; for the present analysis we shall use national income received.

CHANGE IN NATIONAL INCOME ORIGINATING IN PETROLEUM SECTOR

The answer to the question, how sensitive is Venezuela's tax system, depends on whether we assume that the change starts in the petroleum sector and spreads from there to other parts of the economy, or whether it is in the non-oil sector that the depressive—or inflationary—forces originate. We examine the former case first.

Let us suppose, first of all, that the change in the oil sector is one of price alone, not physical volume. The price of petroleum in the world market declines; oil company profits fall, say, by Bs.100 million. And for the moment, let us say that this is all that happens; for the time being, we assume, the oil companies do not cut back on their purchases of domestic labor or supplies. The government's revenue from taxes on the petroleum companies declines, we suppose, by Bs.50 million.[1] The national income received falls by just this amount, Bs.50 million, for national income received embraces only that part of the oil companies' profits that flow to the government in taxation. Here, a decline of Bs.50 million in national income is accompanied, automatically, by a decline of Bs.50 million in tax revenue: the system is 100 per cent sensitive. But there is no accompanying effect on employment or prices in Venezuela, over the short run, assuming that the foreign exchange reserves are adequate to cushion the fall in the flow of foreign exchange to the government.

If the decline in petroleum profits is due to a fall in the physical volume of oil exported, rather than to a decline in the price of oil, the effect on the tax system is somewhat different, and so too is the degree of sensitivity. In this event, the national income available to residents of Venezuela is decreased not only by a fall in the amount of taxes from

---

[1] The decline in taxes payable would in fact be equal to just 50 per cent of the decline in profits only for those oil companies that were paying additional income tax before the fall in price and that were still paying it after the decline. However, whether the decline in total tax payable by the oil companies is in fact just 50 per cent of the decline in profits does not affect the analytical point discussed here.

oil companies;[2] it decreases also by the inevitably smaller total of wages paid to oil company workers as the physical volume of activity necessarily contracts somewhat, and, for the same reason, by a decline in the incomes of domestic concerns that sell to the oil companies.

Meanwhile, what of the fall in tax revenue? It includes not only a decline in taxes paid by the oil companies, but also a decrease of income tax due from oil workers who have become temporarily unemployed, and from domestic contracting firms and others, who have been selling to the oil companies. Because of these latter two sources of decline, the national income received in Venezuela will fall by a larger amount than the tax revenue; we shall have moved away from the strange, limiting, case of 100 per cent sensitivity of the tax system to a fall in national income received. But the percentage might still be close to 100—perhaps 80 or 90. And again, so high a percentage would not mean that the Venezuelan economy was being safeguarded against a depression better than if the tax revenue had declined less, for we are dealing with the case in which the greater part of the decline in national income received is the fall in the tax revenue itself (the tax revenue from the oil companies). We are again reminded that, in the peculiar economic circumstances that characterize Venezuela, where a large income is generated within the country's borders for sharing between (a) owners living abroad and (b) Venezuelan residents through the instrument of government, a sensitive tax system is not an economic stabilizer. This is so, if only because there is no destabilization occurring, on this first round of events, of the economy within Venezuela's borders (again excepting oil workers' wages and like items). There will be a good deal of internal stabilizing to do, to be sure, if the government does not act promptly to draw on its domestic monetary reserves, or does not create money through the domestic banking system, to avoid having to cut back its own expenditures when its tax receipts fall.

A similar analysis applies if oil company profits rise rather than fall. If the tax system proves quite sensitive to this rise, so that revenues from the oil companies increase rapidly, there is still nothing, at that moment, that is acting to destabilize the Venezuelan economy; there is no upward pressure on Venezuelan prices if the government does not increase its own level of spending, or the oil companies, their levels of spending.

Of course, these generalized statements are subject to many excep-

---

[2] The various components of the oil company taxes will behave differently when volume falls, rather than price.

tions that will no doubt occur to the reader; but it remains broadly true that the principle enunciated at the start of this chapter is not applicable when the change in national income received originates from a change in the profits of foreign-owned companies operating within the country.

We turn now to the instances where this general principle does apply. It applies in at least one case where the economic disturbance originates in the oil sector; and to practically any case where it originates in the non-oil sector.

The kind of change in the oil sector that is implied at this point is a change in development activity by the petroleum companies within the borders of the country. This change may or may not be touched off by a fall in profits; whatever its cause (and it is here considered apart from whatever fall in profits or production there may be), it exerts a depressing influence on the economic welfare of Venezuelan residents, one which, moreover, can be mitigated by a tax system that is sensitive. This case is merely an extension of the element already noted above, where the production of oil is assumed to decline.

When exploration, drilling, the construction of pipe lines, storage tanks, etc., drop off, employment in Venezuela declines appreciably; the total of wages and profits may fall substantially. National income received in Venezuela declines accordingly. As to the tax revenues, they decline by the sum of the diminution of income tax revenue from oil workers' wages, oil contractors' profits, and the like.[3] Subsequently, when the oil workers, contractors, etc., spend their now diminished income, they will buy less liquor, cigarettes, etc., and so there will be some fall in consumption-tax revenue. The greater these automatic declines in tax revenue, the less severe will be the net repercussion of the lessened rate of oil development on the economy. But, as will be shown below, the rate of decline in these non-oil tax revenues, relative to the decline in national income received, will not be great. The counter-depression force exerted by the automatic decline in tax revenues is not a strong one.

CHANGE IN THE NATIONAL INCOME
ORIGINATING IN THE NON-PETROLEUM SECTOR

A decline in national income originating in the non-oil sector of the Venezuelan economy is likely to start either with a decline in govern-

---

[3] National income received, and tax revenue, also decline by the fall, if any, in total taxes paid by the oil companies, including customs duties on imported equipment and supplies, but this element has been analyzed above.

ment spending or a fall in the rate of purchase or construction of capital equipment or dwellings, in the private sector. Let us suppose that gross private domestic investment spending on equipment, construction, and so on, declines by Bs.1,200,000 (annual rate), of which Bs.200,000 is a decline in the purchase of equipment from abroad. This latter decline has no effect, for the time being, on economic activity within Venezuela. The remaining Bs.1,000,000, on the other hand, represents a decline in domestic purchase of domestic labor, materials, etc., and is reflected at once in a decline in domestic profits, and, except as it gives rise to an (involuntary) increase in inventories, by a decline in employment and hence payrolls. What happens to tax revenues? Total revenue from the income tax is at present only some 30 per cent from non-oil sources, so we are dealing with a total amount, before the hypothetical decline in revenue, of only some Bs.400 million, perhaps even less. The national income received is running at, say, Bs.15 billion before the hypothetical decline. Thus the non-oil income tax revenue at full employment is equal only to some 2½ per cent of the national income received. The rate of decline in income tax revenue depends, of course, not on this average rate, but on the marginal rates applicable to the several tax-payers. Is the marginal rate, relative to national income, greater than the average rate? Many of the workers who become unemployed under this hypothetical depression pay no income tax even in prosperity; their marginal rate is much less than 2½ per cent; it is zero. Those who have been paying salary tax have been subject only to a 1 per cent rate. But a good many taxpayers will have been paying at a marginal rate appreciably higher than 2½ per cent, particularly under the complementary tax. But again, the highest rates of the complementary tax, the 26 per cent rate and those slightly below it, are paid only by the oil companies, in fact (with very few exceptions), and as we have seen, an automatic decline in the tax revenue from the foreign-owned oil companies does not directly stimulate the Venezuelan economy. Without many more data than are at hand as this is written, no precise estimate can be made of the degree of sensitivity of the non-oil part of the income tax to a decline in the national income received; but if a guess may be hazarded, the figure might be put at about 2 per cent. Thus, an initial decline of Bs.1,000,000 in national income received, reflecting a decline of Bs.1,200,000 in domestic spending on investment, might be accompanied automatically by a decline of income tax revenue equal to some 2 per cent of that decline in national income, that is, a decline in tax revenue of Bs.20,000.

But there are, of course, other taxes, which will also decline automatically with the fall in domestic investment spending. Customs duties and consular fees, which come to almost Bs.700,000,000 a year, and hence equal about 4½ per cent of the national income, will decline immediately as the importation of equipment and supplies declines. The duty rates on such imports are appreciable and the duties paid on those imports account perhaps for not far from half of total customs revenues. The average rate applicable to the imports in question would depend on what we assume about the exact composition of those imports, but let us postulate an average rate of 10 per cent, on some Bs.200,000 of imports. The decline in tax revenue, that is, the decline in the demand being made on the pocketbooks of the domestic taxpayers, would therefore be about Bs.20,000. Subsequent to the initial decline in the non-oil sector[4] consumers would import less also, since discharged workers, and business men whose profits were being squeezed, would buy less abroad for personal consumption. If domestic spending on consumption declined by Bs.600,000 because of the reduced incomes due to the fall in investment spending; if Bs.200,000 of this Bs.600,000 was a decline in import of consumer goods; and if the average duty rate on such goods turned out to be 20 per cent; there would be another Bs.40,000 smaller demand on the taxpayers than before the recession started.

The other taxes in the present Venezuelan fiscal system are either too small to be included in the very rough calculations being made here (e.g. the gasoline tax, yielding only Bs.25 million) or are almost completely resistant to economic change, over the short run (e.g. the municipalities' taxes on real estate rentals). We may therefore add the three estimates of tax decline obtained above: Bs.20,000 (income tax), Bs.20,000 (duties on imports of capital goods), and on the second round, Bs.40,000 (duties on imports of consumer goods). The total thus far of the automatic decline in tax demands on consumers and business men, in the event of an initial fall of Bs.1,000,000 in national spending, in the domestic investment sector, would be only some Bs.80,000, or 8 per cent of the stipulated decline.

Although, to repeat, these computations are incomplete, and subject to error, it does seem certain that the present non-oil segment of the Venezuelan tax system is so small, relative to the demand it makes on domestic firms and consumers even during full employment, and is so little sensitive to changes in business conditions, that it cannot be

---

[4] The multiplier effect of the initial fall in investment spending is not pursued further here, as the aim is merely to illustrate the larger magnitudes initially involved.

counted on to be an appreciable counter-depression influence through the automatic decline in its demands on consumer-producer pocketbooks when depression gets under way. Now this is no reason for making the tax system heavier! But it may be a reason for trying to make the non-oil part of the Venezuelan tax system somewhat more sensitive.

The analysis above has been cast in terms of depression. The same analysis can be applied to inflationary influences. If the private economy goes on an investment spree, bidding up the prices of goods and labor under more-than-full employment, tax revenues will automatically increase somewhat, but not by enough to serve as a substantial check to inflation.

The present analysis has been in terms of domestic surpluses or deficits (automatic increases or decreases in tax revenue) of the Venezuelan Treasury, not in terms of the country's foreign exchange reserve. However, if the economic disturbance originates at home rather than in the world market for oil, a sensitive tax system does aid somewhat in preventing balance-of-payment difficulties. Under inflationary pressure at home, which tends to be accompanied by increased spending abroad, the rising tax revenue siphons off part of the funds that might otherwise have been spent on added imports. But if the disturbance originates in the world market for oil, showing itself in a decline in oil profits and hence Treasury revenue from that source, sensitivity of that branch of the revenue is not a good sign; rather, it reflects the fact that as oil exports and profits slacken, the supply of foreign exchange available to Venezuelan residents decreases, and if the government continues on the same level of expenditures in the face of the deficit in its own revenue caused by the fall in taxes from the oil companies, the continuation of the normal rate of imports by consumers and business men could lead to a balance-of-payments problem. As indicated in Chapter II, however, this fact is no reason by itself for the government to cut back its normal level of outlays and thus induce depression in the domestic economy; the appropriate remedy—assuming that the decline in oil income is not for the long run—is to borrow, not at home, but abroad, if there is no adequate foreign exchange reserve already accumulated that may be drawn upon.

SENSITIVITY IMPLICATIONS
OF RECOMMENDATIONS IN PRESENT REPORT

Scattered throughout the present report on the Venezuelan tax system there are a number of recommendations for change. They have been made, for the most part, for reasons chiefly other than improving the sensitivity of the tax system, but in a final judgment of their accept-ability we have attempted to ascertain whether on balance they also are effective in terms of that goal. Table XIII-1 gives an approximate answer, with respect to the non-oil segment of the Venezuelan tax sys-tem, and it is in the affirmative. Each major recommended change, listed below, is given a plus sign if it tends to make the non-oil part of the tax system more sensitive than the present one; a minus sign indicates the opposite effect. In giving these signs, it is assumed that the new system raises, under full employment at a stable price level, about the same revenue as does the present one.

Although, in general, the recommendations as a group tend to increase the sensitivity of the tax system, the influence is not enough, quantita-tively speaking, to make an appreciable difference in the economy's power to counter automatically the forces of depression or inflation.

Table XIII-1.   Recommended Tax Measures Classed by Effect on Sensitivity of Non-Oil Segment of Venezuelan Tax System[1]

	Increases sensitivity (+)	Decreases sensitivity (—)
Income Tax		
1. A more progressive rate..........................	+ (?)	
2. Lower personal exemptions.......................	+ (?)	
3. Carry-backs of business loss......................	+	
4. Taxation of dividends............................		—
5. Higher rates but less progression in corporation income tax..		—
6. Current payment of tax on estimated income of current year; and extension of withholding................	+	
7. Averaging of capital gains over several years, and carry-forward of unabsorbed capital losses..........		—
Customs Duties		
1. Higher tax rates on certain luxuries................	+	
2. Lower tax rates on certain necessaries..............	+	
3. Extension of ad valorem basis in place of per kilo basis	+	
Gasoline Tax		
1. Higher rates....................................	+	
Real Estate Tax		
1. Improved administration and increased rates........		— (?)

[1] Question mark indicates considerable doubt which category the item belongs in.

INCREASING FURTHER THE SENSITIVITY
OF THE TAX SYSTEM

There are very few measures, unobjectionable or even desirable on other grounds, that can be added to the recommendations given above, in order to increase still more the sensitivity of the non-oil part of the tax system. The most powerful instrument of all, at some future period, might be the carry-back of unused personal exemptions, but this allowance is too much of a task to impose on the Tax Administration at a time when it will have much to do in any case, insofar as the changes recommended in this report are accepted.

By a carry-back of unused personal exemptions is meant the following: Suppose that a family of husband, wife, and two children had a total family exemption of Bs.12,000 under a revised income tax (see Chapter III above), and an income, in one year, of Bs.20,000, which drops in the year following to Bs.9,000. This family will have paid some income tax on the first year's income. On the second year's income they have no tax to pay; their income falls short of their personal exemptions by Bs.3,000. This Bs.3,000 is an unused personal exemption—unused because it is not set off against any income. If it could be carried back and offset against the Bs.8,000 that was taxed the previous year, reducing this Bs.8,000 to Bs.5,000, the family would have a right to a tax refund, calculated at the marginal rate of the previous year's tax on the last Bs.3,000 of the family's income. Such a carry-back might conceivably be extended back over a period of two or three years. But administration of it would require more record keeping and other administrative tasks than seem wise to undertake at this time. Moreover, no other income-taxing country has yet adopted this carry-back of unused personal exemptions, so there is no experience to appeal to. It is a device that might profitably be studied by the tax research division recommended elsewhere in this report for possible use some years from now.

In the section of this report dealing with the income tax, refunds of overwithheld taxes and of taxes overpaid by mistake are of course recommended. It may be added here that the more quickly these refunds are made, the better for the economy. Overwithholding is most likely to occur when a depression strikes early or in the middle of the year, and a prompt refund of overwithheld tax will put money into the pockets of the consumer, to help stabilize the economy.

A SYSTEM OF TREASURY RESERVES

A sensitive tax system, we have seen, tends to build up surpluses in times of boom or inflation, and to place the government in a deficit position in the event of a severe depression.[5] What will the government do with the extra money, in the one case, and where will it get the resources to maintain its level of expenditures, in the other?

The simplest way is merely to let the excess revenue build up, preferably in the Central Bank, to be drawn upon when tax revenues fall off, and this is the procedure we recommend. Alternatively, formulae can be devised by which the government is required by law to set aside certain stipulated amounts (expressed either in absolute terms or as percentages of increase over previous year's revenue, etc.) and by which it is limited, in the same manner, in the degre to which it can draw on the reserves. But these mechanical formulae are on the whole likely to be more troublesome than helpful for a sovereign nation that can borrow when it wishes to do so and is of course not restricted in its power to sterilize temporarily as much of its revenues as it wishes. The chief thing to guard against is that the government be shut in by constitutional restrictions or by Central Bank laws to the degree where an intelligently managed counter-cycle fiscal policy cannot be implemented. We repeat the recognition given in Chapter II above to the reasons that in the past have led to such restrictions, but we suggest a reconsideration of the degree of their severity and inapplicability to a modern fiscal and financial system.

---

[5] The Venezuelan economy might conceivably find itself in an economic state that would call for an indefinite series of government surpluses, to maintain economic stability, or an indefinite series of deficits. Then reserves with the Central Bank should accumulate indefinitely, or borrowing should continue indefinitely. But these chronic states of inflationary or deflationary pressure do not seem likely; at least the chronic deflationary state does not.

CHAPTER XIV : Venezuelan National Government
Accounts and Accounting Reports

This chapter is mainly concerned with the role of the accounting system in Venezuela with respect to the needs of information for financial management and economic analysis, and with the problem of developing a system of reports which will better serve such needs. However, in their planning and management functions, the budget and the financial reports of the accounting system are a part of the same conceptual team. The accounting reports should summarize the outcome of the budget in a manner which permits a comparison of outcome with original plan. Therefore, some consideration will also be given in this chapter to the Venezuelan budget system.

A. Functions of a Modern Accounting System

We may distinguish four main functions to be served by government accounts and accounting reports. These functions reflect the numerous and diverse interests of those who utilize accounting data. The functions, which are somewhat interrelated, are as follows:

1. Accountancy—keeping records of expenditures, receipts, assets, and liabilities in a form that will ensure compliance with legislative intent as to the disposition of funds, preventing the diversion of public funds to unauthorized purposes, and that will ensure proper stewardship of government assets.

2. Planning and policy-making—establishing governmental objectives and goals; attempting to select programs of highest social priority from among the many competing demands upon government funds.

3. Management—checking technical efficiency (input-output relationship) of governmental operations; supervising implementation of legislative and administrative plans; and handling of government funds (cash management).

365

4. Information—providing meaningful data on government operations to government officials and the public, as well as information necessary for functions mentioned in the preceding three paragraphs. One important requirement is that the system furnish information for economic analysis, including data for estimating governmental expenditures on goods and services, consistent with national income and national product estimates.

The purposes which governmental accounts, particularly those of national governments, have been called upon to serve have increased tremendously in the past few years as the result of many developments, among which are the use of social accounting and the concomitant requirements for information on the government's contributions to national income and national product; and the increasing participation of many governments—particularly governments of undeveloped countries—in trading, production and finance, and activities to promote economic development.

Efficient policy-making must rest upon comprehensible and prompt information on government activities. The structure of the government's accounts must be arranged to meet planning and management requirements; these will vary, of course, from government to government, depending upon the requirements of the government concerned. Moreover, no single accounting classification system will yield all the information required by the various functions listed above; several systems of account classification may be required.

B. The Venezuelan Accounting and Reporting System

1. DESCRIPTION OF THE ACCOUNTING AND REPORTING SYSTEM

The Venezuelan accounting and reporting system is prescribed by the Basic Law of National Finance (Ley Orgánica de la Hacienda Nacional). Accounting and reporting responsibilities are assigned by law among:

a. Offices in charge of the administration of revenues (levying offices)
b. Offices in charge of the administration of expenditures (Ministries)
c. Office of the Treasurer of the Finance Ministry (Tesorería Nacional)
d. Receiving offices (Receptorías de Fondos Nacionales)
e. Paying offices

    f. Office of the Controller (Contraloría General de la Nación)
        (1) Centralization Court (Sala de Centralización)
        (2) Section 1 of the Control Court (Sala de Control)
        (3) Section 2 of the Control Court (Sala de Control)

Although not required by law to do so, the Central Budget Office (Dirección General del Presupuesto) of the Finance Ministry keeps accounts of all disbursements of the Ministries; records payments against all long-term contracts, that is, those that go beyond the current fiscal year; and keeps summary accounts of receipts by revenue sources (ramos de producto).

All receipts of the Venezuelan Government are cleared through receiving offices established by the national executive in and outside of Venezuela and through other entities entrusted specifically with Treasury services responsibilities.

The Government's cash accounts are kept in the Central Bank of Venezuela (Banco Central de Venezuela) and in the Bank of Venezuela (Banco de Venezuela). All receipts collected by the receiving offices mentioned in the preceding paragraph are cleared through one or the other of these banks. These banks cash all the pay orders issued by the Government. As will be explained later, they perform important accounting and reporting functions for the Venezuelan Government.

In the Venezuelan fiscal system the functions of levying taxes and of administering all other sources of revenues are completely separated from the function of revenue collection. The former tasks are performed by the offices entrusted with the administration of specific revenues, which have to keep records of all levies made and of the collections against those levies. The second function is performed by receiving offices designated by the national executive. It should be made clear at this point that for all revenue accruing to the Government, a levying document is issued which has to be paid at a receiving office before the payer receives the certificate of tax payment. Seals, stamps, and the like, and some Government publications and services are sold to the public through revenue offices. In these cases, the purchaser receives the stamps, etc., at the same office where he makes the payment.

In the Venezuelan system no checks are issued to pay for goods and services supplied to the Government; permanent and special pay orders are the documents used for this purpose, the former to pay for recurring acquisitions of goods and services such as salaries to employees and the latter to pay for non-recurring acquisitions of goods and services. The function of issuing these pay orders is separated from the function of cashing them. The former function is performed by the Ministries. Pay orders are cashed by the "Banco Central" and "Banco de Venezuela," which are the banking institutions in which the Office of the Treasurer keeps current bank accounts.

The "Ley Orgánica de Hacienda" provides that all governmental revenue shall be covered into the general Treasury and that all expenditures of the general Treasury shall be made out of appropriations approved by Congress. Therefore in the Venezuelan system there are no earmarked revenue funds, revolving funds, or trust funds. All receipts are credited to the general Treasury and all disbursements are made out of appropriations included in the Budget Law.

With these considerations in mind, we turn to a summary description of the way in which accounting for receipts and expenditures is performed by all agencies and banks mentioned and of the reports pertinent to this work turned out by the accounting system. This description is supplemented by Diagrams XIV-1 and XIV-2.

a. Receipts Accounting and Reporting.

(1) OFFICES IN CHARGE OF THE ADMINISTRATION OF REVENUES (levying offices). These offices are required by law to maintain a Revenue Journal (Manual) and a Revenue Ledger (Mayor). Accounts are maintained by prescribed revenue sources (ramos de producto).

Revenue levies are registered in the Revenue Journal on a monthly or other periodical basis, depending on the volume of transactions of the levying office. The levying documents are registered in a schedule of levies in chronological order of issuance, indicating the date and the number of the levying document (planilla), name of the payer, and the revenue source.

The "planilla," source document for these entries, is handed by the levying office to the person to whom issued. This person makes the payment at the receiving office (receptoría de fondos nacionales) indicated in the planilla. The receiving office indicates in the planilla the date of payment and returns the original to the payer. The payer should take the original of the planilla to the levying office as evidence of having made the payment. If he does so, the levying office writes in the original the clause known as Solvency Certificate (Certificado de Liberación).

Using the copy of the planilla received from the receiving office, the levying office registers the revenue collection in the Schedule of Monthly Collections (Relación Mensual de Cobros), in chronological order of collection, indicating the date and number of the planilla,

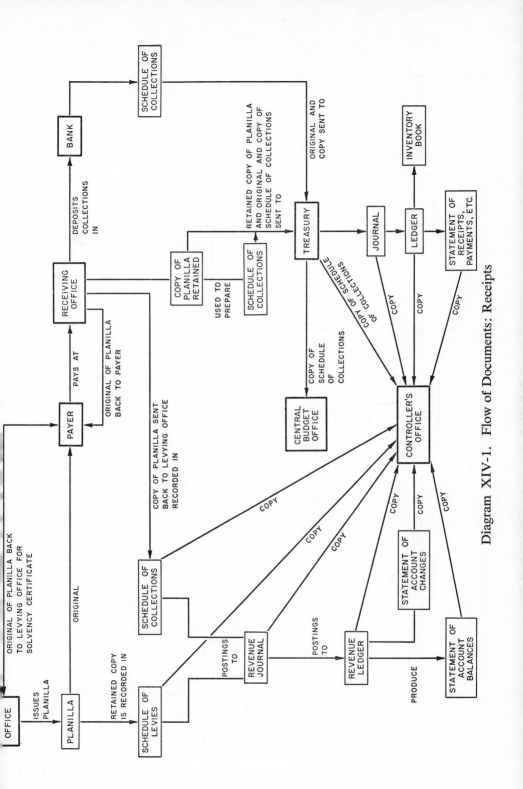

Diagram XIV-1. Flow of Documents: Receipts

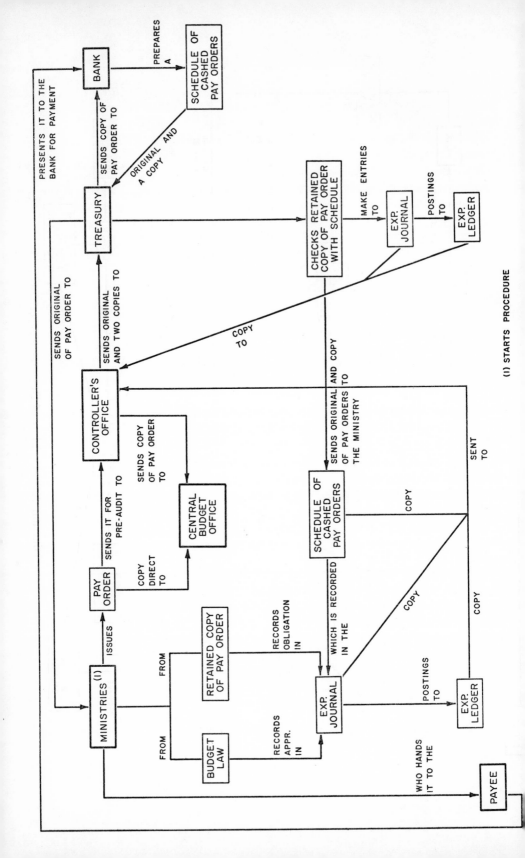

BANK — PREPARES A — SCHEDULE OF CASHED PAY ORDERS

PRESENTS IT TO THE BANK FOR PAYMENT

SENDS COPY OF PAY ORDER TO

ORIGINAL AND A COPY

TREASURY

SENDS ORIGINAL OF PAY ORDER TO

SENDS ORIGINAL AND TWO COPIES TO

CHECKS RETAINED COPY OF PAY ORDER WITH SCHEDULE — MAKE ENTRIES TO — EXP. JOURNAL — POSTINGS TO — EXP. LEDGER

COPY TO

CONTROLLER'S OFFICE

SENDS IT FOR PRE-AUDIT TO

SENDS COPY OF PAY ORDER TO

COPY DIRECT TO

CENTRAL BUDGET OFFICE

SENDS ORIGINAL AND COPY OF PAY ORDERS TO THE MINISTRY

SCHEDULE OF CASHED PAY ORDERS

WHICH IS RECORDED IN THE

COPY

COPY

COPY

SENT TO

PAY ORDER

ISSUES

MINISTRIES (1)

FROM — RETAINED COPY OF PAY ORDER — RECORDS OBLIGATION IN

FROM — BUDGET LAW — RECORDS APPR. IN

EXP. JOURNAL — POSTINGS TO — EXP. LEDGER

WHO HANDS IT TO THE — PAYEE

(1) STARTS PROCEDURE

name of payer, and the revenue source. This schedule is used to make monthly entries to the Revenue Journal by year of levy and revenue source.

Postings to the Revenue Ledger accounts are made from the Revenue Journal. A statement of the balances of the Revenue Ledger accounts (Estado de Valores) is prepared which shows, by revenue source, the amounts levied and not yet paid as of the beginning of the month; and the amounts levied, collected, cancelled, and exonerated, both during the month and accumulated as of the end of the month.[1] A copy of this statement, together with the schedules of levies and collections, is sent by the levying office to the Sala de Centralización de la Contraloría Nacional, the Centralization Court of the Controller's Office.

Offices in charge of the administration of revenue sources are required by law to send to the Sala de Centralización de la Contraloría a statement showing the accounts changes (Estado de Movimiento de las Cuentas) during the reported month. This statement contains the same information contained in the statement of the balances of the Revenue Ledger accounts just described, except the amounts levied but not yet paid as of the beginning of the month and accumulated at the end of the month.

Offices in charge of the administration of revenue send every month to the Sala de Centralización de la Contraloría Nacional copies of the Journal and the Revenue Ledger.

(2) RECEIVING OFFICES. Taxpayers and purchasers of government's goods and services present themselves to the receiving offices indicated in the levying documents issued to them, to make the corresponding payments.[2]

The receiving office, after making the collection, retains two copies of the levying document and hands the original to the payer. One of the copies is sent to the levying office.

If the receiving office is not a bank, it hands the collections made to the Banco Central or Banco de Venezuela and sends directly to the Tesorería Nacional one of the retained copies of the levying document together with a schedule of collections. Collections in Caracas are cleared through the Banco Central while collections outside Venezuela and in the interior of Venezuela are cleared through the Banco de Venezuela. If the Banco de Venezuela does not operate a branch office in

---

[1] The books are closed every six months. Hence only six months are accumulated.

[2] Sometimes payment is made at receiving offices different from the ones indicated in the levying documents.

or near the location of the receiving office, the receiving office sends the money and the schedule of collections, together with the copies of the levying document, to the Tesorería Nacional which in turn deposits the money in the bank.

(3) BANCO CENTRAL AND BANCO DE VENEZUELA. These banks perform Treasury services in two capacities: as receiving offices that make collections directly from the public, and as clearing offices of the collections made by all other receiving offices. As receiving offices these banks work more or less in the same way other receiving offices do. The schedule of collections prepared differs in that it contains all collections made by the banks and all collections made by other receiving offices cleared through the banks.

The banks, using mechanical and electromechanical equipment, prepare a daily statement of collections. This statement indicates, in cases of collections made directly by the banks, the Ministry to which is attached the levying office, the revenue source, the date and number of the levying document, the name of the payer and the amount collected. The statement also includes the total amounts collected by other receiving offices cleared through each bank. No detail of these collections, except by receiving office, is made. The statement also includes sale of stamps by selling office. The Banco Central prepares also a summary of collections made, by revenue source. Original and two copies of the summary, in the case of the Banco Central, and of the schedule of collections, together with the retained copies of the levying documents collected by the banks, are sent to the Tesorería Nacional. The Central Bank reports daily and monthly to the Tesorería Nacional while the Banco de Venezuela reports twice a month.

Every month the Banco Central prepares a summary of collections made, by revenue source. This statement includes the collections during each fortnight of the month, total collections during the month, and accumulated collections during the fiscal year. Original and three copies of the summary statement are sent to the Tesorería Nacional.

Each bank reports daily to the Treasury the beginning cash balance, the total receipts, the total payments, and the cash balance at the end of the day.

(4) OFFICE OF THE TREASURER. This office checks all the copies of the levying documents received from the Banco Central and from the Banco de Venezuela and from all other receiving offices against the schedules of collections received from the banks and other receiving offices.

The Treasurer keeps a Journal (Manual) and a Ledger (Mayor) for government receipts and payments. Receipt entries to the Journal are made from the schedules of collections received from the Banco Central, Banco de Venezuela, and other receiving offices. Receipts are registered by receiving office and by revenue source. In this Journal entries are also made of transactions related to fiscal species (seals, stamps, etc.), receivables, payables, and securities held by the Government. Letters (oficios) from the agencies performing the transactions are the basis of these entries.

Postings to the Ledger Accounts are made from the Journal. From the Ledger Accounts a Monthly Statement of Receipts, Payments, and Cash and other Assets Balances is prepared.

The Tesorería Nacional keeps also an Inventory Book (Libro de Existencias), a sort of subsidiary ledger, where acquisitions and dispositions of fiscal species (seals, stamps, etc.) are registered. The acquisitions are registered from certificates stating the amounts received. The dispositions are registered from issuance orders received from the Internal Revenue Administration. The details of receivables, payables, and securities held by the Government as an owner and as a trustee are carried also in this book.

For each month the Tesorería Nacional sends to the Contraloría de la Nación the following documents:

(a) The Receipts and Payments Journal (Manual) and Ledger (Mayor) accompanied by copy of the schedule of collections and of the summary report of collections by revenue source, received from the banks and from other receiving offices.

(b) The Monthly Statement of Receipts, Payments, and Cash and other Assets Balances (Relación de Ingresos, Egresos, Existencia y Estado de Valores) prepared from the Ledger. This statement classifies the receipt transactions of the month by revenue source and year of levy indicating the accumulated balances as of the end of the reported month.

The Tesorería sends a copy of the schedule of collections to the Central Budget Office.

(5) CONTRALORÍA GENERAL DE LA NACIÓN. Sala de Centralización. This office keeps a Central Revenue Journal (Centralizador de Rentas) in which it records amounts levied, collected, exonerated, or cancelled during the month, by levying office, revenue source, and year of levy, as reported in the monthly statement of changes in account balances (Movimiento y Estado de Valores) received from offices in charge of the administration of revenues.

In the same journal, in the account kept for Tesorería Nacional, monthly collections, as reported in the Tesorería monthly statement of Receipts, Payments, and Cash and other Assets Balances (Relación de Ingresos, Egresos, Existencia y Estado de Valores), are registered by year of levy and revenue.[3]

The Journal "Centralizador de Rentas" is used to prepare the revenue reports included in the "Cuenta de Hacienda" that will be treated later.

(6) CENTRAL BUDGET OFFICE. The Central Budget Office receives daily from the Treasurer's Office information on the cash on hand at the beginning of the day, the receipts by revenue source, the disbursements classified by bank branches in which they were made, and the cash balance at the end of the day. It also receives from the Tesorería a copy of the schedule of collections received from the banks.

The Central Budget Office keeps accounts in which monthly collections are summarized by revenue sources. These accounts are kept for purposes of budget execution and are used to prepare the report "Provisional Liquidation of the Budgetary Receipts and Expenditures" (Liquidación Provisional del Presupuesto de Ingresos y Gastos Públicos).

b. Expenditures Accounting and Reporting.

(1) MINISTRIES. The Ministries keep a record of expenditures through the use of an Expenditure Journal (Manual de Gastos). At the beginning of the fiscal year, in each Ministry the books are opened carrying the balances of all previous fiscal year appropriations into the following two appropriations for the whole Ministry:

(a) Free balances (Créditos Restantes).

(b) Balances to cover unpaid pay orders (Derechos Liquidados).

These appropriations are carried in the books for six months, that is, until December 31, item (a) to cover pay orders issued during the first six months of the current year to meet obligations incurred in the previous year, and item (b) to meet payments against pay orders issued the previous year pending payment as of June 30.[4]

The appropriations approved for each Ministry are recorded in the Expenditure Journal as of July of each year by department (Capítulo) and appropriation (Partida) within department, as they appear in the Budget Law. No further breakdown of appropriations is made, such as

---

[3] Before the entry is made, collections reported by the agencies in charge of the administration of revenues are checked against the Treasurer's report of collections.

[4] Obligations, in the Venezuelan accounting system, are not accounted for when incurred. Only issued pay orders are accounted for.

by object of expenditure or by the different offices the activities of which could be financed from the same appropriation.[5]

The pay orders issued are the source documents for expenditure accounting.[6] They are recorded in the corresponding appropriation of the Expenditure Journal in chronological order of issuance, indicating the name of the payee. The pay order has a detailed description of the object of payment and indicates the place where it should be paid. It has a blank space for the Treasurer to indicate the payment office. All pay orders are sent to Section 1 of the Sala de Control de la Contraloría for pre-audit.

Reductions in pay orders (reintegros) which occur during the same year in which payments were made are recorded in this Journal as increases to the original appropriation.

Each Ministry receives from the Tesorería Nacional original and copy of a monthly schedule of pay orders cashed by the Banco Central, and the Banco de Venezuela, classified by branch office in which payment was made, department, appropriation, and order numbers. After being checked against the issued orders, these payments are registered in detail in the Expenditure Journal.

Postings are made from the Expenditure Journal to the Expenditure Ledger.

For each month each Ministry sends a copy of the Expenditure Journal and Ledger to the Sala de Centralización de la Contraloría, accompanied by a summary by department, of issued and paid orders, and of the copy of the schedule of payments received from the Tesorería.

(2) TESORERÍA NACIONAL AND BANCO CENTRAL AND BANCO DE VENEZUELA. The Tesorería Nacional receives from the Contraloría an original and two copies of all approved pay orders. It indicates in the pay order the bank where the order is to be paid. A duplicate of the pay order is sent to the bank and the original is sent back to the originating Ministries to be handed to the payee. The Tesorería Nacional retains a copy for accounting purposes. When the payee presents the pay order for payment, the corresponding bank, after checking to ascertain that it corresponds to the copy received from the Office of the

---

[5] In the Ministry of Finance pay orders are coded according to a list of objects of expenditures developed by the Ministry. Because of the limitations, we did not visit any other Ministry to determine departures from the prescribed general procedure for recording expenditures.

[6] Contracts for construction or for acquisition of goods and services have to be approved by Section 2 of the "Sala de Control de la Contraloría" before any pay order can be issued against the contract.

Treasurer, pays the order and retains the original.

The banks, using electromechanical equipment, prepare a schedule of pay orders cashed, by Ministry, branch office making the payment, department, appropriation, and order date and number. This schedule indicates the name of the payee. Original and copy of this schedule are sent to the Tesorería where it is checked against the copies retained of the pay orders. The Banco Central attaches to its schedule the originals of the pay orders in the case of special pay orders, and of the receipts signed by the payees in the case of permanent pay orders. The Banco de Venezuela attaches to the schedule the originals of the receipts signed by the payees.

The schedules contain summary totals of payments by departments within each Ministry and by Ministry.

The Tesorería Nacional records the payments by each bank, in the Receipts and Payments Journal, by Ministries and departments, as reported in the schedule of pay orders cashed. Postings are made from this Journal to the Receipts and Payments Ledger accounts.

The Tesorería Nacional sends to the corresponding Ministries the original and the copy of the schedule of pay orders received from the banks. Copies of the Receipts and Payments Journal and Ledger, as explained above in discussing receipts accounting, are sent to the Sala de Centralización de la Contraloría.

(3) SALA DE CENTRALIZACIÓN DE LA CONTRALORÍA. This office centralizes expenditures through the use of a Central Expenditure Journal (Centralizador de Gastos). Pay orders issued and pay orders cashed are recorded in this Journal by department (Capítulo), using the recapitulation of expenditures by department (Capítulo) included in the Expenditure Journal (Manual de Gastos) or attached to it, received from each Ministry.

In the same Journal, in the account kept for Tesorería Nacional, monthly cash payments, as reported in the Statement of Receipts, Disbursements, and Cash and other Assets Balances, are registered by Ministry and department (Capítulo), after being checked against the Ministries' reports.

(4) SECTION 1 OF THE SALA DE CONTROL. In this Section, at the beginning of each fiscal year an account is opened for each appropriation (Partida) within each department (Capítulo) of each Ministry. Reductions in current year pay orders are registered in this account as increases to the original appropriations. When the originals of the pay orders come in, they are checked for appropriateness, that is, to see if

they are properly chargeable to the proposed appropriation (Partida), and for available balance. If found correct, after being registered in the corresponding account, pay orders are sent to the Tesorería Nacional. Advances to disbursing officers (Habilitados) are treated as expenditures and hence a decrease in the amounts originally appropriated. Their refunds are treated as reimbursements and accounted for as revenues.

(5) SECTION 2 OF THE SALA DE CONTROL DE LA CONTRALORÍA. This Section pre-audits and approves all contracts for the acquisition of goods and services, including construction contracts. An account is opened for each approved contract. A copy of each pay order issued against a contract is received in this Section where it is checked for conformance with the contract. Accepted pay orders are deducted from the original amounts of the contracts.

Construction contracts usually contain a provision by which 10% of the contract is advanced to the contractor before he starts work. The pay orders issued to make these advances are charged to the corresponding appropriation (Partida) and no account or record is kept of advances made and reductions in them. Hence, advances to contractors are accounted as expenditures of the year in which the advances are made and not as expenditures of the year in which the construction is actually done.

Subsequent pay orders against construction contracts are issued for 20% less than the value of the portion of the construction certified as completed: 10% as a repayment of the advance originally made and 10% to assure compliance with the contract. The 10% deduction to assure compliance with the contract is retained in the appropriation (Partida) from which the contract is being paid and hence escapes accounting as an expenditure of the current year and as a fund kept in trust by the Government.

(6) CENTRAL BUDGET OFFICE. This office receives directly from each Ministry a copy of all contracts and all pay orders approved by the Controller. It also receives from the Contraloría a copy of all approved pay orders.

For each appropriation included in the Budget Law an account is opened in which the amount appropriated and the total of all pay orders received every day from the Contraloría are recorded. These accounts are used to prepare the monthly report "Executions of the 195_-195_ Budget during the months of _____, 19__ to _____, 19__" (Ejecución del Presupuesto 195_-195_ en los meses _____ de 19__ a _____ de 19__) and the yearly report "Liquidación

Provisional del Presupuesto de Ingresos y Gastos Públicos."

For each approved contract that goes beyond the current fiscal year an account is opened. Payments under the contract are registered in the corresponding contract account using the copies of the pay orders received directly from the Ministries. From these accounts a report of construction contract obligations is prepared, for budget preparation purposes, which shows the part of the obligations to be covered by appropriations of the current fiscal year and the part to be covered by future fiscal years' appropriations.

c. Property Accounting.

(1) MINISTRIES. Property transactions are recorded in the Ministries in a Journal of National Property (Libro Manual de Bienes Nacionales). A description of the properties acquired or disposed of and the offices to which they belong are recorded in the Journal.

Postings are made from the Journal to the National Property Ledger where accounts are carried for each using office and each type of property.

A copy of the Journal and of the Ledger are sent every month to the Sala de Centralización de la Contraloría.

(2) SALA DE CENTRALIZACIÓN. This office keeps a Journal of National Property where the property transactions of each Ministry are accounted for separately. Entries of property transactions are made to this Journal, by type of property, from the copies of the Journal and Ledger of National Property received from the Ministries.

This office also keeps a Ledger of National Property by Ministry and type of property. Postings to this Ledger are made from the Journal.

d. Materials Accounting.

(1) MINISTRIES. Materials transactions are recorded in the Ministries in a Journal of Materials (Libro Manual de Materias). The office to use the materials, the type of materials acquired, and the persons or firms to which payments are made, are indicated for each materials acquisition. Purchases are divided between purchases in Venezuela and purchases outside Venezuela. Dispositions of materials are recorded by offices that use them.

Postings are made from this Journal to a Ledger of Materials. A monthly summary of beginning and end balances and of acquisitions and dispositions is prepared.

A copy of the Journal and Ledger and of the summary are sent monthly to the Sala de Centralización de la Contraloría.

(2) SALA DE CENTRALIZACIÓN. This office keeps a Centralizator and a Journal and a Ledger of Materials by Ministry. From the summary received from the Ministries, monthly entries are made to the Centralizator to record materials beginning and end balances and acquisitions and dispositions.

From the Journal received from the Ministries, entries are made to the Journal by Ministry. From this Journal postings are made to the Ledger accounts by Ministry.

e. Central Reporting for Revenues, Expenditures, Assets, Liabilities, Appropriations, and Balancing Accounts. The Sala de Centralización de la Contraloría General is entrusted by law, among other duties, with the responsibility of preparing the statement of the general accounts that according to law the Minister of Finance has to submit to the National Congress. This report, known as the "Cuenta de Hacienda," contains all the information about revenues, expenditures, assets, and liabilities that the "Ley Orgánica de Hacienda" specifically requires to be submitted to Congress. The following is a summary of the detail pertinent to this study contained in the "Cuenta de Hacienda."

(1) REVENUES. Throughout the "Cuenta de Hacienda" revenues are classified in very great detail by revenue sources (ramos de producto), year of levy, month of collection, receiving offices (receptorías de fondos nacionales), regional levying offices, and by Ministries in charge of the administration of revenue sources. All sorts of combinations of these different classifications are made throughout the report.

(2) EXPENDITURES. Pay orders, both issued and cashed, are presented in summary form by Ministry, by department (Capítulo)[7] and by month of issuance and month of payment.

(3) BALANCE SHEET ITEMS. The "Cuenta de Hacienda" contains a statement of general balances as of the beginning and another as of the end of the reported fiscal year. An analysis of these balances discloses information for the following balance sheet items:

Assets:

Cash Balance (Numerario) in each bank and in each receiving office (receptoría) by month.

Loans to the Federal District, States, Territories, Municipalities, Banks, Farmers, Fishermen, Autonomous Institutes, Hotel Corporations, and other Private Businesses.

---

[7] No detail is presented for payments against previous years' balances (Pagos complementarios).

Special Deposits made for external commerce.
Tax Receivables by year of levy and type of tax.
Other Revenue Receivables by year of levy and revenue source.
Stocks of private enterprises.
Investment in Real Estate.
Investment in Movable Property (Bienes Muebles).
Materials and Supplies Inventory (Materiales).
Investment in Autonomous Institutes.

Liabilities:
Pay orders issued, not cashed, by Ministry and Department.
Postal and Cable Drafts Payable.
Internal and External Public Debt (Principal and Interest)
Certificates of Deposits in Banking Institutions to Guarantee
Contracts with the National Executive.

Appropriations and Balancing Accounts:
Amounts appropriated not disbursed.
Excess of assets over liabilities and appropriations or
Excess of liabilities and appropriations over assets.

2.   THE VENEZUELAN BUDGETARY SYSTEM, ACCOUNTING AND REPORTING SYSTEM, AND ECONOMIC PLANNING

An intensive analysis of the Venezuelan Central Government accounting system shows that it fulfills adequately that part of the functions of accountancy related to the keeping of accurate records of expenditures and receipts, providing the means of complying with budgetary plans, and of preventing the diversion of public funds to unauthorized purposes. On the other hand, it does not measure accurately the assets and liabilities of the Government, does not insure proper stewardship of the Government assets, and does not provide the information needed for planning and policy-making and for management. The reports turned out by the system do not provide meaningful data on government operations to government officials and the public nor do they furnish the information needed for national income and national product estimates, including the proportion of government expenditures representing capital formation. In the following discussion we elaborate more specifically on these limitations of the Venezuelan accounting and reporting system.

The Venezuelan central budgetary system, and as a result the accounting and reporting system, are based on the principle that all government receipts, irrespective of their source, should be credited as general funds of the government and that all expenditures, no matter the direct relation they bear to certain receipts, should only be made out of appropriations included in the Budget Law, to be financed from the general funds of the Treasury. As a result, the Venezuelan budgetary and accounting system fails to distinguish adequately the three functions performed by the National Government of Venezuela:

a. As an operating unit, it provides services to the economy, financed for the most part by taxes;

b. As a proprietary unit, it invests in a wide variety of business enterprises both to serve the government and to serve the public; and

c. As a trustee, it holds private funds.

Separation of the three different activities performed by the Venezuelan National Government is necessary to measure the national government's participation in the country's economic activities as an active operator and as a proprietor. This separation will also make government statistics fit directly into the national product and income accounts, and will facilitate an evaluation of the effects of the government's productive, trading, developmental, and financial operations upon the national economy as a whole.

Recognition of the fact that the government performs different activities that ought to be accounted for separately will also allow the presentation of a more realistic budget document. The inclusion in the budget of recurring operations of a business nature, sales revenue on the receipts side and cost of goods or services sold on the expenditure side, inflates the revenue and expenditure budget estimates, making them unrealistic. Separation of the three government activities, both in the preparation and execution phases of the budget, should enable the administration to relate the proceeds of sales of the services rendered by the government's business-type activities to the cost of producing the services in a way that will supply the basis for the attainment of a more efficient operation.

The principle of unity of the Treasury embodied in the "Ley Orgánica de Hacienda" has been repeatedly circumvented through the creation of autonomous institutes. These autonomous institutes have been authorized to use receipts incidental to their activities to finance in part the cost of such activities.

The Venezuelan central budgetary and reporting system fails to account for expenditures and receipts and changes in the asset position of the autonomous institutes. Most of the activities of these institutes correspond to regular government functions which in the preparation of the budget and accounts reporting should be tied to the transactions of central government agencies entrusted with such functions. Some of the autonomous institutes conduct business-type activities which in the preparation of the budget and in accounting reporting should be tied to central government agencies performing similar activities. The activities of the autonomous institutes managing private funds for the benefit of private parties should be tied to trust transactions performed by central government agencies.

The accounting for disbursements, both at the Ministries and at the Contraloría, is designed to insure that expenditures are made out of authorized appropriations (partidas) to which properly chargeable and that there is an available balance in the corresponding appropriation to cover the expenditures. The lack of a uniform classification of appropriations with detailed descriptions of the objects of expenditures properly chargeable to each one, makes the first goal difficult to achieve. The second one is met successfully by the accounting system.

The budgetary and accounting system provides for expenditures classification by Ministries, departments (capítulo), and appropriations (partidas). Classifications of expenditures needed for economic planning such as by functions, by impact on the asset position of the government, by economic character, by objects of expenditure, and by sector of the economy to which directed, are not made.[8] As a result, no accounting report is or can be turned out which shows the amount of government resources devoted to each government function; the types of goods or services acquired and from whom acquired; the transfers made to the private sector and within the government sector; and the acquisitions of new and of already existing assets.

The Venezuelan accounting system provides for the accounting of receipts by detailed revenue sources (ramos de producto) and regions in which the revenues are collected, classifications which are very useful for economic planning. The system, however, does not provide for the classification of revenues by economic sector in which originated. Revenues such as income taxes, rents of property, some import duties, sales of stamps, and licenses and fees, are liable to come from two or more sectors of the economy. As a result no accounting report is or

---

[8] A sector of the economy might be any part of the economy in which the government is interested. Four sectors, however, could be distinguished for planning purposes: consumers sector, business sector, government sector, and the rest-of-the-world sector.

can be turned out which shows revenues by economic sector from which collected and which identifies properly transactions within and among government sectors.

The Venezuelan accounting system lacks a detailed description of revenue sources. This, added to the fact that no central organization checks on the correctness of the classification of revenue sources, makes errors in classification of receipts liable to occur and limits the reliability of revenue statements produced.

There is not now, in the budget or other regularly published government documents, a separation of permanent investments in public undertakings from government subsidies, no clear separation of earnings from government corporations, and no easy way of determining "reserves" which might be available as "lines of defense" against depression. There is no clear-cut delineation in the budget of how much of the government's expenditures apply to current operations, and how much to increases in capital in the form of (a) investments in new enterprises, (b) acquisition of plant and equipment by the national government, and (c) debt amortization payments.

Finally, the Venezuelan accounting system fails to account accurately for changes in the asset position of the government, that is, changes in current and fixed assets and in short- and long-term liabilities. The principal reason for this lies in the fact that the system does not classify expenditures and receipts by their impact on the asset position of the government. For this reason expenditure transactions such as loans to private and public parties, acquisition of proprietorship interests in public and private organizations, acquisition of real and personal property, and refunds of deposits; and revenue transactions such as repayments of loans, returns of investment in public and private organizations, sales of real and personal property, and special deposits received escape correct accounting. This makes it impossible for the system to turn out accurate reports of assets of the government such as loans, advances to contractors and to disbursing officers (*habilitados*), investment in private and public corporations, and fixed assets (real and personal). Accurate reporting of financial and capital assets is essential, among other purposes, for the development of the governmental sector of the national income accounts.

A consistently developed balance sheet is needed to define as closely as possible the national government's proprietary interest, the various kinds of assets held by the national government, and changes in the government's cash and debt position.

C. Necessary Changes in the Venezuelan Budgetary and Accounting and Reporting System to Meet Economic Planning Needs

1. THE CENTRAL GOVERNMENT AS AN OPERATING, PROPRIETARY, AND TRUST UNIT

Conceptually, the government, for the purposes of a comprehensive system of accounting reports, should be divided into three sectors:

Central Government Sector, comprising the government administrative services, financed entirely or largely by general taxes.

Government Enterprises Sector (including some of the autonomous institutes), consisting of enterprises which are engaged primarily in the production of services for sale to the public.

Trust Fund Sector, concerning any funds (such as social security funds) which are held (by the Central Government or some of the autonomous institutes) for the benefit of persons or parties other than the government, and which cannot be spent on governmental functions.

Under this classification the Central Government performs three essential functions: (a) that of an operating unit in charge of administrative functions, (b) that of a holding company, holding ownership rights in and exercising controls over the public undertakings, and (c) that of a trustee.

A description of the form in which the Venezuelan Government activities should be grouped to attain their proper differentiation follows:

a. Central Government Sector. This sector is what most persons ordinarily think of as "the government." It is made up of functions paid for entirely or mostly out of taxes which are usually considered typical government functions, such as education, highway construction and maintenance, fire and police protection, health and hospitals, and the administration of justice.

(1) GENERAL FUND. This fund is the heart of the accounting system. In it there are accounted for all taxes and other revenues not specifically appropriated by law or contract to special activities. Disbursements are made from this fund out of appropriations included in the Budget Law. Collections of a specific revenue source do not limit the extension of a particular service. The latter is limited only by the priority the government may give it among the competing services to be financed from the resources of the government.

Some of the existing autonomous institutes carry on activities proper to the Central Government Sector. The cost of those activities is financed by transfers from the General Fund of the Government. Examples are the National Sports Institute (Instituto Nacional de Deportes), National Nursing School (Escuela Nacional de Enfermeras), Venezuelan Council for Children (Consejo Venezolano del Niño), National Council for Aged and Invalid (Patronato Nacional de Ancianos Inválidos), and National Council for Student Refectories (Patronato Nacional de Comedores Escolares). In the preparation of the Government Sector account for national income analysis, expenditures of these autonomous institutes should be consolidated with those of the Central Government.

(2) EARMARKED REVENUE FUNDS. The expenditures of some of the existing autonomous institutes that perform general government functions are financed in part from the revenue of the sale of goods and services produced incidental to their activities. Some of these institutes are Workers Training and Recreational Institute (Instituto para Capacitación y Recreación de Trabajadores) and the National Institute of Nutrition (Instituto Nacional de Nutrición). Hence, some parts of the revenues of these autonomous institutes constitute earmarked revenues. Such expenditures and receipts should be consolidated with those of the Central Government in the preparation of the Government Sector account for national income analysis.

b. Government Enterprises Sector. The Venezuelan Government enterprises are of two kinds: (1) those organized to render services to the public and (2) those that render services to other governmental units. The government-enterprise type of organization is common among the existing autonomous institutes. However, some of the organizations directly controlled by the Central Government also have the characteristics of government enterprises.

The autonomous institutes created by the Venezuelan Government that can be classified as government enterprises are authorized by law to use the accrued revenue from the sale of goods and services in the production of new goods and services. Among these are National Institute of Dredging (Instituto Nacional de Canalizaciones), Petrochemical National Institute (Instituto Venezolano de la Petroquímica), Venezuelan Air Mail Line (Línea Aeropostal Venezolana), Autonomous National Railways Institute (Instituto Autónomo de los Ferrocarriles del Estado), Iron and Steel Institute (Instituto del Hierro y del Acero), and the Venezuelan Development Corporation (Corporación Venezolana de

Fomento). The difference between the revenue of these institutes and of those classified as Earmarked Revenue Funds is that in the first case the revenue produced bears a direct relation to the expenditures incurred in producing the goods and services sold. In some cases the cost of producing the goods and services may be a determinant factor in setting the price. This is not so in the second case.

Some of the organizations the expenditures of which are financed from the General Fund are engaged in producing services to other government agencies (the Printing Service) and to the public (some activities of the Communications Ministry). The revenue produced from the sale of goods and services, both to the government and to the public, is covered into the general Treasury, and is employed, along with tax and other revenues, to finance all the appropriations included in the central budget.

In general, the government enterprises should be regarded as separate entities, and their books kept on a commercial accounting basis that will properly account, among other items, for depreciation charges and imputed interest on loans received from the government. Only in this way can the amount of profit or loss of each entity, and the amount of any government subsidy, be accurately measured. Uniform systems of accounts for all undertakings may not be feasible, since the requirements will vary from unit to unit depending on the type of unit (whether it is engaged in production, trading, or financial activities), the degree and kinds of controls exercised by the Central Government, and so on.

Questions may also arise as to the activities to be included in the government enterprise group. Generally, the input-output relation (the imposition of prices or direct charges to cover the cost of the product) is the determining factor. The income of a unit need not cover all its costs for it to qualify as a government enterprise, since the Central Government may subsidize part of its operations. However, there are cases of entities, like a university, which impose direct charges (fees, dormitory rentals, etc.), but do not rely primarily upon such charges for their support; these are ordinarily not considered to be in the business of selling services. Such entities ordinarily will be considered as a Central Government agency, rather than as a government enterprise, although if the commercial operations involved are substantial it may be useful to segregate them and include them in the Government Enterprises Sector.

At the other extreme, there may be entities in which the government has a minor financial interest, but which are mainly owned and controlled by parties outside the government, and for which the Central

Government assumes no accounting responsibility. Ordinarily, there will be no advantage in including such entities in the public undertakings sector.[9]

c. The Trust Unit. The Venezuelan Government, in addition to its general government functions, acts as a trustee of funds belonging to persons or firms outside the government. This trustee function is performed through several autonomous institutes as well as through Central Government agencies. Examples of autonomous institutes performing trustee functions are:

(1) Venezuelan Social Insurance Institute (Instituto Venezolano de los Seguros Sociales) in charge of collecting money from private employers and workers to be used in making insurance payments to workers such as for sickness, accidents, and maternity leaves.

(2) Armed Forces Club (Círculo de las Fuerzas Armadas) in charge of managing a social club for the benefit of the armed forces.

(3) Institute for Armed Forces Social Security (Instituto de Previsión Social de las Fuerzas Armadas) in charge of programs such as the facilitation of the acquisition of houses by members, making loans to members, making contributions to medical payments of members' families, and the organization of a savings plan.

(4) Institute for Social Assistance and Security of the National Education Ministry (Instituto de Previsión y Asistencia Social del Ministerio de Educación Nacional) in charge of managing for the benefit of teachers and their families housing and medical payment plans and commissariats.

All Ministries engaged in construction by contract perform trustee functions inasmuch as they retain 10% of payments to contractors to guarantee compliance with contracts. Monies so retained are not the property of the government. They only are held in trust. By the same token, other types of deposits received from outsiders in compliance with contracts, regulations, and laws are not the property of the government. The government is only a custodian of such deposits.

Although the receipts and payments involved in trustee transactions just mentioned are handled by the Venezuelan Government, they do not concern general government functions of the type usually associated with the Central Government or the government enterprises. Therefore,

[9] The question of which existing governmental units should be regarded as government enterprises for accounting purposes is quite different from the question of whether any given government service should be charged for on a commercial or quasi-commercial basis. Answering the latter question requires extensive and subtle economic analysis.

they should not be shown as receipts and payments transactions of this government sector. They should be accounted for separately.

An intensive analysis of the functions performed by each autonomous institute and by each Ministry of the Venezuelan Government may disclose cases in which an organization is performing all three of the types of governmental functions described. It is essential for economic planning that the operations pertaining to the three functions be distinguished.

2. THE CLASSIFICATION OF RECEIPTS AND DISBURSEMENTS FOR ECONOMIC PLANNING

Receipts and disbursements of the Venezuelan Government should be classified at their origin along lines that make available in readily usable form certain information needed for national income and national product estimates. Valuable perspectives in formulating revenue and expenditure policy are afforded by such data as the following: proportion of gross national product utilized by government (ratio of government purchases of goods and services to total), proportion of national income transferred by government, transfer payments, proportion of personal income taken by tax payments, proportion of total investment accounted for by government investment, etc. Comparisons with other economies, wherever possible, may also afford useful perspectives.

The government accounts at a minimum should distinguish (1) purchases of goods and services on (a) current and (b) capital account, (2) transfer payments, and (3) subsidies.

The accounts should also show the proportion of government revenues which involve no decrease in the purchasing power of residents, such as revenue from foreign oil companies; and government purchases or transfers which do not increase Venezuelan private income (such as purchases direct from foreign suppliers).

Finally, the accounts should show the effects of the expenditures and receipts transactions on the asset position of the government.

Such information requires a set of accounts which follows the conceptual pattern of national income and product accounting. The use of such a set of accounts is not limited to the types of information outlined in this section, of course. In fact this conceptual basis probably is useful for most plannning and economic analysis, as well as in providing general information.

In the following section we elaborate on the needed classifications just explained.

a. By Impact on the Asset Position of the Government. According to their impact on the asset position of the government, expenditures and receipts are classified as follows:

(1) CURRENT EXPENDITURES AND RECEIPTS. Current expenditures are more or less regularly recurring expenditures, which, in the accounting sense, decrease net assets. They include current operating expenses, regular grants and contributions (subsidies, relief benefits, and the like) and interest on debt.

Current receipts increase net assets. They consist mainly of taxes and charges for goods and services.

(2) CAPITAL EXPENDITURES AND RECEIPTS. Capital expenditures include outlays for capital assets—for example, houses, automobiles, machinery, equipment, and other improvements—which render services over long periods of time. They may also include investments which increase the Central Government's proprietary holdings.

Capital receipts include receipts from the disposition of capital assets.

The distinction between current and capital expenditures or receipts thus lies in the effect on net assets. For example, payment of interest on a debt decreases cash, with no corresponding increase in any other government asset. Purchase of a building, however, merely replaces one asset with another. "Receipts" and "Expenditures," in this context, usually refer to cash income and expenditures.

(3) FINANCIAL EXPENDITURES AND RECEIPTS. These transactions are concerned with financial assets and debts. Financial assets are securities —bonds, stocks, mortgages—and other evidences of indebtedness. Financial expenditures include disbursements for loans by the government to others, repayments of government debt, and temporary investments in securities. Financial receipts include repayments of debts owed to the government, proceeds of borrowing, and receipts from the sale of securities held as temporary investments.

Financial transactions resemble capital transactions in that they do not involve net increases or decreases of assets. They represent the exchange of one financial asset for another, or the payment or receipt of cash in return for the cancellation or reduction of a debt. For instance, if the government pays off a bank loan, it exchanges cash for the cancelled evidence of indebtedness, and its net asset position is unchanged.[10]

[10] See *Commonwealth of Puerto Rico, Expenditures and Receipts for Fiscal Years ending June 30, 1953 and 1954,* a report prepared by Lyle C. Fitch and Miss Consuelo Maldonado; Department of the Treasury, Commonwealth of Puerto Rico, San Juan, 1955.

b. By Economic Character. In using the data to analyze economic forces, the foregoing categories of government expenditures and receipts may be subdivided somewhat as follows:

RECEIPTS
> *Current Receipts*
>> Direct Taxes
>> Indirect Taxes
>> Social Security Taxes
>> Licenses and Permits, other than business
>> Business Licenses and Permits
>> Grants and Contributions (Transfer Payments)
>> Charges for Goods and Services
>> Interest and Dividend receipts
>> Fines and Penalties
> *Capital Receipts*
>> Receipts from sale, loss, or damage of real and personal property
>> Repayment of investment in Government Enterprises
>>> For Capital Outlay
>>> For Working Capital
>> Repayment of investment in private enterprises for capital outlay
> *Financial Receipts*
>> Repayment of loans made to others
>> Loans received from others
>> Retained Percentage on Contracts
>> Other Deposits received
>> Proceeds of Bonds

EXPENDITURES
> *Current Expenditures*
>> Compensation of individuals
>>> Salaries, regular positions
>>> Salaries, transitory positions
>>> Salaries, part-time jobs
>>> Salaries, overtime compensation
>>> Salaries, contracted personnel
>>> Compensation to witnesses
>>> Compensation to stamp agents
>>> Compensation to Board Directors
>> Supplements to employees' compensation
>> Other Purchases of Goods and Services
>>> Advertising, printing, and binding

      Materials, supplies, and parts
      Communication services
      Utility services
      Rent of property
    Interest Payments on Government Debt
    Social Security Payments
    Subsidies
    Grants and Contributions (Transfer Payments)
      For Current Expenses
      For Capital Outlays
Capital Expenditures
    Acquisition of new assets
      Equipment
      Buildings and other structures, by contract
      Roads, by contract
    Acquisition of already existing assets
      Land
      Buildings and other structures
    Investment in Government Enterprises
      For Capital Outlay
      For Working Capital
    Investment in private enterprises for capital outlays
Financial Expenditures
    Bond Redemption
    Payment of other Government Debt
    Loans made to others
    Refund of Retained Percentage on Contracts
    Refund of other Deposits

In many of the above cases, it is necessary to distinguish to whom payments are made and from whom money is received. The classification for economic sector, which will be explained later, will meet this need.

c. By Precise Object of Expenditure and Detailed Revenue Source. The classification of receipts and expenditures by economic character just described is not sufficiently detailed for management and control purposes, for providing the information necessary for the preparation and execution of the budget, and for economic planning. To this end uniform classifications of expenditures and receipts by specific objects of expenditure, and by detailed revenue sources applicable to all government agencies, are needed. These classifications should be developed after a study of the detail needed at all levels of management, for control purposes and for fiscal and economic planning. Detail which is useful at low levels of control can be meaningless at economic planning levels. To avoid coding error which might limit the reliability of the reports turned out by the system, detailed descriptions of each minor object and revenue class should be available.

d. By Economic Sector to which Directed or from which Received. The main purpose of this type of receipts and expenditures classification is to make the accounting system provide information needed for economic analysis and for the planning and administration of programs. It also aims at the preparation of financial reports more understandable to executives, legislators, and the general public.

Classification of government expenditures and receipts by economic sector makes possible the elimination of duplicate accounting of transactions, necessary to obtain a real picture of the government receipts and disbursements and to make a better evaluation of the impact of government activities on the general economic activity of the country. An example of this classification, adapted to the Venezuelan Government activities, follows:

CLASSIFICATION OF RECEIPTS AND EXPENDITURES
BY ECONOMIC SECTOR

Domestic Private Sector
Individuals, families, and trusts in Venezuela
Business enterprises, including sole proprietorships
Foreign Private and Public Sector
Domestic Government Sector
Central Government Sector
General Fund
Autonomous Institutes
Government Enterprises Sector
Central Government Enterprises
Autonomous Institutes
Trust Funds
Central Government Trust Funds
Autonomous Institutes
Local Governments Sector
Federal District

States
Municipalities

This classification, like the one before discussed, should be developed in possibly more detail after a study is made of all the economic planning needs of the country. To avoid coding errors, a detailed description of what each sector comprises should be made available to operating personnel.

e. By Region of the Country in which Originated or to which Directed. The Venezuelan accounting system provides this classification to a certain extent. Even though the system produces this information, so far its uses have been limited to control purposes. The information has not been channelled to the government agencies in charge of economic planning.

A careful study of the present system may show that the classification in use, which follows the official paying and receiving offices' detail, is not fitted to the economic planning needs of the country. If so, it should be revised according to economic planning needs.

f. By Function. This classification is of utmost importance in planning the activities of the government. It is intended to show how government resources are distributed among the competing needs for governmental services and identifies the services which the government is emphasizing; for example, how much emphasis the government is putting on defense as compared to investment in human capital (e.g. education). An example of what the Venezuelan functional classification of disbursements can be, follows:

General Administration of the Government
    Legislative Branch
    Judicial Branch
    Executive Branch
Protection of Persons and Properties
National Defense
Correction
Health Conservation
Sanitation
Public Welfare
Housing Development and Slum Clearance
Educational Services

Industrial Development
Agricultural Resources Development
Natural Resources Development
External Transportation and Communication
Internal Transportation and Communication
Parks and Recreation
Debt Retirement
Other

This classification, like all others discussed, should be developed in possibly more detail after a study of all the activities that the government is engaged in, the relative importance of each one, and the needs of information for social and economic planning.

3. THE RECEIPTS AND DISBURSEMENTS EFFECTS ON THE ASSET POSITION OF THE GOVERNMENT

Effects of receipts and disbursements on the asset position of the government are measured through the use of a set of general ledger accounts. These accounts make available, in summary form, information about the resources, liabilities, and operations of the government and make possible the preparation of a balance sheet (statement of assets, liabilities, and surplus) along conventional lines. General ledger accounts are separated between real accounts: assets, liabilities, and appropriations and balancing items; and operating accounts: budget estimates and receipts and expenditures. An example of the detail that could be carried into the general ledger accounts follows:

Assets

Current
    Cash in Bank
    Cash with Disbursing Officers
    Cash Temporarily Invested
    Taxes Receivable
    Other Accounts Receivable
    Inventories
Fixed
    Land
    Mines
    Roads
    Buildings
    Other structures

Equipment
    Office Equipment
    Construction Equipment
    Medical, Dental, and Laboratory Equipment
    Motor Vehicles
    Printing Equipment
    Communication Equipment
    Educational Equipment
    Livestock
    Library Books
    Other

Liabilities

Current
  Accounts Payable
  Retained Percentage on Contracts

Special Deposits
Fixed
  Bonds Payable

Appropriations and Balancing Items

Amounts Appropriated not Disbursed
Excess of Assets over Liabilities and Appropriations

Excess of Liabilities and Appropriations over Assets

Operating Accounts

Estimated Revenues
Revenue Collections
Appropriations

Encumbrances
Expenditures
Budget Liquidation Account

A complete set of general ledger accounts, with detailed explanations of their form of operation, should be developed after a study of all the assets and liabilities of the government, which takes into consideration the needs of summary information about the assets, liabilities, resources and operations of the government at all levels of management.

4. ADJUSTMENTS OF THE PRESENT BUDGETARY AND ACCOUNTING SYSTEM TO MEET ECONOMIC PLANNING NEEDS

The necessary changes in the Venezuelan Budgetary and Accounting System to meet economic planning needs discussed earlier in reality imply the adoption of a new budgetary and accounting system. Although this would prove in the long run the best road to take, some adjustments could be made in the present system so that it would turn out some of the information needed for economic planning. The explanation of these adjustments follows:

a. Budget Law.

(1) REVENUE ESTIMATES. Revenue estimates could be presented in three columns, each one indicating the government sector to which each revenue source will accrue; that is, Central Government Sector, Government Enterprises Sector, and Trust Sector.

The arrangement of the revenue sources could be changed to follow the one explained in Section C–2–a through 2–d, preceding.

(2) EXPENDITURES ESTIMATES. This part of the Budget Law could be separated into three groups, one for each government sector. Under each group, appropriations could be listed classifying the amounts appropriated in three columns, one for current expenditures, another for capital outlays, and the third for financial expenditures.

Appropriations could be detailed by units within each Ministry in charge of developing a significant governmental activity. Within each activity, three appropriations could be detailed: one for Salaries, Regular Positions; another for Other Compensations to Individuals, and a third one for Other Expenses.

The Budget Law could be accompanied by a comprehensive budget document in which more detail is given of the specific objects of expenditures that will fall within the general appropriations "Other Compensations to Individuals" and "Other Expenses." A summary statement of appropriations by function, divided between current and capital appropriations, should also be included. In addition, budgets of the autonomous institutes should be appended to give legislators a comprehensive view of the government finances.

b. Accounting. As explained in Section B of this chapter, the Central Bank and the Bank of Venezuela perform important accounting functions for the government. Through the use of electromechanical equipment they produce schedules of receipts and payments of the government. The following changes could be introduced in the preparation of these schedules to produce the information needed for economic planning:

(1) RECEIPTS. Assign a code to each one of the economic sectors explained in Section C-2-b, preceding. Indicate in all levying documents (planillas) the economic sector code corresponding to the person or firm from which payment is received.[11] In the case of the Central Bank, which uses punched card equipment, punch this code in the detail receipt cards now used. In the case of the Bank of Venezuela, until a decision is made to use punched card equipment for these purposes, make a daily summary of revenue collected from each sector on the daily schedule of collections prepared by each receiving office. At the end of the month, prepare a summary report of receipts by revenue source and economic sector.

(2) DISBURSEMENTS. Assign a code to each one of the types of ex-

---

[11] Instructions should be given to receiving offices to channel the copy of all levying documents they collect, now sent directly to the Tesorería, through the bank in which they deposit the collections.

penditures and to each government function explained in Section C-2-b and 2–f, preceding. In all pay orders indicate expenditure code corresponding to the transaction. Also indicate the economic sector code corresponding to the person or firm to which payment is made. Punch both codes in the detail expenditure cards now used.

At the beginning of the year punch in master cards for each appropriation of the government the functional code to which each appropriation corresponds.

At the end of the month, prepare summary statements of expenditures by object of expenditure and economic sector and by function and object of expenditure. For purposes of budget execution, prepare a detailed statement of expenditures by appropriation and object of expenditure and a summary statement by departments and object of expenditure.

c. Reporting. Designate a Central Government unit to be in charge of receiving the statements recommended above, to develop the final reports needed for budget execution and for economic planning, and to propose necessary adjustments to the system to produce additional information needed.

D. Reporting and Economic Planning

Reports for economic planning demand that the nature and classification of the expenditures and receipts for the whole government be shown, and that surpluses or deficits be related to the cash balance and the debt. The information should be arranged according to a conceptual framework related to the income and product account for the entire economy. The recommended changes in the accounting system discussed in Section C of this chapter will make possible the presentation of financial data in this form. The following procedure can be used to turn out the report:

1. THE THREE-GOVERNMENT-SECTOR REPORTING SYSTEM

The first step is to classify all activities of the government, including autonomous institutes, according to the governmental sectors to which they belong. As explained elsewhere this conceptual framework divides the Venezuelan Government into three units, or sectors: (1) general government activities, financed mostly by taxes; (2) business-type activities, financed mostly by charges for goods and services; and (3) activities pertaining to trust funds managed by the government for the benefit of others. Once this determination has been made, expenditures and receipts transactions within each sector are consolidated. The receipts and expenditures classification by economic sector will be used to eliminate transactions within each government sector. In this way, the accounting reports will show only net transactions—receipts and disbursements—with other government sectors and with the outside world.

2. THE THREE-ACCOUNT SYSTEM

The classifications of expenditures and receipts by economic character and by impact on the asset position of the government, explained in Section C, make possible the arrangement of expenditures and receipts in a way that fits directly into the three-account reporting system needed for economic analysis; that is, a current account for current expenditures and receipts, a capital account for capital expenditures and receipts, and a financial account for financial expenditures and receipts. Some adjustments, however, have to be made:

a. The expenditures made for construction on force account should be included in the current account since the government is actually paying directly for the goods and services acquired. Since these expenditures are for the acquisition of capital assets, they should be accounted for in the capital account. This dual effect is obtained by deducting from all current expenditures of the current account the total representing capital investment and including that amount in the expenditure side of the capital account.

b. In the case of government enterprises, where depreciation charges are made, depreciation is shown as a current expenditure, to measure the amount of existing assets that was used up or consumed during the fiscal year. The same amount is shown as a capital receipt to measure the amount by which capital assets decreased during the year owing to usage, obsolescence, etc.

c. Inventory changes are shown in the current account as increases (in case of a decrease in inventory balances) or decreases (in case of an increase in inventory balances) in purchases of goods and services in order, in the first case, to account for the amount of inventory stock at the beginning of the year used up during the year, and in order, in the second case, to decrease the expenditures of the year by the purchases which went to increase the inventory stock of the government. In the capital account, inventory increases are shown as capital expenditure while inventory decreases are shown as capital receipts.

The balance of the current account expenditures over receipts, or vice-versa, is carried to the capital account. The balance of this last account is carried into the financial account. The significance of the balance of each account is as follows:

Significance of current-account balance. The accounts show the difference between current expenditures and current receipts, as the "current account surplus." The difference would be a deficit if expenditures exceeded receipts.

The relation between current receipts and current expenditures of any economic unit—a family, a business firm, or a government—is a useful indication of whether its economic situation is improving or worsening. If current receipts of a government exceed its current expenditures, the excess may be used to buy new capital equipment or pay off debt, or it may be held in reserve for spending later on. But if current expenditures exceed current receipts, the deficit must be made up by borrowing, by drawing on previously accumulated balances, or perhaps by selling, or, ultimately, failing to replace capital equipment.

However, the current account balance does not tell the whole story of the economic condition of the unit, partly because the distinction between current and capital expenditures is somewhat artificial. The long-run general economic condition of a government might be improving, even if it shows a short-term deficit; for example, it might incur current-account deficits to promote economic development or to improve the nation's educational system, all of which ultimately strengthen the economy.

Significance of the balance of the current and capital accounts. If current and capital receipts exceed expenditures, the capital account shows a surplus, indicating that the firm, family or government has something left over for savings, or for paying off debt. But if current and capital payments exceed receipts, the difference must be made up by borrowing, or by using up savings.

The relation between current and capital receipts and expenditures is used by many governments, including the federal government of the United States, for defining a balanced budget, i.e., the budget is considered to be balanced when current and capital receipts exceed or equal current and capital expenditures. The distinction between current and capital, with respect to economic significance, is in many respects so tenuous that the current account plus capital account balance is more significant than the current-account balance alone. As has been noted, many expenditures ordinarily classified as current, such as educational programs, are potentially more productive economically than physical capital.

Significance of the financial-account balance. This balance shows the effects of the receipts and expenditures transactions on the cash position of the government. If receipts exceed expenditures, there is an increase in the cash surplus. If expenditures exceed receipts, the cash surplus has been decreased.

To illustrate the use of the three-account system, a skeleton statement of Central Government expenditures and receipts of Venezuela, budgeted for the fiscal year 1958-59, is presented in Table XIV-1. These figures are taken from the budget and from an economic analysis of the budget supplied by the Budget Bureau. The classifications employed here are rough, although they are sufficiently accurate to indicate the order of magnitude of the various items. Before such amounts are used for economic analysis and policy decisions, however, concepts must be defined and several major issues of classification decided.

3. ALL GOVERNMENTAL SECTORS ACCOUNTS

Once a set of accounts has been prepared for each governmental sector, the transactions of all three government sectors are consolidated, eliminating transactions among government sectors so as to indicate the magnitude of the government's transactions with the outside world.

4. CENTRAL GOVERNMENT EXPENDITURES BY FUNCTION AND ECONOMIC CHARACTER

This report will be prepared for the Central Government Sector only. The classifications of government expenditures by function and by economic character, explained earlier in this work, will be the basis for the preparation of the report. Transactions within the Central Government Sector will be eliminated to show only Central Government payments to other government sectors and to the private domestic and foreign sectors. The headings of this report will be as follows:

Function
Expenditures of Central Government Agencies
    For Current Operations
    For Capital Outlay

Table XIV-1. National Government, Venezuela, Budgeted Cash Expenditures and Receipts 1958-59

(In millions of Bs.)

Current Account

Expenditures		Receipts	
Purchases of goods and services		Direct taxes	
Wages and salaries............	1,838	Oil production (royalty) taxes...	1,290
Other purchases of goods and		Income and inheritance	
services.....................	771	taxes.......................	1,283
Total...................	2,608	Total...................	2,573
Transfer expenditures		Indirect taxes	
Grants to States...............	512	Excises, customs, misc..........	856
Domestic.....................	154	Profits from foreign exchange	
International.................	8	transactions.................	239
Total...................	674	Total...................	1,095
		Charges for goods and services...	321
		Miscellaneous.................	33
Miscellaneous.................	6		
Total current expenditures	3,288		
Surplus on current account......	734		
Total current expenditures			
plus surplus...........	4,022	Total current receipts.....	4,022

Capital Account

Expenditures		Receipts	
Purchases and construction of			
new capital assets...........	898	Surplus from current account....	734
Purchases of existing capital assets	26	Sale of National property.......	3
Investments in public enterprises.	386		
Grants to Agricultural Bank....	102	Total...................	737
Grants to Venezuelan Develop-			
ment Corporation............	216	Capital account deficit..........	891
		Total capital receipts plus	
Total capital expenditures.	1,628	deficiency.............	1,628

Financial Account

Expenditures		Receipts	
Deficit from capital account.....	891	Proceeds of borrowing..........	1,025
Retirement of obligations.......	902	Balance (equals cash decrease)...	768
		Total financial receipts plus	
Total financial expenditures	1,793	cash decrease..........	1,793

Grants to Autonomous Institutes
  For Current Operations
  For Capital Outlay
Grants to Local Governments
  For Current Operations
  For Capital Outlay
Other Grants and Subsidies
Total
Per cent of Total

In this report, the functional classification will show how the government resources were distributed among the general functions of the government, while the classification by economic character will make it possible to determine the means used by the government to develop each function; that is, as an active operator itself, through autonomous institutes, through local governments, or through the indirect stimulation of private activities, and the amount of expenditures in each function devoted to the acquisition of capital assets that will enhance the future development of each function. This information, coupled with facts about program activities, is very useful in analyzing programs and in planning for the future.

E. Coordination between Budgeting, Accounting, and Economic Planning

The study made of the budgeting and accounting system, and national income accounts, shows a lack of coordination among offices involved in these functions. This lack of coordination has led to duplication of accounting records and may hamper the development of a sound budget and accounting and reporting system. The Central Budget Office, for example, has triplicated accounting records kept at the Ministries and at the Contraloría in an effort to get information about expenditures, receipts, and contract obligations, needed for budget preparation and execution purposes.

Both formal and informal communication among the Budget Office, the Contraloría, and economic planning agencies of the government need to be stimulated in order to avoid records duplication, to improve the accounting system, and to develop a set of accounting reports useful for fiscal and economic planning. Accounting must be looked at as a tool of management, and must be continually studied and revised in order to meet changing needs. The accounting system should also be regarded as the place to get the information needed for budget preparation and for economic planning. Only in this way can budgeting, planning, and accounting fulfill their basic functions.

To initiate the needed coordination among agencies involved in economic planning, budgeting, and accounting we recommend the designation of a committee, composed of a representative from each agency involved, entrusted with the responsibility for making budgeting and accounting keep pace with changes in government functions and in fiscal and economic planning needs.

F. The Venezuelan Fiscal Organization

In Venezuela the responsibility for the preparation of the Central Budget rests on the Ministry of Finance, which is responsible to the President. Budget preparation, in other words, is an executive responsibility discharged through one of the operating Ministries.

Responsibility for the execution of the budget is assigned to the Ministries and to the Controller of the Nation. The Controller is responsible to the Congress. In the execution phase of the budget, the Controller is responsible for approving all contracts for the acquisition of goods and services, including construction contracts, and for auditing pay orders before payment. To fulfill the pre-audit responsibility related to the availability of funds, the Controller keeps an account for each appropriation of the Budget Law.

The Controller is also responsible for centralizing all the financial accounts of the Central Government, for issuing rules and regulations related to accounting, and for post-auditing all the receipts and disbursements transactions of the government, including the autonomous institutes.

The execution phase of the budget and the design of accounting systems and procedures are inherently executive functions. The governmental organization created to fulfill these functions should serve as an arm of the executive in the development of the programs for which it is responsible. The intervention of the Congress, through the Controller, in the day to day operations of the government may result in undue delays and as a result may hamper the development of programs. The lack of authority of the executive in the development of accounting systems and procedures may render accounting useless as a tool of management.

Duplication of efforts, and, as a result, waste of resources, is one of the results of the present Venezuelan fiscal arrangement, followed by delays in payments and in the execution of programs.

An intensive study should be made of this situation, with a view to the design of the fiscal organization that would be most appropriate, efficient, and economical. Consideration should be given in this study to the possibility of assigning responsibilities for the preparation and execution of the budget (including central accounts, pre-audit, and design and installation of accounting systems and procedures) to an organization directly responsible to the President. The bringing together of budgetary and accounting functions will assure coordination between the preparation and execution of the budget. The placement of this body under the direction of the President itself will assure its independence of action.

G. The Autonomous Institutes

In principle, the government should create organizations that stand outside Central Government control, that is, budgetary, pre-audit, purchasing, and personnel controls, when such central controls would presumably hamper the normal operations of the programs entrusted to the organizations so created. Enterprises of a business type which have to be conducted along private commercial lines, to some degree, are examples. A study of the existing autonomous institutes in Venezuela may show that some of them do not meet the criteria that justify autonomy. The general cost of running the government would probably be lowered if functions entrusted to some of the autonomous institutes were brought under the control of Central Government agencies entrusted with similar functions, because of economies in overhead costs and for other reasons.

H. The Local Governments

For economic planning, information is needed regarding the expenditures and receipts of Venezuelan local governments along the same lines suggested above for the Venezuelan Central Government. Because of time limitations, we did not make a study of the accounting and reporting systems of the Venezuelan states and municipal governments. Such a study should be made, so as to determine the capabilities and limitations of those systems to produce the data needed for economic planning and to introduce the changes the conditions may demand.

I. Receipts and Disbursements Procedures, Financial Management, and Accounting Reporting

The Venezuelan receipts and disbursements procedures are very cumbersome, delaying, and complicated. The natural results of this situation are a high cost of operating the government, delays in payments with consequent discredit of the government, higher prices charged to the government because of the delay in payment, and delays in reporting receipts and disbursements, with consequent effects on fiscal and economic planning.

Disbursements procedures should be studied carefully. The possibility of changing the actual pay order system to a system in which checks are issued for paying government debts should be given consideration. A central checks-issuing system might prove more economical to the government and would probably stimulate the use of checks throughout Venezuela. This would tend to facilitate payments of taxes to the government and would reduce the amount of currency needed.

The reports now turned out by the accounting system and presented in the "Cuenta de Hacienda" should be studied to determine their usefulness and reliability.[12] A new set of fiscal reports should be developed, capable of conveying, to Congressmen and the public, information about governmental expenditures and receipts in a way understandable to them and useful for their purposes.

---

[12] Because expenditures and receipts are not tied to the asset position of the government the data on assets and liabilities of the government presented in the "Cuenta de Hacienda" are not accurate.

A. Education

EDUCATION AND ECONOMIC DEVELOPMENT

Education in Venezuela, as in other under-developed countries, is one of the main requisites of economic development. Economic productivity depends on the availability of professional skills—in law, medicine, engineering, business and public administration; and vocational skills—in agriculture, industry, clerical occupations, nursing, and so on. All these must be supplied by the educational system or imported.

Education contributes also to productivity in numerous indirect ways. For example, public health depends heavily upon education in sanitation, balanced diet, and use of medical facilities. An educated electorate is the first essential of democratic government and political stability, and the latter, at least, is essential for the savings and investment that make economic development possible.

Return on Investments in Education. Education pays extraordinarily high rates of return, even in a country like Venezuela where high rates of return are common. From the limited data available, it appears that the average earnings of a primary school graduate are at least twice those of an illiterate person in urban employment, and more than four times those of an illiterate person in agricultural employment; that average earnings of a secondary school graduate are at least twice those of a primary school graduate; and that average earnings of a college graduate are at least three times those of a secondary school graduate (see Table XV-1).

Table XV-2 presents some rough computations of the return on investment in education, for the various levels. The investment in education is computed as the cost of providing schooling at the various levels, plus the income sacrificed by the individual who is going to school in-

406

Table XV-1. Education and Earning Power in Venezuela

(Estimated annual earnings during several age periods)

Level of education	Age period	Average annual earnings (Bs.)
Illiterate		
farm laborer.............................	13–18	1,000
	19–65	1,500
urban laborer.............................	13–22	2,500
	23–65	3,750
Primary school..............................	13–22	5,000
	23–65	7,500
Secondary school............................	18–32	12,000
	33–65	18,000
University..................................	22–35	30,000
	36–50	45,000
	51–65	58,000

NOTE: The above schedules are designed to take account, at least roughly, of the fact that earnings ordinarily increase over the lifetime of the worker.

stead of working. Both school cost payments and sacrificed income payments are cumulated at an annual rate of 10 per cent, under the assumption that the same amounts would otherwise have been invested at 10 per cent. The total investment in education is the sum of these accumulated amounts at the time of graduation.

Table XV-2. Educational Costs and Return on Investment in Education

Direct Educational Costs

				Amount of cost cumulated at 10 per cent interest[3]	
Level of education	Number of years	Cost per year	Total cost	Over period of each educational level	Over entire educational period
		(Bs.)	(Bs.)	(Bs.)	(Bs.)
Primary school.......	6	400[1]	2,400	3,100	3,100
Secondary school.....	5	1,200[1]	6,000	7,300	12,300
University...........	4	5,000[2]	20,000	23,200	41,200

Continued on next page.

Earnings Sacrificed While Attending School

Level of education	Earnings sacrificed	Amount of sacrificed earnings cumulated at 10 per cent interest[4]	
		Over period of each educational level	Over entire educational period
	(Bs.)	(Bs.)	(Bs.)
Primary school.............	0	0	0
Secondary school...........	25,000	30,500	30,500
University.................	48,000	55,700	100,400

Total Educational Costs and Return on Educational Investment

Level of education	Cumulated costs at each educational level[5]			Return on investment in education[6]
	Direct costs	Sacrificed earnings	Total	
	(Bs.)	(Bs.)	(Bs.)	(per cent)
Primary school......	3,100	0	3,100	130[7]–82[8]
Secondary school....	7,300	30,500	37,800	17
University...........	23,200	55,700	78,900	23

[1] Educational cost figures computed as described in text. They include allowances for amortization of cost of school buildings and equipment.

[2] Estimated.

[3] Cumulated amounts as of the completion of the particular educational level. These amounts represent the cumulation of a series of investments at 10 per cent per annum; the computations assume that money spent on education otherwise could have been invested at 10 per cent. For example, as of the end of primary school, the cumulated investment is the first year's cost of Bs.400 invested for 5 years at 10 per cent, plus the second year's cost of Bs.400 invested for 4 years, and so on.

[4] Earnings sacrificed are the amounts which could have been earned if the individual were working instead of going to school. Thus, a secondary school graduate sacrifices five years of earning at a rate commensurate with a primary school education (see Table XV-1). No sacrificed earnings are assumed for primary school pupils, on the assumption that children of primary school age have little or no earning power.

[5] The cumulated direct costs and sacrificed earnings at each educational level represent the investment in education at that level.

[6] The rate of return on the investment in education at each level is the rate which equalizes the investment in education at that level with the present discounted value of incremental earnings corresponding to that level. Incremental earnings at each level are the difference between earnings at that level and at the next lower level. Amounts of incremental earnings are derived from the schedules of Table XV-1.

[7] Computed on basis of incremental earnings of primary school graduate over illiterate agricultural worker.

[8] Computed on basis of incremental earnings of primary school graduate over illiterate urban worker.

So computed, the total investment per pupil, upon his completion of the various levels of education, comes to: primary school, Bs.3,100; secondary school, Bs.42,800; university (four years), Bs.141,600. The incremental returns on these investments are: primary school, between 82 and 130 per cent per annum; secondary school, 17 per cent per annum; university, 23 per cent per annum. The computations of these rates of return are necessarily rough; for instance, they do not allow for the possibility that, as more educated persons come on the market, their advantage in earnings over those without education may decline (but this is not an inevitable result). Even so, when all such qualifications have been allowed for, it seems almost certain that, judged merely from a financial point of view, money put into education in Venezuela will produce a rate of return considerably above the net rate of return obtainable in most businesses, or on real estate mortgages. The rate of return on education is several times the rate of interest that the government would have to pay on money borrowed to finance education.

According to these data, which are presented in Table XV-2, an increase in expenditure on education in Venezuela would be a highly profitable investment for the economy as a whole.

LOW LEVEL OF VENEZUELAN EDUCATION

By exploiting its petroleum resources, with the help of foreign capital and skills, Venezuela has been able to attain a relatively high average level of national income with a relatively low level of education. Education has had such a low priority in the national investment program that the level of education relative to income is one of the lowest in the world.[1] Further progress in the non-petroleum sectors, particularly industry, agriculture, and government, will depend heavily on better education.

In 1957-58, the amount of Venezuelan governmental expenditures on education was less than 2 per cent of the national income. In 1958-59 the figure will approach 3 per cent. But for the United States, the figure is about 4 per cent, and for Puerto Rico, about 4½ per cent. The percentages, education of national income, for Argentina and Chile have been higher than for Venezuela in recent years, but the percentages for several other Latin American countries for which data are available, including Brazil, Colombia, Guatemala, and Mexico, appear to be

---

[1] Opinion expressed by experts of the United Nations Secretariat, based on data on illiteracy and income in various countries.

lower.[2] (However, none of the figures above tell the whole story, for they do not include expenditures on education by parochial and other private institutions.)

A comparison with Puerto Rico is particularly enlightening, in view of the fact that Puerto Rico and Venezuela have the highest incomes per capita of all of the Caribbean regions, and both have under way extensive programs of economic development. The Venezuelan national income is approximately Bs.2,750, or $830 per capita,[3] and the Puerto Rican national income is approximately $500 per capita. The Venezuelan population, 6.3 million, is about 2.9 times that of Puerto Rico (2.2 million).

Puerto Rico has considered education to be an essential component of its economic development program, whereas Venezuela has put more emphasis upon investment in public works and various enterprises.

Comparable data for Venezuela and Puerto Rico are shown in Table XV-3.

Table XV-3. Comparison of Educational Programs, Venezuela and Puerto Rico

	Puerto Rico	Venezuela
Per cent of governmental budget allocated to education, 1958-59	28	10[1]
Per cent of children of school age in school:		
ages 6–12	95	51
13–15	87	33
16–18	46	13
Number of students in secondary, vocational, and normal schools (thousands)	168	79[2]

[1] Including state and municipal governments.

[2] Secondary school in Venezuela includes five years beyond grade six; in Puerto Rico it includes six years beyond grade six.

School Enrollment, by Type of Institution. Estimated enrollment in primary schools in Venezuela in 1957-58 was approximately 750,000 (as shown in Table XV-4), of which about 45 per cent was in national government schools, 25 per cent in state schools, 9 per cent in municipal

[2] See United Nations Statistical Yearbook, 1957.

[3] Based on estimated national income of Bs.17 thousand million for 1958, and estimated population of 6.3 million. Exchange rate of 3.3 bolivars per dollar is used in computation.

schools, and 21 per cent in private schools. Autonomous institutes for disturbed children and other special cases accounted for 2,200, less than ⅓ of 1 per cent.

Secondary school enrollment was estimated at 57,000, of which 59 per cent was in national schools and 41 per cent was in private schools. There are only two small state secondary schools, accounting for about 130 students, and no municipal secondary schools.

Normal school enrollment is estimated at 7,000, 47 per cent of which

Table XV-4. School Enrollment by Type of Educational Institution

Primary, Secondary, Normal and Technical Schools, 1957-58, Estimates

	Government						Total enroll-ment
	National	State	Munic-ipal	Autono-mous insti-tutes	Total govern-ment	Private	
Primary schools....	338,400	185,800	67,900	2,200	594,300	155,400	749,700
Secondary							
Day schools.....	31,000	130	—	—	31,130	22,500	53,630
Night schools....	2,700	—	—	—	2,700	850	3,550
Normal schools....	3,300	—	—	—	3,300	3,700	7,000
Technical schools...	13,800	—	—	—	13,800	1,200	15,000

Kindergarten, University and Adult Education, 1955-56, Estimates

Kindergarten enrollment

National	3,300
State	1,400
Municipal	1,440
Private	6,150
Total	**12,290**

University enrollment

National government	6,995
Private	930
Total	**7,925**

Adult education enrollment

National schools	28,700
State schools	19,400
Municipal schools	6,000
Autonomous institutes	4,100
Private schools	3,800
Total	**62,000**

is public and 53 per cent private. Technical school enrollment is estimated at 15,000, 92 per cent public and 8 per cent private. University enrollment in 1955-56, the most recent year for which published data are available, was about 7,925, 88 per cent in national government schools, and 12 per cent in private schools.

Adult education classes enrolled about 62,000 persons in 1955-56, about 46 per cent under the auspices of the national government; 31 per cent—state governments; 10 per cent—municipal governments; 7 per cent—autonomous institutes; and 6 per cent—private institutions.

To complete the picture, about 12,300 pupils were in kindergarten in 1955-56, 27 per cent in national schools, 11 per cent in state schools, 12 per cent in municipal schools and 50 per cent in private schools.

These data are presented in Table XV-4.

School-Age Population and School Enrollment.[4] We estimate that, in 1957-58, slightly over half the number of children in the age group 6-12 years were attending elementary school and kindergarten. The population of this age group is estimated at 1,235,000, while the estimated enrollment in primary school is 620,000, and in kindergartens, 18,000.

Of the 13-15 age group, numbering 447,000 in all, 114,000 (26 per cent) are estimated to have been enrolled in primary school, and 33,000 (7 per cent) in secondary, normal, and technical schools.

Of the 16-18 age group, numbering 355,000, about 13,000 (4 per cent) are estimated to have been enrolled in primary schools, and 33,000 (9 per cent) in secondary, normal, and technical schools.

Data on school-age population and enrollment, and a description of estimating methods, are presented in Table XV-5.

Population of Legal School Age. Venezuelan law requires school attendance of children between the ages of 7 and 14. The number of children in this age bracket is estimated at 1,313,000 as of mid-1958; the number enrolled in various schools 1957-58 is estimated at 714,000, or 54 per cent of the 1958 population.

High Rate of Drop-out. The data of Table XV-6 show that, of the 677,000 children in primary school in 1956-57, less than one-sixth (15½ per cent) were in the two upper grades, and that more than half were in the lowest two grades (55 per cent). The two middle grades accounted for less than one-third (29 per cent).

---

[4] These figures are for 1957-58 enrollment and 1958 population estimates, so that the percentage of enrolled children to total children in each age group, as of the beginning of the 1957-58 school year, was slightly higher than shown here.

Table XV-5.   Estimated Population by Age Groups and Enrollment, 1957-58

| Age group | Estimated population, 1958 | Estimated enrollment, 1957-1958 | | | Percentage, enrollment of population |
		Elementary school	Secondary school[1]	Total	
6–12.....	1,235,000	620,000	—	620,000[2]	50
13–15.....	447,000	114,000	33,000	147,000	33
16–18.....	355,000	13,000	33,000	46,000	13
Over 18 ...	—	1,000	13,000	14,000	—
		748,000[3]	79,000	827,000	

[1] Includes technical and normal schools.

[2] Omits approximately 18,000 kindergarten pupils; including these would bring the total to 638,000.

[3] In addition there were approximately 2,100 5-year-old pupils enrolled in first grade.

TECHNICAL NOTE: These estimates were compiled from 1950 Census data and estimates of births in the years after 1950.

1. In 1950, there were in the 10-14 age group 575,000
    In 1958, this is the 18-22 age group
    The 18 age group is estimated at 20 per cent
    of the group population..............................   115,000
2. In 1950, there were in the 5-9 age group 687,000
    In 1958, this is the 13-17 age group
    The 1958 16-17 age group is estimated at
    35 per cent of 13-17 age group.........................   240,000

    Total of 16-18 age group, 1958.......................   355,000
3. The 1958 13-15 age group is estimated at
    65 per cent of 13-17 age group.........................   447,000
4. In 1950, there were in the 0-4 age group...................   847,000
5. The 1958 6-7 age group had not been born in 1950
    Live births in 1951 and 1952 totalled 455,000
    The infant mortality rate is estimated at about
    15 per cent, subtracting about 67,000
    This leaves...   388,000

    Total 6-12 age group..............................   1,235,000
6. Deaths other than those classified under infant mortality are assumed to have been offset by immigration.
7. The age distribution of the 677,000 1956-57 primary school pupils is shown in Table XV-6. 1957-58 primary school enrollment, ages 6 and over, is estimated at 748,000. The enrollment was distributed among age groups in the same proportions as was the 1956-57 enrollment.

Table XV-6. Primary School Pupils Classified by Age Groups, School Year 1956-57

Grade	Pupils classified by age															Total
	5	6	7	8	9	10	11	12	13	14	15	16	17	18	19 or older	
1	2,083	20,016	79,132	53,532	33,556	22,934	14,085	9,191	4,367	2,106	633	256	80	22	210	242,203
2		1,517	16,267	30,498	27,431	22,250	14,734	10,551	5,910	2,778	876	354	63	23	73	133,325
3			2,437	13,751	22,091	22,955	18,937	14,348	9,234	4,768	1,831	628	162	51	121	111,314
4				2,104	9,482	16,579	17,227	15,359	11,188	7,120	3,092	1,261	300	86	84	83,882
5					1,396	6,248	11,625	13,083	11,915	9,113	4,897	2,502	735	177	60	61,751
6					—	900	4,290	8,295	9,857	9,219	6,297	3,726	1,492	485	130	44,691
Total	2,083	21,533	97,836	99,885	93,956	91,866	80,898	70,827	52,471	35,104	17,626	8,727	2,832	844	678	677,166

SOURCE: Ministerio de Educación.

As these figures indicate, only a small percentage of those beginning school continue through the sixth grade; the number of those completing sixth grade in the 1956-57 school year was only 18 per cent of the number who had entered first grade in 1950-51. Many schools offer no more than two or three grades, so that children have no opportunity to go further.

Such "wastage" from pupils' dropping out of school before a thorough foundation has been acquired may, to quote from a United Nations report, "detract very largely from the efficiency of the school system and lead to an immense waste of money and of good human material."[5]

MAGNITUDE OF THE PRIMARY SCHOOL PROBLEM

The 1,313,000 children of legal school age in 1958 will be better taken care of than in previous years if the plans of the Ministry of Education for increasing primary school enrollment in the 1958-59 school year by 100,000 are realized. Assuming that the entire 100,000 increase comes from the 7-14 age group, enrollment would be 814,000, plus whatever additional pupils were absorbed by the state and municipal schools, and the private schools. If the latter schools absorbed 10,000 more, total enrollment would reach 824,000, or 63 per cent of the 1958 age 7-14 population. This leaves 489,000 children in this age group who will not be in school during the school year.

By mid-1959, moreover, the school-age population of the 7-14 group will have increased by about 52,000.

Annual Increase in School-Age Population. The population of school age is increasing at the rate of about 4 to 5 per cent a year, as the following data indicate:

Age group, 1958	Population	Percentage increase over next older group
3– 7	1,050,000	24
8–12	847,000	23
12–17	687,000	20
18–22	575,000	—

The age groups cover five years; the annual percentage of increase is approximately an average of the percentage increases for the five-year

[5] *Report on the World Social Situation,* 1957, p. 73.

groups divided by five, or from 4 to nearly 5 per cent. The annual increment in the 7-14 age group is therefore now (1958) at least 52,000, since the 1958 population of this age group is about 1.3 million.

The annual increment will itself continue to increase; by 1963, if the present population trends continue, it will reach 61,000. In 1963, school population will be at least 280,000 larger than in 1958. Moreover, the above figures indicate that the rate of increase is itself increasing.

COSTS OF FIVE-YEAR PROGRAM
TO PUT ALL ELIGIBLE CHILDREN IN PRIMARY SCHOOL BY 1963-64

We next estimate roughly the cost of putting all eligible children of the 7-14 age group into primary school by the school year 1963-64. Such a goal would require a great effort, but it is not impossible.

The mid-1959 population of school age 7 to 14 will be about 541,000 larger than the 1958-59 primary school enrollment. Thus, if enrollments of 1959-60 are no larger than those of 1958-59, there will be 541,000 school-age children not in school in 1959-60. Furthermore, the increase in numbers in this age group from mid-1959 to mid-1963 will be about 228,000. Consequently, the five-year program (1959-60 school year to 1963-64, inclusive) to put all eligible children in this age group into primary school by the school year 1963-64 would necessitate increasing primary school enrollment by 769,000 over the level obtaining in the school year 1958-59. This means an average annual increase in enrollment of 153,800 a year over the five-year period.[6]

What would such an effort mean in costs?

The following estimates are rough because cost data are limited and inadequate. One of the first essentials of a school planning program is better statistics, particularly cost statistics.

The data that we could obtain on cost of construction of primary schools of various sizes and types show a range in per pupil cost of from Bs.575 to Bs.850. Equipment ranges from about Bs.50 to Bs.60 per pupil. We assume an average construction cost of Bs.750 per pupil, and an average equipment cost of Bs.55 per pupil. The total cost per pupil, for construction and equipment, is Bs.805.

The cost of new buildings and equipment, for 154,000 pupils per year

---

[6] These estimates assume an annual rate of increase of 4 per cent in school-age population. As the figures cited in the text show, this figure is a minimum, since the rate of increase appears to be rising.

additional, would aggregate Bs.124 million. This is Bs.21 million more than the total amount allotted for school-room construction in the 1958-59 national budget: Bs.103 million.[7]

With respect to current costs of operation, the average cost per pupil allowed in the 1958-59 national budget is approximately Bs.270.[8] For various reasons the cost of an expanded program to cover all eligible children would be greater than the cost of the program now under way, even assuming no increase in the quality of education. We assume an average annual cost of Bs.300 per pupil; therefore, to provide for an additional 154,000 children annually for the five years 1959-60 to 1963-64 would require an annual increment in current expenditures of approximately Bs.46 million.

Over the five-year period, therefore, the added expenditures of the accelerated program, over the budgeted 1958-59 expenditures, would be as shown in Table XV-7.

Table XV-7. Incremental Cost of Program to Put All Eligible Children in Primary School over Five-Year Period

	Incremental cost (millions of bolivars)		
School year	Current	Capital	Total
1959–60	46	21	67
1960–61	92	21	113
1961–62	138	21	159
1962–63	184	21	205
1963–64	230	21	251

This computation does not allow for the capital expenditures by the states and municipalities, which in 1958-59 may aggregate Bs.30 million or more. We assume, however, that this amount of state-municipal expenditure will be required in any event for betterment of existing schools, many of which are in bad condition.

The figures in the "Total" increment column in Table XV-7 represent a minimum. They allow nothing for increased overhead, nor for rising educational standards; and the amounts allowed for both new buildings

[7] Source: Economic Analysis of the Budget, supplied by the Budget Bureau.

[8] The national budget allocates Bs.118.5 million, which is expected to take care of about 438,000 pupils (338,000 enrolled in 1957-58 plus another 100,000).

and construction, by standards of advanced educational systems, are at the minimum level. The minimum expenditure per pupil in New York schools, for instance, is set by law at approximately $340 a year, or approximately Bs.1,120; this compares with Bs.400 for Venezuela (Bs.300 in current expenses plus an allowance of Bs.100 for interest and amortization of investment in school plant and equipment).

COSTS OF A PROGRAM TO INCREASE ENROLLMENT
IN SECONDARY SCHOOLS AND NORMAL AND TECHNICAL SCHOOLS
TO 300,000 BY 1963-64

Assuming that teachers and qualified pupils can be obtained, what would be the cost of bringing total enrollment in secondary schools, normal schools, and technical schools to 300,000 by 1963-64? The increase involved is approximately 220,000 or 44,000 a year over 1957-58 levels, for the years 1959-60 to 1963-64. It is assumed here that no considerable increase in enrollment will occur in 1958-59. Although national secondary school accommodations will be somewhat expanded this year (1958-59), the increase will simply relieve somewhat the intense overcrowding that now exists in some of the secondary schools; it will not allow an appreciable increase in the number of students. We therefore allow for the lapse of one year before the beginning of an intensive program.

As with primary schools, the objective would require a great effort. However, the figure of 300,000 by 1963-64 is about twice that of Puerto Rico, a country with a population only one-third that of Venezuela. In other words, the goal being considered here would still leave Venezuela considerably short of the level of education in the secondary, normal, and technical fields that Puerto Rico has already achieved.

In the computations below we assume that the costs per pupil of secondary, normal and technical schools are roughly equal.

The capital costs of providing secondary school buildings is estimated, from data on several types of schools, to average approximately Bs.1,600 per student for building, and Bs.150 for equipment, a total of Bs.1,750. For an additional 44,000 students per year, the additional capital costs per year would aggregate approximately Bs.77 million.

Current costs are estimated by dividing the secondary school budget for 1958-59 by the estimated number of students enrolled—the average is approximately Bs.875 per pupil. We assume, in addition, that there are charges now borne by the pupils, which, under an expanded program, will have to be borne by the government. The most important is the cost of books, which is reported to average Bs.250 a year. If the government supplied books, each book could be used for several years, so that the average cost per year would be reduced, perhaps to Bs.100. The total estimated current cost per pupil thus comes to Bs.975. The additional cost of 44,000 additional students would be about Bs.43 million.

There will also be the cost of providing books, at an average of Bs.100 per year, to 51,000 students, the number enrolled in government secondary schools who previously have been buying their own books. This cost amounts to Bs.5.1 million per year.

Under these estimates, total incremental current costs for the program, beginning in the year 1959-60, would be Bs.48 million a year for the first year, and would increase by Bs.43 million a year for the succeeding four years.

The cost schedule over the five-year period would be as shown in Table XV-8.

Table XV-8. Incremental Cost of Increasing Enrollment in Secondary, Normal and Technical Schools to 300,000 over Five-Year Period

	Incremental cost (millions of bolivars)		
School year	Current	Capital[1]	Total
1959–60......................	48	77	125
1960–61......................	91	77	168
1961–62......................	134	77	211
1962–63......................	177	77	254
1963–64......................	220	77	297

[1] Capital costs are assumed to be entirely incremental over the amount of Bs.103 million allotted to school classrooms in the 1958-59 budget, since this entire amount has already been deducted in computing the incremental cost of facilities required for the primary school program.

Combined Cost of Five-Year Programs. The total incremental cost of the five-year programs discussed above begins at Bs.192 million in 1959-60, and rises to Bs.548 million in 1963-64. The combined cost schedule is shown in Table XV-9.

Lack of Teachers: Cost of Teacher-Training Program. We assume that the teachers for the expanded primary school program would be supplied by an expanded normal school program with emergency re-

Table XV-9. Combined Incremental Cost of Five-Year Program

School year	Incremental cost (millions of bolivars)		
	Current	Capital	Total
1959–60..........................	94	98	192
1960–61..........................	183	98	281
1961–62..........................	272	98	370
1962–63..........................	361	98	459
1963–64..........................	450	98	548

cruitment measures. Since an expanded normal program is included in our computation of incremental costs of secondary, normal, and technical schools, we make no additional allowance for this item.

But finding teachers for the secondary, normal and technical schools is a serious, if not insurmountable problem. It cannot be solved simply by spending money. Expanding enrollment by 44,000 students annually will require adding approximately 2,000 new teachers annually. This number is as large as the number of third and fourth year students in the universities and the Instituto Pedagógico in 1955-56.

To turn out 2,000 more trained teachers per year will require greatly increased higher education facilities devoted to this purpose. A student body of at least 10,000 is required for so large an annual output. Assuming an annual cost of Bs.5,000 per student, the cost of such a program would be Bs.50 million per year. Even if the program could be gotten under way immediately, four years would be required for the increased supply of teachers to begin coming out of the pipeline.

It may well be that this teacher-training program should take precedence over other elements of an expanded educational program. Here we come to another obstacle—the lack of staff for teacher-training institutions. If Venezuela is to solve its education problem in the foreseeable future, it may have to break into this vicious circle of shortage by importing trained personnel to fill posts in institutions of higher learning, until the country can develop its own supply.

B. Public Health

Future public health expenditures in Venezuela cannot be estimated so readily in terms of a definite goal as those for education; the public health problem covers many and varied activities, and a great deal of research and planning would be necessary to translate the range of tasks into terms of annual bolivar expenditures. Certain general statements can be made, however.

In relation to other Latin American countries, Venezuela's expenditures on health have ranked higher than those on education. Thus, the percentage of current expenses of government that went to public health, only 7 per cent in 1945, had risen to 12 per cent in 1950 and 1954. Four other Latin American countries ranked higher than Venezuela by this test; five others ranked lower. This showing is in contrast to that for education. In 1954, the percentage of government expenses going to education was lower in Venezuela than in any other of the ten Latin American countries for which data were compiled, except only one; that is, nine countries showed a higher percentage than Venezuela, and only one, a lower.[9]

Public health, however, depends on education—probably more than education depends on public health. (But the need for a school lunch program reminds us that education can be blocked by malnutrition.) Many of the problems in public health arise out of ignorance of the populace, or the power of habit and tradition, especially with respect to proper nutrition and the willingness to seek medical care and advice. Formerly, the great task of the public health authorities in Venezuela was to wipe out yellow fever, malaria, and similar transmittable diseases that were killing on a large scale. This task has been largely accomplished. There remain, among the tasks ahead, campaigns against malnutrition, infant mortality (some of the figures we have had quoted to us are extraordinarily high—one source estimates the rate at 15 per cent), and diseases that flourish where the water supply is impure, or latrines are inadequate.

These campaigns require both more expenditure by government and a higher income level at the disposal of those who are now too poor to afford a sufficiently nourishing, well-balanced diet. The latter requirement can be met, in part, by taking care that the tax system does not reach down into the lowest income levels; and although this aim may not be achieved completely, various other sections of the present report recommend changes in taxation that will be in this direction. An improved and expanded social security system would also be one of the best of public health measures, for the same reason; but this complex task is outside the scope of the present report.

[9] See CEPAL, Estudio Economico de América Latina, 1955.

As to government outlay, there are many items on which expenditure could be increased with substantial benefit to public health.[10] Pre-natal advice and care; assistance in caring for infants and pre-school children; the school lunch program—here are expenditures for services given directly to the populace.

Another type of public health expenditure falls more in the realm of public works, some of them small units of public works, but none the less important for that. For example, at present some 13,000 to 14,000 latrines are being constructed by the government in rural areas; this could well be increased to 50,000 a year. About 10 water systems a year, especially for rural towns of less than 5,000 inhabitants, are now being constructed; so great is the need that a rate of 25 a year would not be excessive. Indeed, it is estimated that the great majority of such rural towns do not have water systems that guarantee water fit for drinking. Anyone who has seen some of the truly poverty stricken towns of the interior of Venezuela will probably agree that public health in those areas is also largely a matter of achieving a minimum level of dwelling accommodation; a program of constructing 70,000 rural dwellings a year for 20 years is estimated to be necessary to eliminate the "rancho" —to say nothing of the problem this type of shack poses in the shanty areas on the periphery of the large cities. The average government contribution to the new dwellings could be about Bs.4,000.

There are at present 10,000 beds in government hospitals. If a standard of 4 beds per 1,000 population is set, Venezuela, with 6,000,000 population, needs 14,000 more hospital beds—and while these are being constructed, the population will be growing. A need for 5,000 more beds for tuberculosis patients has been estimated, 14,000 more for mental patients, and 2,000 more for those being treated for leprosy.

On a more general level, there are now 394 rural medical-service units; at a minimum, 500 units is the estimated need, but still more are required if the aim is to have one unit for each rural village or town of from 600 to 5,000 inhabitants. The more comprehensive health centers are now only 12 in number; they are appropriate for centers of population of from 5,000 to 20,000 inhabitants, and there are at present 58 towns and cities of this population range.

Expenditures for public health as budgeted by the national government have increased steadily in the past five years, from Bs.152 million in 1955-56 to Bs.319 million for 1958-59; but as a percentage of the

[10] Estimates of needs given below (but not the estimate of total cost in bolivars) are from data submitted by la Dirección de Salud Pública.

budget, the public health figure has remained virtually unchanged (10.9 per cent in 1955-56 and 11.5 per cent in 1958-59). Although precise estimates cannot be given at this time, for reasons stated above, it seems likely that a public health program that would be regarded as adequate by competent authorities might well involve an increase in annual governmental outlays of something on the order of Bs.100 million to Bs.200 million, or perhaps even more.

C. Increase in Tax Rates to Cover Estimated Costs

The incremental cost of the first year of the five-year primary and secondary education programs could be obtained without much difficulty from an increase in the income tax alone. The first year's incremental cost is estimated (Table XV-9) at Bs.192 million. If we assume that the corporation income tax could be made to yield some Bs.60 million extra by upward adjustment of rates (after reform of that tax as recommended in Chapter III), Bs.132 million would remain to be raised from other sources. If the structure of the personal income tax is revised as indicated in Chapter III, Bs.132 million could be obtained by the personal income tax rate scale presented immediately below. That is, the yield of such a rate scale would be some Bs.130 million above what the existing (August 1958) personal income tax rates would yield in the same period.

Taxable income before deducting exemptions (approximately) (Bs.)	Taxable income (after exemptions) (Bs.)	Bracket rate, on the part of the taxpayer's income[1] within the range indicated
14,000–19,000	0 – 5,000	6%
19,000–24,000	5,000–10,000	7%
24,000–29,000	10,000–15,000	9%
29,000–39,000	15,000–25,000	11%
39,000–69,000	25,000–55,000	14%
above 69,000	above 55,000	—[2]

[1] Taxable income after deducting exemptions.

[2] The precise income-tax bracket rate or rates to be imposed on these higher personal incomes need not be specified here, as they would not greatly affect the present estimate; these rates in the higher income brackets involve issues of general tax policy, more than the question discussed here, of amount of revenue for a particular purpose.

This computation assumes an average family exemption of Bs.14,000.

The rate scale is for a unitary type of personal income tax. Hence, this scale may be compared with the sum of the schedular rate and complementary rate under the existing system.

The rates are of course marginal rates (bracket rates), each rate being applicable only to that part of the taxpayer's income that is within the range indicated.

At this time, no attempt is made to estimate the rates needed to cover the costs of later years, or to cover the costs of the expanded health program. More analysis of the data is needed before proceeding farther with such revenue estimates.

CHAPTER XVI : Non-Tax Revenues

This concluding chapter contains a brief survey of National Government current revenue in Venezuela from sources other than taxation.

These sources are three in number. The first is prices, charged for the sale of products or services of a kind and produced under such conditions that they could conceivably be offered by private enterprise instead.

The second consists of rentals received from Government-owned property.

The third is fees, charged, like prices, to cover the cost of the service rendered by the Government. But the fees are charged for those services which, given the circumstances under which the service is supplied, could not easily be thought of as being rendered by a private profit-seeking enterprise; it is this characteristic that distinguishes fees from prices. The dividing line between the two, however, is not always easy to draw; hence the classification below is somewhat arbitrary. This classification does not always follow the budget classification respecting fees (*Tasas*).

A. Prices

CIVIL AVIATION FEES AND PRICES

Under the heading *"Derechos de Aviación Civil,"* the budget for 1959-60 lists a revenue of Bs.2,800,000. Data supplied by the Dirección de Aeronáutica Civil for 1957-58 show total revenue of Bs.3,316,074.24.

The income consists chiefly of charges for landing, etc., rights on the Venezuelan airfields operated by the Government, and use of the airways with the assistance of the Government. These charges amounted to Bs.2,345,000 in 1957-58, of which Bs.1,294,000 came from national traffic and Bs.1,051,000 from international traffic.

425

The remainder of the revenue comes from lease of airport land for hangars, office space, etc., Bs.693,000 in 1957-58; sale of electricity, Bs.201,000 in that year; and registration fees, Bs.76,000. The registration fees are imposed when a pilot obtains a license, when ownership of an airplane is transferred, and on similar occasions.

The landing fees were last raised in October, 1958.[1] An increase in revenue might be obtained, in the opinion of some in the Dirección, by higher rental charges. And there are plans to charge for the various radio services: radio guidance, transmission of messages, etc.

But the main problem remains: whether, by a very substantial increase in landing, etc., charges, to recoup a considerably greater part, if not all, of the expenses.

Listed on page 427 are the budget estimates of expenses of the Servicio de Aeronáutica Civil (Chapter 4, in the budget of the Ministerio de Comunicaciones) (figures rounded off here, to thousands of Bs.).

What part of this total of Bs.36 million (1958-59) and Bs.25 million (1959-60) should be recouped from the users of the airfields? In principle we may look upon these services as essentially the same as the supplying of highways: there is then a strong case for recovering a large part, if not all, of these expenses by means of special charges on those who use the airports. Much use of the airfields is made by large business firms that employ their own planes; in June, 1958, for example, there were 637 landings by planes of such companies, on Venezuelan airports (intra-Venezuelan traffic).

A special tax on aviation gasoline might be levied for this purpose. Also, the landing, etc., fees might be increased. What such a tax, or such increases in fees, should be, is a matter for study by aviation experts. There is some Bs.30 million involved; hence the question is fairly important.

TOLL ROADS

Venezuela possesses virtually no railroad system; therefore, the financing of highways is especially important. The gasoline tax has been discussed in Chapter VIII above; here, we analyze toll charges.

Turnpikes and toll roads, after being out of fashion for more than a century, reappeared in the United States a few years ago. A series of toll roads now link Boston, New York, Philadelphia, and Chicago, and a few toll roads have been built in other parts of the country. But al-

[1] See *Gaceta Oficial*, Oct. 13, 1958, No. 25,784. The schedule of fees is too complex to be reproduced here.

Budget No.		*1958-59*		*1959-60*
(63)	Dirección de Aeronáutica Civil...........	666,000	(67)	757,000
(64)	División de Aerovías Nacionales, Caracas..	497,000	(68)	497,000
(65)	Servicio de Control de Tránsito Aéreo en Aeropuertos.........................	2,512,000	(69)	3,196,000
(66)	Estaciones de Comunicaciones en la República...........................	946,000	(70)	1,091,000
(67)	Servicio de Mantenimiento en el Interior de la República........................	1,270,000	(71)	1,560,000
(68)	División de Aeronavegabilidad y Operaciones.........................	1,788,000	(72)	1,409,000
(69)	División de Aeropuertos................	702,000	(73)	
			(74)	859,000
(70)	Jefaturas de Aeropuertos en la República, Aeropuertos de Servicio Internacional Primera Clase......................	747,000	(75-82)	1,321,000
(71)	Aeropuertos de Servicio Nacional Segunda Clase...............................	350,000	(83-91)	793,000
(72)	Aeropuertos de Tercera Clase............	355,000	(92)	324,000
(73)	Aeropuertos de Cuarta Clase.............	360,000	(93)	360,000
(74)	Personal..............................	3,848,000	(95)	4,037,000
(75)	Adquisiciones.........................	2,321,000	(96)	3,197,000
(76)	Diversos[1]............................	19,191,000	(97)	4,878,000
			(94)[2]	572,000
	Total................................	35,552,000		24,850,000

[1] Includes: "Plan de Control de Tráfico Aereo, Bs.14,734,000."
[2] Escuela de Aviación Civil.

ready the new era of toll road construction has come to an end in the United States, and it has not yet touched Europe. Even some of the heavily motorized states of the United States have no toll roads (California is the chief example). The huge new highway program financed by the United States Federal Government is being constructed chiefly with revenue from the gasoline tax; it includes no toll roads.

A special set of circumstances must exist if toll roads designed to recoup the cost are to be justified.

First, let us suppose that a certain prospective highway is still being discussed; a decision to build it has not been made. We suppose further that traffic engineers and economists estimate that enough motorists have a strong enough demand for such a highway, so that its cost of construction and maintenance can be met by toll charges. Finally, suppose that the road is not of great benefit for those who will not use it. Under these conditions, a toll may be an acceptable method of collecting revenue, simply on the grounds that the people who are specially bene-fited by the service, and who are willing to pay for that benefit, should be given an opportunity to do so. The toll is merely a price, not a tax; it is as if the government went into the business of selling furniture, or food, or any other commodity or service. A toll road to the top of a scenic mountain is a good illustration.

Do these circumstances exist in Venezuela today? As to the first two suppositions, general observation suggests that at the moment there are no completely new highways that would pay for themselves through tolls. However, two qualifications must be made to this conclusion.

First, the question is not merely one of completely new highways. Perhaps some existing stretches of road could be rebuilt, and the tolls could pay for the cost of rebuilding, and for later maintenance charges due to the larger, modernized road. For example, the section of the Pan-American highway between Tejerías and Caracas is heavily trav-elled, and, in the opinion of some observers, dangerous in places and inadequate to carry present and potential traffic. An engineering study is needed; and it would not be surprising if such a study showed that a moderate system of tolls would yield enough revenue to cover the cost of improving the highway. The same may be true of the present high-way from Valencia to Puerto Cabello. A bridge over Lake Maracaibo is another possible illustration.

Second, a main highway produces a general benefit for the entire economy. Hence a compromise may be made between a toll charge that would allow the road to pay for itself completely, and a free high-way. The toll charge could be set to cover, say, one-half or two-thirds the cost. Low tolls have the advantage of promoting use of the high-way, thus avoiding waste.

Finally, decisions respecting toll roads in Venezuela depend in part on the policy adopted regarding the gasoline tax. If the gasoline tax is increased, as is recommended in Chapter VIII above, in order to finance a substantial, general increase in highway construction, the case for toll roads grows weaker. The experience of the United States and Europe indicates that the gasoline tax is a more convenient form of collecting tolls than are toll gates. Taxes on tires, on automobile lubricating oil, and directly on the automobile, may be used to supplement the gasoline tax, to finance highway construction. The toll gate would remain only for a very few superhighways of special value to the motorist.

For the privilege of speeding along the super-highway or the park-way (the parkway is a road that can be used only by passenger cars), the autoists who use them are willing to pay a price that they would consider very high indeed if it were collected in the form of a gasoline tax. In the United States, the average toll charge is equivalent to a gasoline tax of about 25 cents a gallon. The toll charges that are being proposed for the Valencia-Tejerías road (see below) are roughly equivalent to a tax of 17 céntimos a litre.

Caracas-La Guaira Toll Road. From the tolls on the *autopista* between Caracas and La Guaira, the Government has been receiving about Bs.10,000,000 a year in gross revenue.[2]

The toll charges were changed on October 6, 1958, from the schedule that had been in effect since the toll road was opened in 1954. The old and new tolls are as follows (in Bs.).

	To October 6, 1958	After October 6, 1958
Motorcycles...	1.00	1.00
Passenger automobiles and ambulances..................	2.00	2.00
Passenger station wagons (*camionetas*)..................	3.00	2.00
Other station wagons.................................	3.00	—
Up to 1½ tons..	—	3.00
Over 1½ tons...	—	5.00
Trucks[1]		
Completely empty (*completamente vacíos*)...............	—	5.00
Loaded: Up to 5 tons capacity........................	—	5.00
5 to 12 tons capacity..........................	—	10.00
12 to 20 tons capacity.........................	—	20.00
Over 20 tons capacity.........................	—	30.00
Loaded or empty: Up to 5 tons........................	5.00	—
5 to 12 tons...............................	10.00	—
Over 12 tons..............................	20.00	—
with trailers		
20 tons or less............................	20.00	—
Over 20 tons.............................	30.00	—
Buses...	—	5.00
Up to 45 seats for passengers.................	15.00	—
Over 45 seats.............................	20.00	—

[1] In the new tariff, no distinction is made for trailer-trucks.

Thus, none of the tolls were increased in October, 1958. The decreases in the charges for buses and for empty trucks of over 5 tons were made (a) to give relief to mass transportation (buses) and (b)

[2] Budget for 1958-59: Bs.11,000,000.

because a number of the empty trucks had been using the old narrow, winding road from Caracas down to the port, which the toll road had been built to supersede.

The toll road cost Bs.268,290,440 to construct (1947-54); this figure includes Bs.2,574,226 for the cost of preliminary studies (1947-49). Income over the first five years of the toll road's operation, February 7, 1954-February 7, 1959, was Bs.51,000,000, an average of Bs.10,200,000 a year. Annual cost of operation and maintenance is estimated at Bs.2,000,000. The balance of the income, Bs.8,200,000 a year, would amortize the original cost in 32½ years, that is by 1987, if there were no change in traffic or costs.[3] No allowance for interest on the investment is made in these figures.

No great importance should be attached to trying to recoup the investment in any particular number of years. The construction expense is now a "sunk cost," it has been incurred; and the chief aim now should be to make the toll road as useful as possible. This can be done by keeping the tolls at a level that will cover current operating costs. A still higher toll is justified if the demand for the services of the toll road is very inelastic. In fact, the demand seems to be fairly inelastic, for there is no good alternative road available. Thus, tolls considerably higher than just enough to cover operating expenses can be imposed, as they are being, without causing much loss of traffic.

All in all, the present tolls probably do not call for change.

Valencia-Tejerías Toll Road. Sometime in the summer of 1959, toll booths will be installed on the stretch of road leading from Valencia to Tejerías. The proposed toll charges are said to have been arrived at by taking a rough average of toll charges now being made on the main toll roads in the United States. But the highway from Valencia to Tejerías has already been built; it is not a question of setting up a schedule of tolls that will allow the highway to be built, by guaranteeing amortization of the cost. The toll charges in the United States were determined before the toll roads were built. They were set at a level that made it financially possible to build the roads. Accordingly, these toll schedules may not be very appropriate guides to a toll schedule for the Valencia-Tejerías highway, even if the past costs of constructing United States highways happen to be close to present costs of constructing Venezuelan highways. The Valencia-Tejerías highway is already there; the question

---

[3] Information on costs and revenue supplied by Dirección de Renta Interna, Dpto. Timbre Fiscal, Cigarillos, Fósforos, Derechos de Tránsito.

now is, how to make the best use of it. Perhaps, on further study, it will be decided that a somewhat lower level of tolls than that copied from the United States is advisable. Indeed, a toll on this already constructed highway begins to look like nothing but a tax, if it does more than cover the cost of maintaining the highway.

For the lightest weight of car, which can go about five kilometers on a litre of gasoline, the proposed toll charge from Tejerías to Valencia is equivalent to a gasoline tax of 17 céntimos per litre. This figure is reached in the following way. The proposed toll charge is Bs.3.25. The distance is 93.62 kilometers. About 19 litres of gasoline is required to drive this distance. Dividing Bs.3.25 by 19 litres, we arrive at 17 céntimos per litre.

For heavier passenger cars, and trucks, the proposed toll charges are heavier. But the number of litres of gasoline used by such cars in travelling a given distance is also greater. Thus the net result, for the heavier car, might be either a higher or a lower "gasoline-tax equivalent" than for the lighter car.

POSTAL SERVICE

The budget heading, "Postal Service" (*Correos*), under the category, "Fees" *(Tasas),* indicates for 1959-60 a revenue of Bs.19,600,000. This is gross revenue, not net. The expense section of the budget (Minister of Communications, Chapter 2, Postal Service) shows an estimated total of expenses for the fiscal year 1959-60 of Bs.41,801,172. Hence the indicated deficit is Bs.22 million. However, certain decisions have been made that, it is said, will reduce the deficit to Bs.7 million. Expenses will be held to about Bs.39 million. Revenue will be increased to Bs.32 million by an increase in postal rates, effective July 1, 1959. The most important change in rates will be that affecting letter mail. On the first 20 grams of weight of any letter (domestic service) the rate will rise from 20 céntimos to 25 céntimos, the rate that was in effect some years ago.

In 1957-58, postal revenues were only Bs.15 million. At that time, all books, periodicals, newspapers and other printed matter originating in Venezuela were carried free of charge. Beginning January 1, 1959, this class of mail pays regular postage rates.

Government mail is carried free of postage (except for a surcharge on air mail). There are no immediate plans for imposing a postal charge on such mail. If Government mail had to pay postage, the post office deficit would be reduced, perhaps eliminated, but the expenses of other departments would be correspondingly increased. The argument employed below regarding Government telegraph messages, namely, that Government departments would be more careful in their use of the service, applies also to the postal service, but probably with less force. The argument is important enough to warrant serious consideration.

The increase in postal rates appears justified, in view of the deficit, and in view, also, of the recent improvement in postal service.

In principle, there should be a certain amount of deficit shown by the postal accounts as long as the Government mail is carried free of charges. The cost of carrying Government mail, which is really part of the cost of operating the other departments, should be carried by taxpayers in general. It would be unfair to ask the user of the mail to pay, through still higher postal rates, part of the cost of operation of the armed forces, the Department of the Treasury, and so on.

The cost of carrying Government mail is apparently as great as the prospective deficit, if not greater. Accordingly, no further increase in the general level of postal rates seems justified at this time. This conclusion must be made with some reservations, because the expenses of the post office, like those of other departments, do not include depreciation, but do include investment expenditures. Also, under Chapter 1 of the budget (1959-60) for the Minister of Communications, there is a total of Bs.10 million for the office of the Minister of Communications. In principle, this amount should be allocated among the several services (post office, telecommunications, etc.).

When the campaign against illiteracy is well under way, some method should be found for encouraging use of the letter mail by low-income families, perhaps through a special, low rate.

SALT

Under the category, "Income from Public Domain" *(Ingresos del Dominio Fiscal),* sub-category "Industrial and Commercial Properties" *(Dominio Industrial y Comercial),* the budget carries a line, "Salt" *(Salinas),* which for 1958-59 was estimated to yield revenue of Bs.9 million, and for 1959-60, Bs.8.2 million. The larger part of the revenue comes from the sale by the Government of salt from its own deposits. The sale of such salt in domestic markets, in bags, grossed Bs.4.0 million; salt not in bags, Bs.2.0 million, in 1958-59. A tax on salt produced by private business firms yielded Bs.1.2 million.

The Government's salt deposits are operated by the Finance Ministry *(Hacienda).* The total cost of the Salt Administration was estimated, for 1958-59, at Bs.36.7 million (Chapter 7 of the Hacienda section of the budget), but this represented an extraordinary year, for, of this total, Bs.20.8 million was for mechanization of the salt deposits of Araya, and another Bs.5.2 million was for purchase of equipment, etc. Over the past few years, some Bs.50 million has been invested in the mechanization and industrialization of the Government's salt marshes.

Again, therefore, we see that failure of Government accounts to compute depreciation, and enter it as a cost of production, in place of the initial cost of plant and equipment, makes it impossible to estimate a normal annual expense total that can be meaningfully compared with revenue from the sale of the product, to ascertain whether the business is being operated at a profit or a loss.

The expense total should be slightly decreased, for comparison with revenue from sales, since a part of the expense under Chapter 7 of the Treasury section of the budget is allocable to the task of enforcing the tax on salt sold from private deposits.

The estimate of expenses in the 1959-60 budget is only Bs.16.9 million, nearly Bs.20 million less than the 1958-59 estimate. There is no large item for mechanization in the 1959-60 estimate.

If we make a rough estimate of Bs.15 million as a normal annual expense of operating the Government salt deposits (assuming depreciation as a cost, in place of initial expenditure on plant and equipment), and compare it with the annual receipts of about Bs.6 million from the sale of Government salt, a deficit of some Bs.9 million is seen to exist.

The price at which the Government now sells its salt is 14 céntimos the kilo, bagged, and 10 céntimos the kilo, unbagged. Salt used by net or line fishermen (*los pescadores a red y a cordel*) is sold for 7 céntimos the kilo.[4]

The tax on salt from private deposits is 5 céntimos per kilo of common salt (raised in September, 1958, from 1 céntimo). Most of this common salt goes for consumption, but some is used by industry, e.g., some parts of the chemical industry, leather tanning, and fish salting. Industrial salt is taxed at 1 céntimo per kilo.

Apparently, the Government controls the domestic market for salt to a sufficient degree to allow a substantial increase in the price of Government-produced salt, without serious loss of markets, provided the tax on privately produced salt were increased at the same time.

However, it is too early to say whether the price of salt needs to be increased, despite the deficits noted above. When the economies result-

[4] *Gaceta Oficial,* Sept. 27, 1958, No. 25,771.

ing from the program at Araya take full effect, the deficit may disappear; conceivably, the price might even be lowered somewhat.

TELEGRAPH AND RADIO SERVICE

In the Ministry of Communications, the Office of Telegraph and Radio (*Dirección de Telecomunicaciones*) operates the domestic telegraph and radio communications system. There are no other companies in Venezuela, public or private, operating such a system for general domestic use. Long-distance telephone service (*Telefonía a larga distancia: Radiotelefonía y Telefonía para el exterior e interior*) was carried on by this office until May, 1958, when it was transferred to the Venezuela Telephone Co. (Administración de la Compañía Anónima Nacional Teléfonos de Venezuela), almost all of whose stock is owned by the Venezuelan Government.

A number of business firms operate, for their own uses, private systems of radio telephones. These systems pay an annual tax, depending on the power of the system: Bs.1,000 a year if under 10 watts; Bs.1,500 if from 10 to 99 watts; Bs.2,000 if from 100 to 199 watts; Bs.3,000 if 200 watts or more.

Private broadcasting stations pay a tax of 1 per cent on their gross income.

These taxes are included in the receipts *(Ingresos)* of the Office of Telegraph and Radio, but by far the larger part of this revenue comes from the charges that the office makes for the services it renders. The rates that the office charges have not been altered since the time, about ten years ago, that they were lowered somewhat. The present telegraph rates, per message, are:

> From   1 to 10 words............Bs.0.75
> From 11 to 15 words............Bs.1.00
> From 16 to 20 words............Bs.1.25
> From 21 to 25 words............Bs.1.50

and so on, at the rate of Bs.0.25 for each additional amount of one to five words. "Urgent" telegrams pay double rate.

The radio service for transmitting messages is at the rate of Bs.0.10 per word (Bs.0.20 per word for "Urgent" messages)[5] for certain stations, and Bs.0.50 and Bs.1.00, respectively, for others. Various rates apply

[5] *Nómina de Estaciones de Telecomunicaciones, Tarifas, Registro de Dirección e Instrucciones Complementarias.* Caracas, Imprenta Nacional, 1955, p. 19.

to messages sent to other countries, the revenue being shared with the cooperating companies.

The number of messages sent in the fiscal year 1958-59 was: telegrams, 7,067,000; radio messages, 1,200,000; cables, 336,672. These figures include official messages (messages sent by any office or branch of the Venezuelan Government), which are handled free of charge. In the fiscal year 1958-59, when Bs.19,141,022 was received in charges for messages sent by private persons and business firms, it is estimated that an additional Bs.5,345,508 would have been received by the Office of Telegraph and Radio if the Government messages had been paid for, at regular rates. Thus, revenue from Government messages would have amounted to about 22 per cent of total income from messages if Government messages had been paid for. In fact, the percentage would have been somewhat less, for a reason to be noted below.

In that same year, 1958-59, the office collected Bs.8,685,284 from the taxes described above. Thus its total cash revenue for the year was Bs.27,826,306. If Government messages had been paid for, at the regular rates, the total revenue would have been Bs.33,171,814. However, the total would in fact have been somewhat smaller, for, if each Government department had been required to pay for the messages it sent, it would no doubt have been more careful, and would have sent fewer words.

The expenses *(Egresos)* of the office in the year 1958-59 amounted to Bs.137,092,982.[6] Thus it incurred a deficit of Bs.109,266,676. But even this large figure is not the true deficit. The revenue includes, as we have seen, Bs.8,685,284 in taxes. A very small part of the expenses was incurred in collecting these taxes. In order to obtain the true deficit of operating the telegraph and radio service, we should compare the expenses, Bs.137 million (or almost all of it), with the receipts from the services, namely Bs.19 million. This comparison reveals a deficit of Bs.118 million, or at least nearly that amount.

The revenues for 1959-60 are estimated by the office at Bs.30 million;[7] the expenses, at Bs.115 million: a deficit of Bs.85 million. If the Bs.30 million income includes, say, Bs.10 million in taxes, the true estimated deficit for 1959-60 is Bs.95 million.

The expenses vary considerably from year to year, as shown by comparing the total for 1958-59 and (estimated) for 1959-60; Bs.137 million and Bs.115 million. Expenses include amounts spent on construction or purchase of plant, facilities, and other capital equipment.

[6] Data supplied by the office.
[7] The estimate in the budget is lower: Bs.24,800,000.

They do not include depreciation. Consequently, in a period when the plant and equipment are being expanded, the total of expenses is overstated, compared with what a private business firm would show. The expenses include about Bs.4 million paid to other companies (*Intercambio*). The expenses also include special items that add to the difficulty of obtaining a clear idea of the normal level of year-to-year expenses. For example: the 1959-60 estimate of expenses includes an item of Bs.21 million in settlement of a debt owed to certain private construction and advisory companies. Another example is the temporary retention of radio-telephone employees on the Office of Telegraph and Radio payroll after that service (and its revenues) were transferred to the telephone company. Nevertheless, it is clear that the telegraph-radio service is operating at a heavy loss, a loss that must be made up, eventually by taxpayers. The rates for telegraph and radio messages could probably be increased by 25 per cent or 50 per cent without causing a severe drop in the number of messages. Perhaps an even larger increase is justified. The consequent shrinkage in number of messages sent would allow a decrease in expenses.

A further decrease in expenses could follow if the Government were required to pay for all the messages it sends. At present, the employees in the Government departments are under no pressure to be careful about how many words they send. They often do not bother to eliminate superfluous words (articles, prepositions, etc.). Whole texts of regulations, decrees, and laws are sometimes thrown on the telegraph and radio. A great waste of manpower and equipment is the result.

In principle, taxpayers should not be called upon to cover the operating deficit of the telegraph and radio company, except that part of the deficit that is due to free use of the telegraph service by the Government. Moreover, as indicated above, there is good reason for eliminating that part of the deficit too, by requiring Government offices to pay for the telegraph and radio service they use. The consequent increased cost to those departments would be met from general taxes.

According to this principle, by how much should the true deficit be reduced, through an increase in rates? Even an approximate figure is difficult to compute; in principle, depreciation and an interest charge should be substituted for expenditures on plant and equipment, in computing the true deficit. And as rates were raised, that part of the deficit attributable to a certain number of free Government messages would be increased. If an approximate allowance is made for these factors, the present deficit should, in principle, be decreased by Bs.70 million, or Bs.80 million, more or less. Since present revenues from messages are only about Bs.20 million, a decrease in the deficit by Bs.70 million or Bs.80 million would require rates four or five times higher, at least. For example, messages now costing 75 céntimos would cost Bs.3.00 or Bs.3.75. This increase in rates would cause a considerable decrease in the number of messages sent; on the other hand it would also allow some decrease in costs. Perhaps the costs would decrease so little that, in fact, the deficit could not be decreased by Bs.70 million or Bs.80 million by rates that were four or five times higher than present rates. Still, considerable progress toward that goal would be achieved.

The resulting decrease in number of messages sent might be considered so harmful to the country that it would be justified to continue to call on taxpayers to meet a large part of the deficit. Such a conclusion seems unlikely; but if that conclusion is reached, it should be reached only after careful consideration.

Even at rates four or five times higher than present rates, telegraph and radio service in Venezuela would not be high relative to that in other countries, in view of the generally high price level in Venezuela. At present, telegraph and radio rates in Venezuela are very low.

The conclusions reached above are subject to one important qualification, namely, that there is evidence that expenses could be considerably reduced without appreciably impairing service. For example, one source informs us that about half the telegraph stations in the interior are used hardly at all. In some cases, no more than two or three messages are said to be sent and received over a two-week period by such a station; yet personnel for the office must be paid, the telegraph wires maintained, and so on. Rates four or five times higher than present rates would of course not be justified if substantial economies can be made. It is not fair to ask the users of the heavily engaged parts of the telegraph system to pay not only the full cost of sending their own messages, but also part of the deficit incurred in maintaining little-used stations. If the latter stations are to be maintained (at a loss), this should be at the expense of the general taxpayer.

B. *Rentals*

NATIONAL PROPERTY (Propiedades Nacionales)

The Government owns certain buildings, such as the passenger terminal at La Guaira, and some rural properties not included under *"Tierras Baldías"* (see below), such as coffee farms and cacao farms, from which it derives a revenue in the form of rentals, or payment for concessions to use the property. This income appears in the budget under the heading *"Propiedades Nacionales."* The estimated revenue for 1959-60 is Bs.2,500,000.

Other items of property under this heading are: the 90 per cent stock holding of the Government in the corporation that owns the buildings in which many of the Government offices are housed, in the center of Caracas (Centro Simón Bolívar); the buildings used by the Customs Administration at the ports; warehouses at the docks; and a cattle ranch.

The expenses of maintenance and operation are said to be only a small proportion, perhaps not more than 5 or 10 per cent, of the gross revenue. Depreciation is not included in expenses.

The proper charge for the use of these properties is simply whatever the market will allow. Their cost of construction is a "sunk cost," and need not figure in arriving at the rental to be charged now.

As current leases expire, the properties can again be put up for leasing at the highest price that can be obtained. No one can forecast whether the resulting revenue will be higher or lower than is now obtained. The important point is simply that the rentals be set by fair competition, among prospective tenants.

In summary, it would not be safe to count on an increase in revenue in future years under this head.

NATIONAL PUBLIC LANDS (Tierras Baldías)

National and state public lands *(Tierras Baldías)* yield revenues, some of which are included under the heading, *"Tierras Baldías,"* in the national budget. Income from municipal public lands *(Ejidos)* is not included under this heading. The budget estimate for *Tierras Baldías* was Bs.800,000 for 1958-59, and is Bs.600,000 for 1959-60.

The term "public lands" excludes those lands acquired by the nation with a definite end in view,[8] classified as *Bienes Nacionales.*

Revenue from the public lands comes largely from taxes, or perhaps they should be called fees or prices, paid by those who cut timber on such lands, or otherwise exploit them. For example, the tax for every cubic meter of fine wood (e.g., mahogany) cut is Bs.50; of hardwood, Bs.30; of softwood, Bs.25. In addition, a charge ranging from Bs.0.50 to Bs.2 per hectare is imposed, depending on the state or territory in which the land is located.[9]

[8] Law of Public Lands (*Ley de Tierras Baldías y Ejidos*), July 26, 1936.

[9] The Forest, Soil, and Water Law (*Ley Forestal, de Suelos y Aguas*), of Aug. 27, 1955, Art. 14, stipulates that the area tax must be between Bs.0.20 and Bs.10 per hectare.

The charges are indeed taxes (*Impuestos,* as they are called), in the sense that they are determined without reference to the initial cost, if any, of obtaining the land and the timber on it, or without reference to the cost that may be incurred in reforestation. The last increase in these rates was in October, 1954.

In the Department of Agriculture and Cattle Raising, the *Sección de Tierras Baldías* is within the *Dirección de Recursos Naturales Renovables.* Revenue paid to the national Treasury under the heading of the various revenue sources listed under that Dirección amounted to Bs.1,715,356 in 1958. This is considerably more than the revenue carried in the budget estimates under the caption *"Tierras Baldías."* The reason for this difference is not clear.

Of this revenue total, the greatest part comes from the exploitation taxes (*impuestos de explotación*): Bs.1,500,000 (in round figures). The area taxes yielded only Bs.50,000.

The revenue from the exploitation taxes has grown steadily from 1953, when it was only Bs.424,000.

Rental income from *Tierras Baldías* was only Bs.12,000 in 1958. This total seems very low. The explanation lies in the fact that the rental charge averages only a few céntimos per hectare. No first-class agricultural lands are under lease at present. The land rented is either second-class agricultural land, for which an annual rental of Bs.1.00 is paid, or cattle lands, paying 20 or 40 céntimos per hectare per year. Perhaps these rental charges should be re-examined; they seem nominal, as if the land were practically worthless.

The expenses of the *Dirección de Recursos Naturales Renovables* were estimated at Bs.11,300,000 (in round figures) for 1958-59, and Bs.11,200,000 for 1959-60. These totals are largely accounted for by an item headed *"Servicios de Guarderías Forestales y de Pesca a cargo de las Fuerzas Armadas de Cooperación,"* which amounted to Bs.7,700,000 in the 1958-59 estimate, and the same in the 1959-60 estimate. This item covers supervision of forest land exploitation, guard duty, and fire control. The guards also see to it that proper fishing techniques and equipment are used.

Evidently it would be a task of some magnitude to allocate the costs attributable to guarding and tending the particular lands on which forest products, etc., are exploited. Lacking such knowledge, we cannot recommend any substantial increase in the present exploitation taxes or area taxes. If the revenue were devoted to a reforestation program, and if the costs of reforestation could be estimated, the taxes could be treated as prices, and fixed accordingly. As noted in other parts of this chapter, while allocating particular taxes to particular expenditures is not good budgetary practice, it is appropriate to devote the proceeds of prices to covering the cost of producing, or reproducing, as the case may be, the thing that is being sold (in the present case, timber).

C. Fees

CARTAGE AND STEVEDORING

The largest single item under "Fees" in the national budget, aside from consular fees, which have been discussed in Chapter IX above, is that for cartage and stevedoring in the customs areas: *Caleta y Estiba.* The 1959-60 budget estimate for revenue under this head is Bs.90 million. However, the estimated expenditures are virtually the same: Bs.90.7 million. In 1957-58, according to the *Cuenta de Hacienda,* the Government obtained a surplus of Bs.15,200,000.[10] There was a slight deficit at four of the smaller ports; the sum of these deficits was only Bs.2.5 million, against surpluses of Bs.5.4 million at La Guaira, Bs.7.3 million at Maracaibo, Bs.3.6 million at Puerto Cabello, and Bs.1.5 million at Guanta-Puerto La Cruz.

This is essentially a commercial service that the Government renders, and the revenues from it should not, in principle, exceed the cost (including in cost a fair interest return on whatever capital is tied up in the enterprise). Accordingly, in view of the estimates for 1959-60, no substantial increase in revenue from this source seems justified.

The estimated cost for 1959-60 consists almost entirely of costs for personnel. Only Bs.9 million of the Bs.91 million is allocated for purchase or construction of plant, equipment, etc.

OVERTIME AT CUSTOMS

The item *"Habilitaciones"* in the budget represents fees paid from importers who want the services of customs inspectors, etc., outside of regular working hours.[11] According to figures supplied by the Customs Administration, the cost of rendering these overtime services is estimated at Bs.1,800,000 for 1959-60. The budget estimates the revenues from *Habilitaciones* for 1959-60 at Bs.8,500,000. If the cost estimate is

[10] *Cuenta de Hacienda,* 1959, for 1957-58, p. 130, Table 53.
[11] The schedule of fees is given in *Gaceta Oficial,* April 21, 1958, No. 189,171.

reasonably accurate, and if it is comparable with the revenue item, the service is earning a large profit, at the expense of importers. On the general principle governing the level of fees, these figures suggest that the present fees should be reduced considerably.

CHANNEL DREDGING

An important case of fees, or price, is found in the National Institute of Channel Dredging (Instituto Nacional de Canalizaciones).

For use of the channel over the bar in Lake Maracaibo, the Institute received Bs.44,208,231 in fees in 1958. All but Bs.507,566 was from oil tankers. The charge for oil tankers is 10 céntimos per barrel of 42 gallons (increased from 9 céntimos in 1958, which was a reduction from a 10-céntimo fee in force in 1957). General freight is charged 70 céntimos per metric ton.

For use of the channel in the Orinoco River that allows iron ore ships to reach the sea, Bs.2.80 per ton is charged. In 1958, Bs.32,500,000 was collected. Ninety per cent of this was paid to the Orinoco Mining Company to cover the expenses it incurred in the maintenance and administration of the channel, and amortization of the capital invested in dredging the channel. The remaining 10 per cent went to the Institute, toward covering its administration expenses.

The Institute's maintenance and administrative expenses for the period January 24-December 31, 1958, totalled Bs.32,033,811. Interest and depreciation on capital outlays made by the Institute itself are not included in this figure. Since revenue from fees for all of 1958 (Maracaibo fees, plus 10 per cent of Orinoco fees) was Bs.47,458,000, there is no evidence from these figures above that the fees are inadequate.

The revenues described above do not appear in the national budget, since they are paid to an autonomous institute.

DOCKS (Muelles)

Under the heading *"Muelles,"* the budget estimates a revenue of Bs.1,500,000 for 1959-60. This revenue comes from fees, or prices, charged to ships, for use of the docks. The scale of fees varies from port to port. At Guanta, for example, the charge is 50 céntimos per ton (*tonelada*) of merchandise loaded or unloaded from ships of Venezuelan registry, of up to 80 tons, and Bs.1.00 for larger ships.[12] Foreign ships

[12] Decree of June 6, 1947.

all pay at Bs.1.00 per ton. Additional rates are imposed for periods outside the ordinary hours of work: from 6 p.m. to 12 p.m., Bs.3.00; from 12 p.m. to 7 a.m., or on holidays, Bs.4.00.

Anchorage fees (*Fondeo*) are levied in addition: 10 céntimos per registered ton (*tonelada de registro*) for all foreign ships, and the same for domestic ships of more than 80 tons capacity.

Owing to the absence of data on depreciation on imputed interest, no meaningful cost figures can be obtained at present, to ascertain whether the dock and anchorage fees are yielding a profit or a loss.

LIGHTHOUSES (Faros)

The budget lists, under "Fees," a small item for lighthouses: Bs.200,- 000 for 1958-59, and again for 1959-60. Information supplied by the Budget Bureau (Sección de Economía de Finanza) is to the effect that only one lighthouse is involved: that at Punta Brava, near Puerto Cabello. Under a law of February 4, 1909, each ship of more than 150 tons arriving at Puerto Cabello must pay a lighthouse fee of 5 céntimos per ton. No data appear to be readily available on the costs of this lighthouse.

PILOTING (Pilotaje)

Under "Piloting" *(Pilotaje),* the 1959-60 budget estimates revenue of Bs.4,300,000; under *"Ingresos Varios,"* the budget carries revenue from Towing Services *(Servicio Remolcadores),* amount unspecified. Information supplied by the operating services supplies a breakdown of these revenues for the calendar year 1958:

	Bs.
Fees for bringing pilot to and from the ship (no charge for the pilot's services during working hours)	3,235,191
Towing services	1,817,206
Other services	28,893
Fines	20,595
Total	5,101,885

The fees are based on the tonnage of the ship being piloted or towed. The schedule is not necessarily the same at all the ports. At Maracaibo, for example, the charge is Bs.20 for boats up to 200 net tons (*toneladas netos*), Bs.40 for those from 201 to 1,000 tons, and so on, to a maximum of Bs.200 for boats over 15,000 tons. These Maracaibo fees are to be increased shortly. They were last changed November 15, 1957.

In other ports for which we have information the most recent changes in the fees were in 1955, 1956 or 1957, except la Vela de Coro, 1944.

The operating department states that a precise allocation of costs is not feasible, but the following estimated costs for the fiscal year 1959-60, which are said to be similar to the costs incurred in calendar 1958, represent a minimum that can be so allocated:

Piloting:	Bs.
Payroll	1,854,576
Pensions	200,520
Uniforms	100,000
Total	2,155,096
Towing	618,240

The figures given above do not afford a basis for recommending a general increase in the fees. However, the question may be raised whether the services of the pilot himself should continue to be supplied free of charge (in regular working hours).

PATENTS AND TRADEMARKS (Patentes de Invención,
Registro de Marcas y Denominaciones)

The 1958-59 budget, under "Fees," showed two items of only Bs.10,000 each, under "Patents" and "Trademarks." The 1959-60 budget does not show these items separately.

The total revenue from these fees in the period Jan. 23, 1958 to Dec. 31, 1958 was Bs.539,200, and from associated taxes, Bs.222,500, according to the Ministry of Development.[13] Thus the income appears to be running at about Bs.800,000 a year. However, we are informed by officials in the Ministry that they are understaffed with respect to billing for these fees and taxes, and, if they had sufficient personnel, the revenue might reach Bs.2,000,000 a year. The schedule of fees, etc., too complex to be reproduced here, may be found in the *Gaceta Oficial* Oct. 14, 1958, No. 24,873.

The annual cost of the office dealing with these matters is estimated at Bs.1,287,280 for 1959-60 and Bs.1,353,192 for 1958-59, according to the budget. Thus this operation is being conducted at a loss at present. But apparently no increase in fees is called for if all those who should pay are required to do so.

[13] *Memoria . . . Cuenta*, 1956-57—1958-59, Ministerio de Fomento, p. 434.

DEPARTMENT OF HEALTH FEES

Under the budget heading, "Servicio Sanitario," there come the fees collected by the Department of Public Health (a) for inspection of ships outside regular working hours, and (b) for analysis of canned foods that is necessary before a certificate is granted to manufacturers and importers.

The inspection fee for ships, a flat amount of Bs.100 per ship per inspection, yields about Bs.600,000 a year. No fee is charged if inspection occurs within regular working hours; consideration might be given to imposing a fee for inspection at those times. Some hundreds of thousands of bolivars, at least, might be obtained from this source. The present fees, on inspection outside regular working hours, are substantially greater than the cost of such inspection. Thus they are to some degree an example of a minor sort of tax. The Bs.100 fee has remained unchanged for many years.

The fees collected for inspection of canned foods just about equal the cost of inspection.

Drugs, imported or manufactured in Venezuela, are inspected. The cost of such inspection amounts to more than Bs.1,000,000 a year. A proposal to impose an inspection fee on drugs is being considered. The proposed fee is Bs.5,000 once every five years for importers of injection drugs, or Bs.2,000 for those domestically produced; and Bs.2,000 once every five years for importers of drugs in the form of pills, or Bs.500 for domestic products. It is estimated that these fees would yield Bs.2,000,000 a year. This much revenue might be justified if the speed of inspection were somewhat increased to avoid delays. The discrimination between imported and domestic drugs can be justified only if there is a corresponding difference in the cost of inspection.

Some of the modern Government hospitals that furnish bed care are charging patients who can afford to pay, a price of Bs.50 a day. The money is retained by the Department of Health and is used to support the hospitals. This procedure of allocating the money to the support of the hospitals is justifiable on the grounds that the revenue is from a price charged for a service, not from a tax. Tax revenue should not, in general, be earmarked; but price revenue may, with economic logic, be devoted to covering the cost of the service that is sold at the price. The price now being charged is no larger than the cost of the bed care supplied, and may be somewhat smaller.

WAREHOUSING AT CUSTOMS

For the use of its warehouses in the customs areas, the Customs Administration charges fees, or rentals. The estimate for this item in the 1959-60 budget is Bs.2,000,000.

The Customs Administration has no figures on costs of operation that might be allocated to these warehouses. Even if they did have such figures, the absence of estimates of depreciation and imputed interest would make impossible a useful approximation of total costs.

D. Summary

In summary, the following possibilities for raising additional revenue from higher prices or fees may be considered:

	Bs.
Civil Aviation	30,000,000.00
Telegraph and Radio	50,000,000.00
Sanitary Service	1,000,000.00
Total	81,000,000.00

These figures are only rough estimates and need to be checked carefully before being used as a basis for policy measures.

Anyone who attempts to gather data on fees and costs must be impressed by the obstacles inadvertently placed in the way of such a study by the existing method of computing costs, and by the difficulty of obtaining figures on actual expenditures (as contrasted with figures on estimated expenditures) that are truly comparable with the figures on receipts referring to the same activity.

Some kind of depreciation costing needs to be installed; uniform terminology on revenues as between the budget document and the *Cuenta de Hacienda* would be helpful. So too would a wider understanding on the part of the officials of the operating departments of just how the budget estimates of receipts are arrived at, and of the exact meaning of the *Cuenta* tables. Finally, there should be drawn up an information table, for use within the Government, showing precisely what office or section possesses the information on fees or prices charged, revenue taken in, and actual costs incurred, for each of the activities for which a charge is made.

Appendices

The petroleum companies operating in Venezuela are required to satisfy their needs for bolivars by purchasing them from the Banco Central at the rate of either 3.09 or 3.046 bolivars per dollar, according to circumstances to be explained below, while the Banco Central sells dollars to the commercial banks at 3.32 and to the public at 3.35 bolivars per dollar. The profits from these transactions are turned over to the Venezuelan Treasury. No comprehensive study of the Venezuelan tax system can ignore this exchange differential, which suggests a disguised tax of some sort. If the Government buys low and sells high, somebody, it would appear, is worse off than he would be if the Government bought and sold at the same price, or stayed out of the market altogether. But is this really so, and, if it is, who suffers from the exchange differential—the petroleum companies, or someone else?

The petroleum companies need bolivars for various purposes, chief among which are the payment of the production tax (sometimes called a "royalty") of 16⅔ per cent on gross value of the oil extracted, and the Venezuelan taxes on income. But the value of the oil, in bolivars, is computed by applying to the dollar value of such oil the exchange rate, not of 3.35, but of 3.09. Moreover, by far the larger part of the taxable income of the petroleum companies is computed in foreign exchange, and this income is translated into bolivars at the 3.09 rate.[1] If the only need for bolivars arose from the production tax, one rate of exchange would be as good as another, for the petroleum companies, provided

---

[1] A company that is able to forecast, with reasonable accuracy, the proportion of its dollars that, in a given year, will have to be sold at 3.046 (see below) may construct a composite rate between that and 3.09 that may be used for computing the production tax and the base for income tax. At least one company does so. Otherwise, the 3.046 rate does not enter into computation of production tax or income tax. See Creole Petroleum Corporation, 1957 Annual Report, p. 29, referring to a rate of "approximately 3.078 bolivars" to the dollar, at which "most bolivar items included in current assets and liabilities were converted into dollars. . . ."

448

always the same rate applied both to their sales of dollars and to the computation of their production tax due. The same is true with respect to the Venezuelan income tax, for which the oil companies also need to purchase bolivars. One exchange rate is as good as another, provided the same rate applies both to the oil companies' sales of dollars, and to the conversion of their income tax liabilities from dollars into bolivars.

In fact, the exchange rate at which the Banco Central purchases dollars from the oil companies is not always the same as the rate used to convert dollars to bolivars in accounting, with respect to production tax and income tax.

If the supply of dollars in a given year turns out to have exceeded the demand for dollars, so that the foreign-exchange reserve of Venezuela has increased, this absolute amount of excess of dollars leads to a readjustment of the price paid by the Banco Central to the petroleum companies to the extent of this same number of dollars. The Banco Central has been selling bolivars to the petroleum companies during the year for 3.09 bolivars per dollar; at the end of the year it finds that the excess of dollar purchases for the economy as a whole over dollar sales is, say, x dollars. The buying rate on these x dollars (subject to certain minor adjustments) is retroactively adjusted downward to 3.046; the oil companies have to make a refund (in bolivars, of course) to the Banco Central. The bank, or the Government, does not undertake the task of specifying how much of the total refund is to be made by each petroleum company; the refund is an industry-wide assessment, and an allocation among the companies at the end of the year is made on an agreed upon basis, namely, proportional to the amount of dollars that each company has brought in. Occasionally a year will turn out to be a deficit-dollar year; Venezuela experiences a drain on its dollar reserves. But no carry-over from one year to the next is allowed; the amount of refund required from the oil industry because of a dollar surplus in one year is not affected by the existence of a dollar deficit in a preceding or later year.

A year in which much exploration and development work and expansion of capital equipment is accomplished in Venezuela is likely to be one in which the dollar surplus is large, hence one in which the industry must pay a substantial refund. The excess demand for bolivars may of course result from the activity of only one or a few companies.

To the extent to which the oil companies must, from one year to another, sell at 3.046 instead of 3.09 (while computing production tax and income tax at 3.09), they are of course disadvantaged, compared with being able to sell at 3.09.

The rationale for the 3.09 and 3.046 rates seems to have been as follows. After the dollar was revalued downward in 1934, the gold par of the bolivar stood at 3.06 to the dollar. At that time the gold export point was approximately 3.09. The gold import point (as computed at a somewhat later date) was about 3.046. The Venezuelan Government may be viewed as saying to the petroleum companies: if it were not for the dollars that you supply us, we might have to pay for our imports by shipping some of our gold abroad. Given the cost of transporting that gold, we would have to surrender, not 3.06 bolivars, but 3.09 bolivars for every dollar of those imports. Accordingly, we are willing to pay you 3.09 bolivars for every dollar. But of course if you insist on selling us more dollars than we need, we might well refuse to purchase that excess, and you would have no recourse but to buy gold with your dollars and ship it to Venezuela, there to exchange it for bolivars; and, given the cost of transporting gold, you would end up with only 3.046 bolivars for every dollar, instead of 3.06. Accordingly, in a year when there is an excess of dollars offered on the market, we shall pay you only 3.046 on that excess.

The need for bolivars by the petroleum companies in fact exceeds that represented by the production tax and income tax payments. Customs duties, fixed at so many bolivars per kilo, must be paid in bolivars; labor engaged in Venezuela must be paid in bolivars. Some of the oil companies' equipment and supplies may be purchased in Venezuelan markets, instead of being brought in from abroad after direct purchase with dollars. Moreover, there are other payments to the Government; the successful bidder for an oil concession, for example, needs bolivars. To be sure, some of the petroleum companies sell part of their output in the Venezuelan market, and get bolivars that way. A hypothetical case can be made of a company that receives more, in bolivars, from sale of its products on the Venezuelan market, than it needs to spend on the Venezuelan market and to pay the Government for other than the production tax and the income tax. Such a company would be better off, the fewer the bolivars needed to buy a dollar, since it would have what might be called an economic excess of bolivars, which it would want to change into dollars, to pay dividends to its foreign stockholders, or to pay for purchases abroad, or to pay some of its executives' salaries. By economic excess is meant net bolivar accretion during the year, disregarding the bolivars "spent" on the production tax and the income tax. These latter bolivars, we have seen, are a source of no concern to the company so far as the exchange rate is concerned. With respect to these bolivars, an exchange rate of 3.09 is no better or worse than one of 3.35. Putting to one side, then, those dollars arising from sale abroad, to the extent they are sold to the Banco Central to get bolivars for production tax and income tax, we ask whether bolivars receipts from sales within Venezuela fail to cover, or exceed, the remaining bolivar needs of the petroleum companies; and the answer in fact is that in every case so far there has remained a net need for bolivars. Accordingly, in real life, no petroleum company would be harmed, and all would be benefited in varying degrees, if they could buy and sell bolivars freely at a rate that gave somewhat more bolivars per dollar than 3.09.

To say all this, however, is not to demonstrate any substantial burden on the petroleum companies. Up to this point the reasoning is fairly straightforward, and, it is hoped, not open to serious objection. But in the paragraphs to follow we deal necessarily in conjecture, for the profit the Government gets from the differential exchange rate—if it is a profit —need not be entirely at the expense of the oil companies. The heart of the problem lies in specifying the alternative situation for the exchange rate that is assumed, or implied, if one thinks of what would be the case if the differential rate did not exist.

If we assume that, were there no differential exchange rate, there would be but one, equilibrium rate, and if the economic state of the oil companies at present is compared with what it would be under such a free rate, it can be seen at once that the customary determining factors in any economic problem, the relative elasticities both of demand and of supply, must be known before an answer can be given. An analogy may be drawn with an ordinary excise tax, which drives a wedge between the price received by the seller and the price paid by the buyer. These two prices used to be the same; now, they differ, by the amount of the tax. But whether the wedge drives down the price received by the seller, or forces up the price paid by the buyer, or—the usual case— drives the one down somewhat and forces the other up somewhat, depends on the elasticities of demand and supply. The quantitative measures of these elasticities are in fact usually unknown.

To attack the problem, let us start with some extreme assumptions, to define a limiting case. Suppose that (a) the same amount of petroleum would be produced, exported, and sold at the same price abroad, from Venezuela, whether the exchange rate were 3.09 or 3.35, and that (b) Venezuelan purchases of goods abroad are quite sensitive to the exchange rate, and that (c) the present differential exchange rate procedure is producing an equilibrium—no excess of dollar purchases and sales. Under these circumstances, let us suppose that the oil companies were allowed to sell their dollars at any rate they could obtain. At first, this rate would be 3.35. At this rate, would the oil companies offer fewer dollars, in the course of a year, than they did under the 3.09 rate? Supporting an affirmative answer is the following assumption: the oil companies would be producing no more oil than under the 3.09 rate. To this extent, they would have no more need for bolivars than before. On the other hand, supporting a negative answer, is the likelihood that the oil companies would be buying more equipment that was manufactured in Venezuela and correspondingly less equipment manufactured abroad, in view of the new exchange rate. At 3.35 it is more expensive, in bolivars, to buy abroad than at 3.09.

Which of these opposing forces will predominate? To answer, we need information on the elasticity of substitution of Venezuela-produced goods for foreign-produced goods.[2] Lacking such information, let us make the assumption that the net result would be that at 3.35 the oil companies would offer somewhat fewer dollars than at 3.09, though not fewer by the full amount of this difference in exchange rates.

Since the oil companies would be offering fewer dollars than before, Venezuela would have to decrease its rate of imports, compared with what it had been doing under the 3.09 regime. If Venezuela did not decrease its imports, it would incur a deficit on current account, and sooner or later would run out of dollars. How would Venezuela be induced to reduce its imports? In a free market, the answer is: by a rise in the dollar exchange rate to, for example, 3.40 or 3.50 bolivars to the dollar. If, as we assume, Venezuelan imports (we are speaking now of imports other than by the oil companies) would drop off rapidly under the less favorable exchange rate, a new equilibrium could be reached. To be sure, the oil companies would be supplying still fewer dollars at 3.40 or 3.50 than at 3.35. Conceivably, then, no equilibrium could be reached, at least within a short range of exchange rates. But let us suppose it is reached, say at 3.50.

Now we can see how, under the assumption made above, the burden of the existing differential exchange rate is distributed. We follow our chain of reasoning back. The hypothetical free, equilibrium rate is 3.50. Suppose that the Government moves again, back to its original policy of controlled differential rates of 3.09 and 3.35. Venezuelan consumers are not only not harmed by the new arrangement of 3.09–3.35; they are better off than before. The oil companies are worse off since they must pay out more dollars, and that is what counts for them.

Thus, under the supposition of extreme inelasticity of supply of oil,

[2] See W. J. R. Woodley, "The Use of Special Exchange Rates for Transactions with Foreign Companies," International Monetary Fund, Staff Papers, Oct., 1953.

and a zero, or at least very small, elasticity of substitution of Venezuela-produced oil equipment and supplies for those from abroad, the foreign exchange "tax" is one that rests entirely on the oil companies. Part of the tax proceeds goes as a "subsidy" to the Venezuelan consumer. But we must recall that this conclusion is reached by, and is used here only on the basis of, certain assumptions about elasticities of supply and demand. The truth probably lies somewhere in between the extremes of (a) all the burden is on the oil companies; (b) all the burden is on Venezuelan consumers.

No one, so far as we are aware, has attempted to compute the relative elasticities, and we are certainly not equipped to make such an estimate. The point to emphasize is this: the differential exchange rate is economically a tax, though not legally so. At one extreme it is even a combination of tax and subsidy. The burden of the tax is probably, in practice, borne partly by the oil companies (with respect to their purchases of bolivars other than for production tax or income tax payments) and partly by the Venezuelan consumer of imported goods, or of goods made with the aid of imported capital goods. But in precisely what proportion the tax burden of the differential exchange rate is distributed, we do not know.

Coffee and cocoa exports have in the past received still other exchange rates, these being differentially in their favor. By parity of reasoning, these rates can be seen to have represented a subsidy. Since we are concerned at this point with positive taxes, not negative taxes (subsidies), these exchange rates will not be examined here.

A significant point concerning the Government's financial accounts is involved. It will be recalled that, to the extent the petroleum companies do pay a "tax" through the differential exchange rate, they do so only aside from their bolivar needs for paying production tax and income tax. A very large part of the profit the Government gets through selling bolivars to the oil companies at only 3.09 to the dollar is in effect, though not so shown on the books, offset by having the royalty and income tax also computed at 3.09. Thus, if the Government paid the oil companies 3.35 for all the dollars they sold, its budgetary accounts on the income side would shrink by elimination of the item, "profits on foreign exchange," but, since 3.35 would now be required for computing royalty and income tax, those two lines on the revenue side would at once show an increase. While it is proper for the Government to list its exchange profits as an item of revenue, we must keep in mind that it is a peculiar sort of revenue, in this respect: eliminate it, and two other items of revenue automatically increase substantially.

The differential exchange rate encourages petroleum companies to buy abroad directly, rather than through a Venezuelan importer. Suppose that an oil company wants a piece of equipment that is made in the United States, and that costs $1,000 there. For simplicity, let us disregard transportation costs and customs duties. A Venezuelan importer, paying 3.35 bolivars for a dollar, must spend 3,350 bolivars for the equipment, and would have to charge the oil company at least that much. To get 3,350 bolivars, the oil company would have to sell $1,084.14 to the Central Bank. The oil company can buy the equipment more cheaply by purchasing it directly from the United States manufacturer for $1,000.

Still more important in the long run is the rate of substitution of Venezuela-produced goods for foreign-produced goods that the oil companies use. The fewer bolivars the oil companies get in exchange for a dollar, the cheaper it is for them to buy oil field equipment, etc., that is produced abroad (whether they buy it directly or through a Venezuelan intermediary) than it is to buy similar goods produced in Venezuela. If the oil companies' demand for such goods were very sensitive to differentials in price, and if there were enough potential production of such goods in Venezuela, the 3.09 rate could be a threat to the economic development of a part of Venezuela's industry.

Moreover, if the exchanges were freed, the equilibrium rate might be this side of 3.35—say, 3.20, or even 3.00—if the elasticity of substitution were great enough, and the amounts involved large enough.

Probably this factor is not of enough immediate importance to warrant concern. But in the long run, and if Venezuela succeeds in developing a substantial industry sector, any pressure on the oil companies (through the differential exchange rate) to buy foreign-produced instead of Venezuelan-produced goods will have to be carefully considered.

Finally, to the extent that under the present system there is a tendency for foreign-currency reserves to accumulate, an elimination of the multiple rate structure might cause very little depreciation in the exchange—perhaps only to 3.40, or even not at all.

Note: Much of the information given here was obtained from the article by Dr. Carlos Rafael Silva, "La incidencia del Régimen Venezolano de Cambios Diferenciales," in *El Trimestre Económico,* XXII, No. 2, April-June, 1955. Dr. Silva is not, however, to be held responsible for whatever errors there may be in the analysis here of the division of the burden between oil companies and consumers in accordance with elasticities.

: **Total Taxes Paid, Directly**
: **and Indirectly, by Twelve**
: **Hypothetical Venezuelan Families**

Every family in Venezuela is subject to some taxation. Many Venezuelan families are probably not aware of the fact that they are paying any tax, since many of them pay only indirectly, through the higher prices of the things they buy, or through lower incomes than they would otherwise be receiving. To others, however, taxation is all too familiar, in the form of income tax and other direct taxes.

If we had complete information, we could take the Bs.4 billion in taxation, more or less, that is paid to the national, state and municipal governments in Venezuela in a year, and allocate it among the families in Venezuela. We could ascertain that so much is borne by this family, in direct and indirect taxes, so much by that family, and so on. If we possessed, not complete information, but fairly precise estimates on income distribution and family consumption expenditures, we might be able to estimate the tax bill (direct and indirect) for each of several income groups in the community: so many hundreds of million Bs. is paid, directly and indirectly, by the aggregate of families with income less than, say, Bs.5,000 a year; so much, in the aggregate, by those with incomes from Bs.5,000 to Bs.10,000 a year—and so on, until all the Bs.4 billion was allocated among income groups. There is not yet enough information about the Venezuelan economy to make a firm estimate in detail, along these lines. A provisional estimate, dividing the economy into three income groups only, is given in Table I-9 of Chapter I above. That table is based in part on the information presented in Tables B-1 to B-3, below. These tables are based on another, complementary approach to the problem, implying the following technique: a hypothetical Venezuelan family is described in detail. The family is assumed to have a certain specified pattern of consumption and saving, out of a stipulated income. For example: let us construct a hypothetical family consisting of a worker at an iron mine, who is married and has four children, and whose annual wage is Bs.11,000, plus fringe benefits and extraordinary cash payments totalling Bs.8,000. Let us make some assumptions about the consumption pattern of his family: they spend only Bs.20 a year on imported ham and bacon, Bs.10 a year on imported preserved fish (and so on), Bs.2,400 a year on housing, Bs.1,240 a year on furniture, appliances, and home furnishings.

Given these assumptions, and others, also, noted in the table, and knowing the rates of income tax and the rates of indirect tax on the goods and services the family consumes, we should be able to compute the annual amount of tax the family pays, directly and indirectly. Assumptions are made too, of course, about the shifting of taxes: for example, it is assumed that the taxes on imports are passed on to the consumers in higher prices. The full effects of the fiscal system on the family, to be sure, would include the effects of higher prices for articles produced by domestic firms that are in existence only because they have tariff protection. These indirect burdens are ignored in the present study, as are a portion of the cinco por mil and local gross receipts taxes.

Now if the assumptions—and there are a host of them, indeed—are reasonable, and especially if the figures used for consumer expenditures are based on family budget studies or the observation of knowledgeable persons, the answers we get are almost surely more helpful than misleading.[1] Beyond this very modest statement we cannot go. We must warn against the appearance of precision that the figures give. They are no better than the quality of the data from which they were constructed. The temptation to draw the precise inference becomes strong when one reaches the last column (Table B-3), which expresses the total of taxes on the family, direct and indirect, as a percentage of the family's income. Here we seem to have a very useful figure indeed. We can compare the different families. We note that Family A, with Bs.20,750 of income (Table B-1), pays a little over 11 per cent of income in taxes, direct and indirect, while Family B, with only Bs.14,780 of income, pays more than 13 per cent—so, the tax system as a whole appears to be regressive, instead of progressive. But then we note that Family C, with Bs.28,000 of income, pays almost 18 per cent in taxes; the system begins to appear progressive. And so we run down this last column, receiving what seem to be definite impressions.

The impressions are useful, but they should not be allowed to become definite. The basic data on the Venezuelan economy are still too scanty to allow us the luxury of certainty. Nevertheless, some value, we hope,

---

[1] The only complete budget information available was for iron and oil workers' families. Many of the weighting procedures employed in the table were based on the data for these middle income families. Reasonable guesses were then used to vary the magnitudes according to income for the other families.

attaches to the tables presented in this appendix, which create hypothetical families and lead them through the tax maze, to a final figure expressed as a percentage of the family income. They certainly show how complicated is the task of understanding, even in a rough way, the distribution of taxation. And, if the reader will check the reasonableness of each of the assumptions made, he can decide for himself how much weight he will want to place on the final percentage figure. More, he can recompute the percentage by varying the assumptions.

The accompanying tables need refinement by further study, a task that was not feasible within the resources of our Commission. The percentage for some of the higher income families are especially liable to error, because of the important part played by luxury consumption, the substantial taxes that are imposed on that kind of consumption, and the almost complete lack of data on how wealthy families do in fact spend their incomes. The housing columns were especially difficult to fill because of the impossibility, in view of the scanty data, of calculating that portion of yearly housing cost upon which a customs duty burden should be applied. It is quite possible that a reworking of the assumptions would show that the final percentage (tax as per cent of income) in the present computation should be somewhat lower than Table B-3 indicates.

Is the present tax system of Venezuela, as a whole, progressive, regressive, or proportional? The data here, as we have seen, give no clear answer. But from them we may infer that, if the basic data were available, and if a thorough study were made, it is likely that the tax system would be shown to be slightly progressive with respect to income, at least within certain income ranges, and that substantial differences would be found, at any one income level, between the tax burden on large and small families, and on urban and rural families.[2]

All money figures in Tables B-1, B-2 and B-3 are in bolivars.

[2] A slight downward adjustment, less than one percentage point in all but one case (and zero in three cases), is called for in the last column in view of the fact that the customs duty of Bs.2 per kilogram on eggs was, we now learn, suspended.

Table B-1. Hypothetical Budgets and Tax Burdens of Venezuelan Families: Family Data and Direct Tax Computations

Primary Occupation	Identification Letter	Location	Parents[3a]	Children	Other	Total	Source of Income or Occupation	Income[7]	Social Security Deduction[8]	Income (after S.S.)	Relationship	Source of Income or Occupation	Income[9]
				Family Size			Head of Family				Other Income Earners		
Iron Mine Worker	A[1]	Estado Bolivar	2	4	0	6	regular from work	11,000			1st child	part time work	600
							fringe & extraord.[4]	8,000			2nd child	part time work	400
							Total 19,000	19,000	250	18,750		Total	1,000
Petroleum Field Worker	B[2]	Estado Zulia (living in camps)	2	2	2	6	regular from work	9,000					
							fringe & extraord.[4]	6,000					
							Total	15,000	220	14,780			0
Wholesale Grocery Executive	C	Caracas	2	2	0	4	regular from work[5]	24,000					
							ext. & fringe[4]	3,000					
							net cap. gain	1,000					
							Total	28,000	0	28,000			0
Bookkeeper, Food Factory	D	Barcelona	2	3	0	5	regular from work[5]	13,300			child	occasional work	15,750
							ext. & fringe[4]	2,450					
							Total	15,750	0	15,750			1,500

Occupation		Location					Income source				
Machine Tender, Textile Mill	E	Valencia	2	3	1	6	regular from work[5]	7,000			
							ext. & fringe[4]	1,220			
							Total	8,220	220	8,000	0
Attorney	F	Caracas	2	4	0	6	legal practice	60,000			
							shares	10,000			
							net rents	10,000			
							Total	80,000	0	80,000	0
Domestic	G[3]	San Cristóbal	1	2	0	3	regular from work[5]	2,500			
							ext. & fringe[4]	0			
							Total	2,500	0	2,500	0
Unskilled Laborer, e.g. Construction	H	Caracas (e.g. ranchero)	2	7	0	9	regular from work[5]	3,400			
							ext. & fringe[4]	420			
							Total	3,820	90	3,730	0
Real Estate Speculator and Owner	I	Caracas	2	3	1	6	rents	200,000			
							cap. gains	100,000			
							director's salary	50,000			
							Total	350,000	0	350,000	0
Large Land Owner, e.g. Cane, Cotton, Corn	J	Estado Aragua	2	5	1	8	net profit from farming[6]	49,000			
							land rents	51,000			
							Total	100,000	0	100,000	0
Independent Farmer, e.g. Cattle	K	Estado Anzoátegui	2	4	0	6	net profits from farming[6]	35,000			
							Total	35,000	0	35,000	0
Conuquero (peon)	L	Estado Cojedes	2	7	1	10	net profit from farming[6]	500			
							wages[6]	1,000			child occasional wages 500
							Total	1,500	0	1,500	

Continued on next page

Table B-1 (cont.)

Primary Occupation	Identification Letter	Location	Total Family Income (after S.S.)	Personal Exemption: Amount	Income Taxes												Disposable Income
					Income Taxable Under Complementary Tax	Cedular Deduction	Taxable Income Under Cedular Tax	Cedular Rate	Amt. of Cedular Tax	Complementary Rate	Amount of Complementary Tax	Total Amounts: Ced. & Compl. Taxes	Other Direct Taxes	Total Direct Taxes	Total Direct Taxes as % of Total Income	
Iron Mine Worker	A¹	Estado Bolívar	19,750 gambling, 1,000 Total 20,750	28,000	0	12,000	7,000	salary .01	70	0	0	70	gambling, 100	170	0.3514 0.8215	20,580
Petroleum Field Worker	B²	Estado Zulia (living in camps)	14,780	28,000	0	12,000	3,000	salary .01	30	0	0	30	0	30	0.20	14,750
Wholesale Grocery Executive	C	Caracas Total	28,000	22,000	6,000	12,000	27,000 0	salary .01 cap. gain .03	270 0 270	.015	90	360	0	360	1.28	27,640
Bookkeeper, Food Factory	D	Barcelona	17,250	25,000	0	12,000	3,750	salary .01	40	0	0	40	0	40	0.23	17,210
Machine Tender, Textile Mill	E	Valencia	8,000	28,000	0	12,000	0	salary .02	0	0	0	0	0	0	0.0	8,000

Occupation		Location					Tax item							%	Total
Attorney	F	Caracas	80,000	28,000	42,000[10]	0	60,000 prof. .02	1,200		880[11]	2,330	0	2,330	2.91	77,670
		Total				0	10,000 rents .025	250	11						
								1,450							
Domestic	G[3]	San Cristóbal	2,500	18,000	0	12,000	0 salary .02	0	0	0	0	0	0	0.0	2,500
Unskilled Laborer, e.g., Construction	H	Caracas (e.g. ranchero)	3,730	37,000	0	12,000	0 salary .02	0	0	0	0	0	0	0.0	3,730
Real Estate Speculator and Owner	I	Caracas	350,000	322,000		0	200,000 rent .0250	5,000		14,600[12]	23,100	0	23,100	6.60	326,900
			28,000 Total			0	100,000 cap. gain .0300	3,000	12						
						0	50,000 salary .0100	500							
								8,500							
Large Land Owner, e.g. Cane, Cotton, Corn	J	Estado Aragua	100,000	66,000		30,000	19,000 agri. .0200	380		1,160[13]	2,815	0	2,815	2.81	97,185
			34,000 Total			0	51,000 rent .0250	1,275	13						
								1,655							
Independent Farmer, e.g. Cattle	K	Estado Anzoátegui	35,000	7,000		30,000	5,000 agri. .0200	100	.015	105	205	0	205	0.58	34,795
Conuquero (peon)	L	Estado Cojedes	2,000	40,000		30,000	0 agri. .0100	0	0	0	0	0	0	0.0	2,000
						12,000	0 .0200	0							

NOTE: All footnotes to Tables B–1, B–2, and B–3 are numbered consecutively and will be found following Table B–3.

Table B-2. Hypothetical Budgets and Tax Burdens of Venezuelan Families: Indirect Tax Computations

| | | Food and Beverages | | | | | | | | | | | | | | | | |
| Identification Letter | Imported Ham and Bacon | | | Imported Preserved Fish | | | Imported Cheese | | | Imported Canned Fruit and Veg. | | | Imported Eggs | | | Wine | | |
	Amount	Tax Rate	Tax Amount	Amount	Tax Rate	Tax Amount	Amount	Tax Rate	Tax Amount	Amount	Tax Rate	Tax Amount	Amount	Tax Rate	Tax Amount	Amount	Tax Rate	Tax Amount
A	20	.12	2.40	10	.23	2.30	25	.18	4.50	40	.30	12.00	300	.62	186.00	130	.15	19.50
B	15	.12	1.80	30	.23	6.90	100	.18	18.00	120	.30	36.00	200	.62	124.00	90	.15	13.50
C	40	.12	4.80	40	.23	9.20	150	.18	27.00	300	.30	90.00	400[17]	.62	248.00	150	.15	22.50
D	15	.12	1.80	10	.23	2.30	100	.18	18.00	200	.30	60.00	350	.62	217.00	100	.15	15.00
E	10	.12	1.20	20	.23	4.60	20	.18	3.60	50	.30	15.00	100	.62	62.00	70	.15	10.50
F	50	.12	6.00	75	.23	17.20	200	.18	36.00	400	.30	120.00	600[17]	.62	372.00	200	.15	30.00
G	10	.12	1.20	0	.23	0	15	.18	2.70	40	.30	12.00	50	.62	31.00	30	.15	4.50
H	15	.12	1.80	15	.23	3.50	20	.18	3.60	50	.30	15.00	100	.62	62.00	100	.15	15.00
I	200	.12	24.00	250	.23	57.50	400	.18	72.00	800	.30	240.00	800[17]	.62	496.00	250	.15	37.50
J	50	.12	6.00	100	.23	23.00	150	.18	27.00	300	.30	90.00	0[16]	.62	0	200	.15	30.00
K	0[16]	.12	0	75	.23	17.30	50	.18	9.00	100	.30	30.00	0[16]	.62	0	150	.15	22.50
L	0[16]	.12	0	10	.23	2.30	0	.18	0	20	.30	6.00	0[16]	.62	0	80	.15	12.00

Identification Letter	Food and Beverages (cont.)									Housing			Furniture, Appliances, Home Furnishings[25]			Clothing (incl. Yard Goods)[26]			Education Expenditure[36]
	Beer			Other Food															
	Amount	Tax Rate	Tax Amount	Amount	Tax Rate[18]	Tax Amount	Amount	Tax Rate[23]	Tax Amount	Imputed Rent	Real Estate Tax[24]	Tax Amount	Amount	Tax Rate	Tax Amount	Amount	Tax Rate	Tax Amount	
A	0	.35	0	7,770	.04	310.80	2,400[21]	.04	96.00	2,160	.04	86.40	1,240	.27	334.80	2,500	.21	525.00	300
B	0	.35	0	4,480	.04	179.20	2,675[21]	.04	107.00	2,408	.06	144.50	1,300	.27	351.00	1,905	.21	400.00	420
C	80	.35	28.00	7,400[19]	.06	444.00	5,150[19]	.05	257.50	4,770	.065	310.00	2,700[19]	.32	864.00	3,000[19]	.35	1,050.00	1,500[19]
D	10	.35	3.50	6,200[19]	.04	248.00	3,900[19]	.04	156.00	3,510	.05	175.50	1,350[19]	.27	364.50	1,700[19]	.21	357.00	800[19]
E	0	.35	0	3,530[19]	.03	105.90	2,000[19]	.04	80.00	1,800	.04	72.00	320[19]	.20	54.00	1,000[19]	.15	150.00	100[19]
F	300	.35	105.00	14,175[19]	.08	1,134.00	22,900[19]	.06	1,374.00	21,068	.065	1,369.40	6,400[19]	.39	2,496.00	6,700[19]	.45	3,015.00	10,300[19]
G	0	.35	0	1,195	.03	35.90	700	.03	21.00	650	.04	26.00	140	.15	21.00	200	.15	30.00	0
H	0	.35	0	1,700[19]	.03	51.00	300[19]	.03	9.00	0	0	0	250[19]	.15	37.50	400[19]	.15	60.00	100[19]
I	600	.35	210.00	22,350	.08	1,788.00	100,000	.10	10,000.00	95,000	.065	6,175.00	21,000	.41	8,610.00	15,000	.55	8,250.00	45,000
J	200	.35	70.00	9,100[20]	.06	546.00	20,000[22]	.06	1,200.00	18,400	.04	736.00	4,100	.39	1,599.00	7,000	.45	3,150.00	15,000
K	60	.35	21.00	6,350[20]	.05	317.50	5,000	.04	200.00	4,500	.04	180.00	1,550	.27	418.50	4,000	.35	1,400.00	4,000
L	0	.35	0	600[20]	.02	12.00	200	.02	4.00	0	0	0	160	.05	8.00	490	.08	39.20	75

NOTE: All footnotes to Tables B-1, B-2, and B-3 are numbered consecutively and will be found following Table B-3.

Table B-3. Hypothetical Budgets and Tax Burdens of Venezuelan Families: Indirect Tax Computations, Total Tax Figures, Tax as a Per Cent of Income Figures

Identification Letter	Amount[27]	Automobile			Transportation						Cigarettes			Liquor		
					Gasoline			Other Transp.								
		Amount of Fees[28]	Tax Rate[29]	Tax Amount	Amount	Tax Rate[30]	Tax Amount	Amount	Tax Rate[31]	Tax Amount	Amount[32]	Tax Rate[33]	Tax Amount	Amount[32]	Tax Rate[33]	Tax Amount
A	610	115	.12	73.20	300	.08	24.00	550	.02	11.00	370	.30	111.00	200	.33	66.00
B	570	165	.12	68.40	280	.08	22.40	200	.02	4.00	210	.30	63.00	135	.33	44.50
C	2,000	287	.15	300.00	400	.105	42.00	250	.02	5.00	500	.30	150.00	270	.33	89.00
D	600	115	.12	72.00	350	.08	28.00	200	.02	4.00	0	.30	0	250	.33	72.50
E	0	0	—	0	0	—	0	150	.02	3.00	200	.30	60.00	150	.33	48.50
F	4,000	367	.13	520.00	500	.105	52.50	500	.02	10.00	400	.30	120.00	600	.33	198.00
G	0	0	—	0	0	—	0	50	.02	1.00	0	.30	0	0	.33	0
H	0	0	—	0	0	—	0	200	.02	4.00	200	.30	60.00	100	.33	33.00
I	20,000	734	.13	2,600.00	1,200	.105	126.00	1,500	.02	30.00	600	.30	180.00	3,000	.33	990.00
J	10,000	215	.13	1,300.00	800	.105	84.00	1,000	.02	20.00	300	.30	90.00	1,000	.33	330.00
K	3,000	165	.15	450.00	500	.105	52.50	400	.02	8.00	250	.30	75.00	300	.33	99.00
L	0	0	—	0	0	—	0	100	.02	2.00	80	.30	24.00	75	.33	24.80

Identification Letter	Admissions Amount	Admissions Tax Rate[34]	Admissions Tax Amount	Other Recreation Amount	Other Recreation Tax Rate[35]	Other Recreation Tax Amount	Personal Care & Household Operation Amount	Tax Rate[37]	Tax Amount	Medical Amount	Medical Tax Rate[38]	Medical Tax Amount	Other Expenditures[39] Amount	Tax Rate[40]	Tax Amount	Net New Savings (+) or Debt (−)	Total Indirect Taxes	Total Indirect Taxes as a % of Total Income	Total Indirect Taxes as a % of Disposable Income	Total Taxes: All Forms	Total Taxes as a % of Total Income
A	85	.13	11.00	335	.26	87.10	490	.13	63.70	310 [21]	.02	6.20	985	.02	19.70	+1,385	2,167.60	10.97 [14] / 10.44 [15]	11.01 [41] / 10.53 [42]	2,237.60 [43] / 2,337.60 [44]	11.33 [43] / 11.26 [44]
B	110	.13	14.30	410	.26	106.60	410	.13	53.30	500 [21]	.02	10.00	610	.02	12.30	−20	1,945.80	12.97	13.19	1,975.80	13.17
C	250	.13	32.50	600 [19]	.28	168.00	900 [19]	.15	135.00	690	.02	13.80	750	.02	15.00	+30	4,592.30	16.40	16.61	4,952.30	17.67
D	100	.13	13.00	300 [19]	.26	78.00	350 [19]	.10	35.00	500	.02	10.00	400	.02	8.00	−690	2,064.10	11.96	11.99	2,104.10	12.20
E	50	.13	6.50	150 [19]	.16	24.00	200 [19]	.11	22.00	75	.02	1.50	150	.03	4.50	−345	739.80	9.25	9.25	739.80	9.25
F	400	.13	52.00	2,000 [19]	.31	620.00	2,000 [19]	.17	340.00	1,300	.02	26.00	1,900	.01	19.00	+1,653	12,399.10	15.49	15.96	14,729.10	18.41
G	20	.13	2.60	0	—	0	50	.11	5.50	0	.02	0	10	.03	0.30	−10	194.70	7.79	7.79	194.70	7.79
H	50	.13	6.50	30	.11	3.30	100 [19]	.11	11.00	0	.02	0	50	.03	1.50	−50	377.70	10.13	10.13	377.70	10.13
I	1,500	.13	195.00	12,000	.36	4,320.00	4,000	.21	840.00	3,500	.02	70.00	6,000	.01	60.00	+66,216	46,105.00	13.17	14.10	69,205.00	19.77
J	250	.13	32.50	2,000	.31	620.00	1,500	.17	405.00	2,000	.02	40.00	2,000	.01	20.00	+19,920	10,633.50	10.63	10.94	13,448.50	13.45
K	150	.13	19.50	500	.28	140.00	500	.15	125.00	1,000	.02	20.00	500	.02	10.00	+6,195	3,779.80	10.80	10.86	3,984.80	11.38
L	10	.13	1.30	0	—	0	50	.09	4.50	80	.02	1.60	10	.03	0.30	−40	142.00	7.10	7.10	142.00	7.10

NOTE: All footnotes to Tables B–1, B–2, and B–3 are numbered consecutively and will be found following Table B–3.

FOOTNOTES TO TABLES B-1, B-2, AND B-3

[1] All data on iron workers are based on Ministerio de Trabajo, Dirección de Trabajo, *Encuesta Sobre Condiciones y Costo de Vida de las Familias de Obreros en la Industria de Hierro*, Caracas, 1957, unless otherwise noted.

[2] All data on petroleum workers are based on National Industrial Conference Board, *Indice de Precios al Consumidor para los Empleados Petroleros en Venezuela*, New York, 1955, unless otherwise noted.

[3] It is assumed that the domestic maintains her own domicile, i.e., does not "live in."

[3a] "Parents" refers to head of family cited plus spouse.

[4] Under fringe and extraordinary benefits (prestaciones) there were included only those items which would be considered taxable income. These were:
    a) 20 days of paid holidays and vacations
    b) 17% of base wage under "utilidades"
    c) for oil and iron worker, housing and medical subsidies.

[5] Estimated from information returns submitted to Ministerio de Trabajo.

[6] Estimated from information provided by Consejo Bienestar Rural, Caracas.

[7] All wage and salary income is considered to be earned in equal monthly portions.

[8] Calculated from Venezuelan Social Security Law.

[9] All income in this category is considered tax exempt for purposes of the schedular tax but is included in family income for complementary tax purposes.

[10] The Bs.10,000 of dividends is not taxable.

[11] Computation of complementary tax for F:

Amount of income in bracket (Bs.)	Tax rate	Tax (Bs.)
10,000	.0150	150
4,000	.0175	70
6,000	.0200	120
8,000	.0225	180
10,000	.0250	250
4,000	.0275	110
		880

[12] Computation of complementary tax for I:

Amount of income in bracket (Bs.)	Tax rate	Tax (Bs.)
10,000	.0150	150
4,000	.0175	70
6,000	.0200	120
8,000	.0225	180
10,000	.0250	250
12,000	.0275	330
14,000	.0300	420
16,000	.0350	560
20,000	.0400	800
40,000	.0450	1,800
60,000	.0500	3,000
80,000	.0550	4,400
42,000	.0600	2,520
		14,600

[13] Computation of complementary tax for J:

Amount of income in bracket (Bs.)	Tax rate	Tax (Bs.)
10,000	.0150	150
4,000	.0175	70
6,000	.0200	120
8,000	.0225	180
10,000	.0250	250
12,000	.0275	330
2,000	.0300	60
		1,160

[14] Excludes gambling from total income.

[15] Includes gambling in total income.

[16] It is assumed that all products of this category that are consumed are produced on the farm.

[17] The wealthier, non-farm families, C, F, I, tend to consume a larger proportion of domestic eggs, the price of which is considerably greater but the freshness of which is superior to imported eggs.

[18] Graduated duty-paid percentages are applied to the families according to income, the higher income families consuming larger proportions of imported foods. Some shifted cinco por mil and other taxes are also included.

[19] Expenditures on broad consumption categories are estimated from DATOS materials.

[20] Food expenditure data for rural families are estimated from various publications of the Venezuelan Institute of Nutrition.

[21] Includes both direct outlay by family and subsidy by employer.

[22] Data from Consejo Binestar Rural.

[23] The duty burden for housing and house maintenance materials is assumed to be a graduated percentage of yearly expenditures, based on income.

[24] To ascertain real estate taxes, the local rate on imputed rent for the year is taken.

[25] In computing the furniture and appliance tax burden, a weighted average of the constituent items is taken (the weights from oil and iron workers' budget studies). Assuming that 33% of furniture is imported, 50% of home furnishings, and 100% of appliances, and assuming 1% for shifted cinco por mil and other taxes, gives a figure of 27% for tax burden on middle income families. Adjustments are made for higher and lower income families.

26 The weighted average of duty burden on clothing and yard goods is 68% of the retail price. A proportion, varying with income, of total expenditure on imported clothing and yard goods for each family is assumed, and thus a net duty burden for each is arrived at.

27 Estimated from DATOS materials (cars are of varying ages as well as types).

28 Local license fee plus Bs.15, federal license fee.

29 Since one-half of all cars purchased in Venezuela are assembled in the country, and auto parts imports bear only a nominal duty, then only one-half of the duty-as-a-percentage-of-retail-price that might apply to the given car is charged against the given family. It is assumed that families A, B and D each own one cheaper type of U.S. car; C and K each own one medium-price U.S. car; F and J each own one expensive U.S. car, and I owns two expensive U.S. cars. Shifted cinco por mil is included.

30 It is assumed that families A, B, and D, use standard grade gasoline and that families C, F, I, J, and K use super grade. Shifted cinco por mil is included. Gasoline tax estimated from Chapter VIII.

31 Assumes a 2% tax rate due to cinco por mil and other shifted taxes.

32 Estimated from DATOS materials.

33 Using estimates from Chapter VIII.

34 Thirteen per cent appears to be an average admission (plus cinco por mil, etc.) figure.

35 About one-third of the "other recreation" expenditures in middle income families is on goods that bear a weighted average tax percentage of 75% (includes such items as sporting goods, toys, photographic equipment, musical items, but not phonographs or radios). Thus 25% would give the "other recreation" tax burden in these families (plus 1% for cinco por mil, etc.). Graduated percentages, depending on income, are applied to the other families.

36 No indirect tax on education expenditure is assumed.

37 The duty burden on "personal care and household operation" expenditure for middle income families was arrived at in the following way: In middle income families, of the 0.4% of the budget going to personal care, about 75% is on imported items which bear an average duty rate of 7%. This gives 5% as the duty burden on this portion. Of the 0.9% of the budget going to household operation about 25% is on imported items which bear an average duty rate of 60%. This gives 15% as the duty burden on this portion. The weighted average of the two is 12%, to which is added 1% cinco por mil etc. Graduated percentages, depending on income, are applied to the other families.

38 Since about 27% of typical medical expenditures are on pharmaceuticals, which bear about 7% in duty, a flat 2% on medical expenditures is assumed as the duty burden.

39 Includes dues, gifts and donations, and occasional miscellaneous purchases.

40 In this catch-all category the tax rate is likely to be regressive because, the larger the income, the larger would tend to be the proportion going to dues and donations which, of course, are not taxed.

41 Excludes the amount (gambling income minus gambling tax) from disposable income.

42 Includes the amount (gambling income minus gambling tax) in disposable income.

43 Excludes gambling tax from direct taxes.

44 Includes gambling tax in direct taxes.

NOTE: The figures in the tables in this Appendix B are provisional and are subject to later revision. A probable scaling down of some of the expenditure items will result in a lower total duty burden for some families.

Supplementary Table. Families Ranked by Income

Family code letter	Total income (Bs.)	Total direct taxes (Bs.)	Total direct tax as % of total income	Total indirect taxes (Bs.)	Total indirect tax as % of total income	Total taxes (Bs.)	Total tax as % of total income (Bs.)
I[1]	350,000	23,100.00	6.60	46,105.00	13.17	69,205.00	19.77
J[2]	100,000	2,815.00	2.81	10,633.50	10.63	13,448.50	13.45
F[1]	80,000	2,330.00	2.91	12,399.10	15.49	14,729.10	18.41
K[2]	35,000	205.00	0.58	3,779.80	10.80	3,984.80	11.38
C[1]	28,000	360.00	1.28	4,592.30	16.40	4,952.30	17.67
A[1,3]	19,750	170.00	0.35	2,167.60	10.97	2,337.60	11.84
D[1]	17,250	40.00	0.23	2,064.10	11.96	2,104.10	12.20
B[1]	14,780	30.00	0.20	1,945.80	12.97	1,975.80	13.17
E[1]	8,000	0	0	739.80	9.25	739.80	9.25
H[1]	3,730	0	0	377.70	10.13	377.70	10.13
G[1]	2,500	0	0	194.70	7.79	194.70	7.79
L[2]	2,000	0	0	142.00	7.10	142.00	7.10

1 Urban.

2 Rural.

3 Ignores gambling transaction.

APPENDIX C : **Income Tax Revision**
: **of December, 1958**

The income tax law was amended by Decree No. 476 of December 19, 1958. This decree in form repealed the prior law and enacted an entire income tax law. However, its actual effect was to change only several articles of the prior law, the principal change being that of an increase in the rates of the complementary tax. The new complementary tax rates, and one other provision, were applicable commencing with the year 1958; other changes were applicable commencing with 1959. The changes are briefly summarized below.

1. Complementary Tax

NEW RATE SCALE

The new complementary tax rate scale is as follows:

Brackets (Bs.)	Rate (%)	Brackets (Bs.)	Rate (%)
0– 8,000	2.00	280,000– 380,000	11.50
8,000– 10,000	2.50	380,000– 500,000	12.50
10,000– 14,000	3.00	500,000– 640,000	14.50
14,000– 20,000	3.50	640,000– 800,000	15.50
20,000– 28,000	4.00	800,000– 1,000,000	17.00
28,000– 38,000	4.50	1,000,000– 1,400,000	18.50
38,000– 50,000	5.00	1,400,000– 2,000,000	20.00
50,000– 64,000	5.50	2,000,000– 2,800,000	21.50
64,000– 80,000	6.50	2,800,000– 3,800,000	23.00
80,000–100,000	7.50	3,800,000– 5,000,000	25.50
100,000–140,000	8.50	5,000,000– 6,400,000	28.00
140,000–200,000	9.50	6,400,000– 8,000,000	30.50
200,000–280,000	10.50	8,000,000–10,000,000	33.00
		10,000,000–14,000,000	35.50
		14,000,000–20,000,000	38.00
		20,000,000–28,000,000	40.50
		Over 28,000,000	45.00

Tax burden tables under these new rates, Tables C-1 and C-2, may be compared with Tables III-1 and 2 in Chapter III.

The revenue estimates for 1958 income respecting the change in complementary tax rates are as follows:

Gross increase in complementary tax for all
taxpayers Bs.873,000,000

Less: amount of additional (50-50) tax that would
have been paid but was not paid due to the increase
in complementary tax rates 160,000,000

Net increase in complementary tax.............. 713,000,000

Portion of net increase paid by oil companies....... 578,000,000

Reductions for Reinvested Income. In the case of the last three brackets, following the pattern of the prior law, special rate reductions apply to reinvested income: "investments made in the country by the taxpayer in the expansion of his means of production." In the case of taxpayers in the bracket Bs.14,000,000-20,000,000, the rate is 36% on the amount of income in that bracket equal to the amount of such investment made during the year, up to Bs.3,000,000 of income, with any balance of income in that bracket being taxed at the regular rate of 38%; in the case of taxpayers in the bracket Bs.20,000,000-28,000,000, the rate is 37.50% on the amount of income in that bracket equal to the amount of such investment, up to Bs.4,000,000 of income, any balance of income being taxed at the regular rate of 40.50%; in the case of taxpayers with incomes over Bs.28,000,000, the rate is 41% on the amount of such investment up to one-half the difference between the total taxable income and Bs.28,000,000, the balance of income in that bracket being taxed at the regular rate of 45%. These lower rates are not cumulative.

In addition, the 1958 law in a new provision grants reductions in tax rates to taxpayers in all brackets for reinvested income. This new provision applies to investments in fixed assets for businesses engaged in the manufacture of industrial products, the generation and distribution of electric power, transportation (if these activities are taxed under Schedule 3, business income), and for agriculture (Schedule 5). In the case of the above businesses, the tax reduction applies only if the manufactured articles sold or services rendered represent 80% of the total gross earnings of the taxpayer under Schedule 3. Businesses engaged in bottling or packaging of articles manufactured by others, or engaged in like activities, are not eligible for the reductions. Oil and mining activities are also not eligible since they are not classified under Schedule 3. The acquisition of land is not considered an eligible reinvestment.

The tax reductions for reinvested income are as follows:

Investment as percentage of complementary tax net income	Reduction of complementary tax
From 10% to 20%	10%
20% to 30%	11%
30% to 40%	12%
40% to 50%	13%
50% to 60%	15%
60% to 70%	17%
70% to 80%	19%
80% to 90%	22%
90% to 100%	25%

If a taxpayer is entitled both to the tax reduction granted in one of the last brackets for reinvested income and to the percentage tax reductions granted for all taxpayers who reinvest income, then he obtains only the benefit of the provision which results in the larger reduction in tax.

Loss Carryovers. In the computation of income for the complementary tax the new law permits the applications of any net loss carryovers existing under Schedules 3, 4 and 5. For this purpose a loss carry-over under one schedule may be applied against income from another schedule, including schedules other than Schedules 3, 4 and 5.

Applicable Date. The above changes were applicable commencing with 1958 (tax years ending after December 19, 1958).

2. Schedular Rates

The following changes in schedular rates were made, commencing with 1959:

Schedule 6, Non-Commercial Professions. The rate applicable to non-residents was increased from 7% to 12%.

Schedule 7, Salaries and Wages. The rate applicable to non-residents was increased from 4% to 6%.

Schedule 9, Lottery Prizes and Other Chance Winnings. The rate was increased from 10% to 20%.

3. *Sales of Real Estate on Installment Basis*

In the case of sales of real estate on an installment basis, falling under Schedules 3 or 8, if the income from the sales represents more than 40% of the taxpayer's total gross income under the respective schedule, the taxpayer at his option need only include in income the proceeds of sale when received. As respects any amount so included, a part of the cost or other allowable expenses is allowed on a proportionate basis. This provision is applicable commencing with 1958.

4. *Tax Court*

The new law does not contain the requirement that one of the members of the Tax Court shall be an accountant. The three present members are lawyers.

5. *Interest on Appeals to Tax Court*

If an appeal to the Tax Court is "completely without grounds," interest is due on the amount of tax appealed at the rate of 1% per month, commencing with the end of the 30-day period in which the Tax Administration could have reconsidered the taxpayer's objections. The payment of interest is excused only if the Tax Court expressly states that the taxpayer had rational motives for presenting the appeal. The provision is applicable to appeals filed after December 19, 1958.

Table C-1. Income Tax at Various Income Levels: Individuals
(Money figures in Bs.)

Net Income (before exemptions)	Salary & Wages			Per cent of tax to net income	Business Incom	
	Schedular tax	Complementary tax	Total tax		Schedular tax	Compl mentar tax
Single person:						
12,000....	0	0	0	0	0	0
15,000....	30	60	90	0.60	75	60
19,200....	72	144	216	1.12	180	144
19,201 (Bs.1,600.08 monthly)...	192.01	144.02	336.03	1.75	480.02	144.
25,000....	250	300	550	2.20	625	300
30,000....	300	470	770	2.56	750	470
50,000....	500	1,310	1,810	3.62	1,250	1,310
50,001....	500.01	1,310.05	1,810.06	3.62	1,250.02	1,310.
75,000....	750	2,625	3,375	4.50	1,875	2,625
100,000....	1,000	4,320	5,320	5.32	2,500	4,320
200,000....	2,000	13,180	15,180	7.59	5,000	13,180
500,000....	5,000	47,720	52,720	10.54	12,500	47,720
1,000,000....	10,000	125,580	135,580	13.55	25,000	125,580
Married person, two children:						
12,000....	0	0	0	0	0	0
15,000....	30	0	30	0.20	75	0
19,200....	72	0	72	0.37	180	0
19,201....	192.01	0	192.01	1.00	480.02	0
25,000....	250	60	310	1.24	625	60
30,000....	300	160	460	1.53	750	160
50,000....	500	860	1,360	2.72	1,250	860
50,001....	500.01	860.04	1,360.05	2.72	1,250.02	860.
75,000....	750	2,075	2,825	3.76	1,875	2,075
100,000....	1,000	3,590	4,590	4.59	2,500	3,590
200,000....	2,000	12,230	14,230	7.11	5,000	12,230
500,000....	5,000	46,470	51,470	10.29	12,500	46,470
1,000,000....	10,000	123,880	133,880	13.38	25,000	123,880

(1958 Law Tax Rates)

Total tax	Per cent of tax to net income	Farm Income		Total tax	Per cent of tax to net income
		Schedular tax	Complementary tax		
0	0	0	0	0	0
135	0.90	0	60	60	0.40
324	1.68	0	144	144	0.75
624.04	3.25	0	144.02	144.02	0.75
925	3.70	0	300	300	1.20
1,220	4.06	0	470	470	1.56
2,560	5.12	400	1,310	1,710	3.42
2,560.07	5.12	1,000.02	1,310.05	2,310.07	4.62
4,500	6.00	1,500	2,625	4,125	5.50
6,820	6.82	2,000	4,320	6,320	6.32
18,180	9.09	4,000	13,180	17,180	8.59
60,220	12.04	10,000	47,720	57,720	11.54
150,580	15.05	20,000	125,580	145,580	14.55
0	0	0	0	0	0
75	0.50	0	0	0	0
180	0.93	0	0	0	0
480.02	2.50	0	0	0	0
685	2.74	0	60	60	0.24
910	3.03	0	160	160	0.53
2,110	4.22	400	860	1,260	2.52
2,110.06	4.22	1,000.02	860.04	1,860.06	3.72
3,950	5.26	1,500	2,075	3,575	4.76
6,090	6.09	2,000	3,590	5,590	5.59
17,230	8.61	4,000	12,230	16,230	8.11
58,970	11.79	10,000	46,470	56,470	11.29
148,880	14.88	20,000	123,880	143,880	14.38

Table C-2. Income Tax at Various Income Levels: Corporations
(Compañías y Sociedades Anónimas) (Money figures in Bs.)

Net income before taxation	Business Income			Per cent of tax to income
	Schedular tax	Complementary tax	Total tax	
12,000....	0	270	270	2.25
15,000....	75	365	440	2.93
19,200....	180	512	692	3.60
19,201....	480.02	512.03	992.05	5.16
25,000....	625	740	1,365	5.46
30,000....	750	950	1,700	5.66
50,000....	1,250	1,910	3,160	6.32
50,001....	1,250.02	1,910.05	3,160.07	6.32
75,000....	1,875	3,395	5,270	7.02
100,000....	2,500	5,220	7,720	7.72
200,000....	5,000	14,320	19,320	9.66
500,000....	12,500	49,220	61,720	12.34
1,000,000....	25,000	127,620	152,620	15.26
5,000,000....	125,000	1,029,620	1,154,620	23.09
10,000,000....	250,000	2,569,620	2,819,620	28.19
20,000,000....	500,000	6,269,620	6,769,620	33.84
30,000,000....	750,000	10,409,620	11,159,620	37.19

(1958 Law Tax Rates)

Farm Income			Per cent of tax to income
Schedular tax	Complementary tax	Total tax	
0	270	270	2.25
0	365	365	2.43
0	512	512	2.66
0	512.03	512.03	2.66
0	740	740	2.96
0	950	950	3.16
400	1,910	2,310	4.62
1,000.02	1,910.05	2,910.07	5.82
1,500	3,395	4,895	6.52
2,000	5,220	7,220	7.22
4,000	14,320	18,320	9.16
10,000	49,220	59,220	11.84
20,000	127,620	147,620	14.76
100,000	1,029,620	1,129,620	22.59
200,000	2,569,620	2,769,620	27.69
400,000	6,269,620	6,669,620	33.34
600,000	10,409,620	11,009,620	36.69

: **The Law of Public Credit**

Venezuela has been operating under a Law of Public Credit[1] which has proved to be both too restrictive and too loose.

It is too restrictive, in that it requires Congressional approval of all money borrowings (*empréstitos*); and, when a public works project is involved, there must be submitted to Congress the detailed plans for the project. This procedure is very cumbersome. Moreover, no continuously outstanding short-term debt is practicable under the present law.

On the other hand, the law does not regulate incurrence of debt on contracts, as contrasted with issuance of debt for money. Moreover, the autonomous institutes (e.g. the Development Corporation: Corporación de Fomento) are not mentioned in the existing law.

Consequently, Government departments, by contracts, and autonomous institutes more generally, have in recent years issued more or less short-term notes, without approval by Congress, or by any central office in the national Government. It is the large volume of such notes issued under the recent dictatorship that has faced the new Government with a financial problem of some magnitude.

As of Dec. 31, 1957, the direct public debt of the national Government of Venezuela was almost negligible: Bs.23 million.[2] But the obligations incurred by the various Ministries and autonomous institutes were Bs.4,578 million. Of this latter total, only Bs.915 million is directly attributed to the autonomous institutes, but in fact their role was much larger, for the debt listed as incurred by the Ministry of Development includes large amounts borrowed by the Development Corporation, for construction of a steel mill, the Caroní hydro power plant, and other similar projects.

Of the Bs.4,578 million in these obligations, Bs.1,658 million was to

[1] Ley de Crédito Público, June 27, 1941, as amended by Ley de Reforma Parcial de la Ley de Crédito Público of June 19, 1944.

[2] These and succeeding figures on the public debt are from Banco Central de Venezuela, *Memoria,* 1957, pages 284-86.

fall due in the fiscal year 1957-58, Bs.1,294 million in 1958-59, and Bs.559 million in 1959-60. The remainder was spread over the four succeeding years.

The first problem noted above, concerning debt procedures that are too restrictive, can be met by dispensing with the requirement for submitting detailed plans of public works, and by allowing the Government to issue a certain amount of short-term debt without obtaining prior approval by Congress. The proposed law stipulates that short-term debt (e.g. *Bonos de Tesorería, Letras, Pagarés*) may be incurred up to 10 per cent of the ordinary revenue (*los ingresos ordinarios*) as estimated in the current budget.[3]

Ultimately, it may prove advisable to expand this limit, but for the time being the 10 per cent appears sufficient to give the flexibility needed, and to begin the development of an active market in short-term government obligations.[4]

The second problem, that of preventing uncontrolled incurrence of obligations, is to be met in two ways.

Government departments or other public entities *(ente público)* are to be forbidden to incur obligations on contracts, purchase of equipment, etc., without prior authorization by the National Executive, after consultation with the Central Bank; but an exception is made for an amount up to 5 per cent of the total income of the entity's budgeted revenue for the current year.[5]

Secondly, the new law will prohibit the autonomous institutes (Los Institutos o Establecimientos Oficiales Autónomos) from contracting debt without previous authorization from the National Executive, given by the Council of Ministers.[6] Before such authorization is granted, the advice of the Central Bank must be obtained. Exception is made for short-term debt incurred in anticipation of ordinary receipts. This exception may pose some problems, but it is unlikely that a more restrictive plan would be practicable.

States and municipalities, not mentioned in the old law on public credit, will be subject, under the proposed law, to national Government approval for any incurrence of debt.[7] As with the national Government, short-term debt will be authorized up to 10 per cent of the budgeted income, without the need of approval by the National Executive.

[3] Article 15, Special Paragraph.
[4] Exposición de Motivos del Anteproyecto de Ley de Crédito Público (1959), page 1.
[5] Article 4.
[6] Article 30 of proposed law.
[7] Article 35.

Index

Accountants, viii, 352

Accounting, 90
  basis of, cost or accrual, 90, 102, 110, 172-73
  fiscal-year or calendar year, 102, 110, 199, 205-206
  governmental, 1, 365-405
  in income tax administration, 177, 241
  see also Professions

Ad valorem basis, customs, 285, 287-90, 291

Administration
  customs duties, 18-19, 281-88
  income tax, 16-17, 176-201, 202-41
    cost of, 199-200
  inheritance and gift taxes, 248-50
  liquor taxes, 256-57
  local taxes, 334-35, 344-45
  sales tax, 297-99, 304
  taxes generally, 366-74

Admissions, 319, 321, 323, 324, 465

Advertising, 323

Aeronáutica Civil
  Dirección de, 425
  Servicio de, 426

Aged and Invalid, National Council for, 385

Agriculture, 75
  administration of income tax on, 179
  amount of tax on, at various levels, 129, 131, 473, 475
  earnings in, 26-27, 29-31, 37-39, 41, 407, 459
  equipment used in, 266
  government expenditure on, 320
  income, amount of, 138
  in national income, 7, 24
  productivity in, 65-68, 82
  reform of, 327

treatment of
  under gross receipts tax, 296
  under income tax, 88, 89-90, 92, 104-106, 162-63, 231, 469
  under inheritance tax, 242, 247

Agriculture, Ministry of, 34, 77, 439

Aguerrevere, P. E., viii

Air freight, 282-83, 290, 294

Air lines, *see* Transportation companies, international

Air Mail Line, Venezuela, 385

Alaska, 326

Alcohol, *see* Liquor

Amazonas, 315, 329

Ambulances, 429

American Municipal Association, 352

Annuities, 88

Antoni, J., vii

Anzoátegui, 315, 329

Appeals, by taxpayers, 17, 196-98, 224-26, 230-31, 284

Apples, 269, 276

Appliances, electric, etc., 18, 79, 268, 270, 277, 288, 292, 463

Appropriations, 374-75, 382

Apure, 315, 328, 329

Aqueducts, *see* Water Supply

Aragua, 315, 329, 459

Araujo, A., vi

Araya, 433, 434

Architecture, *see* Professions

Argentina, 303, 307, 311, 312, 409

Armed Forces Club, 387

Aspirin, 270, 277

Assessment
  income tax, *see* Liquidation
  other taxes, *see under names of taxes*

Audit
  of government expenditures, 374-380,
    see also Pre-audit
  under gross receipts tax, 298

479